# THE EVOLVED STRUCTURE OF HUMAN SOCIAL
# BEHAVIOUR AND PERSONALITY

# THE EVOLVED STRUCTURE
# OF HUMAN SOCIAL BEHAVIOUR
# AND PERSONALITY

## Psychoanalytic Insights

*Ralf-Peter Behrendt*

**KARNAC**

First published in 2012 by
Karnac Books Ltd
118 Finchley Road
London NW3 5HT

British Library Cataloguing in Publication Data

A C.I.P. for this book is available from the British Library

ISBN-13: 978-1-78049-115-8

Typeset by V Publishing Solutions Pvt. Ltd., Chennai, India

Printed in Great Britain

www.karnacbooks.com

# CONTENTS

*CHAPTER SIX*
Anxiety                                                               139

**Ralf-Peter Behrendt** studied medicine and biophysics (medical cybernetics) in Moscow, Russia. He came to England in 1997, where he trained in psychiatry, pursuing special interests in psychoanalysis and neuropsychiatry. He now works as a consultant in old-age psychiatry. He has published several articles and book chapters in the field of psychopathology and neurobiology of mental illness, especially in the interface with philosophy. He is the author of *Neuroanatomy of Social Behaviour: An Evolutionary and Psychoanalytic Perspective* (Karnac, 2011).

# CHAPTER ONE

# Introduction

Insights gained by psychoanalytic theory need to be harnessed if we want to understand the way in which interrelated processes of anxiety, aggression, avoidance, submission, and care-seeking/care-giving behaviour give rise to the complexities of interpersonal behaviour, mental illness, and social structure. Here, we are concerned with psychoanalytic conceptualisations insofar as they help us to lay the foundation for a biologically and evolutionarily sensible model of human social behaviour and personality; the aim is not to provide a critique of psychoanalytic writings.[1] There is a need for a model of the mind that allows us to discern the relevance of animal data for human behaviour and that advances our understanding of functional neuroanatomy, neurophysiology, and neurochemistry as well as of the evolution of the nervous system (insofar as it subserves social behaviour and personality). The functions of hippocampus, ventral striatum, amygdala, and their interconnectivity are still poorly understood; but it has long been recognised that, whatever the nature of the involvement of these ancient structures in social behaviour, their contribution is critical. Eventual success in efforts to illuminate brain-behaviour relationships will depend on our ability to anchor the complexities of human behaviour and psychopathology in the evolution of defensive, offensive (territorial), and parental behaviours in animals. Apart from psychoanalysis, ideas that have emanated from the field of ethology, in particular, open the prospect of arriving at an internally consistent and evolutionarily grounded model of the mind—a model that has the potential to explain neuroscientific data more parsimoniously. Complementing a recent review of findings from functional neuroanatomy, neurophysiology, and neurochemistry relevant to attempts to shed light into the regulation and evolution of social behaviour (Behrendt, 2011), the intention here is to take a top-down approach towards understanding how the brain could have evolved to generate social behaviour and personality (as well as their variations into psychopathology).

---

[1] Inconsistencies, contradictions, and sometimes contrived conceptualisations can be shown, and have been shown, in the works of Freud, Freudian pioneers (such as Bergler, Burrow, Federn, Hartmann, Schilder), or Kleinian theoreticians (such as Fairbairn and Bion), however a critical emphasis likely overshadows, or distracts us from, valuable insights gained, and important contributions made, by these writers.

Psychoanalytic and ethological concepts support the notion that human social behaviour reflects an interplay of unconscious processes, namely (i) active solicitation of affiliative reward (reward that is related to maternal ministrations of care) from increasingly abstract derivatives of the primary love object (the mother); (ii) the aversiveness of social unconnectedness and rejection (related to the infant's separation distress), which promotes the acquisition of attachment behaviours; (iii) maintenance of attachment to derivatives of the object and active solicitation of social inclusion—unconsciously in order to increase the probability of receiving affiliative reward; (iv) the aversiveness of social punishment (displays of others' offensive aggression), which promotes the acquisition of socially normative behaviour; (v) expression of normative and complying behaviours (including culturally ritualised variations of innate appeasement gestures)—unconsciously in order to inhibit the innate offensive aggressiveness of other individuals who compete for attention and care provided by the derivative of the primary object (such as a group leader's attention); (vi) expression of offensive aggression (rooted in evolutionarily older territorial aggression), which—when expressed in culturally sanctioned forms—serves to maintain a social position or rank associated with protection against punishment and access to affiliative reward; and (vii) anxiety relating to the unpredictable exposure to others' offensive aggression. All of these interacting processes can be shown to contribute to the constitution of the self (an experience that manifests a control mechanism of social behaviour); and all of these processes can be related to neural structures, neural systems, and global regulatory mechanisms studied in experimental animal paradigms that capture essentials of evolutionary precursors of these fundamental processes (Behrendt, 2011).

Psychoanalytic theory inspires and enriches a conceptual framework within which we can understand human social behaviour deterministically. No other species has such high needs for relatedness on a background of such profound latent insecurity (anxiety), and no other species uses such complex methods of escaping anxiety and maintaining relatedness. These are factors that critically contribute to mental illness in humans. Psychoanalytic theory has revealed the dynamics involved in various forms of personality disorder and mental illness—insights that have to merge with a conceptualisation of social behaviour in terms of interacting defensive and parental-care systems that are deeply rooted in evolutionary history. Object relations theory, which has provided many critical insights into the ontogenesis of social behaviour and the pathogenesis of mental disorders, has to be made accessible to those who are concerned with the scientific study of human behaviour but unfamiliar with psychoanalysis. Concepts such as introjection, ego splitting, or projective identification seem to be irrelevant to the challenges facing behavioural neurosciences, but they contain fundamental insights into the organisation and regulation of human social behaviour—insights that are critical for an evolutionarily founded model of personality and for our ability to map normal and pathological human behaviour onto brain anatomy and physiology.

Psychoanalysis reveals the hidden structure underlying social behaviour and psychopathology; and it is this structure that needs to be mapped onto what we know, and what we still need to find out, about the brain. It is argued that a perspective informed by psychoanalysis will help us to integrate an accumulating wealth of neurobiological data pertaining to normal behaviour and mental illness and overcome a sense of theoretical confusion. The relationship between consciousness (including the phenomenal world as it is constructed subjectively) and unconscious processes (the discussion and conceptualisation of which is dependent on, and embedded in, conscious awareness) needs to be made clearer if we are to succeed in efforts to deterministically and parsimoniously relate brain processes to social and psychopathological phenomena; and here again, psychoanalysis provides important leads. The approach taken here is not related to, or borne out of, the field surrounding cognitive neuroscience and cognitivist-analytical philosophy. It may be time to give credit to theoretical achievements of psychoanalysis and ethology and to reemphasise the role of psychoanalysis as a conceptual framework for understanding brain-behaviour relationships (especially insofar as social behaviour is concerned), rather than engage with the tradition of cognitive theory and neuroscience, which has very many advocates. It is also time to revive a deterministic framework (as opposed to the teleological one implicit in cognitivism) for psychiatry and psychology that would be more compatible with evolutionary views and recent advances, made by the natural sciences, in understanding the self-organisation of matter on progressively higher levels of complexity. Alongside the need to reground our understanding of human behaviour and psychopathology in a biologically and evolutionarily feasible framework, enshrined assumptions underlying social policy making and psychiatric "service development" may need to be challenged.

# CHAPTER TWO

# Deterministic metapsychology

One meets with passionate opposition from non-biologists when one attempts to explain that, in spite of its universal tendency to develop from the simple to the complex, from the probable to the improbable—in a word, from the lower to the higher—the whole of organic life is governed by the laws of chance and necessity. ... To realize that the great laws of nature admit of no exceptions seems to conflict with our consciousness of free will and with the value we attach to it as one of the supreme human possessions and an inalienable human right. (Lorenz, 1973, p. 232)

Psychoanalytic theory helps us to map psychic, psychopathological, interpersonal, and social phenomena onto a network of ancient motivational processes, which, in turn, can be subjected to experimental study in behavioural neuroscience. Phenomena on every level of organisation of matter require their own explanatory framework. Determinism is a fundamental principle that should apply to whatever level of organisation of matter we consider. Behaviourism understands behaviour, in general, deterministically.

Behaviourism maintains that no agent can be held responsible for our thoughts, feelings, or actions. The notion of an agent as "an originator of action" is rejected (Zuriff, 1985). All behaviour can be traced *causally* to environmental and internal physical variables. In what appears to be "voluntary" behaviour, the relationship between environment and overt behaviour is mediated by chains of covert behaviour (including "anticipatory goal reactions") (Zuriff, 1985). Psychoanalysis provides a framework within which psychopathological and social phenomena can be understood deterministically. In psychoanalysis, human beings are conceived as being motivated "not by rational desires to achieve ends and to fulfil purposes envisaged by the imagination as desirable, but as impelled by a drive from below whose strength is derived from forces which are both incalculable and irrational" (Joad, 1955, p. 189).

## 2.1 Instinct and drive

Nietzsche (1886) considered human behaviour and thought to be expressions of an interplay of natural forces that seek discharge. According to Freud (1915), "psychic energy" or "tension"

5

that originates in instinctive needs is expressed in behaviour or psychological performance. The aim of instinctive behaviour is to eliminate an underlying instinctive need; and satisfaction of the need leads to a reduction in tension. Freud distinguished between "instinct" and "drive", suggesting that "instincts" are intermittent sources of motivation, while "drives" (such as libido and aggression) are constant sources of motivation (sources that are not dependent on environmental and physiological stimulation) (Kernberg, 1992). "Affects", in Freud's system, are discharge processes of drives; affective behaviour reduces "tension" associated with drives. Nevertheless, "instinct" and "drive" are often used synonymously in the psychoanalytic literature. McDougall (1924) saw instincts as the "prime movers of all human activity". An instinct "determines the outflow of energy into all bodily organs that take part in the instinctive activity" (p. 106). Motor mechanisms, which "require to be 'driven' by some impulse, by a stream of energy derived from some instinct", are the "channel[s] of outlet for the energy liberated from any of the instincts" (McDougall, 1924, p. 117). "Instinctive energy" is discharged and redistributed in the course of behaviour, and persists for as long as the instinct has not reached its end. Instinctive action strives towards "a change of situation of a particular kind, which alone can satisfy the impulse and allay the appetite and unrest of the organism" (p. 119). It is "the kind of change of the animal's situation which its movements, whatever they may be, tend to bring about" that defines the instinct and that "when it is achieved, brings the train of behaviour to a close" (McDougall, 1924, pp. 118–119).

From an ethological perspective, instincts are inherited, relatively fixed patterns of behaviour (and communication) that are activated by appropriate environmental and/or physiological stimulation (Lorenz, 1963). Bowlby (1973) spoke of "causal factors" that are required to either activate or terminate "systems" responsible for instinctive behaviour. "Causal factors" that activate or terminate a "behavioural system" include

hormonal levels, proprioceptive stimuli, and environmental stimuli. Behaviour that results from activation of a "behavioural system" is considered to be "instinctive" insofar as "it follows a recognizably similar pattern in almost all members of a species" (Bowlby, 1973, p. 81). Each "behavioural system" serves a "biological function" that "promotes the survival of the species" (p. 82). The "biological function" is served "when a system is active in the organism's environment of evolutionary adaptedness" (Bowlby, 1973, p. 82). The notion of "drive" is more closely related to learned appetitive (preparatory) behaviour, which *prepares* the organism for the release of innate instinctive patterns. Hull (1943) considered "drives" as important "intervening variables" in a behavioural input-output (stimulus-response) system. Learning, according to Hull, takes place when needs (that is, deviations from homeostasis) are satisfied and drives undergo reduction. It was a rapid drive reduction that was considered to strengthen the association between stimulus and response (Hull, 1943).

### 2.1.1  Cathexis

Husserl (1928) suggested that instincts derive their satisfaction from "stable experiential units". Instincts play a crucial role in constituting increasingly complex and stable objects of our perception. By giving perception its "intentional directedness", instincts institute the world as experienced by the subject. For Husserl (1928), our consciousness of the world is but an explication of our endowment with instincts (reviewed in Smith, 2003). McDougall (1924) thought that an instinct "renders possible the perception of the specific object" that acts as "the key to the instinct" (p. 106). According to Freud (1915), "psychic energy", or "tension", is "invested" into objects (cathexis). "Cathexis" refers to the investment of libidinal or aggressive instinctual energy ("psychic energy") into a representation of an object or the self. Through the object, "the instinct attains its external aim"; while "its internal aim is always a somatic modification which is experienced as satisfaction" (Freud, 1933, p. 126). Each instinct is directed onto, or invested into, *its* object. "Displacement" refers to the shifting of instinctual energy onto a substitute for the object into which the energy is normally invested. In Kleinian theory, libidinal energy is projected outwards to create good objects, while aggressive energy (death instinct) is projected outwards to create bad objects. Good and bad objects are thence "reintrojected" to produce an inner representational world (reviewed in Cashdan, 1988).

Toman (1960) thought that objects signify conditions under which "desires", that is, drives, can be satisfied. Not only the perception of objects, and generally the perception of conditions for the satisfaction of desires, but also the experience of ideas are automatic consequences of resurging desires. Object cathexis, as a learning process, occurs as we satisfy desires. By means of cathexis and object formation, "the Ego builds up a person's world or reality in which desires can be satisfied" (Toman, 1960, p. 32). Early in development, desires are still primitive and the efficacy of behaviour is limited. We learn to control primitive desires and to satisfy them under an ever increasing range of conditions. Behaviour becomes instrumental to the satisfaction of desires (that is, instrumental to the procurement of reward). Echoing reinforcement learning theory, Toman (1960) stated that "as cathexis of conditions under which desires can be satisfied progresses, those forms of behavior that can influence and even create any of these conditions are more and more likely to be among the cathected" (p. 64). Thus, we gain control over conditions under which we can satisfy our desires (Toman, 1960).

> It looks as if a person's world and what he can do in it gets ordered into a network of "instrumentality", as he grows up. Part of a person's knowledge of the world as a whole, which includes himself, is to know in ever so many ways what leads to what. (Toman, 1960, p. 65)

Countercathexis

As Toman (1960) realised, other people "are inevitable and indispensible conditions of all satisfactions that we can ever hope to attain" (p. 60). Satisfaction of our desires depends on other people's desires, however, in satisfying their desires, others may deprive us of the satisfaction of our desires. According to Toman (1960), deprivation of a desire produces anxiety, pain, and/or aggression. A desire may become impossible to satisfy. The individual has to learn not to respond to objects or situations that have previously led to deprivation and anxiety. This form of learning—reminiscent of avoidance learning—is called countercathexis. Countercathexis "means 'learning how to avoid' or 'learning how to fear'" (p. 24). Anxiety is a cue suggesting that countercathexis has been insufficient and further countercathexis (that is, avoidance learning) is necessary. Countercathexis, which, like cathexis, is a function of the ego, prevents the recurrence of anxiety. When the individual is faced with resurging desires, he "scans" the situation for action possibilities. How the situation is perceived is determined by all previous cathexes and countercathexes "of conditions under which the desires in question could or could not be satisfied, respectively" (p. 76). The situation is perceived—in accordance with all pertinent previous cathexes and countercathexes—"before any action can even be contemplated" (p. 73). The perceived situation "will represent a specific 'opportunity profile' in accordance with the individual's cathexes and counter-cathexes of previous situations", as well as "in accordance with the 'intensity profile' of his desires at that time" (Toman, 1960, p. 79).

*2.1.2  Objects and emotions*

> There is no perception, no imagination, no thought which is not action, which does not contain in itself motility, i.e. action. When we see an object, the perception is based upon the preceding and subsequent

movements of the eye muscles and of the body. Without motility we would not see at all. A perception without motility is of no account. Perception and movement cannot be separated. We should not take as a unit in psychology either perception or movement but a sensory-motor unit, or still better, a sensory-motor-vegetative unit. Even this formulation is incomplete in so far as the sensory-motor-vegetative unit gets its meaning merely in a specific total situation of which the personality is part. Whatever we may experience as individuals, we live in actions; and the action has its basis in the world which we perceive. (Schilder, 1951, p. 314)

Objects—insofar as they are characterised by meaning and embedded in a spatial and situational context—are perceived (consciously) within a particular emotional or drive state (consistent with the notion of cathexis). "Conative" experience, being the "felt impulse to action", is integral to all "sense impressions" (in proportion to the strength of the underlying drive or instinct); an "object recognised or thought about" "evokes in [the subject] an impulse to effect some change" (McDougall, 1924, p. 265). Consciously perceived objects may not induce sensorimotor transformations directly, as external stimuli (including features of objects) would do, but allow for the engagement of another emotional behaviour mode or a task mode, or a mode of expectancy, that flexibly constrains actions. In other words, objects may precipitate the replacement of a general emotional state with a specialised emotional state or task mode. For instance, perception of an object associated with danger transforms a state of anxiety (the emotional state concerned with expectation of uncertain or poorly defined dangers) into an emotional state of fear or rage, depending on whether the identified external danger is more likely to be overcome by flight or fight behaviour. Emotional states of fear or rage describe behavioural *tendencies*, namely tendencies to withdraw from,

or placate, the external danger or to attack the source of fear. For a child, the danger is generally connected with, and attributed to, "mother and father, who may punish or withdraw tenderness and affection" (Arieti, 1970, p. 14).

> In general, the organism prefers to feel dangers as threats from without rather than from within because certain mechanisms of protection against overly intense stimuli can be set in motion against external stimuli only. (Fenichel, 1946, p. 147)

Similarly, perception of a motivationally relevant object or cue can mediate the transition from a state of hunger to appetite. Appetite, if understood as an emotion, is a feeling of expectancy that is accompanied by "a tendency to move forward, contact, grab, or incorporate an almost immediately attainable goal" (Arieti, 1970, p. 8). The role of consciously perceived objects, in this regard, is the same as that of internal images. An image is "an internal quasi-reproduction of a perception that does not require the corresponding external stimulus in order to be evoked" (p. 13). An image of the mother would evoke feelings that the child also experiences when perceiving the mother. The image of the mother can act as a substitute for the externally perceived object. Both, the image of the mother and perception of the external object, can evoke a "longing or appetite for the corresponding external object". The motivational effect of the mother's image is to lead the child "to search out the actual object, which in its external reality is still more gratifying than the image" (p. 14). In general, when imagery emerges (phylogenetically or ontogenetically), "the individual becomes capable of wishing something that is not present and is motivated toward the fulfilment of his wishes" (Arieti, 1970, p. 25).

### 2.1.3 Transformations

Instinctual drives, such as aggression or libido, are thought to have properties such as impetus ("psychic energy") and direction. Affective behaviours as well as affectively neutral motor functions and cognitive processes expend instinctual energy ("psychic energy"). Instinctual energy is said to be diverted into indirect channels if direct channels are blocked. External reality imposes delays and restraints on the expression of instinctual drives, as Freud realised. Processes that, in dealing with these impositions, modify and divert instinctual drives constitute the "secondary process" ("reality principle") and the ego. Thus, the ego is a representative of external reality. When instinctual drives are expressed through affectively neutral cognitive and motor functions, instead of being expressed through emotional or affectively charged behaviour, instinctual energy is said to be "neutralised". Neutralisation of the aggressive drive, for instance, is integral to many mechanisms of defence, especially those mechanisms of defence that can be seen to have aggressive meanings in interpersonal situations. Hartmann and Loewenstein (1962) suggested that functions attributable to the ego and superego serve to expend aggressive and libidinal energies of varying degrees of neutralisation. The "id", by contrast, may refer to "a way of acting erotically or aggressively that is more or less infantile in its being irrational, unmodulated, unrestrained, heedless of consequences and contradiction" and that is "associated with those vivid and diffuse physiological processes that fall under the common heading of excitement or arousal" (Schafer, 1976, pp. 195–196).

Baudouin (1922) thought that "affective life, including the higher feelings, represents an evolution of instincts" (p. 81). He pointed out that an "instinct is often at work in matters with which at first sight it seems to have no concern" (p. 79). An instinct can be suppressed and "transformed", giving rise to "secondary tendencies" (Baudouin, 1922). Secondary or derived tendencies determine many aspects of psychological life, such as interests and dreams. Freud chiefly considered the sexual instinct (or drive) with its pathological suppressions and transformations in neurosis. Indeed, the sexual instinct must be

of "exceptional importance in the genesis of our feelings" because of its potency and the repressions imposed by social life. However, energy relating to other instincts (drives) can be shown to "flow in lateral channels, and may there give rise to new derivatives which are sometimes of great moral and social value" (Baudouin, 1922). For McDougall (1924), "reasoning, like all other forms of intellectual process, is but the servant of the instinctive impulses"; it is an activity through which "we discover new means for the attainment of our goals" (p. 215). Already Nietzsche (1886) proposed that conscious thinking is secretly guided and forced into certain channels by instincts. Rational understanding, self-deception, and morality are nothing but the instruments of man's innermost drives (Nietzsche, 1886, sections 3 and 6).

> By itself, reason can only devise means to achieve otherwise determined ends; it cannot set up goals nor give us orders. Left to itself, reason is like a … wonderful system of wheels within wheels, without a motor to make them go round. The motive power that makes them do so stems from instinctive behaviour mechanisms much older than reason and not directly accessible to rational self-observation. (Lorenz, 1963, p. 240)

## Reality principle

Freud emphasised the importance of pleasure and punishment in the organisation of instinctually "driven" behaviour ("pleasure principle"). Freud's "reality principle" refers to the organism's ability to give up momentary pleasure in order to gain—along a new path—pleasure at a later time. Hartmann (1964) agreed that "the reality principle [is] the natural opponent, or at least modifier, of the pleasure principle" (p. 244). The reality principle "imposes restrictions on the pleasure principle" (p. 248). It "represents a tendency to wrest our activities from the immediate need for discharge inherent in the pleasure principle" (Hartmann, 1964, p. 244). The ego, incorporating the reality principle, promotes a "safer form of adjustment by introducing a factor of growing independence from the immediate impact of stimuli" (p. 115).[1] In ontogenesis, "goal-directed" and organised actions gradually replace immediate reactions. Importantly, the child learns to approach reality "in constant relation to the adult's approach to it" (p. 257). Frustration of actions plays an important role in the development of the reality principle, but so does the experience of reward (pleasure). Sublimated activities have "pleasurable potentialities"; "functions that constitute the reality principle can be pleasurable in themselves" (Hartmann, 1964, p. 244).

> The ego is, then, a substructure of personality and is defined by its functions. The instinctual aspect of personality is today conceptualized as the id. Through development of the ego it becomes possible that the pleasure principle, dominant in the realm of the instinctual drives, can be modified to that consideration of reality, in thinking and action, that makes adaptation possible and is termed, as I said before, the reality principle. (Hartmann, 1964, p. 329)

Neutralisation

"Neutralisation" (sublimation) refers to the deflection of instinctual drives "from instinctual aims to aims which are socially or culturally more acceptable or valued" (Hartmann, 1964, p. 217). Neutralisation also describes "a change in the mode of energy, away from instinctual and toward a noninstinctual mode" (p. 223), that is, a "deinstinctualization of both aggression and libido" (p. 227). Nevertheless, in neutralisation, "the ego allows a certain amount of discharge of the original tendencies, provided that their mode (and, often, their aims) have been modified" (Hartmann, 1964, p. 231). The ability "to neutralize considerable amounts of instinctual energy" is "an indication of ego strength" (p. 129). The ego is defined by its functions—functions that are "fed" by neutralised energy. Energies that "the ego uses for its specific functions are as a rule not instinctual", they are "desexualised" and "deaggressivised", that is, neutralised forms of energy (p. 226). Hartmann (1964) emphasised that "the ego has from its start the tendency to oppose drives, but one of its main functions is also to help them toward gratification" (p. 139). Although ego aims are usually "fed by neutralized energy", they "may, under certain conditions, also be cathected with instinctual energy", especially when "ego aims lie in the direction of id tendencies" (p. 230). Thus, "the ego accepts some instinctual tendencies and helps them toward gratification", while, in other cases, the ego "will substitute ego aims for the aims of the id" (Hartmann, 1964, pp. 229–230). Many "ego functions" are object-directed. The formation of object relationships "presupposes some degree of neutralisation" of instinctive drives (Hartmann, 1964).

> The formation of constant and independent objects, the institution of the reality principle, with all its aspects, thinking, action, intentionality all depend on neutralisation. (Hartmann, 1964, p. 235)

### 2.1.4  Instinctive motor patterns

Instincts (innate actions), according to Lorenz (1935, 1937, 1952), are autonomous, rigid and stereotypical, and genetically determined species-specific behaviour patterns. Selective environmental stimuli or stimulus configurations define suitable circumstances under which each instinctive behaviour pattern is performed.

---

[1]As behaviour becomes organised in accordance with the reality principle, "anticipation of the future" "enters the process as an independent variable" (Hartmann, 1964, p. 40). Hartmann (1964) thought that, in goal-directed action, "anticipation of the action's outcome plays a role in its setup" (p. 41), however, the action's goals or aims are not "fixed ends" but "merely turning points in activity" (p. 44).

Although selective environmental stimuli trigger instinctive behaviour sequences, the absence of a trigger does not prevent an innate behaviour from being performed. In the absence of the releasing stimulus, the threshold for the releasing stimulus is progressively lowered until the innate behaviour pattern expresses itself spontaneously. In other words, the threshold that a releasing stimulus has to reach in order to elicit an instinctive motor pattern decreases with longer periods of passivity, while, at the same time, the organism's restlessness may increase, motivating the animal to seek out the missing stimulus (Lorenz, 1963).

Releasers and releasing mechanisms

The stimulus configuration that selectively elicits an innate behaviour, or the "device" that emits this stimulus configuration, is called a "releaser". Each releaser activates a specific "innate releasing mechanism" (the perceptual correlate of the releaser) and, thereby, sets off the innate behaviour sequence (instinct). The "innate releasing mechanism" ("innate releasing schema") is activated by a configuration of only a few simultaneously occurring stimuli. Many innate behaviour sequences (instincts) are object-directed and are activated by only a few stimuli which their object emits (Lorenz, 1935). Two or more intrinsic releasing mechanisms (schemas) may share a common object but are not necessarily activated by the same stimulus configuration associated with that object. Thus, when two or more intrinsic releasing mechanisms respond to stimulus configurations emitted by a common object, different instinctive activities can be centred on the same object. This allows the object of instinctive behaviour to be "treated as consistently in natural living conditions as it would be if its identity were conceived subjectively" (Lorenz, 1935, p. 118).

Fellow members of the species are the object of many instinctive actions. Conspecifics are also the releasers of instinctive actions performed in social situations. "Social releasers", which, by definition, elicit social reactions in fellow members of the species, include conspicuous morphologic features and conspicuous (ritualised) behaviour patterns. Social releasers, their perceptual correlates ("innate releasing mechanisms"), and the responses elicited by them "constitute a sort of 'understanding' within a species" (Lorenz, 1937, p. 148). Once a social releaser, such as an individual's ritualised performance, has activated an "innate releasing mechanism" and elicited an innate social reaction in another individual, the latter individual comes to act as a social releaser in its own right and elicits a matching social response in the former individual (feedback). Lorenz (1935) envisaged that, in social species, "the interlocking performances of individuals, the releaser in one animal and the released reaction in the other, make up the complex function of society" (p. 125).

> I have called releasing instinctive movements, and the colors and structures supporting them, "social releasers". The entire sociology of many animals, and particularly of birds, is based on complex systems of releasers and innate mechanisms, which guarantee consistent and biologically adequate handling of the sex partner, the young, in brief, of all the fellow members of the species. (Lorenz, 1937, p. 141)
>
> The entire sociology of higher animals is built up on social releasers and corresponding innate mechanisms. They should be the main building stones of all sociological research, because the thin coating of acquired behavior amounts to very little in proportion. (Lorenz, 1939, p. 257)

Phylogenesis

Social releasing stimuli, social actions that produce them, and "innate releasing mechanisms" (perceptual schemas) through which these stimuli control other individuals' behaviour are not acquired in ontogenesis but develop in the course of the species' phylogenesis (Lorenz, 1935). When an animal is in a state of general motor excitation, innate reactions may not be discharged fully, or other reactions ("displacement actions") may be discharged out of context. Displacement actions tend to be performed under conditions of conflict and may lower tensions (having a cathartic effect) (Lorenz, 1952; Tinbergen, 1951). In the phylogenesis of a social species, "incipient actions" (incomplete discharges of actions) and displacement actions "may acquire a secondary meaning through conveying a mood from one individual to another" (Lorenz, 1937, p. 149). Developing into expressive movements ("Ausdrucksbewegungen"), intention and displacement actions undergo a process of "ritualisation" to heighten their effect. While an originally senseless intention or displacement action becomes a "social releaser", an initial readiness to "understand" the action develops into an innate releasing mechanism or schema (the perceptual correlate of the releasing action) (Lorenz, 1935).

### 2.1.5   Ritualisation

"Intention movements" and "displacement activities" are the most frequent sources of ritualised "expressive movements" ("Ausdrucksbewegungen") (Tinbergen, 1951; Lorenz, 1952). Many ritualised expressive movements with a communicative function are "based on movements of intent which convey an appetency toward specific modes of behavior" (Hass, 1968, p. 112). Displacement activities are aimless motor patters that occur in animals under conditions of *conflict*. "Expressive movements" ("rites") often develop in the course of phylogenesis when, during typical encounters between individuals, opposing or conflicting impulses seek expression. "Ritualisation" creates new instinctive motor patterns by welding together motor expressions of conflicting impulses (Lorenz, 1963). The display of new instinctive motor patterns ("rites") acquires signal function in the species. Their phylogenetic formation is mirrored by the formation of "innate understanding" on part of the individual receiving, and reacting to, the signal (Lorenz, 1963). "Unritualised behaviour" refers to those sequences of postures and movements

that are employed in the course of purposeful activities, such as nest building, self-grooming, feeding, drinking, or hunting (Moynihan, 1998). "Ritualised performances" are behaviour patterns that, in the course of evolution, have been derived from unritualised forms of behaviour and that have become specialised "to convey information, and perhaps in some cases to do nothing else" (p. 30). Ritualised behaviour patterns are also called "displays". In addition to conveying information, ritualised performances "provide 'emotional relief' for internal stress" (Moynihan, 1998, p. 30). Providing emotional relief, displays may at the same time communicate the performer's emotional state to other individuals.

### Communication

Ritualised patterns of behaviour (displays) are *specialised* for the conveyance of information. However, all overt behaviours, including unritualised patterns, encode information, information that may be conveyed to a receiver. Transmission of information "is an act of communication, and the information in the signal is a message" (Moynihan, 1998, p. 97). The "message" of a signal is the sum of information encoded in a pattern of behaviour. The "meaning" of a message is the information received by an observer; it is the information that the observer infers from the message. The meaning perceived by the observer "is derived from a reading, partial or complete, of the message in its actual context" (p. 95). Communication is directional; signals are designed to induce responses. Meanings perceived by observers "produce results, changes in the attitudes or activities of the observers" (p. 95). These effects on observers are what determine the function of a message and reveal the significance of its meaning. Messages and meanings of ritualised patterns (displays) change in the course of evolution (Moynihan, 1998).

> Naturally occurring social behavior patterns may be varied or variable because they are responses to multiple stimuli, not

only signals from interlocutors but also input from other features of the surroundings that differ from one event to another. (Moynihan, 1998, p. 99)

## Modalities

Visual communication "can be encoded in all sorts of postures and movements, again ranging from unritualized to highly ritualized" (Moynihan, 1998, p. 98). Postures and intention movements that express tendencies to advance or retreat can function as signals, communicating, for instance, intentions to attack or escape during hostile encounters. Unritualised patterns of advance or retreat that are displayed in a hostile context can become, in the course of evolution, ritualised patterns (displays), which are only performed in processes of communication. All acoustic performances of all animals (presumably including aspects of language in humans) "may be assumed to be displays in this sense" (p. 30). The primary function of acoustic patterns "can only be communication" (Moynihan, 1998). Vocalisations "express all kinds of motivation, aggression, and other tendencies, at all levels of intensity, in various combinations and permutations" (p. 97). Vocalisations "can signal probabilities of attack or escape or other activities with great precision", and they can "reveal, even advertise, individual identities and physiological states" (p. 98). Olfactory signals (scent marking), too, "can encode information about identity, mood, probabilities of performance, status, social relations, and associated factors such as the distribution and abundance of food and other resources" (Moynihan, 1998, p. 98).

Many nonhuman animals have the physical capabilities to discuss many subjects. They do not seem to do so frequently or extensively on most occasions. But, even when their statements are basically simple, they can be conveyed with many inflections and, presumably, remarkable precision. (Moynihan, 1998, p. 99)

## Ontogenetic and cultural ritualisation

There are three forms of ritualisation: phylogenetic, ontogenetic, and traditional (cultural) (Eibl-Eibesfeldt, 1970). Traditional ritualisation is transmitted in the course of cultural evolution from generation to generation. Ontogenetic and traditional ritualisation play a particular role in humans. Unlike phylogenetic rituals, ontogenetic and traditional rituals are acquired through learning, however, similarly to phylogenetic ritualisation, behaviour patterns that become ritualised in ontogenesis or cultural evolution "are exaggerated in pantomime and accentuated through additional equipment" but also simplified and rhythmically repeated (Eibl-Eibesfeldt, 1970, p. 50). Thus, behaviour patterns are turned into signals, whereby, in the process of phylogenetic ritualisation, "this is often accompanied by the development of special physical structures" (p. 54). Modifications that original behaviour patterns undergo in the process of ritualisation are "designed to make the signal striking and unmistakable" (p. 54). Simplified behaviour patterns are effective signals. All three processes of ritualisation are constrained by the same requirement, namely that the receiver of a signal (that is, the perceiver of a ritualised behaviour pattern) has to determine the meaning of the behaviour pattern (Eibl-Eibesfeldt, 1970).

The complex of impressions received from the personality of one individual—his ideas, his appearance, his moods, gestures, intonation of voice, his interests, his enthusiasms and his doldrums—may constitute the symbolic system of stimuli by which one is conditioned. (Burrow, 1949, p. 136)

Without having recognized it, man has become conditioned socially through gradual subjugation *as a species* to a social *system* of symbolic stimuli. Though experimentally unpremeditated, these symbolic stimuli are present to-day in the vicarious mechanism of the spoken word, or language. These verbal stimuli have artificially produced in us endless conditioned reflexes. ... For not only has man been gradually trained over generations to respond reflexly to certain selective words or symbols, but the conditioned reflexes thus induced by these systems of stimuli have become *socially consolidated into affectively conditioned systems of reaction.* (Burrow, 1949, pp. 135–136)

### 2.1.6   Appetitive behaviour

Noninstinctive (acquired) behaviours include orienting reactions, conditioned reflexes, and goal-directed or appetitive behaviour. Conditioned reflexes change or refine innate behaviour patterns, adapting them to concrete environmental conditions. Goal-directed, purposive, or appetitive behaviour refers to the animal's striving to achieve a "stimulus situation" ("Reizsituation") in response to which an instinctive act can be discharged (Lorenz, 1937). The goal of appetitive or goal-directed behaviour is the attainment of a stimulus situation needed to release an instinctive act. In appetitive or goal-directed behaviour, the animal can be said of have an appetite for a particular releasing "stimulus situation" (Lorenz, 1937). The stimulus situation releases an instinctive act when it is recognised by an "innate releasing mechanism" (the perceptual correlate of the stimulus situation). Thus, appetitive behaviour can be followed, once an appropriate stimulus situation is attained, by a consummatory act ("Endhandlung").[2] A functional unit of behaviour has purposive (adaptively modifiable) and instinctual (rigidly innate) components that may alternate in direct succession. Most long chains of behaviour are intricate integrations of innate and acquired elements, but the final component of a behavioural sequence is always an instinctive (usually consummatory) act (Lorenz, 1937) (Figure 2-1).

---

[2]Consummatory action is always innate.

Lorenz (1935) thought that innate (instinctive) behaviour and acquired behaviour develop along two divergent phylogenetic and ontogenetic lines. Instinctive reactions are fundamentally different from actions acquired through learning. In particular, stimuli to which an animal responds with innate behaviour are different from stimuli to which the animal responds with acquired behaviour. "Innate releasing mechanisms" are tuned to simple sets of stimuli, whereas acquired behaviour responds to very complex sets of stimuli (Lorenz, 1935). The response to complex stimulus qualities must be acquired by conditioning. Although instinctive acts are often released by an unconditioned reflex to a small set of stimuli (and, in this sense, instincts are related to unconditioned reflexes), in some cases, the releasing mechanism (recognition of the releasing situation or object) has to be acquired (Lorenz, 1935). For example, the releasing mechanism for reactions to fellow members of the species may not be innately determined, even though the motor mechanism involved in these reactions is innate. The schema (object) that releases an innately determined reaction to conspecifics has to be acquired during a "critical period" in the animal's ontogenetic development (in a process known as "imprinting"). Once "imprinting" has occurred, the animal will react to the relevant object as if its recognition is innate (Lorenz, 1935). A similar mechanism may account for ontogenetic ritualisation.

A conditioned reflex may be interposed between conditions of the environment and a rigid automatism (instinctive action). This means that a chain of innate behaviour can be set off by a conditioned reflex or by an unconditioned reflex. Conditioned reflexes may not only act to "release innate behaviour patterns in specific situations where they fulfill their biological function"; they may also spatially orientate the organism to a releasing stimulus situation (Lorenz, 1939). In the latter case, conditioned reflexes respond to *complex* spatial stimuli. Orienting reactions that are based on conditioned reflexes to *complex*

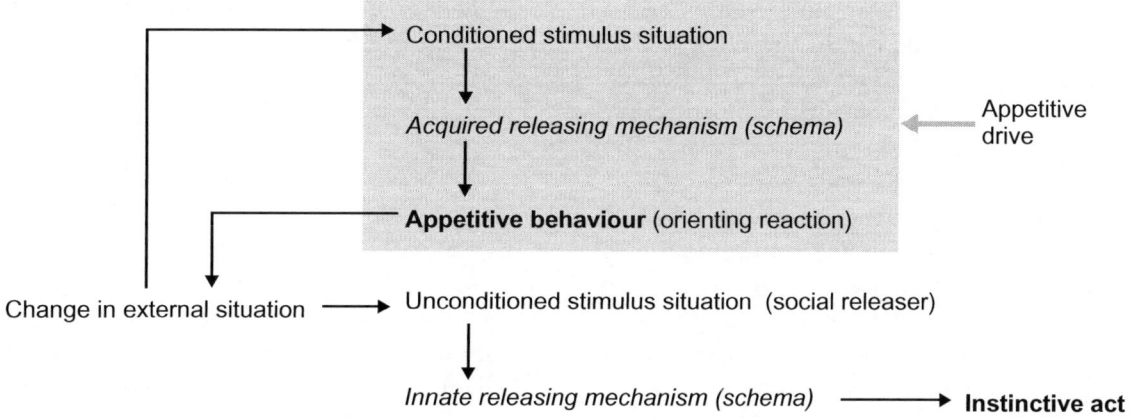

Figure 2-1.   Relationship between instinct, drive, and appetitive behaviour.

spatial stimuli are the most primitive form and the forerunner of all appetitive and intelligent behaviour (Lorenz, 1937). Appetitive, purposive, or goal-directed behaviour not only consists of orienting reactions but also employs subordinate locomotor patterns, which, too, help to attain a releasing stimulus situation. Locomotion, balancing mechanisms, and other simple innate patters (grasping, glancing, pecking) are tools of purposive behaviour that can be applied in the service of different appetences. The animal can use the same simple motor patterns as means to attain stimulus situations related to different instinctive activities (Lorenz, 1937).

Orienting reactions

Orienting reactions, which are elicited by complex, spatially defined stimuli, adapt the organism's motor state to spatial conditions in the environment (Lorenz & Tinbergen, 1938). Orienting movements play a critical role in directing or orienting the animal towards a goal in the environment. Orienting reactions help to create "the stimulus situation in which the instinctive action is released and, at the same time, the spatial relationship required for its biologically effective discharge" (p. 207). Appetitive behaviour may be limited to a mere orienting movement. In the simplest form of appetitive behaviour, an orienting reaction

establishes a postural relationship between the animal and the object of its instinctive action (Lorenz & Tinbergen, 1938). Instinctive action in itself is a purely automatic performance. Instincts, representing centrally coordinated motor patterns, "cannot function adequately unless the animal is also adjusted spatially to the object of each action" (p. 183). In order to ensure adaptation to spatial conditions in the environment, orienting reactions often alternate with innate reactions in a functional unit of behaviour. A functional unit of behaviour integrates centrally coordinated instinctive motor patterns with receptor-controlled "topic taxes" (orienting mechanisms) (Lorenz & Tinbergen, 1938).[3]

Tool reactions

"Tool reactions" ("tool activities") are simple hereditary motor patterns that are useful for various purposes. Various instincts can make use

---

[3]Not all orienting reactions respond to complex, and presumably allocentric, spatial stimuli. Orienting reactions may have their own innate releasing mechanism, perhaps especially if they respond to simple egocentric stimuli. Although orienting reactions implicated in appetitive behaviour were suggested to be fundamentally different from instinctive actions, it seems that both, orienting reactions and instinctive actions, can depend on innate releasing mechanisms that select opportunities for their employment (Lorenz, 1939).

of these simple motor patterns (including loco-motor patterns), "each within the context of its particular motor flow" (Hass, 1968, p. 48). "Tool reactions" are also available to orienting reactions and appetitive behaviour (Lorenz, 1939). Tool reactions are instinctive actions (Lorenz, 1937). Thus, there are two types of instinctive action, representing extremes on a spectrum: tool reactions and consummatory actions (Lorenz, 1939). Consummatory actions ("Endhandlungen") are specific with regard to their releasing circumstances and are rarely activated. An instinctive act that is the goal of appetitive behaviour "nearly always has only a single highly specific function, and correspondingly only one releasing mechanism which unerringly selects the unique biologically adequate situation" (p. 253). Tool reactions, by contrast, are elicited by comparatively unspecific and frequently occurring stimulus situations—in accordance with the fact that tool reactions are general in purpose (Lorenz, 1939).

### Hierarchical organisation

Appetitive behaviour of a general nature does not usually lead directly to a consummatory act but has to be followed by appetitive behaviour of a subordinate nature (Lorenz, 1952). Appetitive behaviour is organised hierarchically. The hierarchically organised system of appetitive behaviour guides the animal from one acquired releasing stimulus situation to another, always from a more general and accessible releasing situation to a more specialised one (Tinbergen, 1951). General appetitive behaviour continues until a stimulus situation is attained that elicits appetitive behaviour of a more specialised type. This, again, continues until the next releasing stimulus situation is achieved. As the animal encounters a releasing stimulus situation, an acquired releasing mechanism switches from appetitive behaviour of a more general nature to appetitive behaviour of a more specialised nature, until, eventually, a stimulus situation is attained that activates an innate releasing mechanism

and, hence, an instinctive (consummatory) act (Lorenz, 1952) (Figure 2-1).

### 2.1.7   Drive as energy

"Drive" refers to the process that makes the animal seek a key stimulus, that is, a stimulus situation or object that elicits a consummatory action. Drive "spurs the animal to search, directedly or at random, for a specific stimulus situation (the only one in which the innate releasing mechanism of the craved reaction will respond)" (Lorenz, 1937, p. 171). Thus, drives ("instincts" in McDougall's sense) motivate appetitive behaviour. Drives do not motivate instinctive motor actions; instead, by motivating and coordinating appetitive behaviour aimed at achieving a releasing stimulus situations or object, drives *prepare* for instinctive action (Figure 2-1). Emotional feelings, other than perhaps pleasure, are correlated with drives ("instincts" in McDougall's sense) but not with instinctive actions. Pleasure, being the subjective manifestation of reward, is associated with the attainment of a stimulus situation (or object) that can release an instinctive action (or it is associated, as Lorenz thought, with the performance of the instinctive action itself).

Instincts cannot be changed by experience; the adaptiveness of behaviour does not reside in the instinctive act but *precedes* it (Lorenz, 1952). Appetitive behaviour becomes gradually more adaptive or "goal-directed" through trial-and-error learning based on repeated exposure to reward and punishment (reinforcement learning). Appetitive behaviour may search for a stimulus situation more or less "aimlessly". Exploration and play are appetitive behaviours of high variability. In the presence of a more general drive, appetitive behaviour may take the form of random search or exploration (Lorenz, 1952). Through trial-and-error learning (reinforcement learning), appetitive behaviour becomes more specialised. Specialised appetitive behaviour is perhaps accompanied by a specialised drive in form of a state of expectation.

Reaction tendencies

Drives have nondirective properties; they cannot be said to be directed towards or away from objects (Brown, 1953). Instead, drives play an energising or activating role. Drives function in concert with "reaction tendencies" (habits) to determine overt behaviour. Brown (1953) ascribed guided and directed aspects of behaviour to "reaction tendencies" and to the directive function (response-eliciting function) of stimulus cues. "Reaction tendencies" refer to the *capacities* of stimulus cues to elicit specific reactions. A drive engages one or another "potentiality" for behaving in specific ways in the presence of given stimuli. In other words, a drive activates one or more "reaction tendencies" (habits); but it cannot in itself determine behaviour. Likewise, reaction tendencies cannot produce overt behaviour in the absence of a drive. *Goal objects* (including incentives) are stimulus cues that have acquired strong approach-response-evoking tendencies (specific reaction tendencies); they can elicit approach strivings, or steer behaviour in other ways, but do so only when behaviour is energised by a drive. Drawing on existing action tendencies, the drive produces whatever behaviour is called for by the specific environmental situation (Brown, 1953).

## 2.1.8    Drive reduction

Drives, such as hunger or thirst, impel the organism to make responses to cues (Miller & Dollard, 1941; Miller, 1948). Whether responses to cues will be repeated in a similar situation depends on whether they are rewarded. There is variability in drive-imposed responding; and it is this variability that may lead to a response that produces a rewarding event, that is, an event that occasions a reduction in drive (Miller & Dollard, 1941; Miller, 1948). Similarly, a more or less random response can bring about the cessation of a fear-arousing stimulus or the cessation of pain, frustration, or noxious stimulation. A sudden reduction in fear or pain following a more or less random response strengthens the connection from fear or

pain, and other relevant cues in the situation, to the response (Miller, 1948). In general, a reduction in a drive will increase the probability that behaviour preceding the drive reduction will occur again in a similar situation. Learning, in this instance, is due to the reinforcement of a link between a cue constellation embedded in a situation and a response. Experience of pain or exposure to punishment following a response will weaken the bond between stimulus situation and behaviour. What the organism acquires in this manner is a set of habits or "modes of responding to complex stimulus situations composed of both external and internal elements" (Brown, 1953).

Drive stimulus

The situation to which an organism responds can be regarded as a composite of external and *internal* discriminable stimuli, which would be consistent with the notion that emotional feeling (if it represents an internal discriminable stimulus) is but an abstract aspect of the situation to which the organism responds. "Drive stimuli" are internal discriminable stimuli that accompany emotional states or drives. It is thought that behaviours that precede a reduction in drive can become attached to these "drive stimuli" (Brown, 1953). Perhaps, it is a stimulus configuration consisting of both drive stimulus and sensory cues that is linked, through reinforcement learning, to the behavioural response that occasioned a drive reduction (or that is linked to the class of behaviour to which this response belongs). Drive stimuli, in combination with external events, acquire the capacity to elicit responses directed towards objects—responses that are capable of reducing drives (Brown, 1953).[4]

---

[4] Alternatively one could argue that, while discriminative aspects of a situation are connected with particular classes of motor responses, emotional aspects of the situation are connected with drive and affective arousal. The situation will have acquired an emotional dimension as a result of conditioning, but it would be the discriminative or sensory dimension of the situation that, as a result of drive reduction and reinforcement, is linked to an overt response.

## 2.2   Situation and emotion

Animals actively strive to attain stimulus situations ("Reizsituationen") in response to which an instinctive act can be discharged (Lorenz, 1952). Appetitive or goal-directed behaviour brings the animal into contact with a stimulus situation (or a stimulus object) that releases an instinctive behaviour pattern (usually a consummatory act). In other words, the goal of appetitive behaviour is to attain a stimulus situation (or object) needed for the discharge of an instinctive act. Orienting mechanisms, interacting with locomotor mechanisms, direct the organism towards a releasing stimulus situation or an object of instinctive behaviour (Lorenz & Tinbergen, 1938). An orienting movement that turns the organism towards a releasing stimulus situation (or stimulus object) constitutes the simplest form of appetitive behaviour. Orienting reactions are conditioned to complex stimuli in the environment. All appetitive behaviour is steered by complex spatial stimuli. Appetitive behaviour may not strive directly for a stimulus situation that releases an instinctive act but strive for an acquired (conditioned) situation that releases appetitive behaviour of a subordinate nature, which, in turn, may succeed in attaining a stimulus situation that releases an instinctive act (Lorenz, 1952). Drive and emotion accompany appetitive behaviour in search of a releasing stimulus situation (or stimulus object). In the presence of a more general drive, appetitive behaviour may take the form of more or less random search or exploration (Lorenz, 1952). Drive and emotion of a specific nature may be attached to layers of complex spatial stimuli that, via orienting and locomotor reactions, move the animal from one acquired releasing stimulus situation to the next, until an innate stimulus situation has been attained that releases an act of consumption. Thus, emotional feelings that accompany behaviour that responds to, and creates, complex spatial stimulus constellations may have come to pervade the experience of space itself.

Affective processes are motivational in the sense that they play an essential role in organising, activating, regulating, and sustaining behaviour patterns (Young, 1959). Affective processes are anchored to physiological events, but they can also be anchored to events within the physical environment. Environmental situations can have an *innate* capacity to arouse an affective process; or they *acquire*, through conditioning, the capacity to arouse an affective process. A situation may produce positive or negative affective arousal (Young, 1959). Affective arousal orientates the animal towards or away from stimulus cues and objects. If a situation produces positive arousal, the animal reacts positively to stimulus cues in the environment. If the situation produces negative affective arousal, then the animal makes cognitive discriminations or choices and performs actions that are consistent with fear, distress, or anxiety (Young, 1959). States of pain or discomfort are often inhibitory in their effect on the generation of actions, whereas states of pleasure and satisfaction tend to facilitate various modes of action. Moreover, animals strive to attain and preserve satisfying states of affairs, and they avoid or abandon discomforting or annoying states of affairs (Thorndike, 1911). Discomforting or annoying sates of affairs are characterised by negative affective arousal in the form of pain, fear, or anxiety.[5] Goal-directed behaviour was suggested to be organised in such a way that its performance minimises negative affectivity (e.g., distress due to a state of deprivation) and, at the same time, maximises positive affectivity (Young, 1959). When positive affectivity is present, the animal tries to increase it, such as by employing approach patterns of behaviour. When negative affectivity is present, the animal tries to reduce it by employing behaviour that aims to terminate an aversive condition or escape from it (Young, 1959).

---

[5]Separation from the mother or the herd is anxiety-arousing and, hence, represents an intolerable state of affairs for mammalian infants and members of gregarious species, respectively.

## 2.2.1  Contextual conditioning

> The pleasure principle, then, is a tendency operating in the service of a function whose business it is to free the mental apparatus entirely from excitation or to keep the amount of excitation in it constant or to keep it as low as possible. (Freud, 1920, p. 62)

The acquisition of conditioned avoidance responses capitalises on the primitive urge to attain a state of quiescence (Lorenz, 1973). An animal remains in a state of agitation for as long as an aversion-producing situation persists. Behaviour patterns are acquired that remove the animal from the harmful situation. In agreement with Hull (1943), it is the waning of irritation that acts as the conditioned reinforcement (reinforcement by relief of tension) (Lorenz, 1973). In a related fashion, more or less random exploration or search (appetitive behaviour of a more general nature) is shaped, through reinforcement learning, into instrumental behaviour that is more or less habitual. Drive reduction or relief of tension, which occurs whenever a reward is encountered and a situation is experienced as pleasurable, reinforces the link between the preceding situation and the orienting reaction and locomotor behaviour that was applied in this situation. Thorndike (1911) proposed that, in the process of learning, connections are formed between situations and responses. According to the "law of effect", the response made to a situation is connected to that situation if the response was followed by "satisfaction". Similarly, the link between a situation and the (orienting or appetitive) response made in that situation is weakened if the response was followed by discomfort or pain, meaning that the response will be less likely to be repeated in the future whenever similar circumstances prevail (Thorndike, 1911). The greater the satisfaction or discomfort, the greater the strengthening or weakening of the link between situation and response. Different responses may differ in their readiness to be connected with a particular type of situation; and some responses may form a more intimate connection with a situation than others (Thorndike, 1911).

Young (1959) suggested that laws of conditioning apply to affective processes, too, so that links can be formed between environmental situations and affective processes, similarly to the formation of links between discrete stimuli and motor responses (stimulus-response learning). Thus, representations of environmental situations may acquire the capacity to elicit an affective process that is appropriate to the animal's environmental circumstances and physiological context. Affective processes, in turn, play a role in the acquisition of approach-maintaining and avoidance-terminating patterns of behaviour. They may do so in two complementary ways. First, affective processes constrain the generation of orienting and locomotor behaviours in such a way that a suitable innate releasing stimulus situation is likely to be encountered and an instinctive act called for under the animal's circumstances is likely to be released. Second, the drive associated with a negative affective process (relating, for instance, to a state of deprivation) undergoes an acute reduction following an orienting and locomotor response that successfully instates the releasing stimulus situation for an instinctive consummatory act. Drive reduction reinforces the link between spatial aspects of the preceding situation and an approach-maintaining or avoidance-terminating pattern. Approach-maintaining and avoidance-terminating behaviours that have become habitual and automatic are affectively neutral (Young, 1959).

## 2.2.2  Bodily resonance

Moore (1926) thought that the subject's emotional state is dependent on the perception of an exciting fact or an "intellectual insight" into the situation (and that the "insight into the situation is the cause of the emotion" (p. 132)). A fact or situation would cause an emotional reaction that is *merely*

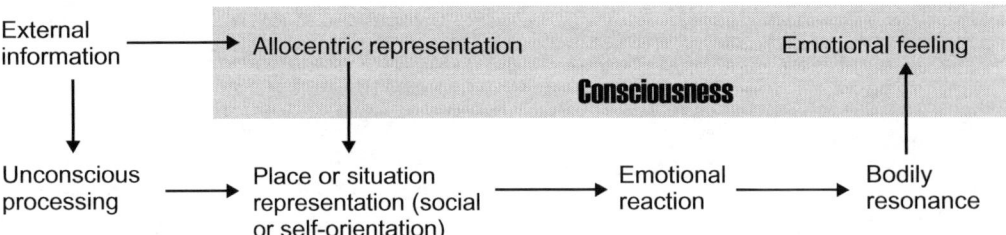

Figure 2-2.   Appreciation of the situation, operating unconsciously, evokes an appropriate emotional reaction, however bodily resonance (which forms part of the emotional reaction) is required for emotional feelings.

*accompanied* by "complex and extensive bodily resonance" (Moore, 1926, p. 106). James (1890) however had argued that emotional *feeling* (which we have to distinguish from emotional reactions or emotional behaviour modes) is the *perception* of a complex pattern of bodily resonance—a hypothesis that does not preclude the possibility that emotional reactions (unconscious) depend on the organism's appreciation (unconscious or perhaps conscious) of its external situation or the perception (unconscious) of an "exciting fact". For James (1890), it is the perception of an exciting fact that causes a state of bodily resonance (an unconscious emotional state), which secondarily gives rise to a conscious feeling state. The subject consciously experiences the emotional feeling only after an external or internal event (having been processed unconsciously) has induced (via a hypothalamic centre) a pattern of emotional bodily resonance. James' theory is often taken as implying that cognition does not mediate in the generation of emotion, however, if we distinguish between emotional reaction (unconscious) and emotional feeling (conscious), then both would be true: (i) cognition (in the sense of unconscious processing of external information or perhaps conscious appreciation of the situation) precedes the generation of emotion, that is, the emotional reaction (unconscious); and (ii) the emotional feeling (conscious) is secondary to a pattern of bodily resonance (constituting part of the emotional reaction). Emotional feeling, in turn, colours ongoing formation of event memories (allocentric

representations) and, thereby, influences ongoing assessment of the situation and the physiologically relevant learning of behaviour applied in the situation (Figure 2-2).

### 2.2.3   Emergency emotions

Pain promotes behaviour that seeks to rid the organism "of the source of suffering" (Rado, 1956, p. 243). A close relationships between pain, fear, and rage is suggested by the fact that present pain can elicit reactions of rage or fear. Rado (1956) suggested that pain, acting as a warning signal of damage, "is the very basis upon which the entire organization of emergency behavior has evolved" (p. 243). The "emergency emotions" of fear and rage, working "in the same adaptive direction as pain", "are based on the anticipation of pain from impending damage" (p. 219). The aim of fear is "to escape from the threat", while the aim of rage is "to eliminate it by combat" (Rado, 1956, p. 219). Fear, in particular, is a warning signal elicited by expectancy of impending damage. Exploration by distance receptors enables the animal to foresee pain from damage likely to occur in the location (or situation) *ahead* of its movements (p. 244). It is this expectancy of pain that elicits fear. In the course of evolution, "the range of foresight (expectancy of pain from damage) increased, and so also, through the cumulative effect of repetition, did the automatization of operating patterns" (p. 234). Rage, unlike fear, is not "an immediate response to the threat of pain from damage" (p. 244). To Rado (1956) it looked "as if the organism has to be primed to rage by a shot of fear" (p. 244). Fear can be converted into rage, and vice versa; and "the organism is often seen to oscillate between fear and rage until one or the other prevails" (Rado, 1956, p. 244).

Rado (1956) established that, even though "the feeling aspect of fear or of rage may be completely absent", "the emotions of fear and rage may nonetheless be present in the organism and exert their motivating (integrative) influence on the patient's actions and thoughts" (p. 246). We can discern the subject's underlying motivation even in the absence of emotional feelings, given that "patterns of thought and action motivated (integrated) by the various emotions characteristically differ from one another" (p. 246).[6] Behaviour of the fearful or enraged animal or man is not limited to escape or combat. The expressive aspect (outward display) of "emergency emotions" evolved "presumably for the purpose of broadcasting the warning to other members of the herd" (Rado, 1956, p. 244). Displays can be acoustic (vocalisations) as well as visual (gestures and facial expressions). In the infant, "fear tends to elicit a cry for help" (p. 245). Submission to authority, visually communicated by ritualised movements, can be seen as a form of escape behaviour that is employed in "social dependency relationships" (pp. 219, 245). Submission to authority and the infant's cry for help would share the same motivational origin: fear prompting escape to safety (Rado, 1956).

### 2.2.4  Emotional action modes

To fear is, among other things, to engage in fantasies of harm coming to one from some source of danger; to develop ideas of fleeing from that danger or else attacking its source; to make incipient movements

of attack or escape, both of which involve setting off physiological and muscular changes that enable the anticipated exertions to be performed; to be restless; and either to be hypervigilant and jumpy or to avoid representing the danger consciously (denial, repression, counterphobic activity). (Schafer, 1971, p. 285)

Moore (1926) emphasised that emotions contain a characteristic impulse. Sadness, for example, seeks to procure others' sympathy; it contains a "craving for sympathy", an impulse to solicit "tender caresses" (Moore, 1926, p. 189). Schafer (1971) conceived affect or emotion as an action to be done or as a mode of such actions. Emotive actions ("emotion-actions") are actions performed as part of an "emotion-mode". We can conceive "emotion-modes" as abstract kinds of action, accepting that "actions may be designated on every conceivable level of generality or abstractness" (p. 274). An emotion-mode, such as fear, is an action "because it subsumes a number of more concrete actions or modes, such as to flee, to avoid, to act timidly or placatingly" (Schafer, 1971, p. 275). Anger ("the mode of acting angrily") "includes tensing muscles, clenching teeth, biting fiercely, hitting, soiling, thinking of attack, and subjectively defining it as vengeance or defence or even pleasure" (pp. 282–283). Thus, emotions refer to "our actions, including thought-actions, and the modes in which we perform them, including modes of thinking" (p. 279). Situations, ascertained by cognitive and orienting actions, set the occasion for acting emotionally in or on the environment. The concepts of emotion-action and situation are inseparable. We can define "a person's emotion-action, and emotion-modes by stating his or her situation in a certain way" (Schafer, 1976, p. 340).

Emotion-actions and emotion-modes are performed only in their own situations, that is, during the doing of them under specific subjective circumstances. (Schafer, 1971, p. 313)

---

[6]Rado (1956) listed "escape pattern, combat pattern, submission pattern, defiance pattern, brooding pattern, expiatory pattern, pattern of self-damaging defiance, etc". (p. 246).

Under certain conditions, people perform certain emotion-actions or act in certain emotion-modes. The conditions include the person's own actions of one sort or another, among them the actions of defining and estimating environmental circumstances as threats, opportunities, etc., and of estimating oneself relative to these. In a general sense, the conditions refer to the personal action of constructing and maintaining situations of certain sorts. (p. 339)

Emotion is: an emotion-action or emotion-mode of action that people perform in the situations they define. (Schafer, 1976, p. 356)

Accepting that emotion or affect is an abstract form of behaviour—an action mode—, we could go on to argue that one's conscious emotional feeling is an aspect of one's awareness of the situation to which one responds emotionally, contrary to Schafer's position. Hence, we can explain "the frequent resemblance, and the occasional apparent exact likeness, between one's remembered emotionality in some situations and one's perceived or subjectively experienced emotionality upon thinking of it in the present" (Schafer, 1976, p. 313). The subjectively experienced emotionality of situations predisposes to certain emotive actions or action modes in a way that is similar to how meaningful objects in a situation map onto instrumental task modes. Whether the situation is experienced emotionally or affectively neutrally, we tend to respond to it in a manner that was previously reinforced, tending to repeat the past in the present.

... we use the idea of old feelings to say that we are presently in an actual situation that seems so similar to the old one or is so evocative of it that we necessarily react in it and to it in a way we did in the past. (Schafer, 1976, p. 314)

## Controlling emotions

We respond to emotional situations (situations imbued with emotional feeling), in different ways. First, one may refrain "from performing some or all of the emotive actions one wishes to perform in a certain situation" (Schafer, 1971, p. 295). Emotive actions from which one refrains, or the public visibility of which one limits, "include frank statements, facial expressions, gestures, exclamations, tones of voice, postures, and movements in space relative to other people, objects in the environment, and parts of one's body", all of which are constitutive aspects of one's acting emotionally (p. 295). By refraining from emotive actions, "the person will be acting differently than would be the case were he or she simply, unconcernedly, and visibly acting emotionally" (p. 295). Second, one may "engage in cognitive actions by which one transforms one's situation, hence one's occasion for acting emotionally" (Schafer, 1971, p. 295). Remembering, anticipating, and imagining are "thought actions that may be carried out in various emotion-modes" (p. 313). By comprehending, integrating, reviewing one's previous impressions, attending, gathering more information, anticipating, and taking stock of one's prospects ("cognitive actions"), "one develops one's situations, thereby establishing the occasions and significances of one's emotions" (p. 296). As a result, one may "have less reason or no reason to be emotional in the way or to the extent one has judged undesirable" (p. 297).

Seeming merely to keep control of an emotion, one may go so far as to eliminate it (except in its conditional mode) or transform it into its opposite, as, for example, the paranoiac does in transforming homosexual love to hate and then fleeing or provoking persecution by others, and as the obsessional neurotic does in finding or constructing situations that call for acting kindly when otherwise he or she would be "filled with rage". But never is it really a matter of transforming an entity, emotion, by ones actions: the *it* that is transformed refers to a situation and the actions appropriate to it. (Schafer, 1971, p. 298)

Third, one may take "action socially and physically to change one's position in one's given environment or else to change the environment itself" (Schafer, 1971, p. 295). Emotive actions that alter one's position in the social environment include "confronting an antagonist overtly, offering or demanding an explanation, and finding a friend or a shelter or a weapon" (p. 297). Many physical and social actions one performs "in and on the environment … cannot be called emotive actions" (Schafer, 1971, p. 297). These may be the instrumental or affectively "neutralised" actions or modes of action that have been associated, through reinforcement learning, with particular situations. Emotive or instrumental actions one performs may alter the physical environment or "affect the actions of others in the environment" (Schafer, 1971, p. 297). Others' actions, in turn, alter one's situation and one's perception of it. In perceiving others' emotive actions, one may be unconsciously disposed to mirror their emotive actions or action modes. One's observation and interpretation of the immediate social situation may be influenced by one's automatic mirroring of others' affective expressions. One may become angry or anxious in a social situation if one sees somebody acting angrily or anxiously. One's observation of others' emotional actions (involving subtle imitation of their actions or action modes) may not differ in principle from observation of one's own emotion actions, leading in both cases to a change in one's emotional feeling state, consistent with James' (1890) notion that one's consciously experienced emotionality is secondary to one's performance, albeit subliminal performance, of emotive actions.

> Among the observers of acting angrily may be one who is possibly, but not necessarily, in an especially favourable position as observer; this is the one who performs the actions and modes in question—the agent. (Schafer, 1971, p. 283)

## 2.2.5   Psychic reality

> [The] assumption is that whenever one sees oneself as being in the same situation, one will react in the same way. … we cannot absolutely separate the definition of a situation and the definition of a reaction to it, for the two are correlative. … *there cannot be more than a relatively narrow range of similar reactions to a group of relatively similar situations.* Clearly different actions must imply clearly different situations. The concept of situation is the same as the concept of psychic reality, … (Schafer, 1971, p. 231)

Kernberg (1992) regarded affects as "complex psychic structures indissolubly linked to the individual's cognitive appraisal of his immediate situation" (p. 12). In interpersonal situations, cognitive appraisal always concerns the relationship between representations or images of oneself and another person (an object) (Kernberg, 1992, 1996). Affects give rise to an impulse or "action tendency" towards a stimulus or object in the situation. The affect that is linked to the individual's appraisal of his immediate situation implements an "action tendency" that is appropriate to the situation (a tendency to emit situationally appropriate responses to stimuli embedded in the situation). This is to say that an emotionally coloured situation implements an *action mode* in accordance with a previously reinforced association. Thus, the situation sets the occasion for one's responding to discrete stimuli. One's responding to a stimulus depends on the situation, and one "might be continuously redefining the stimulus in terms of his or her changing situation" (Schafer, 1971, p. 317).

The social situation in which one finds oneself, and to which one is disposed to respond emotionally or instrumentally, is a constellation of social symbols and representations of others' actions, intentions, and social status as well as one's knowledge of others' relationships with each other and with oneself. One perceives the constellation of social cues insofar as it relates to one's competitive position or status in the group and to one's seeking of attachment to an individual or the group as a substitute for the primary love object. The meaning one attributes to social stimuli and the social situation is self-relevant. In perceiving others' actions, intentions, or status, one indeed shows a "tendency to replace the actuality of an individual with one's own social image of him" (Burrow, 1949, p. 16).

> There *is* a reality in the sense of there being some inescapable limits to possibility, which means some necessity that is being encountered, interpreted, and allowed for. But there is no single right way in which this reality must be observed, even though there are many irrational ways. ... *How* we observe *what* we observe will depend on whether we are acting needfully, desperately, submissively, etc.; on our level of cognitive development and our task orientation ... and the implicit or explicit theoretical model we are using. (Schafer, 1976, p. 239)

The observed social situation ("psychic reality") can be "distorted by biased or defensive action" (Schafer, 1976, p. 239), or it can be cognitively reinterpreted, possibly by incorporating ideas that pertain to, but are not directly evidenced by, the social situation. The social situation we encounter extends well beyond what is observable. Situations can be transformed by orienting reactions or cognitive actions into other situations. Orienting reactions, when monitoring the external environment, change the external situation to which one is exposed, while thinking (covert orienting and remembering) modifies the situation in imagery. Cognitive actions by which we reevaluate situations internally may be derived evolutionarily from orienting reactions by which we gather self-relevant information from the situation. Cognitive transformation of a situation may be followed by transformation of the situation by way of a social action or action mode. In any event, transformation of the situation would dispose us to a different mode of action. According to Schafer (1976), "making environmental changes is like cognitively transforming one's view of a given situation:

one is seeing to it that one no longer defines a sufficient reason or indeed any reason to begin or continue acting in a certain emotional way" (p. 298).

Cognitive theory

Individuals spontaneously interpret their present social situation by means of what Beck called "automatic thoughts". Cognitive theory of social behaviour and personality maintains that the "spontaneous interpretation of the situation" plays "a central role in eliciting and shaping an individual's emotional and behavioral response to a situation" (Pretzer & Beck, 1996, p. 45). We respond to the immediate situation by invoking an emotional state and employing a certain type of interpersonal behaviour. "Automatic thoughts", contributing to spontaneous interpretation of the present situation, determine one's emotional response to the situation and one's interpersonal behaviour. While "the individual's interpretation of events shapes his/her emotional response to the situation", the emotional response to the situation, in turn, "has important effects on cognition" (p. 51). It has been shown experimentally that a person's mood (emotional response) tends to bias his or her perception and memory recall (aspects of cognition) in a mood-congruent way. For instance, anxiety biases attentional processes in favour of signs of threat (reviewed in Pretzer & Beck, 1996). Increased vigilance for interpersonal threats not only maintains the state of anxiety but codetermines the person's social behaviour. On the other hand, individuals strive to avoid unpleasant emotions. They "may attempt to avoid thoughts, memories, or situations that they expect to elicit the emotion"; or they "may seek to escape from experiencing the emotion as quickly as possible" (Pretzer & Beck, 1996, p. 52), making again the point that not only interpersonal behaviour but also cognition, involving derivatives of orienting reactions, can effect regulation of emotional states via altered perception and interpretation of the situation.

## 2.2.6   Compulsion to repeat

> It has always surprised us that the forgotten and repressed experiences of early childhood should reproduce themselves in dreams and reactions during analytic treatment, especially in reactions involved in the transference, ... (Freud, 1933, p. 138)

Freud discovered that, in the formation of interpersonal relationships, one is compelled to repeat forgotten (repressed) events of one's childhood as contemporary experience. The repetition of the past in the present is called "transference". The emergence of the patient's repressed material in the process of psychoanalysis, insofar as this material manifests itself in the patient's behaviour towards, and relationship to, the analyst, is called "transference neurosis". Patients in psychoanalysis repeat "unwanted situations and painful emotions in the transference and revive them with great ingenuity"; "they contrive once more to feel themselves scorned, to oblige the physician to speak severely to them and treat them coldly"; or "they discover appropriate objects for their jealousy", objects that are of interest to the analyst (Freud, 1920, p. 21). Crucially, the patient undergoing psychoanalysis repeats aspects of his past relationships within the present analytic relationship and, at the same time, avoids to consciously "remember" these aspects. The task of the analyst is to help the patient "to recognize that what appears to be reality is in fact only a reflection of a forgotten past" (Freud, 1920, p. 19)—a recognition that the patient is "resisting". Freud thought that the patient's resistance to remembering arises from his ego. The compulsion to repeat, on the other hand, may be due to a fundamental tendency to remove or reduce tension that has been raised in the organism. The same fundamental tendency may also find expression in the "pleasure principle" (Freud, 1920, p. 56).

Interpersonal situations may be linked with emotional or instrumental action modes in a manner that resembles the more familiar linkage between discrete stimuli and discrete actions. Transformations of situations into emotional actions or action modes would be subject to reinforcement learning, similarly to the conditioning processes involved in the acquisition of stimulus-response patterns. Representations of salient environmental contexts or more abstract interpersonal situations would elicit emotional or instrumental behaviour modes in accordance with previously reinforced associations. Situations and modes of responding to situations cannot be separated. Emotional actions and modes "are correlative of the infant's creation of projects and situations" (Schafer, 1971, p. 356).

> The child has no clear and objective sense of the relation between action and aim, hence an aspect of the situation brings to mind the recollection of the whole procedure, ... (Shapiro, 2000, p. 72)

In an interpersonal situation, the individual's behaviour is designed to reinstate a previously gratifying interpersonal situation (object relation) or escape from the situation (if previous exposure was painful). Seeking to reinstate a desired state or avoid a painful situation, the individual is motivated "to respectively reinstate or avoid similar affective experiences" (Kernberg, 1992, p. 13). It is, according to Kernberg (1992), "the juxtaposition of an evoked remembered state with a future desired state in the context of a current perception that activates the desire for change" (p. 13). Appetitive or goal-directed behaviour does not move towards a "goal" or strive for a "purpose". Instead, a goal, insofar as it is experienced as a remembered state of a desired outcome, operates as an "internal" contextual stimulus, in accordance with a deterministic model of behaviour. We respond to complex contextual information characterising a particular interpersonal situation by displaying appropriate submissive or assertive behaviours—behaviours that are designed to avoid exposure to aggressive gestural signals, inhibit others' potential for intraspecific aggression, or solicit others' attention or appreciation or other aspects of primarily maternal behaviour. Social situations become meaningful in individual development in that they acquire the ability to compel us to enact a situation (outcome) in which we are *likely* to obtain social reward or avoid exposure to social punishment. We navigate towards situations that allow us to reexperience, in "unconscious fantasy", aspects of our primary object relation. Much of acquired social behaviour is instrumental to this aim. Whether instrumental behaviour is designed to minimise the probability of punishment or maximise the occurrence of social reward (grooming and reassuring eye contact and vocalisations—primarily maternal signals), instrumental behaviour, including seemingly voluntary social behaviour, is always a repetition of the past.

### 2.2.7   Hippocampus

> So much, if not all, of our social inter-
> change consists in saying the "right" thing
> to the "right" person at the "right" time.
> (Burrow, 1949, p. 285)

There has to be a system that translates the location or situation in which the animal finds itself within its environmental habitat and temporal cycles into behaviour dispositions that are appropriate to the location or situation. The hippocampus evolved as part of a system that was concerned with ascertaining the chemical composition of the environment (Lathe, 2001). Initially, the appreciation of the location that the animal occupies within its environment may have been based on olfactory information. Increasingly, environmental circumstances that adaptively bias the animal toward engagement of a specific set of behaviours (e.g., foraging or safety seeking) came to be characterised by visual information. Accurate characterisation and recognition of the animal's location, in particular, came to rely on characterisation and recognition of visual landmarks and their spatial constellation, although it would have continued to draw on visual nongeometric and other sensory

information (Anderson & Jeffery, 2003). This hypothetical evolutionary development would explain a shift of hippocampal function from processing olfactory information to the integration of visual information about landmarks and their spatial context. The hippocampus receives spatial and nonspatial (identifying) information about landmarks (and objects in general) via the lateral and medial entorhinal cortex and may use this information for the characterisation of the animal's location within its habitat (reviewed in Behrendt, 2010, 2011).

Location representations (place memories) may be encoded by hippocampal region CA1 and, to some extent, the subiculum (with which region CA1 is continuous). Location information encoded by the hippocampus translates into loco-motion across the environment via a multisynaptic pathway connecting the subiculum with the nucleus accumbens (German & Fields, 2007) and then ventral pallidum, which, in turn, projects to brainstem centres that coordinate forward locomotion (Floresco, 2007). Location information has to be stored sequentially as the animal moves across its environment in order to allow subsequent reward or punishment exposure to strengthen or weaken preliminary associations between location representations and locomotor impulses. This may have provided the impetus for the evolution of hippocampal place memories. Region CA1 and subiculum also project to the medial prefrontal cortex. Interaction between CA1 of dorsal (posterior) parts of the hippocampus and the anterior cingulate/prelimbic region of the medial prefrontal cortex may determine the animal's locomotor response to its current location in space, especially if the animal enters a known location. Sequential responding to known locations may underlie complex instrumental behaviour, brining the animal back into contact with a previously explored source of reward. Output from ventral (anterior) parts of CA1/subiculum, which encode affective and object-related information, to the ventromedial prefrontal cortex may play a greater role in determining the animal's response to a novel or motivationally ambivalent location. Affective and object-related information processed by the ventral hippocampus, in conjunction with spatial information processed in dorsal CA3 and CA1, may elicit motivational processes (such as incentive arousal) via subicular input to the ventromedial prefrontal cortex (reviewed in Behrendt, 2010, 2011).

Characterisation or recognition of visual landmarks and their spatial constellation not only involves the processing of spatial and nonspatial visual information (received by the hippocampus via the entorhinal cortex from the dorsal and ventral visual streams, respectively) but also depends on sequences of orienting reactions. The hippocampus may use spatial and nonspatial information about landmarks (and objects in general), which, again, it receives via the lateral and medial entorhinal cortex, respectively, for the guidance of orienting reactions (Sokolov, Nezlina, Polyanskii & Evtikhin, 2002). Thus, there may be a parallel system that translates allocentric view-dependent information (event information) into orienting reactions and, perhaps, behaviours that evolutionarily derived from orienting reactions (such as complex appetitive behaviour (Lorenz, 1952)). The episodic memory system may have evolved from the animal's capacity to characterise its current spatial location by appreciation of the nature and constellation of landmarks visible from its current location. In other words, landmark recognition and characterisation may have laid the foundation for the capacity to form event memories encoding landmarks in their visual and other sensory context. Event memories, encoding feature-rich landmarks in their visual and other sensory context, may be formed in hippocampal region CA3 and linked into episodic memories by hippocampal region CA1. Event memories or episodic memories may have to be mapped onto location memories (place memories), which may be formed and represented in CA1 or subiculum, to inform the animal about its location and enable situationally appropriate behaviour. Output from dorsal (posterior) regions of the hippocampus to medial *parietal* cortices may play a role in biasing orienting reactions to landmarks relevant

to the animal's current location. Alternatively, or in addition, CA3 of the dorsal hippocampus interacts with the anterior cingulate/prelimbic cortex in controlling the animal's orientation to landmarks in its environment. Activity in the anterior cingulate/prelimbic cortex ensures that the animal responds to the composition of landmarks (by changing its orientation or position) in a manner that was previously reinforced by reward contact or punishment avoidance.

It is argued that neural representations of social situations are a derivative of location representations. Research into hippocampal, ventral striatal, and medial prefrontal cortical functions provides evidence consistent with a model according to which representations of salient environmental contexts or more abstract social situations can elicit instrumental or emotional behaviour modes in accordance with previously reinforced associations (reviewed in Behrendt, 2010, 2011). Moreover, hippocampal activity, integrating nonspatial information about landmarks (or objects) with information about their spatial context, and hence enabling the animal to define or recognise its location or situation within the wider environment, may organise into complex patterns that underlie conscious experience (in the autoassociation network of cornu ammonis region CA3). When the animal pauses and its brain is in "default mode", activity in dorsal CA3 can represent *nonlocal* compositions of landmarks and may give rise to conscious imagery (simulation of outcomes), while activity in dorsal CA1 can represent *nonlocal* positions in the environment. It may be the symbolic representation of self-organising activity patterns in CA3 that is reflected in the content of conscious experience, whether conscious experience takes the form of perception of the seemingly external world, hallucination, or dream imagery (Behrendt, 2010, 2011).

## 2.3   Inner world and self

The evolution of appetitive or goal-directed behaviour is intricately linked with that of the episodic memory system. For appetitive behaviour to be acquired and modified by experience, the circumstances in which each individual action in a chain of actions is performed "must be recorded in some sort of memory, and this record must be brought into relation with the success attained" (Lorenz, 1973, p. 85). There is another reason for assigning to the hippocampus a central role in the organisation of goal-directed behaviour. Lorenz (1973) pointed out that "motor learning, even on the highest level, does not differ in principle from the path learning of lower mammals" (p. 103). Path finding and path habits may well be evolutionary forerunners of voluntary behaviour. Path conditioning is "the most elementary form of motor learning"; and "more complex behaviour patterns are probably also learnt in the same way" (Lorenz, 1973, p. 139). Similarly to path navigation, appetitive or goal-directed behaviour consists of a chain of locomotor pattern performances (and other tool reactions). Each acquired stimulus situation releases a movement, which, in turn, creates another stimulus situation, which, if the animal is still on the right path (that is, if the created stimulus situation corresponds to the anticipated stimulus situation), releases a further movement in the chain (Lorenz, 1973). Similarly to path navigation, voluntary behaviour is interspersed with, and guided by, orientation reactions. Not only path learning, "there is scarcely any form of learning that is not, from its very beginning, guided by orienting processes" (p. 163). The evolution of orienting reactions led to "an ever increasing ability to form precise and detailed images of space" (p. 132). Phylogenetically, "perception of space and adaptability of motor activity are closely related to the demand made by the structure of the environment" (p. 163). Primates living in trees were required to develop their faculties of spatial orientation most fully (Lorenz, 1973).

### 2.3.1   Thought

It has to be understood that "the interplay of motor learning and the development of a conception of space is of vital importance for

learning the shapes of physical objects" (Lorenz, 1973, p. 143). The development of a conception of space and, hence, of a conception of objects in space is likely to be an essential step in the evolution of thought. Another important step in the evolution of thought is the emergence of a capacity to monitor the external environment, and objects located therein, before deciding on a course of action. Such monitoring of outer space may have come to lapse, for brief moments, into a monitoring of an inner "visualised space", representing a "model of outer reality". Lorenz (1973) regarded thought as "action" taking place in a "visualised space" "that is, in a model representation of the present environment" (p. 163). Thinking is "tentative exploratory action" performed on objects located in a "neural 'model' of outer reality" (p. 128). The fact that anthropoid apes "first explore their environment with their eyes, then make the appropriate movement, gives the impression of remarkable 'intelligence'" (Lorenz, 1973, p. 127). When facing a problem in an experimental set-up, an anthropoid ape, such an orang-utan, "looks around in all directions and collects information on the spatial situation" (p. 130). It appears to perform "imagined acts in an imaginary space with models of spatial objects", looking for a solution to the problem "by pushing the central representation of a box around in a centrally represented space" (Lorenz, 1973, p. 128).

> The anthropoid sits down quietly, reviews the situation most carefully, gazing attentively from one part of the experimental set-up to the other. Its inner tension becomes apparent only by its frequent gestures of 'embarrassment', such as scratching its head like a man in thought, or other 'displacement' activities. (Lorenz, 1973, pp. 127–128)

Hartmann (1964) and Freud, too, regarded thinking as internalised "trial activity".[7] As we

---

[7] Thought is one of the "ego functions" described by Hartmann (1964).

anticipate danger or reward, we engage in inner experimentation concerning actions relevant to the danger or reward. Thinking comprises actions that have originally occurred in relation to the external world and have been internalised in the process of phylogeny. Trial activities "with whose help we attempt to master a situation, to solve a problem, are gradually internalized" (Hartmann, 1964, p. 41) in individual personality development. The development of language, phylogenetically and ontogenetically, is inseparable from that of thought (Lorenz, 1973). The capacity for thought is not acquired in its own right; instead, "we learn the symbols for things, like a vocabulary, and the relationships between them" (p. 187). These symbols are "set into a preformed framework without which we would be unable to think"—a framework that has evolved in the history of our species (Lorenz, 1973, p. 187). This framework may derive from the "visualised space" that represents a "model of outer reality". Our "extremely visual way of thinking", which evolved as an adaptation, earlier in human phylogeny, to an arboreal way of life, "finds expression in our language" (Hass, 1968, p. 109). It is a remarkable insight, discussed by Lorenz (1973), that language translates nonvisual relationships between things, such as their relationship in time, into spatial relationships.

### 2.3.2 Introspection

Thought is perhaps a derivative of the attentional monitoring mode used to ascertain contextual information from the immediate surroundings, covering sections of environment stretched out in the animal's head direction.[8] With the aid of thought, "man became able to calculate and foretell dependably events lying beyond the "shell of the immediate future" surrounding his head, and has thus vastly expanded the spatial and temporal range of his expectancies" (Rado, 1956, p. 220). Thought and broad attention to the environment are modes of attention that allow the weighing and setting of goals for subsequent behaviour. Internally experienced goals, in turn, determine modes of exploratory or instrumental behaviour—modes that are associated with feelings of expectancy. In goal-directed behaviour, including "goal-searchings, goal-findings, goal-pursuits, and goal-attainments", "the organism's own expectancies enter as components into the causal mechanism of its behavior" (Rado, 1956, p. 217).

> At a higher stage of development man became capable of taking time out to think and contemplate the *future* consequences of his reactions. His growing foresight thus taught him to absorb present pain for the sake of future pleasure and, conversely, to abstain from such pleasure as would result in future damage and pain. He also learned to subdue pain and substitute it for the anticipation of pleasure, and to substitute the fear of pain to come for deceptive pleasure. (Rado, 1956, p. 341)

Emotions constrain attention not only when monitoring or assessing the external situation but also during introspection and thought. Emotional thought "tends to justify and thus to feed the emotion from which it springs and by which it is controlled" (Rado, 1956, p. 340). Objects or events perceived in their environmental context during emotional states of fear or rage may prompt situationally appropriate fear or rage responses. Responses "prompted by the new set of warning signals", contained in "apprehensive thought and angry thought", "remain substantially the same: escape, submission and cry for help on the one hand, combat and defiance on the other" (p. 220). Repression, for instance, is an escape response to painful thought and feeling. Similarly to other pain-related behaviour, repression effects a "riddance from painful thought and feeling" (Rado, 1956, p. 244).

> At the high level of unemotional thought, the organism responds to danger with a purely intellectual expectancy of pain

---

[8] The dorsal hippocampus and circuit of Papez (of which the dorsal hippocampus forms a part) play an important role in orienting reactions by head movement.

from threatening damage. Unhampered by the emergency emotions, the intellect safeguards the organism in the superior manner of a computing machine. Yet, the moves prompted by these new sets of warning signals remain substantially the same: escape on the one hand, and combat on the other. (Rado, 1956, p. 245)

## 2.3.3   Voluntary behaviour

The impression that behaviour is directed towards the future or is under control of a goal that has not yet been achieved is misleading (Skinner, 1953). Skinner (1953) pointed out that man does not behave because of the consequences which are to follow, but because of the consequences which *have* followed similar behaviour in the past. The "law of effect" states that, of several responses made to a situation, those responses which were followed by satisfaction are firmly connected with the situation and are likely to recur in that situation (Thorndike, 1911). In other words, man is likely to emit responses that in the past have been reinforced in a similar situation by drive reduction (Brown, 1953). It is not the particular instance of the response preceding drive reduction that is learned; instead, reinforcement increases the probability of future responses being selected from the class to which the response that preceded the drive reduction belongs. This means that conditioning concerns a class of behaviour (Skinner, 1953). Owing to a learning process that involves reinforcement—contingent on drive reduction—of links between a situation and a class of behaviour (which includes the instance of behaviour that produced the drive reduction), the organism acquires *modes* of reacting to complex *situations* composed of both external and internal stimulus components (Brown, 1953). These ideas explain goal-directed behaviour deterministically, but they fail to account for the phenomenon of outcome imagery, which often seems to precipitate goal-directed action. Purposive action seems to be governed in some degree by *prevision* of its effects, that is, by the

prevision of events which have not yet happened but which are likely to happen as a result of the action itself (McDougall, 1924).

## Suspension of action

"Conative experience", according to McDougall (1924), is "the felt impulse to action" that is present in, and an essential feature of, all perceptual experience. "Conative experience" "takes the form of mere craving for some undefined goal, of definitely directed desire, of conflict of desires, of resolving, choosing, willing" (McDougall, 1924, p. 320). Impulses are often checked by difficulties encountered or foreseen and, hence, cannot express themselves immediately in action. When facing difficulties, instinctively *driven* action should be suspended but not aborted. Under these circumstances, an impulse will continue to work as "desire". According to McDougall (1924), "desire", in the widest sense, denotes a striving or "an impulse directed toward a remote object" (p. 207). The "higher animal" should be capable of "imagining the remote food or the remote danger" (p. 207). Although most "trains of behavior of an animal are initiated by sense-impressions" relating to the present environment, imagining the remote object (often an object that is "located in a known position") can maintain the animal's "continuity of effort or behavior" (p. 206). "Desire", in the narrow sense, "denotes our state when imagination of an object evokes in us an impulse to action, yet action is suspended" (McDougall, 1924, p. 207).

> Such suspension of action, while the impulse to action continues to work in the form of desire kept alive by imagination of its object, is the essential condition of all higher intellectual activity, of all our thinking in the fuller and more usual sense of the word. (McDougall, 1924, pp. 207–208)

Volition is intricately linked with decision making. Shapiro (2000) thought that "the capacity for volitional direction brings with it the sensation of active intention, the consciousness of choices and decisions, and the experience of agency and personal responsibility" (p. 48). Volition is an experience akin to emotion. Both, volition and emotion, allow the suspension of action for the purpose of decision making. Shapiro (2000) suggested that in "the infant's earliest reactiveness there is hardly a separation between" emotion and reaction. As the infant develops, emotion separates from reaction. Emotional feelings "continue to be immediately reactive to the external event, but with development they no longer are sufficient to trigger action"; "immediate emotional reaction may tempt action, but can no longer trigger it" (Shapiro, 2000, p. 59). Then, as action becomes increasingly instrumental and planful, volition separates from emotional feeling. Thus, while emotion, that is, emotional feeling, may continue to mediate between an external event (that is, a situation encountered by the subject) and the behavioural emotional reaction to the event, volition comes to mediate between external event and instrumental action.[9]

## Passive reactiveness

Both, emotional experience and volition, are developmental achievements. According to Shapiro (2000), impulsive psychopaths and hysterics retain or regress to a "prevolitional mode" wherein agency experience is diminished and action is not clearly differentiated from emotion. In other words, action is insufficiently preceded by emotional or volitional experience, which means that a deficit in emotional or instrumental (volitional) decision making causes impulsive actions. Such deficiency in reflectiveness (deficiency in agency experience or conscience) would go hand in hand with a reduction in anxiety, insofar as decision making in situations characterised by approach-avoidance conflict is an essential function of anxiety, although Shapiro

(2000) argued that the reduction in agency experience (deficiency of reflectiveness) in character pathology is often *due to* an active avoidance of such experience—an avoidance that is "exaggerated in the interest of forestalling anxiety" (p. 62). As Shapiro (2000) put it, "the process of volitional self-direction and the consciousness of one's own agency … seem directly to evoke anxiety" (p. 133); and he spoke of a "defensive motivation to avoid consciousness of agency or personal intention" (p. 127).

> To avoid a mode of planful and deliberate purpose, with its sensation of agency and, for some, anxiety, is to embrace a mode of passive reactiveness. (Shapiro, 2000, p. 65)

## Default mode and decision making

In a situation characterised by conflicting motivational imperatives, different options of behavioural responding to the situation, that is, different behaviour modes, may compete with each other in a process of decision making. A brain state that facilitates observation and monitoring of the external environment may enable consideration of competing behavioural response options, such as competition between a tendency to flee a dangerous situation and another tendency to attack the source of threat. If appropriate behavioural response options are not discernable, the brain system that primarily enables monitoring and assessment of the external situation (default-mode network) switches to a state of thought or internalised cognition to enable goal imagery and the simulation of action outcomes (Addis, Wong & Schacter, 2007; Schacter & Addis, 2007). During restful wakefulness, internalised cognition, enabling goal imagery and outcome simulation, alternates spontaneously with conscious perception and monitoring of the external environment. Both are forms of default-mode network activity (reviewed in Behrendt, 2011). To enable high-level decision making, an internal goal image or simulated outcome must not automatically translate into an instrumental or

---

[9]Events are spatiotemporally, but also emotionally, defined micro-situations. Principles of responding to situations should apply to responding to events, too.

emotional behaviour mode, just as an object observed externally must not translate immediately into action. Eventually, imagery of an outcome would translate into engagement of an emotional or instrumental behaviour mode. Thus, thought or goal imagery would have the same effect on behaviour as appreciation of the external situation (consisting of external objects and their context) encountered by the animal. The brain's default mode network, including the hippocampus, has been implicated in both, internalised cognition and assessment of the external environment during periods of rest. Both, thought and external monitoring, are dependent on "behavioural inhibition" (which is another function attributed to the hippocampus). Conscious emotional experience (emotional feelings) would accompany internal thought or external environmental monitoring insofar as we abstain from, or withhold, the direct expression of emotional behaviour during decision making in an emotionally significant situation. Eventually, it is imagery of a motivationally relevant object, similarly to its perception, that allows switching from the default mode to a task mode (accompanied by feelings of expectancy or volition) and that sets goal-directed behaviour into motion. Imagery of a motivationally relevant object may also switch from one emotionally tinged mode of monitoring (default mode), such as anxiety, to a more focused emotional attention mode, such as fear or anger.

### 2.3.4   Fantasy

Fantasy, as a process of conscious imagery or imagination (predominantly pictorial, in the form of visualisation), provides an avenue for constructive planning for the future (Laughlin, 1970). We respond to an anticipated situation as if this were a present situation. By responding with incentive arousal to an incentive cue embedded in an anticipated situation (outcome), the organism energises appetitive movements towards the anticipated situation. The adaptiveness of anticipatory imagery is due to the fact that the anticipated situation is somehow connected, via a *path* through time and space, with the present

situation. In other words, imagined outcomes are approachable (retraceable) from the present. Conscious imagery, utilised for the purpose of anticipating future events or outcomes or exploring consequences of actions, is related to daydreaming fantasy with which psychoanalytic theory is concerned. The content of fantasy in daydreaming draws on past experiences, much like conscious simulation of action outcomes is constituted by recollection and recombination of past events or situations (Addis, Wong & Schacter, 2007; Schacter & Addis, 2007).

Fenichel (1946) distinguished between "creative fantasy, which prepares some later action, and daydreaming fantasy, the refuge for wishes that cannot be fulfilled" (p. 50). Creative fantasy is involved in "abstract preparatory thinking"; it provides the ground for the development of obsessive ruminations, when the patient's "thinking is a kind of eternal preparation for actions that never are performed" (p. 50). The second type of fantasy, magical pictorial daydreaming, "becomes a real substitute for action in the state of 'introversion', when 'small' movements accompanying fantasy become intense enough to bring discharge" (Fenichel, 1946, p. 50). These "small" movements are remnants of orienting movements that were originally performed when the organism was monitoring the outside world.

Fantasy in the form of more or less vivid daydreaming comprises a sequence of imaginary events or mental images that is advanced and directed by unconscious forces in the service of substitute gratification or wish fulfilment (satisfaction of difficult or impossible goals). Fantasy as an "ego aid" enables retreat into self-absorption. Fantasy, featuring emotionally significant content, may provide an unrealistic "emotional aura" within which realistic action is avoided (Laughlin, 1970). Fantasy is "a potent means for the avoidance of conflict" (p. 119). It may seek to resolve emotional conflict, such as by blocking or aiding partial expression of frustration or rage. Fantasies about revenge help to restrain actions, in that they "serve as caution or break to oneself" (Laughlin, 1970, p. 116). It is perhaps anticipation of punishment that holds emotional behaviour in check and provides escape from difficult situations.

The content of fantasy, whether it is concerned with wish fulfilment or revenge, is private and secret; its revelation outside a nonjudgmental therapeutic context is *unsafe*, because revelation to others would invite judgement or criticism (social punishment). The manifest content of fantasy can be viewed "as the outward shadowy reflection of more potent and meaningful underlying *unconscious* material" (Laughlin, 1970, p. 117). The latent content and significance of fantasy is referred to as "unconscious fantasy". Fantasy can be fleeting or even instantaneous, its emergence being rapidly and automatically repressed. Fleeting fantasies that hardly reach conscious awareness can also be considered as unconscious fantasies. The nearly instantaneous "repression" of fantasies serves defensive purposes (Laughlin, 1970).

### 2.3.5   Internal object relations

Kernberg (1996) defined "object relations" as "real or fantasied interpersonal interactions that are internalized as a complex world of self and object representations in the context of affective interactions" (p. 115). Internal object relations are structures in the mind that organise interpersonal experience. This is to say that we enact object relations in day-to-day life by treating others (external objects) as replicas or instances of internal objects or the self and treating them in a way that corresponds to an internalised (internal) object relation. Internal objects and internal object relations are abstract concepts; they can give rise to *imagery* of an object with which one has a relationship (in conscious fantasy), much as they can be projected into instances of external objects with which one has a relationship, but internal objects (in the sense of abstract representations) are not to be confused with *imaginary* instantiations of objects.[10] In Kleinian theory, instinctual impulses

are represented in the mind by ideas about objects and the self as well as by conscious or unconscious fantasies concerning the relationships between objects and self. At other times, instinctual impulses are represented by external objects that are replicas of internal objects or the self (conscious instances of unconscious representations of objects and self). For instance, the expression of libidinal impulses leads to cathexis of, and pleasurable contacts with, gratifying objects. Objects invested (cathected) with libido, in turn, are introjected (internalised) as good internal objects. The ego or self assimilates good internal objects. In another example, aggression expresses itself in form of unconscious fantasy, such as the fantasy that the object wilfully frustrates the infant's desires and wilfully withholds its supplies. Objects, including fantasised objects, become the target of aggressive impulses (i.e., they are cathected with aggressive instinctual energy) when they have been the cause of frustration. Generally, feelings of tension, such as anxiety or frustration, are expelled and invested into persecutory objects. The projection of inner tension states constitutes the origin of paranoid fears. Thus, anxiety gives way to fear, and, similarly, frustration gives way to anger, once a suitable object has been identified (projected). Persecutory objects, which have allowed the transformation of anxiety into fear, or of frustration into anger, can be internalised (reintrojected) as internal bad objects. Inner bad objects (inner persecutors) are the origin of primitive superego anxiety. In Kleinian theory, internal persecutors constitute the early superego (reviewed in Kernberg, 1980).

### 2.3.6   The ego

The ego, according to Freud (1923), refers to a coherent organisation of mental processes. The ego "gives mental processes an order in time and submits them to 'reality-testing'" (Freud, 1923, p. 55). The ego not only performs an *integrative function*, integrating perceptions of reality (as well as integrating behaviour), it also enables "discrimination between inner and outer reality" (Fairbairn, 1952, p. 9). The ego is the

---

[10] "Introjects" or "internal objects", according to Schafer (1976), on the other hand, are "dreamlike experiences of the nearness and influence of other persons or parts of persons" (p. 164).

representative of the external world (especially its objects) to the "id" (the seat of instincts). It mediates between the external world and the "id", trying "to make the world fall in with the wishes of the id" (Freud, 1923, p. 56). Thus, the ego's *adaptive function* relates "primal instinctive activity to conditions prevailing in outer reality, and more particularly social conditions" (Fairbairn, 1952, p. 9). Being answerable to the id, the ego controls instincts and inhibits them. At the same time, the ego defends itself against reproaches from the superego.[11] Trying to appease the superego, the ego is concerned with repressing intolerable wishes and memories of traumatic events ("repression"). The repressed material is "cut off sharply from the ego" (p. 24) and prevented from accessing consciousness. In psychoanalytic therapy, the ego is responsible for the patient's "resistances" against gaining insight into the repressed material (Freud, 1923). Federn (1952) preferred to think about the ego as an actual mental experience, rather than an abstract concept. "Ego feeling", as a continuous mental experience and a permanent feature of one's being conscious, discriminates between the ego and the external world (non-ego). The "mental ego feeling" coincides usually, but not always, with the "bodily ego feeling" (motor and sensory memories). Depersonalisation (estrangement), characterised by reduced bodily ego feeling, "commences just when the subject is alone, or feels lonely on meeting with strangers or in social situations which are not flattering to his vanity" (Federn, 1952, p. 34). Thus, ego feeling is a function of our relatedness to, or appreciation and appraisal by, others.

The redirection of libidinal energy to parts of the ego can be observed in narcissism.[12]

---

[11]The superego, which arises from "an individual's first and foremost identification, his identification with the father" (p. 31) (an identification that stems from the resolution and repression of the Oedipus complex), acts aggressively against the ego (Freud, 1923).
[12]Similarly, the "instinct of destruction" can be redirected against the ego, if "discharge" against the external world and other organisms is obstructed (Freud, 1923). In masochism, aggressive impulses that have fused with libidinal impulses are directed against the ego or an object introjected into the ego.

The "transformation of object-libido into narcissistic libido" (p. 30) is contingent on a withdrawal of libidinal cathexis from external objects (Freud, 1923). Freud (1923) thought that "the character of the ego is a precipitate of abandoned object-cathexes and it contains the history of those object-choices" (p. 29). Federn (1952) argued that ego feeling is created and sustained by investment of libido in the ego (narcissistic cathexis). The ego is also thought to be the seat of anxiety. How can we reconcile these notions? Perception of others' care, approval, and appreciation towards us (narcissistic sustenance) provides a sense of satisfaction, alleviates anxiety, and arrests, for a period of time, our approval-or attention-seeking behaviour, which is motivated, in part, by anxiety. It is conceivable that *imagery* of others' care-giving or approving behaviour has a similar effect. Imagery of approval or care is a pleasurable experience that can be said to be cathected with ego libido (narcissistic cathexis); and it is a form of fantasy that can be said to take place in the ego (as opposed to the non-ego). Hence, ego libido, according to Federn (1952), allows us to gain pleasure from our own ego.

### 2.3.7  Narcissistic cathexis

The self, according to Kohut (1971), is a "comparatively low-level, i.e., comparatively experience near, psychoanalytic abstraction" (p. xv). Constituents of the "mental apparatus", namely the ego, id, and superego, by contrast, belong to a higher, experience-distant level of abstraction in psychoanalysis. The self is a content of the "mental apparatus"; it is "not an agency of the mind" (p. xv). Self-contents (self-representations) vary; they can have the character of grandiosity or inferiority. The self is "cathected with instinctual energy" (Kohut, 1971, p. xv); more precisely, it is cathected with "narcissistic libido". Stable self-esteem reflects a reliable "narcissistic cathexis" of the self-image. Objects that participate in the regulation of self-esteem, too, are cathected with "narcissistic libido". From early childhood, the subject "invests other people with narcissistic cathexes and thus experiences

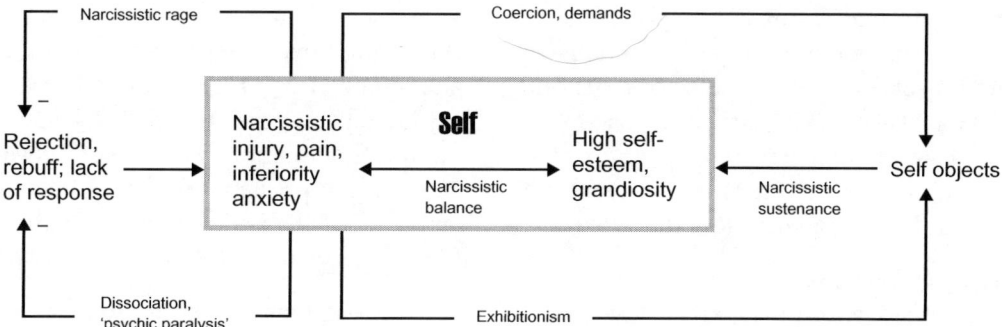

Figure 2-3.    Regulation of "narcissistic homeostasis" in Kohut's terms. The self is cathected with "narcissistic libido" supplied by selfobjects. Selfobjects are provoked by the subject to provide "narcissistic sustenance," that is, to enhance the subject's self-esteem. If selfobject experiences are not forthcoming, the subject feels hurt and employs defensive behaviours (withdrawal or rage).

them narcissistically, i.e., as self-objects" (p. 26). Selfobjects are objects that are either used in the service of the self or that are part of the self. Self-esteem depends on the presence of selfobjects, their confirming approval, or their admiration (Kohut, 1971).

There is a crucial difference between narcissistically experienced objects (selfobjects) and "true objects (in the psychoanalytic sense) which are cathected with object-instinctual investments, i.e., objects loved and hated" (Kohut, 1971, p. 51). Mature objects, which are cathected with "object libido" (as opposed to narcissistic libido), respond to the subject's care, affection, or love with reciprocal care, affection, or love and, thereby, enhance or maintain the subject's self-esteem. Thus, self-esteem can be controlled via "selfless" investment in mature object relations or via the creation and manipulation of selfobjects (through exhibitionism and solicitation of approval), although in most instances these processes likely interact. Objects that are experienced narcissistically (objects of "narcissistic love") tend to feel "oppressed and enslaved by the subject's expectations and demands" (p. 33) for approval or admiration. A "narcissistic imbalance" arises when objects withdraw their love, threaten punishment, or threaten the subject with their "temporary absence or permanent disappearance" (Kohut, 1971, p. 21). This may

be experienced by the subject as a "narcissistic injury", which, in turn, can precipitate "narcissistic rage" (Figure 2-3).

### 2.3.8   Mnemonic processes

The hippocampus plays a critical role in the formation and recall of episodic memories. Stern (1985) implicated episodic memory in the formation of representations ("internalisation") of early relationships. He argued that episodes of "lived experience" in an infant's life become episodes for memory (episodic memories). This applies to subjective experiences of being with a "self-regulating other" (similar to Kohut's (1971) concept of "selfobject" experiences) (Stern, 1985). Episodes of interactive experience (with the "self-regulating other") generalise across several actual instances (thereby forming an average across similar instances) and are, thus, gradually consolidated into a mnemonic representation (called "representation of interactions that have been generalized"—a concept that is somewhat similar to Bowlby's (1973, 1988) "working models"). The processes envisaged are reminiscent of processes involved in spatial learning: the recording of spatial experience (in form of episodic memories) and their gradual consolidation into map-like representations (processes that critically involve the hippocampus and its interaction with the medial prefrontal cortex). A "representation of interactions that have been generalised" is "a representation of a specific type of interaction" (Stern, 1985, p. 114), but it may be seen as referring to a class of interpersonal situations (an abstract interpersonal situation), that is, an object relation (or "role relationship" (Sandler, 1976)).

> The self-regulating other is not a given …; it is an active construct, and it forms alongside the forming sense of self … (Stern, 1985, p. 241)

## Lived experience and evoked companion

A "representation of interactions that have been generalized" is retrieved whenever one of the attributes of the encoded interpersonal situation is present. The attribute of the encoded situation acts as a *retrieval cue* and precipitates the reactivation of a "lived experience" (Stern, 1985). Lived and retrieved experiences of being with a "self-regulating other" have affective attributes. Feelings can be attributes of situations, so that feelings, perhaps in conjunction with spatio-temporal attributes of an encoded situation, can precipitate the reactivation of a lived experience. When a memory representing a specific type of interaction (i.e., a type of interpersonal situation) is reactivated in the here-and-now, the currently unfolding interactive episode is apprehended in light of this memory, and so the infant encounters an "evoked companion" (Stern, 1985). The "evoked companion" is an activated episodic memory and an actual experience of being with the "self-regulating other". The evoked companion is an active exemplar of a class of past happenings, whereby the actual experience puts "some experiential flesh on an abstract representation" (pp. 112–113). "Evoked companions" "represent the accumulated past history of a type of interaction with an other"; and "they serve a guiding function in the sense of the past creating expectations of the present and future" (Stern, 1985, p. 115). "Lived experience" (current experience) is, to a large part, an instantiation in the form of an activated memory, although each "lived experience", being different in some way from similar past experiences, also serves to update the memory (the "representation of interactions that have been generalized"). Retrieval cues can activate this memory when the "self-regulating other" is not present, "resulting in an imagined interaction with an evoked companion" (Stern, 1985, p. 113).

> Evoked companions can also be called into active memory during episodes when the infant is alone but when historically similar episodes involved the presence of a self-regulating other. (Stern, 1985, p. 113)

Whether the infant engages with a real external partner (external object) or with a companion evoked in imagery (fantasised object), "the memory of past experiences with self and other in exploratory contexts" creates trust and security, allowing the infant to feel trustful and *secure* in his explorations (Stern, 1985, p. 118). Stern (1985) thought that, in the actual presence of the other, "the infant needs only recognition memory to call to mind the evoked companion that is stored in memory, since the actual episode is happening now before the infant" (p. 116). When a lived episode of being with an other is recalled in the other's absence, cued recall memory ("evocative memory") is required, of which infants are capable from the third month of life and which "improves greatly toward the end of the first year of life" (p. 117). Recall (evocative) memory function is closely related to "the ability to generate future-representations of possible events; and the ability to generate communicative or instrumental responses to deal with the uncertainty and distress that are caused by incongruencies between present events and future representations of events" (Stern, 1985, p. 117).

### 2.3.9 Self-idealisation

> A child's idea of himself and his future life is often built upon parental example. From parental example children turn to their teacher, and to a greater or lesser

degree they are influenced by everyone with whom they come in personal contact. (Moore, 1926, p. 176)

Parental example is one of the factors that determines one's "self-ideal" (part of which is unconscious); and, thereby, also determines one's actual self. In the formation of one's sense of self, according to Moore (1926), "the external ideal of what one aims at" is "transformed into the more or less subconscious idea of what one is" (p. 176). Moore (1926) thus suggested that a person makes two estimates of his abilities or position: "what he would like to be" and "what he fears he really is" (p. 174). The self-ideal, being the person's estimate of "what he would like to be" (p. 174), is intimately linked with the subject's estimate of what he really is (Moore, 1926); and it carries with it the impulse to transcend one's current being and to attain a desired position.

> One cannot separate one's estimate of himself from what he wants to be, for the idea that we have of ourselves is an ideo-motor concept. We conceive an ideal of ourselves and this conception carries with it a tendency towards its own realization. The actual living out of the personal ideal is often a very difficult matter. We cannot be what we want to be because external factors are often necessary for the realization of the self-ideal. (Moore, 1926, p. 175)

Defeat or frustration in the course of self-realisation, showing us "that there are lines of development that for us at least are impracticable or impossible", modifies our self-ideal (p. 175). Defeat may not be tolerable. The desire of self-realisation and the encounter, in the pursuit of self-realisation, of external hindrances "are the sources of life's severest conflict, a conflict which lies at the root of the mental breakdown" (Moore, 1926, p. 175).

The neurotic person, according to Horney (1950), conceives his goals or aspirations in the form of images of an "idealised self". This is likely to be true for the nonneurotic person, too.

The neurotic (or nonneurotic) person seeks to actualise or realise his "idealised self", which is to say that he has "to prove [his self] in action" and model himself "into this special kind of perfection prescribed by specific features of his idealised image" (p. 25). Imagination plays a critical role in the process of self-idealisation. Imagination, in general, shows us what our possibilities are—whenever "we wish, hope, fear, believe, plan" (Horney, 1950, p. 31). Imagination conjures up social contingencies of our social and nonsocial actions. The idealised self, when fleetingly experienced in the realm of imagination, envisages a goal in terms of interpersonal security and reveals a prospect of potential access to resources of narcissistic supplies. Social goal imagery consists of an idealised self-image (derived from the ego ideal) in nonneurotic persons, too, however what distinguishes social goal imagery in neurotic persons (from that in nonneurotic persons) is "the fantastic nature of their self-glorification" (Horney, 1950, p. 32). Imagery of an idealised self represents an anticipated outcome of appetitive behaviour aiming to procure narcissistic supplies (outcome simulation) (Figure 4-2). It is perhaps the intensity of narcissistic needs that renders the neurotic person's self-imagery fantastic and glorious. Although the difference may be one of degree rather than quality (contrary to Horney's position), consequences for intrapsychic and interpersonal processes are likely to be qualitatively different when comparing the neurotic with the healthy person.

> By dint of his intellect and the power of his imagination, man can visualize things not yet existing. He reaches beyond what he is or can do at any given time. He has limitations, but his limits are not fast and final. Usually he lags behind what he wants to achieve within or outside himself. ... Man under the pressure of inner distress reaches out for the ultimate and the infinite which—though his limits are not fixed—it is not given to him to reach; and in this very process he destroys himself, shift-

ing his very best drive for self-realization to the actualization of his idealized image and thereby wasting the potentialities he actually possesses. (Horney, 1950, p. 377)

The idealised image of the self derives from a process of *identification* with significant others who (acting, in part, as rivals) have been successful in attracting the primary object's love and attention (narcissistic supplies) or the love and attention of a derivative of the primary object. In particular, the idealised image of the self, and hence one's ability to imagine one's self, is a developmental consequence of the triangular oedipal constellation (in which rivalry with the paternal other played a role). The person may fleetingly imagine himself in a situation that allowed a significant other (a third person, such as the father) to obtain praise or affection from the primary object (or its derivative). Such imaginary scenarios, involving the idealised self, a derivative of the maternal object and, perhaps, competitors, can, as Horney (1950) put it, "take the form of imaginary conversations in which others are impressed or put to shame" (p. 33).

### 2.3.10   Self as another

Being familiar with the work of Lorenz and Tinbergen, Lacan (1966) understood that instinctive behaviour patterns are released in response to specific visual images. Recognition (unconscious) of a visual image ("imago" or perceptual Gestalt) of another member of the species (in accordance with a "mental schema") mobilises a primitive impulse towards that member of the species (whereby the impulse may be related to attack, territoriality, courtship, or mating). Lacan (1966) assigned the visual image ("imago") and the reflexive response to it to a fundamental plane or dimension of experience and behaviour that he called "the imaginary" ("the register of the imaginary"). The "logic" of the imaginary plane is one of acting and being acted upon (Lacan, 1966). The individual is manipulated by others; and it is through these manipulations that the infant's

first attitudes take shape. The power of looking at others or being looked at by others can be ascribed to the power of "the imaginary". The imaginary mobilises primitive "drives" (or instincts, strictly speaking). The genesis and action of the libidinal "drive", for instance, is associated with "the imaginary"; the cycle of sexual behaviour, too, is centred on the function of the imaginary. By fixing libidinal and other drives to visual images (perceptual registrations), the imaginary establishes the initial conditions under which objects in the world can be predictably experienced. The relation to "the other" (another individual) is rooted in the imaginary plane (Lacan, 1966).

In the "mirror stage" of development, the infant's relationship to "the other" is one of "primary identification"—a relationship in which self and other are indistinguishable (and notions of self and other remain meaningless) (Lacan, 1966). "Primary identification" is based on recognition of primitive imagos, giving rise to transformations in the infant (on the imaginary plane). In the "mirror stage", primitive formations of libido come into being (attesting to reflexive transformations in the infant) through the recognition of imagos. These primitive formations constitute the early ego. For Lacan (1966), the ego is a formation of "the imaginary"; it is an "imaginary" structure that has libidinal value.[13] The "imaginary formation" that is called the ego is modelled on "the other" (the object). This is to say that the ego is formed through "primary identification" with the other. On the imaginary plane, the ego is coupled to the other in a relationship that is interchangeable and *reflexive*. While the ego has libidinal value, it is structured in a way that defends against anxiety. Anxiety threatens the integrity of the ego; anxiety manifests a breakdown of the imaginary form of the ego (Lacan, 1966).

---

[13]The ego, which has to be distinguished from the human subject or the self, must be taken, according to Lacan (1966), to be an internal object.

The symbolic plane

The ego, depending on "the other", generates frustration when its libidinal formation faces an obstacle (Lacan, 1966). "Desire" stems from frustrated or inhibited drives (i.e., from a deficit or gap that drives cannot bridge). Desire finds a guide beyond "the imaginary" on the plane of "the symbolic". Libido is constrained to pass through the imaginary stage, however when libido is brought under the influence of "the symbolic", the potentialities of desire can be accessed. Desire manifests itself in and through a process of symbolisation (Lacan, 1966). The symbolic plane is the register of language and linguistically mediated cognitions. Desire comes into being through symbols; it unfolds on the plane of the symbolic through the "signifying chain" of language. Human desire (the desire of the subject) is passed along a chain of signifiers, meaning that it is expressed in language. The symbolic opens an access to "the real" via a representation of the real (although the real in itself cannot be comprehended).[14]

The imaginary ego has to be distinguished from the speaking subject, much as drives (or instincts, to be precise) have to be distinguished from desire (Lacan, 1966). The speaking subject inhabits the symbolic plane. On the imaginary plane, a sense of identity is given by the perceptual imago; the subject is the other to the ego. This otherness of the subject is inserted into the symbolic plane. All dyadic (bipolar) relations are of an "imaginary" style; for a relation to take its "symbolic" value, it is necessary for there to be a mediation by a third person (Lacan, 1966). Human desire is the desire of a third person to whom the self (the speaking subject) is linked. Although human desire is expressed on the plane of the symbolic, language is not only at

the service of desire. Routinised, empty speech, flattened out in day-to-day use, draws resources of the symbolic onto the plane of the imaginary. Routinised speech allows for unthinking reflexes in conversations (Lacan, 1966).

Time

Not only the signifying chain of language but also memory retrieval and recollection mediate desire. Unlike the imaginary, which is restricted to the *present* experience of the individual, the symbolic plane extends over time (Lacan, 1966). The symbolic plane is characterised by intentionality and temporality. Goal-directed, appetitive processes are suggested to unfold on Lacan's symbolic plane. Consistent with this suggestion, experiences of expectation, discovery, and surprise are associated with the function of the symbolic. The "imaginary" sense of identity is represented in an instant of time, whereas the symbolically mediated subject (the self or speaking subject) is bound to past, present, and future. The subject is stretched out over time in the succession of the signifying chain (emphasising the temporalised character of subjectivity). The speaking subject (the self) cannot be abstracted from its extension over time (Lacan, 1966).

## 2.4   Summary

Motor expression of an instinct is contingent on receiving sensory input that is consistent with a releasing stimulus situation ("Reizsituation"). Let us assume that coordination of instinctive motor expression is the function of a dedicated neural centre (in the hypothalamus). Such centre would also control autonomic or vegetative aspects of instinctive behaviour. In the course of evolution, it must have become possible for the autonomic or vegetative segment of the instinctive control centre to be activated under sub-threshold conditions, so that autonomic aspects of instinctive behaviour could be implemented without producing the related motor pattern. This would have been an important evolutionary

---

[14] "The real", being the third plane in Lacan's system, is a wholly indeterminate and unorganised domain—a domain that is inaccessible to experience, unknowable. The notion of "the real" encapsulates the wholly undifferentiated impact of the material world (including the needs of the organism) on the organism's behaviour mechanisms.

achievement with respect to appetitive (purposive) behaviour ("Appetenzverhalten"). Spontaneous activity of an instinctive centre may be enhanced by specific patterns of endocrine or homeostatic information. Such activation does not necessarily entail motor expression of the instinct, since the latter is generally codependent on a releasing stimulus situation. However, activation of the instinctive centre reduces the threshold which a stimulus situation has to reach in terms of its intensity or clarity in order to elicit the innately programmed instinctive motor pattern. At the same time, activation of the instinctive centre may lead to specific emotional arousal and recruitment of nonspecific arousal functions that are integral to appetitive behaviour (incentive motivational arousal). Appetitive behaviour would eventually lead to the perception of the very stimulus situation that releases the innate motor pattern. Restlessness when seeking out a stimulus situation is an excellent example of appetitive behaviour. This alone may make the occurrence of, and exposure to, the releasing stimulus situation more likely. Importantly, subthreshold

activation of an instinctive centre inhibits other instinctive centres (in the hypothalamus). Due to suppression of competing instinctive centres, an ambiguous stimulus situation approximating that of the primed instinct is more likely than that of other instincts to precipitate instinctive motor action (Figure 2-4).

### 2.4.1 Consciousness

What could be the role of consciousness in this regard? First, conscious awareness of the spatially and temporally extending world can be seen as a sequence of contextual events, that is, as a sequence of symbols representing acquired stimulus situations. Perhaps, conscious events are complex cues (cue constellations) that act as—or rather refer to—acquired releasing stimulus situations for orienting movements (such as head direction adjustments) constitutive to appetitive behaviour. Events—that is, neural patterns underlying event memories (neural patterns that are symbolically represented by conscious events)—may help to guide appetitive (preparatory or

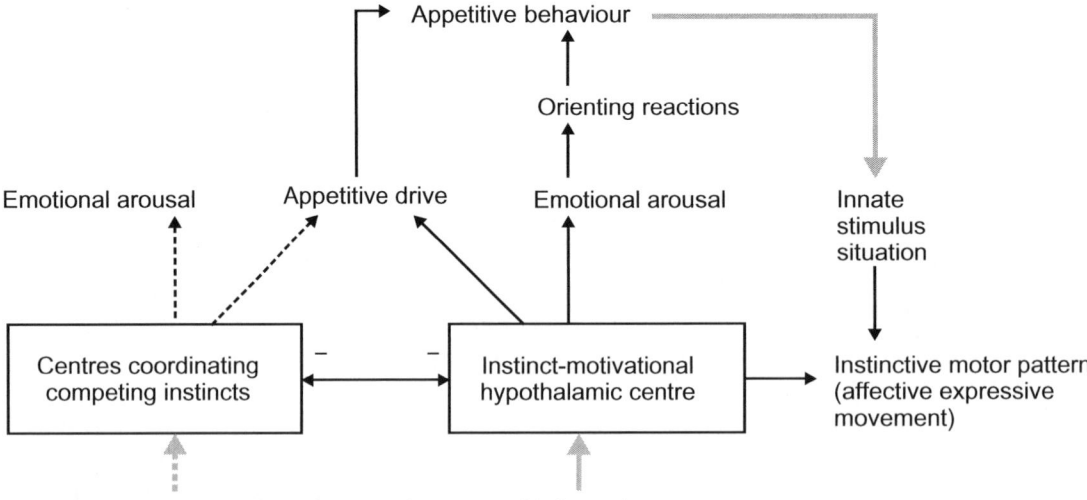

Figure 2-4. A hypothalamic centre coordinating autonomic and motor aspects of instinctive behaviour may, when activated in the presence of an innate stimulus situation, produce an instinctive motor pattern or, when activated in the absence of an innate stimulus situation, energize both general and directional aspects of appetitive behaviour.

purposive) behaviour through probabilistic adjustment of the animal's orientation in its environment. In fact, orienting reactions to events are a critical component of appetitive behaviour. Orienting reactions to contextual information may be required to give directedness to general appetitive arousal or drive. Approach locomotion is the archetype of all appetitive behaviours and manipulations instrumental to accessing resources of reward and obtaining reward itself. Withdrawal behaviour can also be regarded as purposive or appetitive, especially insofar as it serves to approach locations of safety or create situations of safety (perhaps habitually so, in which case we can speak of active avoidance behaviour). *Spatial aspects* of objects appear to *guide* appetitive approach behaviour by prompting appropriate orienting reactions. Generally, conscious (contextualised) perception of objects in space and time may play an important role in ensuring the directedness and adaptiveness of locomotor and manipulative interactions with the external physical world. Objects that are perceived in their spatial and temporal context act like, and are evolutionarily derived from, perceived landmarks that enable self-localisation and that guide locomotor navigation in the external environment. The contention is that a system that has evolved to control social behaviour in a manner that resembles landmark-based navigation can bring the organism into contact with stimulus situations that release innate patterns of social interaction.

Second, conscious perception, recollection, or imagery—or, strictly speaking, neural processes underlying these conscious phenomena (or neural processes that are symbolically represented by these phenomena)—may influence behaviour via alteration of emotional arousal and appetitive drive. *Semantic aspects* of objects are predictive of punishment or reward. Conscious perception or imagery of a reward-related object may dispose to (or, strictly speaking, reflect a disposition to) incentive motivational arousal and, thereby, potentially energise appetitive behaviour. It is the meaning (semantic aspect) of

objects that is suggested to activate autonomic segments of instinctive centres (in the hypothalamus), and, through them, produce an appetite drive. Consciously perceived or imagined objects may also dispose to (or, strictly speaking, manifest a disposition to) an aversive motivational state that, in turn, can translate into withdrawal or avoidance behaviour. Contingent on decision making, perceived or imagined objects (that are embedded in a spatiotemporal, that is, conscious, context)—insofar as they are motivationally significant (rather than just acting as landmarks)—may control appetitive (approach or withdrawal) behaviour indirectly via activation of autonomic segments of instinct control centres, which, in turn, activate centres controlling incentive arousal (positive or negative) and appetitive behaviour. By inducing incentive or aversive motivational arousal, object perception or imagery helps to define the framework within which the organism responds to contextual cue constellations, thereby sequentially advancing appetitive behaviour and eventually manoeuvring the organism to a stimulus situation that innately releases an instinctive behaviour pattern. Activation of an instinctive centre would not only energise appetitive behaviour but also affect consciousness and orienting behaviour via emotional arousal. Emotional feelings, perhaps being derived from autonomic aspects of instinctive activations, may have adopted the function of constraining or codetermining orienting behaviour used in the service of appetitive behaviour (Figure 2-4). Emotional feelings that accompany appetitive drive may also manifest a neural process that is important for the ongoing modification, through reinforcement learning, of appetitive behaviour.

Objects are consciously perceived *not* because they are "out there"; they are "created" because they are relvant to one or another motivational drive (relating to one or another form of appetitive behaviour) that is presently active (consistent with the notion of cathexis). The relative motivational, that is, approach- or avoidance-related, value of objects is gleaned from evaluation of their context. For instance, the adaptiveness of approaching, controlling, or avoiding another individual depends on his or her social and historical context, such as one's relationship with the other individual and his or her social standing in the group. Such contextual information is embedded in conscious perception of other individuals or gleaned from recollections of past events or simulations of future events concerning them. If motivationally relevant objects or cues embedded in conscious space-time favour both approach and withdrawal tendencies (resulting in approach-withdrawal or approach-avoidance conflict), then the animal hesitates, that is, it exhibits a state of behavioural inhibition. It may transpire that all conscious phenomena are evidence for a degree of hesitation and decision making; consciously perceived or imagined objects would be linked with behavioural options only probabilistically (much as appetitive behaviour in relation to these objects always has to bridge space and time). Behavioural inhibition may be accompanied by recurrent reorientation. Objects that are concurrently or sequentially perceived, recalled, or anticipated (as the external or internal context is explored) may prompt incompatible approach and withdrawal reactions. High-level decision making processes during states of behavioural inhibition (involving default mode activity) are concerned with weighing the approach and avoidance value of various simultaneously present or successively perceived or simulated objects.

### 2.4.2   Hippocampus

The hippocampus evolved as a system of responding to diffuse external chemical stimuli. Characterisation of the animal's location within the wider environment by olfactory information was increasingly complemented and replaced by characterisation of the animal's location in terms of its visual features. Much like olfactory investigation and characterisation of a location, orienting reactions to visual or auditory stimuli help to elaborate a representation of the environment that encapsulates its basic aversiveness or resourcefulness. Information about the animal's present location would then modulate (via the lateral septum) thresholds for expression of various instinctive motor patterns encoded in hypothalamic centres, much like shifts in the organism's metabolic and endocrine status would be expected to have this effect. In the course of evolution, the ventral hippocampus (corresponding to the anterior hippocampus in primates) would have become specialised for this function. Motivationally meaningful objects (semantic information) may modulate instinctive behaviour partly via this ventral hippocampal-lateral septal-hypothalamic route, too (Figure 10-1).

Gradually, characterisation of the animal's present location in terms of nonvisual and nongeometric visual information was complemented by geometric characterisation of the animal's view ahead of itself. Such geometric information controls the animal's head movements, and, thereby its appetitive direction or directedness in it's environment, via structures connected through Papez's circuit, including the dorsal (posterior) hippocampus. Thus, on the one hand, investigatory orienting behaviours would enable the animal to form a dynamic representation of its location in its environment, while, on the other hand, spatial view-dependent information gathered and integrated by the dorsal hippocampus is translated into directional movements that shape and adjust the animal's appetitive behaviour trajectory. In other words, characterisation of the external environment by the hippocampus controls two aspects of appetitive behaviour: view-independent information, ascertained by the ventral hippocampus, regulates activity levels in hypothalamic centres (devoted to the control of emotional arousal and instinctive motor expressions) as well as activity in the ventral striatum (generally concerned with appetitive behaviour), while view-dependent information, ascertained by the dorsal hippocampus, guides the implementation of appetitive behaviour by giving directedness to general psychomotor agitation (appetitive drive) (reviewed in Behrendt, 2011).

In order to learn goal-directed behaviour, allocentric view-dependent information has to be memorised in form of event memories. Event memories also encapsulate view-independent, emotional and semantic information about the environment. As a consequence of learning associations between events (acquired releasing stimulus situations) and orienting movements (including head movements) within a specific emotional framework, appetitive behaviour can bring about (or make more likely) the animal's exposure to a releasing stimulus situation for the instinctive motor pattern related to the specific emotional arousal that was engaged in previous learning situations. The hippocampus closely interacts with the amygdala. The primary evolutionary function of the amygdala may be to link *innate* releasing stimulus situations with instinctive motor and autonomic patterns. Thus, the amygdala may have come to link innate releasing stimulus situations with ritualised affective displays ("expressive movements") that play a communicative and interindividually coordinating function in social behaviour (Figure 10-1). Dyadic social interactions are based on instinctive motor patterns that are released by an innate stimulus situation with which the organism is spontaneously presented or which is aligned with the organism (and brought into a suitable perspective) by a preceding epoch of appetitive behaviour (and it is in the latter case that an interaction with the hippocampus would be required).

## 2.4.3   The self

There are two types of self, a narcissistically cathected self-image and the experience of self-esteem. First, the self that emerges in states of introspection or imagination is based on one's ego ideal. This type of self-experience is derived from one's history of identifications with significant objects, including usually identifications with one's father (in the oedipal period) and one's teachers. One's self-image or imagined self (the self in one's fleeting imagery and daydreaming)—derived, as it is, from one's identifications—is a narcissisti-

cally cathected object, which, during phases of conscious fantasy, arises alongside, or in alternation with, libidinally and narcissistically cathected objects that are derived from one's primary love object. As one emulates—in the here-and-now—an object derived from one's history of identifications (that is, as one emulates one's self-image), relationships similar to the ones envisaged in fantasy are established with external replicas of the primary love object (Kernberg, 1996). In other words, the idealised image of the self is actualised (Horney, 1950).

The second form of self arises when one observes the present social situation or when one is immersed in a social situation. This is an integrative abstraction of signals or cues (embedded in the social situation) that relate to one's potential for attracting praise and affection (narcissistic sustenance) from others and, at the same time, to one's level of protection against offensive attack from others. This type of self is a dynamic representation of one's degree of relatedness to and acceptance by others. This self, manifesting not as an object but as a vague feeling of self-esteem (or "ego feeling" (Federn, 1952)), is diametrically opposed to the state of anxiety—the emotional feeling that signals an increased likelihood of conspecific attack (and a decreased likelihood of instinctive libidinal interactions or the receipt of narcissistic supplies). In a state of anxiety, one feels that others are disapproving of oneself and are, therefore, disposed to attack oneself; and the integrative sense of self, derived from contextual information that positively confirms one's potential to be approved and accepted by others, is lost. The sense of self disintegrates or fragments in states of anxiety, as phenomenologically appreciated by Kohut (1971), Federn (1952) and Laing (1960), for instance.

It has long been recognised that the self is one's reflection in the mirror provided by the social situation (James, 1890). The self that captures one's relatedness to, and security in, the immediate social situation forms an important part of one's conscious awareness of that situation. Consciously guided behaviour is appetitive behaviour constituted of orienting reactions and locomotor actions moving the organism through space or orienting and manipulative actions moving the organism through time (time being an evolutionary derivative of space). Orienting movements, which are responsive to allocentric spatial information (spatiotemporal events) and can be regarded as the simplest form of appetitive behaviour (Lorenz & Tinbergen, 1938), can be performed outside sequences of navigational locomotor actions or social normative and manipulative actions. Reorientation to the present location or situation is implemented by head movements and more subtle orienting movements (as may be the case when the default or resting mode of brain activity is engaged). Social contextual information pertaining to others' attitudes towards oneself and, hence, to one's sense of self, can be controlled directly by subtle orienting movements alone or indirectly by behaviour that actively manipulates others' views

of oneself and/or expresses one's compliance with social norms (Figure 2-5). There is an automatic tendency to enhance one's self-esteem (to move towards a secure interpersonal situation or to implement a securing object relationship); and there is a matching tendency to only discern self-supporting information from the social environment (as long as one is not in an anxious mood). "Repression" is a manifestation of this automatic process; it ensures that others regard oneself favourably, albeit at the price of self-deception. Repression is effected directly by orienting to favourable aspects of the situation (i.e., by social reorientation) when one observes or monitors the social situation; or it is effected indirectly by more complex appetitive behaviours—in the form of defence mechanisms, interpersonal manipulations, or active compliance with social norms—that are borne out of (and evoked by) the situation one presently occupies. "Defence mechanisms" are behaviours

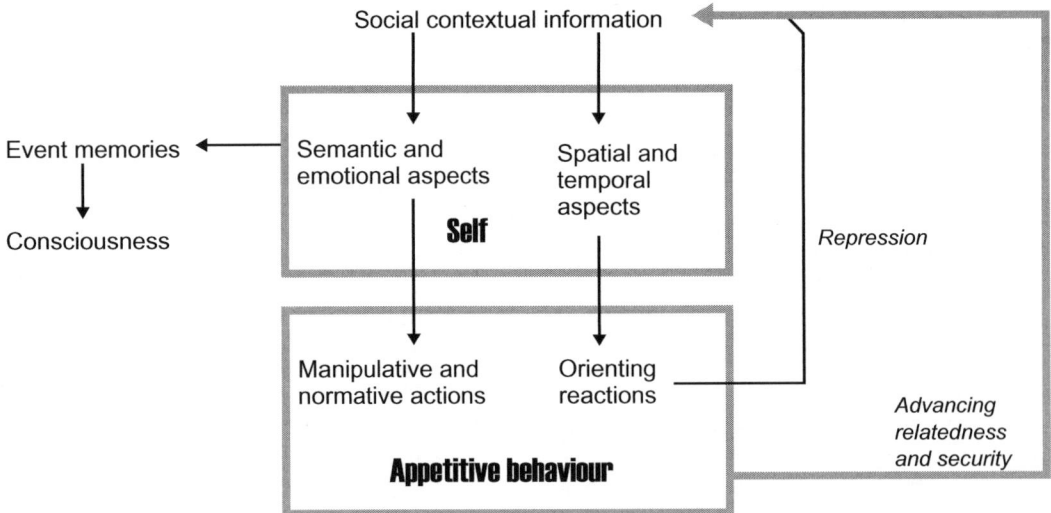

Figure 2-5.   Movement across time to a secure or resourceful *situation* (aided by orienting reactions as well as effort, assertiveness, and instrumental aggression) is evolutionarily related to navigation across space from a dangerous to a secure or resourceful *location*. A secure social situation is one in which offensive challenge from conspecifics (social punishment) is unlikely, while libidinal interactions and affective attunement are likely. The self is an emotional-semantic derivative of the situation (distilled from the context as a whole) to which one responds and, as such, is involved in the induction of appetitive modes of normative or manipulative behaviour.

that support repression, often helping to deceive oneself about others' attitudes towards oneself and, thereby, to keep anxiety at bay.

### 2.4.4 Synthesis

Consciousness is intricately linked with appetitive behaviour. Insofar as consciousness reflects one's being accepted and positively recognised by others in the social environment, appetitive behaviour takes the form of normative social and assertive or submissive interpersonal actions (some of which can be regarded as "defence mechanisms" and some of which involve "projective identification"). Normative social and manipulative interpersonal behaviours (as well as defence mechanisms) facilitate acceptance and recognition of oneself by others (that is, one's awareness of this acceptance and recognition), and thereby enhance one's self-esteem and safeguard one's access to libidinal resources and, indirectly, to other resources (resources of rewards satisfying basic physiological needs, for instance). Appetitive social behaviour effects a navigation across time from a less favourable to a more favourable situation, from an anxiogenic to an interpersonally secure situation or relationship (characterised by one's acceptance or recognition by a derivative of the primary object). Socially normative behaviours and defence mechanisms can also be regarded as forms of active avoidance behaviour, aiming to prevent fragmentation of the self or a shift back to anxiety and deprivation. What is reflected in consciousness, and what is recorded sequentially in the form of event and episodic memories, serves the acquisition of sequences of orienting reactions and sequences of actions moving the organism across space from location to location (navigational locomotor actions) or across time from situation to situation. Conscious awareness of aspects of the present social situation accompanies, and underlying neural activity informs, each step of appetitive navigation towards relatedness and away from unrelatedness (insecurity). Event memories (the substrate of consciousness) capture spatial and temporal determinants of orienting actions constitutive to socially normative behaviour as well as semantic and emotional determinants of higher-level strategies (task modes) and attitudes, so that optimal sequences of social navigational behaviour can be acquired (through reinforcement learning) (Figure 2-5). Thus, there is proposed to be a deep link between self-awareness, social behaviour, self-localisation, navigation, and hippocampal function.

# CHAPTER THREE

# Aggression

The "instinct of combat", or aggressive instinct, is "evoked by the behavior of any other creature that tends to thwart or obstruct him in the pursuit of any natural goal, that is, in the working out of any instinctive train of behavior" (McDougall, 1924, p. 140). The instinct of combat was thought to be unique in that "the key that opens its door is not a sense-expression or a sensory pattern of any kind, but rather any obstruction to the smooth progress toward its natural goal of any other instinctive striving" (pp. 140–141). Behavioural expression of the instinct of combat is accompanied by an emotional excitement of anger, rage, or fury (representing degrees of intensity) (McDougall, 1924). This instinct operates in two successive phases: the phase of threatening and the phase of attack. The most widely used behavioural expressions of the threatening phase are "sounds produced by the voice or other means" (McDougall, 1924, p. 141). Fear (including "timidity" and "terror", representing fainter and more intense variations of fear) is the "characteristic emotional accompaniment" of the "instinct of escape". A loud and sudden noise "is perhaps the most nearly universal key" to the "gates of fear"; others being "the sudden move of a large object", certain odours

of predators, and pain (McDougall, 1924, p. 152). Coevolution of instincts of aggression and escape may have ensured that expression of the former (threatening vocalisation) serves as the key to the latter (fearful reaction) in another individual. Escape is a two-phase instinct, comprising, first, "a running to shelter" and, second, "a lying hid when the shelter has been attained" (pp. 150–151). For gregarious species, shelter may be represented by "the mass of the congregated herd" (McDougall, 1924, p. 151).

McDougall (1924) also discerned instincts of self-assertion and submission, which he thought are crucial for the maintenance social order within the group, pointing out that combat, fear, and punishment alone would be "wasteful of energy" and "little conducive to harmonious social existence" (p. 158). Lorenz (1963) thought that it is the intertwining of intraspecific aggression with fear impulses in processes of phylogenetic and cultural ritualisation that produces displays of self-assertion and submission. Lorenz (1963) argued that social group behaviour in higher vertebrates is based on ritualised forms of aggression. Group behaviour is determined, from a drive-motivational point of view, by successive impulses of "aggression, fear, protection-seeking and renewed aggressiveness" (Lorenz, 1963, p. 55). These motivational forces contribute to a varying extent to a great variety of acquired stereotypical motor patterns that express interpersonal assertion or submission. Intraspecific aggression, according to Lorenz (1963), constitutes the driving force behind social manners and customs as well as social ambition, competitiveness, enthusiasm for a cause, envy, and the use of status symbols.

> What is certain, is that with the elimination of aggression … the tackling of a task or problem, the self-respect [in] everything that a man does from morning till evening, from the morning shave to the sublimest artistic or scientific creation, would loose all impetus; everything associated with ambition, ranking order, and countless other equally indispensable behaviour patterns would probably also disappear from human life. In the same way, a very important and specifically human faculty would probably disappear too: laughter. (Lorenz, 1963, p. 269)

Freud (1933), too, recognised that our civilisation and cultural achievements are founded upon aggressive as well as sexual impulses—the very impulses that are often "inhibited by society" (p. 143). Freud (1933) thought that the taming of aggressive impulses, in particular, is achieved by the "setting up of the super-ego, which makes the dangerous aggressive impulses its own" (p. 143). Insofar as the ego has to "submit itself to the destructive impulses of aggression", aggression becomes self-destructive (Freud, 1933). The superego, which, according to Freud, is a developmental achievement (the "heir") of the Oedipus complex, inhibits the expression of aggression in certain situations, namely when there is a risk of incurring retaliation or punishment from the social environment; it does not abolish aggression as a potent force in social interactions. With the resolution of the Oedipus complex, aggression becomes a means for controlling the object's

attention and devotion *in competition with others*. The form of aggression that emerges from the triadic oedipal constellation can be distinguished from a preoedipal form of aggression that is used, in part, to control the attachment object directly. Kohut (1972) discerned two types of manifestation of the "death instinct" (aggression): "competitive aggressiveness, directed at objects that stand in the way of cherished goals, and narcissistic rage, directed at selfobjects who threaten or have damaged the self" (reviewed in Wolf, 1988, p. 78). While "competitive aggressiveness derived from the oedipal complex is a nonpathological and often constructive force in human relations" (Wolf, 1988, p. 79), narcissistic rage in response to an injury to one's self-esteem—an injury that opens the abyss into existential anxiety—may be continuous with the preoedipal infant's rage at his absent mother.

### 3.1  Ethology

Aggressive behaviour patterns are inherited as fixed action patterns (Eibl-Eibesfeldt, 1970; Lorenz, 1973). In the process of natural selection, variable behavioural sequences are compressed into new rigid motor patterns. An emotional expression will progressively become transformed into a ritualised behaviour pattern (signal) "if it is of advantage to the transmitter of the expression for another animal to understand him" (Eibl-Eibesfeldt, 1970, pp. 46–47). Ritualised movements are often based on "movements of intent". Movements of intent "convey an appetency toward specific modes of behavior" (Hass, 1968, p. 112). Some of our ancestors defended themselves by biting. Teeth grinding is a "movement of intent which conveys a readiness to bite" (p. 112). As a result of phylogenetic ritualisation, teeth grinding became "a forewarning of the intention to bite" (Hass, 1968, p. 112). Acting as a signal, teeth grinding "may alone be sufficient to intimidate an opponent and provoke a withdrawal" (p. 112). For the communicative effect to occur, a "receptive mechanism" had to evolve, which, at the sight of teeth grinding, prompted the appropriate behavioural response in the opponent. Our ancestors also possessed well-developed canines, and, in humans, the lowering of the corners of the mouth, originally to reveal these canines, is still part of the expressive movement ("Ausdrucksbewegung") of anger evolved from teeth grinding (Hass, 1968).

> Baboons, which are equipped with particularly long upper canines, pull their lower lips down at the far corners when threatening, so that the canines are exposed to their full extent. We do just the same, although we do not possess long upper canines. Thus the motor pattern has outlived the reduction in size of the organ that was originally displayed. (Eibl-Eibesfeldt, 1970, p. 19)

Fighting behaviour is activated (released) by specific signals received from conspecifics (Eibl-Eibesfeldt, 1970). A perceived or actual threat to one's own group is a "highly effective releasing stimulus situation" (p. 79). Aggression, perhaps of a different kind, is also aroused when the satisfaction of a need is frustrated. An aggressively *aroused* animal searches for a rival it can attack. This shows that animals can be in a fighting mood (anger). Eibl-Eibesfeldt (1970) spoke of appetitive behaviour for fighting. Appetitive behaviour for fighting points to the existence of an innate drive for aggression. The drive for aggression is aroused not only by frustration but also by pain—occasionally to the point that aggressive motor patters are expressed spontaneously, that is, in the absence of a suitable releasing "stimulus situation" (e.g., swearing when hitting one's thumb with a hammer). Aggressive readiness (aggressiveness) may refer to the ease with which any frustration or pain can arouse the animal's aggressive drive, which—when aroused—prompts the animal to seek out (appetitively) a "stimulus situation" ("Reizsituation") that *releases* an aggressive motor pattern ("expressive movement") (Figure 3-1). Aggressive readiness fluctuates with the level of testosterone

in birds and mammals. Moreover, aggressive readiness is regulated by previous experience in agonistic encounters. Repeated victory makes a mouse more aggressive, whereas repeated social defeat reduces aggressiveness (reviewed in Eibl-Eibesfeldt, 1970) ("conditioned defeat"). In humans, periodic fluctuations of aggressive readiness manifest as irritability. The more irritable a person, the more readily he is provoked to anger (Eibl-Eibesfeldt, 1970).

### 3.1.1  Phylogenetic ritualisation

Expressive actions and gestures ("expressive movements" or displays) are innate patterns of behaviour that have a communicative function. In higher social animals, "the great majority of expressive actions and gestures reflect an urge to threaten or appease" (Lorenz, 1973, p. 213). Hostile performances in birds and mammals are sequences of visual and acoustic patterns that have become ritualised in the course of evolution (Moynihan, 1998). Visual "displays" ("ritualised patterns") of hostile valence are often accompanied by vocalisations. Vocalisations, in general, are ritualised patterns that have a communicative function (Moynihan, 1998).

Most "expressive movements" (phylogenetically ritualised patterns of behaviour with a communicative function) have evolved from "intention movements" or "displacement activities" (gestures of embarrassment) (Lorenz, 1973). Highly ritualised displays of agonistic behaviour, in particular, have "evolved from intention movements and ambivalent behaviour patterns derived from instinctive conflicts" (pp. 211–212). Expressive movements signalling the *intention* to attack are often ineffective remnants of functional ("unritualised") behaviour patterns involved in overt attack behaviour. The evolution of intraspecific aggression necessitated that "the effectiveness of the original motor patterns should be considerably reduced and with it the danger of physical injury to the combatants" (Lorenz, 1973, p. 211). In all likelihood, *interspecific* (predatory and defensive) aggression is the evolutionary precursor of *intra*specific aggression (hostility), which, rather than aiming to kill prey or protect against predators, serves to control competition for resources between rival conspecifics. There is "a high survival value in limiting and channelling" the effects of "the weapons and behaviour patterns for killing a prey or for defence against predators", for they "are far too powerful, cruel and effective for rival fighting" (Lorenz, 1973, p. 211). *Inter*specific aggression is dangerous; and, for it to play a role in controlling *intra*specific competition, it has to be made safe; it has to be controlled in its turn (Moynihan, 1998). Under these circumstances, "selection will favour the development of precautionary measures" (Moynihan, 1998, p. 96).

In birds, hostile "displays" incorporate elements of overt hostility but predominantly consist of elements of nonhostile origin (Moynihan, 1998). Hostile visual displays in birds often contain elements derived from components of feeding, self-grooming, nest-building, and similar behaviours ("displacement patterns"). Displacement patterns, which are nesting-type and other movements produced apparently out of context, tend to occur at moments of stress, including stressful hostile encounters. Displacement patterns become ritualised patterns, namely "hostile, distinctly unfriendly expressions of attack and escape tendencies" (p. 92). In mammals, hostile performances are often traceable to "intention movements" of attack, defence, or withdrawal, and much less to displacement patterns (Moynihan, 1998). Intention movements performed during hostile encounters can become ritualised attack and escape patterns (displays), which is to say that they become specialised for the communication of attack and escape between individuals. Intention movements can be combined, in phylogenesis, with other behaviour tendencies into new rituals. Many hostile displays, not only in birds but also in mammals, incorporate elements derived from allogrooming, copulation, or parent-infant interactions. Diverse behaviour "tendencies such as attack, escape, to be friendly, to form pair bonds, can be accommodated

together—one might almost say reconciled with one another—at low to moderate intensities of activation" (Moynihan, 1998, p. 91).

> Advance, retreat, appeasement, transferred sexual or parental patterns, and so on can all be used to form, regulate, and maintain all sorts of social relations, large groups or small groups. (Moynihan, 1998, p. 103)

### 3.1.2   Defence and offence

Defensive behaviour, as studied in rats, is determined by the distance between the subject and a predator or other threat ("defensive distance") (Blanchard & Blanchard, 1989). At greater "defensive distance", the subject flees or, if escape routes are not available, "freezes while oriented to the predator" (p. 97). Freezing (active immobility) is accompanied by increased muscle tension and enhanced startle reactivity to sudden stimuli. As the predator comes close to contact, freezing behaviour "gives way to defensive vocalisation, and jump attacks and bites at the predator's head" (p. 97). Defensive attack only occurs when, at near-contact defensive distances, "freezing and flight are no longer useful" (Blanchard & Blanchard, 1989, p. 98).[1] Defensive attack "is normally preceded by ample warning to the predator or conspecific attacker" (p. 98). This warning, being effected by weapon display (teeth, in the case of rats) and defensive vocalisations (screams), communicates "the power and high motivation of the defender" (p. 98). Defensive screams are "extremely noxious" and may elicit in the opponent "a strong reluctance to continue" predatory or offensive behaviour (Blanchard & Blanchard, 1989, p. 98).

Situations that elicit offensive aggression in rats and other animals typically involve resource

---

[1] Human pathologies of specific components of defensive behaviour may include "freezing in catatonia", "greatly exaggerated fear to specific stimuli" (phobias), and "heightened defensive attack in the 'dyscontrol' syndromes and (perhaps) paranoia" (Blanchard & Blanchard, 1989, p. 100).

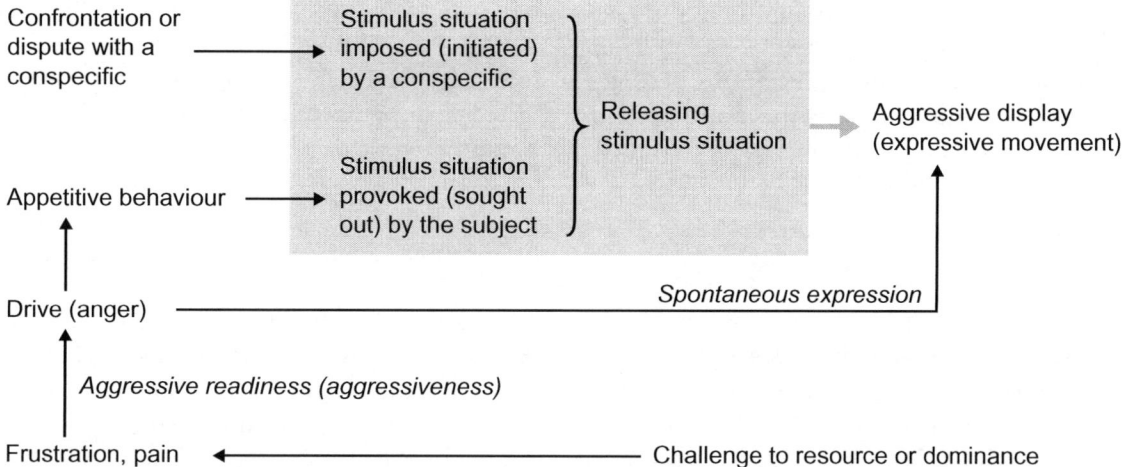

Figure 3-1.   When anger is aroused (by pain or frustration), the subject seeks out a stimulus situation that can release his innate aggressive displays. Alternatively, innate (instinctive) motor patterns may express themselves spontaneously in the absence of a releasing stimulus situation (Lorenz, 1935, 1937).

disputes or dominance claims (Blanchard & Blanchard, 1989). These "situational elicitors" are interrelated, in that an animal's dominance status regulates its access to resources. In both situations (resource and dominance disputes), "a challenge from a conspecific" serves "as an immediate elicitor of offence … regardless of the resource/dominance focus of any actual dispute" (p. 102). Even in the absence of a resource/dominance dispute situation, "some highly aggressive animals seek out opponents to attack" (Blanchard & Blanchard, 1989, p. 103), consistent with the postulation of an aggressive drive (responsible for appetitive aspects of behaviour) collaborating with instinctive motor mechanisms (ritualised displays) (Figure 3-1). The animal's motivation "directed toward attack on an opponent in disputes over resources or dominance" can be considered as "a primitive functional analogue of human anger" (Blanchard & Blanchard, 1989, p. 103). The reinforcement value of victory in a conspecific dispute may be due, in part, to a reduction in anger (Blanchard & Blanchard, 1989), consistent with the hypothesised role of drive reduction in learning, in general (Brown, 1953; Miller, 1948).

Resource disputes (including disputes over property) and disputes over "rights" (being

a proxy for dominance status) are sources of offensive (angry) aggression in humans (Blanchard & Blanchard, 1989). Violations by others of "one's own personal views of 'how things should be'" are another (and possibly related) source of anger and offensive (angry) aggression in humans (p. 110). Through offensive aggression, one aims "to gain access to, control of, or possession of, the disputed property" or "to assert one's right *vis-à-vis* the other" (p. 111). If the goal is achieved, offensive aggression is reinforced and, henceforth, more likely employed in a similar situation.[2] Disputes are usually limited to a verbal exchange of threats and the mutual display of fighting abilities. Perceived challenges to one's rights or resources may provoke in oneself explicit threats or insults (aggressive displays) directed against the "intruding" individual, whereby these threats or insults may elicit reciprocal offensive (angry) aggression in the "intruder" (presumably by being perceived, by the "intruder", as innate releasing stimulus situation). Explicit challenges and insults, expressed

---

[2]Inflicting pain or hurting the other person can be a goal of angry aggression; and this is likewise reinforcing (Blanchard & Blanchard, 1989).

verbally and through gesture, allow opponents to display their agonistic capabilities (Blanchard & Blanchard, 1989). Unlike other forms of affective interaction, angry exchanges usually involve vocalisations, which may be important to understanding the origin of language.

### 3.1.3    Affective cost–benefit analysis

Offensive attack tends to be "inhibited by fear of the physical or social consequences of the attack" (Blanchard & Blanchard, 1989, p. 113). In other words, punishment that is contingent on offensive attack inhibits offensive attack (operating through the fear of punishment).[3] Unlike defensive aggression, offensive aggression usually ensues after complex "affective cost–benefit analysis". "Affective cost–benefit analysis" compares possible outcomes of offensively aggressive versus defensively submissive reactions to the present situation; it "compares the relative values of offence-promoting emotional/motivational states (a primitive analogue of human anger) and fear" (Blanchard & Blanchard, 1989, p. 104). Anger and fear arising in a situation of conspecific challenge depend "in considerable degree upon the specifics of the situation" (p. 104), such as the presence of a disputed resource, the nature of the challenge, the behaviour of the opponent, the status of the opponent, and the opponent's size, strength, and weapons (Blanchard & Blanchard, 1989). Some of these factors (such as the opponent's challenging behaviour) preferentially impact on anger, while others (such as the size and strength of the opponent) impact on fear. In situations involving strangers or "closely matched familiar individuals" or some other ambiguity, "considerable time may be devoted to the process in information gathering and affective analysis" (p. 105). Duration of affective cost–benefit analysis and latency to offensive attack are increased in "situations in which there is some degree of fear,

uncertainty, or novelty" (Blanchard & Blanchard, 1989, p. 106). The need for complex analysis prior to engagement with an opponent may have provided an impetus for the evolution of the default-mode network and high-level decision-making abilities.

Assessment by opponents of each other in a resource/dominance dispute situation is accompanied by ritualistic displays of agonistic capabilities. Threatening displays do not in themselves elicit fear and submissive behaviour in an opponent; they likely elicit both, anger and fear. Contextual information is vital in assessing the probability of winning or losing a dispute or fight. The dispute ends (without a fight) whenever the "affective cost–benefit analysis" in one of the opponents concludes, from the information gathered, that there is a high probability of defeat. From the perspective of the defeated animal, the situation has become an unambiguously dangerous one, so that submissive behaviour is automatically engaged. The defeated animal does not simply disengage from the confrontation; it actively inhibits the opponent's aggression through its submissive behaviour. Especially in humans, angry verbal expressions (and other threatening displays) may change the subject's ongoing "affective cost–benefit analysis" not only by having an impact on the opponent's behaviour but also by attributing blame to, or denigrating, the opponent. Affective cost–benefit analysis includes contextual evaluation of the opponent's strength and social status, and both can be diminished in the eyes of the subject.

### 3.1.4    Macaque behavioural development

In the third month of macaque behavioural development, mothers start to reject their infants' nursing attempts who are now forced to search for food independently. As infants are weaned, they engage in social interaction with other individuals (mostly play) and increase their repertoire of distinct vocalisations (reviewed in Machado & Bachevalier, 2003). At the time

---

[3]These are inhibitions that do not affect defensive attack propensities (Blanchard & Blanchard, 1989).

of increased independence, infants become more fearful of objects. New stimuli that would previously have provoked curiosity with explorative and play behaviour now come to evoke anxiety and defensive reactions. Infants also develop a fear of strangers, which is conveyed by fear grimace and other behaviours such as withdrawal, rocking, and screaming. In human infants, by comparison, fear of strangers and shyness emerge only around one year of age. Until macaque infants are four to six months of age, play is the predominant way of social interaction. Between the sixths and sevenths month, maternal protection disappears completely. This allows infants to be punished more severely by others; and infants learn to judge aggressive signals from others. Around the same time, infants themselves start to show more aggression to control the behaviour of others. Between the sixth and eighth months, infants also start to initiate more grooming with others, especially with peers. As maternal bonds are broken, adult male leaders of the troop take over the care of male infants. In the process of their interaction, male infants appear to adopt the personality traits of their mentor. During the second year of their lives, male and female macaques acquire their dominance rank in the troop (reviewed in Machado & Bachevalier, 2003).

In the first year of life, interactions with other individuals become increasingly more complex and macaque infants have to learn that each individual has a "unique set of intensions determined by the combination of kinship, dominance, gender, environmental conditions and the current social context" (Machado & Bachevalier, 2003). "Infant macaques must learn to accurately assess the emotional state and intensions of others and choose the most appropriate behavioural reactions for that situation". Development of the ability to modulate behavioural responses to social stimuli with respect to the physical and social context, as seen in the macaque after the age of one year, may be related to the maturation of the orbitofrontal cortex and its connections to amygdala

and dorsolateral prefrontal cortex (reviewed in Machado & Bachevalier, 2003).

### 3.1.5    Distrust and contempt

The interest a member of a group shows in an event occurring in the environment is communicated to others by "a widening of the eyes", accompanied by a turning of the head "in the appropriate direction" and, perhaps, an opening of the mouth (Hass, 1968, p. 113). These movements convey "a potentially important piece of information to those out hunting or in danger" (p. 113). If a member of a group of primates, especially the leader of a group, "had noticed something, the ability to indicate its position silently might well be crucial in the next few moments" (p. 113). The opening of the mouth may be "an aid to keener hearing" or represent "a deep reflex intake of breath" in readiness for defensive action (Hass, 1968, p. 114). The widening of the eyes is also part of expressive movements of trust. Deliberately facing another and regarding him "with an open gaze" is a ritualised expression of trust that is innately understood by conspecifics (p. 114). Distrust, "as we call interest which is overlaid with fear", is communicated by subtle ritualised movements of head, body, and eyes that have evolved from "movements of intent denoting a readiness to turn away and flee" and a concurrent narrowing of the eyes (in order to protect the eyes) (Hass, 1968, p. 113). Hass (1968) established (in correspondence with Darwin's views) that "a raising and half-turning of the head, a narrowing of the eyes, and a simultaneous expulsion of air through the nose"—reflecting a combination of "turning away from someone", *rejecting* his smell, and "the wish to impress", or *dominate*, him—became ritualised into a special signal conveying disdain (Hass, 1968, p. 114).

We monitor the social environment for signs of trust, distrust, and contempt; our security within the group (and relatedness to the group) depends on these signs. Sudden loss of trust in a person upon whom one relies (such as the mother) generates "basic insecurity" (Storr, 1968, p. 40), which, in turn, mobilises one's aggression. Others may also lose trust in us. Expressions of distrust and contempt are forms of offensive aggression, the target of which we can become quite readily, unless we inhibit these tendencies in others through our compliance and normality (Laing, 1960). People may feel "some distaste or even hostility" for individuals who are handicapped or unattractive (Berkowitz, 1989, p. 51). These "unfortunate individuals are basically aversive stimuli for others" (p. 51). There is evidence to suggest that an unattractive or handicapped individual is more likely "to draw aggressive reactions from those who are disposed to be aggressive for some reason and do not restrain themselves" (Berkowitz, 1989, pp. 52–53).

### 3.1.6   Expulsion reaction

Laughter, "characterized by an open mouth and the rhythmic emission of sound", is a ritualised threat gesture (Hass, 1968, p. 125). The retraction of the corners of the mouth and concurrent raising of the upper lip cause a baring of the teeth—a movement of aggressive intent. Laughter has "a strongly infectious quality" (p. 127). In primates, concerted threats directed at an enemy or outsider are "accompanied by a rhythmical emission of sounds strongly reminiscent of human laughter" (p. 127). Hass (1968) pointed out that it is often "the spectacle of others' misfortune and the agreeable realisation that we have been spared the thing that has befallen them" that impels us to laugh (p. 126). Moreover, "laughter within a closed group is more likely to excite an outsider's annoyance, especially if he is ignorant of its cause, because he assumes it to be directed at himself" (Hass, 1968, p. 127). Joint mockery, inherent in human laughter, is related to animal behaviour effecting the expulsion of outsiders from the group.

> Joint derision is related to the expulsion reaction commonly observed in animals, which is usually elicited by malformation or, in more general terms, by the quality of being different, physically or behaviourally, from the group. The result of this reaction is that the outsider is not only expelled but in certain circumstances killed. (Hass, 1968, pp. 126–127)

Concerted laughter and the "expulsion reaction" directed at an individual not only "afford an opportunity of working off pent-up aggression" but also "lead to the forming of united fronts" (p. 127). Joint laughter strengthens a pact between individuals and cements the bond within the group. In general, alliances or bonds of friendship can be created by forming a common front of aggressive behaviour towards a third party (Hass, 1968). A threatening gesture directed at a *third party* can become ritualised into a greeting or appeasement gesture used in bond formation. Greeting ceremonies that arise in this way consist in the individual's directing a threat gesture past a potential partner towards a nonexistent third party, whereupon the potential partner reciprocates the act by directing a threat gesture past the first individual. Lorenz (1963) observed patterns of bond formation in geese, called "triumph ceremonies", that likely evolved through ritualisation of a redirected threat.

## 3.2   Control of the attachment object

As pointed out by Bowlby (1973), "small changes in a situation can have great influence on the form of behaviour shown" (p. 137). A strange or novel situation "can elicit either withdrawal or exploration or both together", whereby often "an interested approach and an alarmed withdrawal are shown either simultaneously or in rapid succession" (Bowlby, 1973, p. 137). Similarly, an anxiogenic situation can evoke either withdrawal (flight) or attack behaviour, depending on species-related, individual (organismic), and situational factors. Whether, in an anxiogenic situation, "an animal responds with attack or withdrawal, or with a combination of both, depends on a variety of factors that have the effect of tipping the balance either one way or another" (p. 253). There is "an analogous type of balance" between "anxious attachment" and "angry attachment" (p. 253). A child may be "furiously angry with a parent", at one moment, and "seeking reassurance and comfort from that same parent", at the next (Bowlby, 1973, p. 253) (Figure 6-1).

Separation from an attachment figure amounts to an anxiogenic situation, in response to which withdrawal or attack behaviour may be engaged. Separation anxiety (distress) may be evolutionarily related to pain (Panksepp, 2003). Anxiety is aroused in situations predictive of danger, whereas pain is a response to actual danger and harm. Anxiety promotes withdrawal or attack behaviour, and, similarly, when an animal or person experiences pain, "there is immediate and unthinking retreat, or, alternatively, attack" (Bowlby, 1973, p. 141). Separation anxiety may arise in response to, or be exacerbated by, threats of abandonment (p. 256). Threats of being abandoned or actual abandonment or rejection can cause intense distress and pain. As a result of such intense pain, the abandoned or threatened person can feel "furiously angry with the person who inflicts it" (Bowlby, 1973, p. 249).

> The reason that anxiety about and hostility towards an attachment figure are so habitually found together, it is therefore concluded, is because both types of response are aroused by the same class of situation; and, to a lesser degree, because, once intensely aroused, each response tends to aggravate the other. As a result, following experiences of repeated separation or threats of separation, it is common for a person to develop intensely anxious and possessive attachment behaviour simultaneously with bitter anger directed against the attachment figure, and often to combine both with much anxious concern about the safety of that figure. (Bowlby, 1973, p. 256)

### 3.2.1    Frustration and punishment

Hostility may arise or increase when the child is anxious "that an attachment figure may be inaccessible or unresponsive when needed" (Bowlby, 1973, p. 255). Anger that is engendered by separation, or by the threat of separation, tends to be directed at the attachment figure. If the child's hostility is "directed towards a parent or parent-substitute", then it may take "the form of a reproach for his having been absent when wanted" (p. 246). The child's aggression may act as a "forceful reminder", seeking to ensure that the parent or parent-substitute "would not err again" (Bowlby, 1973, p. 247).

> In the schema proposed, a period of separation, and also threats of separation and other forms of rejection, are seen as arousing, in a child or adult, both anxious and angry behaviour. Each is directed towards the attachment figure: anxious attachment is to retain maximum accessibility to the attachment figure; anger is both a reproach at what has happened and a deterrent against it happening again. (Bowlby, 1973, p. 253)

Anger and hostility can be understood as a response to frustration. Rather than arsing directly in response to an anxiogenic situation, such as one that is engendered by separation or the threat of separation, anger and aggression may be "reactive to frustration of some kind" (Bowlby, 1973, p. 254). Fairbairn (1952), for instance, had argued that frustration or deprivation of the infant's libidinal relationship causes him to become aggressive towards his loved object. The attachment figure may *frustrate* the infant's libidinal striving wittingly or unwittingly. Perhaps, in this situation, anger has the function of coercing the attachment object to display affectionate or attentive behaviour towards the infant, while angry punishment of the attachment object modulates the latter's future behaviour (through avoidance learning).

### 3.2.2 Loss

As emphasised by Bowlby (1973), anger arising in situations of temporary separation has two functions: "first, it may assist in overcoming such obstacles as there may be to reunion; second, it may discourage the loved person from going away again" (p. 247). In other words, whenever separation is believed to be temporary, "anger is expressed as reproachful and punishing behaviour that has as its set-goals assisting a reunion and discouraging further separation" (Bowlby, 1973, p. 248). Separation can be permanent, rather than temporary, in which case it is designated as "loss" (p. 178). Following a bereavement, "anger and aggressive behaviour are necessarily without function" (p. 247). However, anger aroused by loss seems to be linked to hopes of recovering, or attempts to recover, the lost person. During the early phases of grieving, "a bereaved person usually does not believe that the loss can really be permanent; he therefore continues to act as though it were still possible not only to find and recover the lost person but to reproach him for his actions" (Bowlby, 1973, p. 247).

> For the lost person is not infrequently held to be at least in part responsible for what has happened, in fact to have deserted. As a result, anger comes to be directed against the lost person, as well as, of course, against any others thought to have played a part in the loss or in some way to be obstructing reunion. (Bowlby, 1973, pp. 247–248)

Anger may be redirected against the self, especially insofar as the self is unconsciously identified with the lost object. In melancholia, "an object that was lost has been set up again inside the ego"; in other words, "an object-cathexis has been replaced by an identification" of the ego with the lost object (Freud, 1923, p. 28). The setting up of the object inside the ego, as it occurs in melancholia, leads to an alteration of the ego. The ego "assumes features of the object", so that

it is in a position of "forcing itself, so to speak, upon the id as a love-object" (p. 30). The redirection of libidinal energy to parts of the ego is paralleled by a redirection of anger against the ego. Generally, the "instinct of destruction" can be redirected against the ego if "discharge" against the external world and other organisms is obstructed (Freud, 1923).

### 3.2.3 Hatred

Bowlby (1973) recognised that angry behaviour "has coercion as its function" (p. 248). However, angry coercive behaviour expressed towards a parent or partner normally "acts to promote, not to disrupt, the bond" (p. 248) (Figure 6-1). Anger is dysfunctional "whenever a person, child or adult, becomes so intensely and/or persistently angry with his partner that the bond between them is weakened, instead of strengthened" (pp. 248–249). Anger becomes hatred "whenever aggressive thoughts or acts cross the narrow boundary between being deterrent and being revengeful" (p. 249). Bowlby (1973) thought that "hostile impulses, whether conscious or unconscious, directed towards a loved figure can greatly increase anxiety" (p. 255). A vicious circle may develop, wherein "separation or rejection arouses a person's hostility and leads to hostile thoughts and acts; while hostile thoughts and acts directed towards his attachment figure greatly increase his fear of being further rejected or even of losing his loved figure altogether" (p. 254). Following repeated separation or threats of abandonment, thoughts about, or acts of, revenge may go as far as concerning themselves with the killing of the attachment object (Bowlby, 1973).

> Thus not only may angry discontented behaviour alienate the attachment figure but, within the attached, a shift can occur in the balance of feeling. Instead of a strongly rooted affection laced occasionally with 'hot displeasure', such as develops in a child brought up by affectionate parents, there grows a deep running resentment,

held in check only partially by an anxious uncertain affection. (p. 249)

The most violently angry and dysfunctional responses of all, it seems probable, are elicited in children and adolescents who not only experience repeated separations but are constantly subjected to the threat of being abandoned. (Bowlby, 1973, p. 249)

Hatred is an affective response to danger felt to be emanating from the object (Kernberg, 1992). The aim of hatred is to destroy or devalue (dehumanise) the "object, a specific object of unconscious fantasy, and this object's conscious derivatives" (p. 23). Hatred allows the individual to reenact his early identification with a hated object. Identification with a betraying object early in life "initiates the path to a revengeful destruction of all object relations" (Kernberg, 1992, p. 28). Hatred of one's objects may derive from "rationalized identification with a strict and punitive superego" (p. 24). Hatred may take the form of "aggressive assertion of idiosyncratic but well-rationalized systems of morality" or of "justified indignation" (p. 24). Obsessive-compulsive patients seek "to control and dominate others to feel protected against threatening outbreaks of aggressive rebelliousness and chaos in others" (p. 29). In milder forms of hatred, one desires to dominate the object and exert power over it, so that "attacks on the object tend to be self-limited by the object's submission" (Kernberg, 1992, p. 24).

## 3.3   Social control

The shrine of normality at which all of us devoutly worship must on no account be examined into. … The least infringement upon it calls forth a reflex defence-reaction in individual and community. (Burrow, 1949, p. 50)

We help to enforce social norms (internalised by the individual as "superego") by displaying anger (offensive aggression) and directing punishment towards those who deviate from social and cultural norms. "Normality", as recognised by Burrow (1949), "is the measure by which we judge all behaviour and indict as subversive or pathological whatever behaviour deviates from this popularly cherished 'norm'" (p. 50). Others' socially deviant behaviour automatically induces within ourselves anger and disposes us to displaying offensive aggression. We show "automatic defence-reactions in support of the accustomed habits and mores characteristic of the normal level of adaptation" (Burrow, 1949, p. 51). At the same time—when trying to attract others' attention and validation, induce their submission, and improve our social standing, and thus be closer to the affection of the symbolic primary object—we cannot but infringe on social norms, so that "in all our interpersonal relationships", manifest "conformity and manifest defection are at loggerheads" (Burrow, 1949, p. 303).

### 3.3.1   Induction of submission

Intraspecific aggression requires an object. The object is perceived or sought by the subject as he or she experiences a feeling of anger. Anger encompasses "ideas of having been wronged and of doing something more or less violent about that"—ideas or fantasies that "may be repressed altogether or replaced by "tamed" ideas or fantasies of some sort of retaliation against someone or other" (Schafer, 1976, p. 166). Retaliation or revenge may be achieved when the other is suffering but, perhaps, the aim of intraspecific aggression is generally to induce submission or "respect" in those who are attacked. When confronted with another person's angry actions, one may signal submission by abandoning (undoing) a challenge one has implicitly levelled against the other person's social role or standing. The subject expressing aggression or anger "is not likely to go on acting angrily if she has done something that signifies to her adequate revenge or retaliation, or adequate communication and effectiveness of action with regard to her grievance, for then she will see her situation as having changed for the better, and she will no longer find provocation to think or behave angrily" (Schafer, 1976, p. 166).

Submissive expressions one has induced in others by means of offensively aggressive or dominant gestures are evolutionarily related to supportive and validating expressions that one habitually solicits from others (Figure 3-2). Much of social behaviour is designed to elicit supportive and companionable interactions, if necessary by exerting pressure on others (in which case companionable interactions become dominant-submissive interactions). Hostile aggressive behaviour may arise if one does not receive the expected effective support or companionship. Then, hostile aggression is a defensive strategy "to handle fear concerning survival" or prevent the distress associated with the loss of support (Heard & Lake, 1986, p. 436).

### 3.3.2   Neutralisation and attitudes

Hartmann (1964) thought that there is "a neutralized form of aggressive energy working in the ego" (p. 87). "Neutralisation" (sublimation) of aggressive as well as sexual energy "takes place through mediation of the ego" (Hartmann, 1964, p. 128). This is to say that aggressive and sexual energy are absorbed in the evolvement

of "ego functions". Ego functions (psychic structures) provide aggressive and other instincts with "specific modes of expression" (p. 87) that accord with the "reality principle" (social reality). Self-assertion is one of the ego functions that depends on neutralised aggressive energy. Defence mechanisms, too, are ego functions that absorb aggressive energy as they develop. Adaptation to reality generally presupposes "neutralisation" (sublimation) of aggressive energy, although reality situations "appeal sometimes to the unmitigated expression of aggression" (Hartmann, 1964, p. 87). Neutralised aggressive energy permeates our prejudices and attitudes, the expression of which helps to maintain social traditions and socially approved principles of conduct.

> Our habits of living, our habits of feeling and thinking and doing are largely governed by prejudice. So are our traditional virtues, our apocryphal precepts, our cherished "principles of conduct". (Burrow, 1949, p. 31)

Prejudices and attitudes, as well as social norms and traditions, have their motivational origin in the interplay, on a group or societal level, between

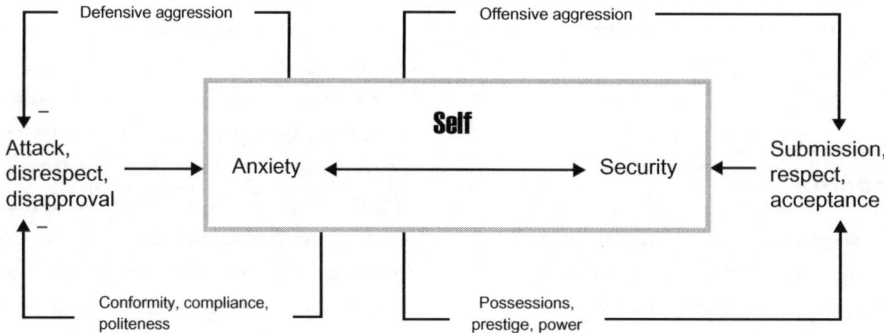

Figure 3-2.   Offensive aggression, evoked by inadvertent conspecific challenge, aims to assert one's claims over resources via the induction of submissive behaviours in others. Power, prestige, and possessions protect against anxiety (Horney, 1937), in part by facilitating one's efforts to induce in others submissive or validating gestures towards oneself. Defensive aggression is a reaction to others' offensive attack, and it may be engaged when others' attack evokes intense anxiety and pain in oneself. One avoids becoming the object of others' offensive attack by behaving in conform and normative ways.

offensive aggression and submission, between anger, fear, and avoidance. One's endorsement of commonly held prejudices and attitudes not only serves to inhibit others' offensively aggressive tendencies but also mediates one's own offensive aggression, self-assertion, and striving for dominance. The expression of prejudices and attitudes may implement offensive aggression in a habitual and nonemotional way. However, in novel and unpredictable situations, the expression of prejudices and attitudes may be accompanied by overt anger and agitation. Burrow (1949) spoke of a "monstrous *social mood* of systematized prejudice and absolutism", a "social mood begotten of partitive feeling, or affect"; and it became clear to him that "this impervious mood of competitive affectivity or prejudice", "whether manifesting itself singly or collectively", "was of one cloth throughout the entire social structure" (p. 52).

> The difference between the partitive response of the animal and the partitive response of man is that man's symbolic or partitive reaction has become socially or interrelationally systematized throughout the organism of the species. This systematization, as I have said, is represented subjectively in the pseudo-identity each of us reflexly impersonates as the "I" or "I"-persona—a constellation of affects and prejudices ... (Burrow, 1949, p. 140)

### 3.3.3   Internalisation of social status

> What man really fears and is ever abjectly dependent upon is the prevalent social image begotten of social opinion or approval. (Burrow, 1949, p. 145)

Offensive (intraspecific) aggression, which evolved for the purpose of acquiring and defending individual territories (and, hence, maintaining an equal distribution of the species across its habitat), came to serve the establishment and maintenance of social hierarchies in group-living species, including primates. We use offensive

aggression—as well as our ability to control others' "attention" (that is, attention in the form of approval, respect, or submission) directed towards us—in the service of efforts to establish and maintain a social position or status within the social group or network to which we relate. The boundaries of our "social territory", outlining the social position or status we occupy, are defined in terms of social norms, rights, and traditions; and we devote offensive aggression (especially in neutralised forms of prejudice and attitudes) to the aim of upholding these norms, rights, and traditions, thereby ensuring the stability of our social territory. Social status or position, which is behaviourally measureable (or phenomenologically describable), is likely a major determinant of our seemingly private self-image. Self-esteem, being the antithesis of anxiety, reflects others' positive evaluations (appraisals) of ourselves, evaluations that are partly enshrined in cultural symbols signifying our social position or status. Anxiety arises when, in a social situation, one is not anchored in the social position one expects or does not have the social status one expects. It is then that the danger of attack from others arises; and it is especially then that we become acutely aware of our self (in the form of heightened self-consciousness or a defensively grandiose self-image) (Figure 3-2).

> In our social relationships we seem ever at pains to preserve what is known as our *amour propre*, our mental and social "right" or prestige. ... The measures we adopt for its protection and security now operate automatically among us. These measures are both defensive and offensive. The defensive mechanism is seen in one's effort to achieve credits, to be thought approvingly of, to be "somebody". The offensive aspect of the mechanism is shown in the tendency to disparage others, to indulge in personal criticism and irritation towards them. Thus one shows a reflex readiness to uphold at all costs this affective image he calls his "character". ... one insists upon

preserving at all times this social image of his "right", his "character" or prestige, and by the same token he belittles the rights and deprecates the prestige of others. We demand our rights with special virulence when the rights of others conflict our own magnified self-image, when the opinions or the prejudices of others are not sympathetic to our own and so do not contribute to sustain our *amour propre* or private prerogative. (Burrow, 1949, p. 39)

### 3.3.4    Projection

Freud (1920) regarded "projection" as a tendency to treat experiences of "unpleasure" "as though they were acting, not from the inside, but from the outside" (p. 29). Feelings or characteristics that are consciously intolerable and disowned can be ascribed to another person (Laughlin, 1970). Projection "attributes to others aspects of one's own disclaimed and personally objectionable character traits, attitudes, motives, and desires" (p. 228). As a result of projection, emotions from which one tries to escape are experienced as being outside the ego, however, "the hatred ascribed to and experienced as coming from another is really one's own" (p. 227). We are critical of attributes in others which we are unable to recognise in ourselves (Laughlin, 1970). Burrow (1949) spoke of "the universal rule that defects of behaviour which one cannot tolerate in others are precisely those which are most often present in himself, though seldom ever disclosed" (p. 33).

> It is also characteristic of an individual that, while he feels entirely at liberty to criticize the conduct, the opinions or the habits of others, he himself is painfully sensitive to and even bitterly resentful of criticism directed towards him. Indeed, it is precisely the criticism one directs at others that he most strongly resents having others direct at him. (Burrow, 1949, p. 33)

As a result of projection, feelings of self-condemnation can be directed outwardly towards others (Laughlin, 1970). Condemnation and hatred of consciously disowned aspects of the self are transformed into rejection, dislike, or anger for another person. The individual consciously experiences dislike, hatred, or anger toward the person to whom the projection has been made. Through projection, the individual secures "a substitute and more tolerable target for his resentment, accusations, and recriminations" (p. 228). The individual may respond, more or less appropriately, to the hostility or aggression attributed to the other person, although behaviour directed against projected aspects of critical self-appraisal can progress to violence (Laughlin, 1970). Through "projective identification", we may unconsciously engineer interpersonal situations in which other people, instead of ourselves, can be regarded as "bad". Others are thus manoeuvred into taking on unacceptable and intolerable aspects of ourselves.

> We divide people into "good" and "bad"—some we like and love, others we dislike or hate; we try thus to isolate and localise these feelings and keep them from interfering with each other. This outlet also enables us to get pleasure by gratifying our aggressive feelings, without, we hope, incurring any corresponding damage to ourselves. So we provide ourselves with objects which can safely be made the targets of our aggression and hate, … (Riviere, 1937, pp. 14–15)
>
> Once we see evil in someone else it becomes possible and may seem necessary to let loose pent-up aggression against that person. It is here that the large part played in life by condemnation of others, criticism, denunciation, and intolerance generally, comes in. What we cannot tolerate in ourselves we are not likely to tolerate in others. In so condemning others we can obtain gratification, too, both directly from discharging our aggressive impulses, and from the reassurance obtained that we ourselves conform to and uphold the standards of rightness and perfection.

… This very important expression of aggressive impulses in civilised life is seen in countess everyday situations … (Riviere, 1937, p. 38)

We suppress certain attitudes and withhold certain social behaviours because we have learned that these attitudes and behaviours are disapproved by others. It is the fear of social disapproval that causes us to suppress these attitudes and behaviours and to shape the outward appearance of our personality accordingly. Stated more succinctly, we have learned to avoid inciting others' aggression by means of not displaying certain attitudes and behaviours in certain situations. "Projection", in one sense, means that we readily perceive in others inappropriate attitudes and characteristics that we have to actively suppress within ourselves. The paradox is that we hate in others attitudes or behaviours that we had to unlearn and likely still have to suppress in ourselves. We tend to criticise or attack others for attitudes and behaviours for which we, too, had been punished. The perception in others of these attitudes and behaviours seems to disinhibit our potential for aggression. Perhaps, perception of these attitudes or behaviours in others constitutes a *challenge* to our social position or security and, hence, to our *self*; or, perhaps, it simply provides an opportunity for *unpunished* expression of hostility. By criticising or offensively attacking others for attitudes and behaviours that we suppress (or fail to acknowledge) in ourselves, we help to eradicate these attitudes and behaviours from our social environment. This is part of the origin of social norms and conformity.

## 3.4   Regulation of self-esteem

Intraspecific aggression serves the purpose of establishing the animal's ranking position or defining its territory (Lorenz, 1963). Territorial aggression spaces out members of a species in order to optimise the utilisation of resources. Storr (1968) had "no doubt that man, too, is a territorial animal" (p. 33). Therefore, man "possesses a great deal of innate hostility towards his neighbour" (p. 36), be it in the form of a neighbouring tribe or clan or another nation. Both, territoriality and ranking order, define our identity and self. Storr (1968) thought that "there exists within us an aggressive component which serves to define the territorial boundaries of each individual personality" (p. 77). Furthermore, self-esteem reflects a "confident conviction of being lovable"—a conviction that is based on the infant's earliest experience of his mother, namely the receipt of "sufficient loving care" from her (p. 77), enabling the introjection of a good mother (Storr, 1968).

### 3.4.1   Striving for superiority

Superior behaviours often conceal underlying feelings of inferiority (Adler, 1965). Feelings of inferiority produce a state of stress that demands action; they generate compensatory movements towards feelings of superiority. The individual tries to rid himself of feelings of inferiority by changing his current situation, sometimes by changing the perception of the situation to the point of self-deception (Adler, 1965). Every neurotic person, according to Adler, has an inferiority complex. Enduring feelings of inferiority determine the neurotic person's life choices in terms of pathways to power, prestige, or possessions. Once the goal of superiority has been defined, all the habits and behaviours of the person will be consistent with that goal. These efforts will be only partially successful, insofar as feelings of inferiority will continue to constitute the undercurrent of the neurotic person's psychological makeup (Adler, 1965).

> If they fail to reach a superior position in real life, they continue to hope that they will do so, and lead a secret life of phantasy in which they imagine that they are so powerful as to be invulnerable. (Storr, 1968, p. 83)

The "striving for superiority" or "will to power" is an important motive of human beings in general, whether or not this striving constitutes part of an "inferiority complex". Adler (1965)

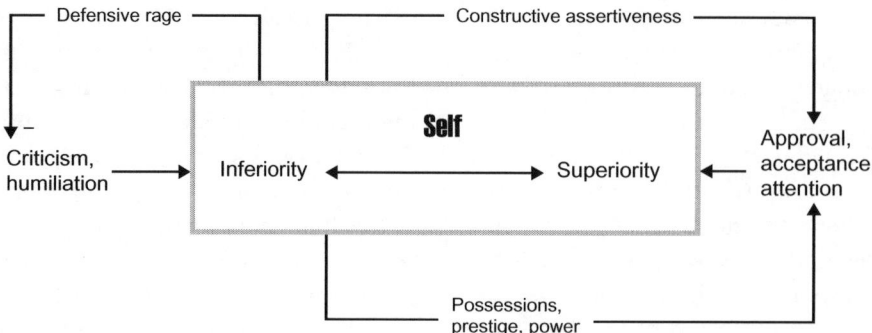

Figure 3-3.   Inferiority leads to excessive striving for superiority and increased vulnerability to criticism.

recognised that "striving for superiority" is based upon a primary instinct of aggression. Aggression in the service of "striving for superiority" is generally not destructive, however aggression can manifest as anger, rage, or hatred when the person's progress towards his goal of superiority is frustrated or when his underlying inferiority is uncovered (Figure 3-3).

Schizoid persons, who avoid close relationships for fear of abandonment or attack, have "a strong desire for power and superiority, combined with an inner feeling of vulnerability and weakness" (Storr, 1968, p. 83). Schizoid persons feel "attacked and humiliated" by any criticism; and their defeat in competitive striving may produce "extreme and vindictive rage" (Storr, 1968, p. 86).

### 3.4.2   Desire to impress

The human "urge to dominate" "prompts us to aspire to positions of eminence and esteem" (Hass, 1968, p. 138)—positions that impress others, that is, induce in them an approving or admiring attitude (which is related to the submissive attitude). A "pleasurable sense of power" was said to be associated with impressing other people "with the attainment of superior positions, titles, decorations, and marks of distinction" (p. 205). Behaviour motivated by the "desire to impress" has two objectives. First, it impresses a prospective mate. Second, "among creatures which live in groups", it "demonstrates the individual's

standing within the group" (Hass, 1968, p. 179). The ability to impress depends on self-assertion and "the influencing of receptive mechanisms in fellow members of the species" (p. 182) ("innate releasing mechanisms"). Man enhances his ability to impress "with the aid of handsome clothing, jewellery, and the like" (p. 182). Man surrounds himself with possessions and symbols designed to "accentuate the impression he makes on others and intensify his pleasurable sense of power", whereby "the desire to acquire them increases his willingness to work" (Hass, 1968, p. 183). The instinctively motivated "striving for success, esteem, and power, for social acceptance and standing, for recognition, superiority, and admiration" deeply influences man's behaviour towards other people (p. 179). It "influences the course of conversations and negotiations" and "hounds a man into the recesses of his imagination" (p. 179). Failure in this striving has "a particularly corrosive effect"; it breeds "contempt and repudiation on the part of others" (Hass, 1968, p. 179).

> To be vanquished or inferior, to be condescended to, to be mocked, ignored, or looked at askance by others—all these things provoke unpleasant tensions against which we are comparatively powerless. If people work far harder than is necessary just to maintain life and security, if they are ruled by a restless impulse to improve their lot, the underlying motive

is often that of the urge to impress. (Hass, 1968, p. 179)

### 3.4.3   Status and security

> I must not be a failure, is the very loud-est of the voices that clamor in each of our breasts: let fail who may, I at least must succeed. (James, 1890, p. 318)

James recognised the link between the sense of self and our ability to hold on to a social position in the group or society. Self-feelings are related to "one's actual success or failure, and the good or bad actual position one holds in the world" (James, 1890, p. 306). Automatic tendencies to enhance our social position (striving for superiority) and to conform to the rules of the group in which we hold a position are importantly mirrored by to our instinctive tendency to react with aggression against those who do not conform with the social structure to which we relate and who, thereby, challenge our position within this structure (Burrow, 1949). As Lorenz (1963) noted, the "nonconformist is discriminated against as an outsider".

> Aggression elicited by any deviation from a group's characteristic manners and mannerisms forces all its members into a strictly uniform observance of these norms of social behaviour. (Lorenz, 1963, p. 76)

Failure to conform to the norms of society, and failure to dynamically maintain our position in the social hierarchy, exposes us to others' aggression, social rejection and, hence, existential anxiety—unless we resort to psychological defences that seek to reframe, within our own mind, our standing in the group (and hence, in unconscious fantasy, our proximity to the primary caregiver) or our dependence on the group (and hence, in unconscious fantasy, our dependence on the primary caregiver). For instance, if we fail to attract recognition from others and fail to occupy the desired social status, then, in order to protect the self, we tend to deny the value of others (looking upon them with indifference or "chill negation, if not positive hate") and deny that the goods we fail to obtain "are goods at all" (James, 1890, p. 312).

Low self-esteem may indicate that the individual anticipates that others will frustrate his efforts to gain others' attention and positive regard (derivatives of signs of maternal care). Low *self*-esteem is associated with anxiety, a latent fear of punishment that is anchored in a contextualised matrix of *other*-awareness. The individual's abilities to avoid others' aggression—subtly motivated by "fear"—and to induce in them submission (or aggressively coerce them into submission) have an essential bearing on his self-esteem as the antipode to existential anxiety. Successful attraction of social approval, sustaining high self-esteem, will depend on the individual's conformity and dominance. What might be the motivational force that drives us to influence others' good opinion of us and avoid their disapproval? While fleeing anxiety (or rather the aversive state of social unrelatedness), we create situations that replicate aspects of primitive object relations within which we were assured of the object's love and care. Our security within the group and our access to its libidinal resources are regulated by our social status or ranking position in the group, which we have to maintain dynamically through appropriately targeted affirmative and submissive gestures manifesting the workings of intraspecific aggression and the "instinct of escape". While competing for social status, in an attempt to maintain in unconscious fantasy our relationship with the primary care giver, we have to conform to the norms of society in order to *avoid* becoming the victim of collective punishment and being driven into social exclusion or unrelatedness (proxy for maternal separation).

### 3.4.4   Humiliation

An insult—being humiliated by others—causes pain. When one's self-esteem or "pride" is "hurt", secondary reactions of rage and fear may arise (Horney, 1950). Neurotic pride (as opposed to healthy self-esteem) renders us vulnerable to humiliation; and "any hurt to our pride may provoke vindictive hostility" (p. 99). Thus, if pride (or self-esteem) is hurt—and the person feels humiliated—rage or "irrational hostility" ensue (p. 99). Pride and self-esteem are linked to an abstract territory or position one occupies in social space, a position that is defined with reference to social norms and laws. Frank insults, aiming to humiliate a person, are expressions of offensive aggression to which the person responds offensively or defensively (depending on the intensity of an insult), whereas others' careless disrespect of the norms and laws to which the person himself adheres represents an infringement upon his territory, an infringement to which he reacts in an offensively aggressive way. Both forms of aggressive response may seem vindictive and irrational. Vindictive or irrational hostility, described by Horney (1950), "has ingredients of derogation, contempt, or intent to humiliate", suggesting that what "operates here is the straight law of retaliation" (p. 99). Offensive behaviour, stemming from hurt pride (Horney, 1950, p. 100), endeavours to restore pride, that is, to reclaim the lost territory or position (Figure 3-4).

> The need to save face is urgent, and there is more than one way of effecting it. … The most effective and, it seems, almost

ubiquitous one is interlinked with the impulse to take revenge for what is felt as humiliation. … vindictiveness may … be a means toward self-vindication. It involves the belief that by getting back at the offender one's own pride will be restored. This belief is based on the feeling that the offender, by his very power to hurt our pride, has put himself above us and has defeated us. By our taking revenge and hurting him more than he did us, the situation will be reversed. We will be triumphant and will have defeated him. The aim of the neurotic vindictive revenge is not "getting even" but triumphing by hitting back harder. Nothing short of triumph *can* restore the imaginary grandeur in which pride is invested. (Horney, 1950, p. 103)

The power to retaliate "can itself be invested with pride" (Horney, 1950, p. 103), much as inability to retaliate can itself constitute a humiliation. Experiencing a humiliation, the neurotic person "suffers a double injury: the original 'insult' and the 'defeat' as opposed to the vindictive triumph", if "the situation or something within him does not allow him to retaliate" (p. 104). The situational context may favour a fearful or submissive response (to a humiliation) over an assertive or angry one.

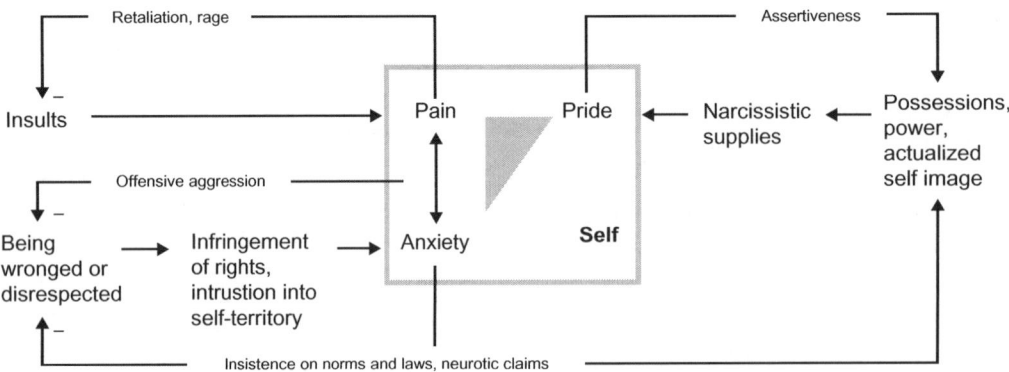

Figure 3-4.    Feeling wronged or disrespected may be associated with pain or anxiety. Anxiety promotes behaviour that reestablishes order, which indirectly restores one's pride. Pain is a predominant component in the response to insults (other's displays of offensive aggression) and facilitates defensive, more violent reactions.

Humiliation can thus give way to fear, or it can cause anxiety or panic; and similar emotional reactions can arise in *anticipation* of a humiliation "because a hurt to our pride constitutes a terrifying danger" (p. 102). The neurotic person not only fears "failure, disgrace, ridicule" but also dreads "all that falls short of glory and perfection"; he "is afraid of not performing as superbly as his exacting shoulds demand, and therefore fears that his pride will be hurt" (Horney, 1950, p. 101). An embarrassing or humiliating incident may lead to the avoidance of situations in which similar incidents are likely to occur; the person avoids "an activity because it might hurt his pride" (p. 107). Having experienced a humiliation and painful injury to his pride, the person henceforth avoids "to take the risk of exposing [his] pride" (Horney, 1950, p. 108).

### 3.4.5   Identity

Relationships between people in organisations and associations are often "based upon identification and mutual reassurance" (Storr, 1968, p. 57). Identification with others means dependence; "and dependence means vulnerability to attack from those upon whom one is dependent" (p. 56). Identification may entail attempts to have one's opinions or beliefs affirmed by others. Religious, philosophical, or political beliefs "constitute a vital part of a man's sense of his own identity" (p. 54). We obtain reassurance and security from other people who "think and feel exactly like ourselves", whereby "the more insecure we are, the more we look for this kind of affirmation of our own identities" (p. 54). The person who feels insecure within himself "will look for people with whom he can identify himself in order to affirm his own identity" (Storr, 1968, p. 56). A difference in beliefs and opinions between oneself and the person with whom one identifies will be felt as an attack. The expression by others of beliefs and opinions that diverge from one's own beliefs and opinions is felt as a threat to one's inner security and, hence, produces offensive aggression, often with the apparent aim of asserting one's beliefs and opinions. Ultimately, however, aggression in these situations serves to preserve and redefine one's identity (Storr, 1968). Others are manipulated, through more or less overtly aggressive means (i.e., means that are partially "neutralised" (Hartmann, 1964)), into supporting the cultural and political framework within which one's identity is defined and within which one's self-esteem is regulated. One's identity (self) is established and defended in a manner that is not dissimilar from the role played by aggression in territoriality.

### Lovability

Love is an important source of self-esteem. Having acquired in childhood "an inner source of self-esteem derived from parental love" (Storr, 1968, p. 70), we will constantly renew our "sense of value through loving and being loved" (p. 69). Most of us are dependent upon "recurrent affirmation of our value as lovable human beings" (p. 70). Threats to one's self-esteem, that is, to one's confidence in one's own identity, can result in intense rage. Rejection by a partner or potential partner represents such threat. Failure in a love relationship, withdrawal of love, or bereavement can be experienced as an attack upon the self, to which we react with violent feelings of hate towards the rejecting, or even the deceased, person. Alternatively, we react with hurt and misery. Despair and self-denigration may result from "a turning against the self of destructive anger which would normally be directed towards the rejecting person" (Storr, 1968, p. 70).

The belief in one's masculinity or femininity "is a fundamental part of human identity" and a basic source of self-esteem (Storr, 1968, p. 68). Persons who, due to emotional difficulties in their childhood, are uncertain "that, as man or woman, they are both able to love and be loved" (p. 68), may "translate their disappointment into creative work"; or they may, "by feverish competition in the world of power, achieve wealth and status" (p. 69). Their "achievements which single them out from their fellows" (p. 69) provide an alternative, albeit less secure, source of self-esteem.

Persons, who "possess no inner sense of self-esteem", however successful they may be in life, "will remain intensely vulnerable to failure, rejection or disappointment" (Storr, 1968, p. 78).

> People who are liable to severe depressive reactions find difficulty in personal relations because they are ultimately looking for something which they should have had in infancy from their mothers, and which it is impossible for them to obtain in an adult relationship. … They hate those whom they love since they cannot get from them what they really need, and since they dare not to show this hate for fear of losing even that which they have, they turn it inwards against themselves in self-torment and despair. (Storr, 1968, pp. 80–81)

### 3.4.6   Self-deception

The self can be seen as a device that allows estimation and evaluation of other people's feelings and attitudes ("personal yardstick") (Laughlin, 1970), especially others' attitudes that concern oneself. Others' attitudes and feelings that are critical of oneself (others' disapprovals) are anxiety-provoking. Others' disapproval and blame "can be mitigated if responsibility can be successfully assigned to another" (p. 226). In a similar fashion, feelings that are self-critical tend to be projected. Projection serves to unconsciously resolve anxiety-provoking conflicts by relocating unacceptable and intolerable aspects of oneself, such as hate, envy, or sexual desires, into an object. Externalisation of danger situations is one of the ego's earliest methods of defence against anxiety. We tend not to "recognize traits about ourselves that have personally and socially handicapping consequences" (Laughlin, 1970, p. 224). Projection enables us to remain blind to these traits and, thereby, avoid feelings of vulnerability to social disapproval and hostility (and, hence, avoid anxiety).

We dynamically construct a representation of our social environment that enhances our social acceptability (self-esteem). Thus, we ensure our security (and remain free of anxiety)

in an inherently hostile world. Socially inacceptable impulses, attitudes, or feelings are disowned because they would decrease our acceptability and, hence, our security. Hostile, socially inacceptable impulses arise within us nevertheless, so that we have to reconstruct our image of the social environment—and reconsider our position therein—in a way that allows for the safe enactment of hostile impulses. We require a target toward which justifiable outrage can be directed. We look for a legitimate outlet for our aggression, an outlet that perhaps allows us to strengthen our position and enhance our security at the same time. In order to create such outlet, we perceive socially inacceptable qualities or attitudes in others. Perhaps anxiety intervenes in this process. An inappropriate, hostile impulse may briefly evoke an image of social unacceptability, causing us to feel vulnerable, insecure, and anxious. Anxiety is quickly externalised into perception of an external threat, providing us with a target against which we can safely express our hostility in a modified form. Externalisation would be facilitated by a similarity between our suppressed impulse and the threatening impulse attributed to another person. Evidence "or what may be interpreted (or perhaps rather misinterpreted) as such by the individual" serves to "reinforce the projected image of hostility and persecution" (Laughlin, 1970, p. 231). In general, evidence in support of one's self-appraisal, prejudiced beliefs, projections, and paranoid system is "eagerly seized upon" (p. 231). Delusions of persecution, in which the individual elaborates beliefs of being hated and plotted against, are the most malignant manifestations of projection.[4] Projection serves as psychodynamic "basis for most of the paranoid delusions in schizophrenia" (Laughlin, 1970, p. 232).

### 3.5   Neurotic manifestations

By exerting power, gaining success, or piling up possessions, one achieves greater security

---

[4]"Paranoid indifference" may accompany paranoid delusions, much like *"la belle indifference"* typically accompanies somatic conversions.

and independence and, hence, protects oneself against "basic anxiety" (Horney, 1937). What Horney (1937) emphasised in her discussion of the neurotic personality, but what may be true in general, is that the "striving for power serves as a protection against the danger of feeling or being regarded as insignificant" (p. 166)—a danger that may rooted in man's vulnerability to conspecific attack (as it is reflected in feelings of anxiety). As a method for obtaining reassurance against anxiety (and as a way of achieving "protection against helplessness and against insignificance" (p. 171)), the quest for power, prestige, and possessions is deeply embedded in Western culture (Horney, 1937). Self-assertion is "the act of asserting one's self or one's claims" (p. 37), including one's claims for power, prestige, and possessions. Power, prestige, and possessions may provide reassurance against anxiety by "fortifying one's own position" (Horney, 1937, p. 162), that is, one's social position, as it is reflected in one's self-image and self-esteem. One's social position may, at the same time, serve to facilitate one's efforts to control others, that is, to induce in them submissive, approving, or affectionate gestures (caregiving behaviours) directed towards oneself, which, then, render the immediate situation secure (as opposed to anxiogenic) (Figure 3-2). While "the normal striving for power" protects against anxiety, "neurotic striving for power … is borne out of anxiety … and feelings of inferiority" (Horney, 1937, p. 163). In neurotic persons, the striving for possessions and similar tendencies "are highly charged with emotion" (p. 180). The neurotic person's striving for possessions is the more compulsive, the more it is associated with anxiety. Having power, success, or possessions guards against the possibility of being hurt by others (Horney, 1937), precisely inasmuch as power, success, or possessions protect against, or reduce, anxiety. By accumulating power, success, and possessions, we learn to avoid the *immediate* pain of rejection as well as the predictive fear of rejection (anxiety), much as we learn to avoid physical pain (inflicted by noxious stimulation) and the fear of such pain

(prospective pain) in our dealings with the external physical world (Mowrer & Lamoreaux, 1946; Rado, 1956).

### 3.5.1 Grandiosity and entitlement

The quest for prestige is related to "a stringent need to impress others, to be admired and respected" (Horney, 1937, p. 171). Neurotic persons, in order to establish or maintain their social position or self-esteem, "have to be able to talk about the latest books and plays, and to know prominent people" (p. 172). If their "self-esteem rests on being admired", it "shrinks to nothing" if they do not receive admiration. Typically, neurotic persons "have to know everything better than anyone else"; they "want to be right all the time, and are irritated at being proved wrong, even if only in an insignificant detail" (p. 168). Correspondingly, "when confronted with a question to which they do not know the answer, [they] may pretend to know, or may even invent something, even if ignorance in this particular instance would not discredit them" (Horney, 1937, p. 168)—as it would seem to a less insecure observer.

The neurotic person feels "entitled to be treated by others, or by fate, in accord with his grandiose notions about himself"; he "feels entitled to special attention, consideration, deference on part of others" (p. 41), "entitled never to be criticized, doubted, or questioned" (p. 43), "entitled to everything that is important to him" (Horney, 1950, p. 42). What, for the healthy person, would be an understandable wish or need turns into a "grandiose claim", a sense of entitlement to have one's needs met. If the neurotic person's grandiose claims are not satisfied or duly respected, if others do not "cater to his illusions", he experiences a deep sense of unfairness (p. 41), and he can become "furiously indignant" (p. 42). Nonfulfilment of a grandiose claim "is felt as an unfair frustration, as an offense about which we have a right to feel indignant" (p. 42). This is perhaps not dissimilar to our reaction to an intrusion into our spatially defined territory or to an infringement upon an abstract territory that is delineated by our "rights". The neurotic person takes benefits "accruing from laws or regulations … for granted" (p. 44); and, in accordance with his tendency to deceive himself about his position in the world, the neurotic person tends to adopt "a right, a title, which in reality does not exist" (Horney, 1950, p. 42). Neurotic claims are irrational because they assume a nonexistent right or an exceptional status (immunity) at the outset.

Claims can be regarded as a projection, into the future, of one's rights. Claims are thus linked to idealising self-imagery (the "idealised self"), much as nonneurotic wishes and expectations are linked to fleeting imagery of one's relation to others, that is, linked to goals one anticipates in the pursuit of security and narcissistic supplies (Figure 4-2). The more compelling the need to actualise the idealised self, the more intense is the reaction to frustration. Severe reactions to frustration and failure "are indicated by the terror of doom and disgrace", by panic, despair, or "rage at self and others" (p. 31). The difference between neurotic claims and healthy expectations is perhaps one of degree (contrary to Horney's (1950) views), although consequences for interpersonal relations are different in quality.

> Considering all the energies invested in justifying the claims, and in asserting them, we cannot but expect intense *reactions to their frustrations*. There are undercurrents of fear, but the prevailing response is anger or even rage. This anger is of a peculiar kind. Since the claims are subjectively felt as fair and just, the frustrations are experienced as unfair and unjust. The ensuing anger has therefore the character of a righteous indignation. The person feels, in other words, not only angry but the right to be angry—a feeling which is vigorously defended in analysis. (Horney, 1950, pp. 55–56)

### 3.5.2   Vindictiveness

Rejection or frustration, by others, of one's efforts to obtain others' approval or affection incites hostility. Neurotic persons, whose "self-esteem has been wounded by humiliation", feel hurt and may become vindictive; their hostility would take "the form of a desire to humiliate others" (Horney, 1937, p. 178). Hostile reactions occur not only in response to a rejection "but also to the anticipation of a rejection" (p. 136). Neurotic persons are prone to a "bossing attitude", of which they may not be aware (p. 169). They may show a "plain anger reaction to a lack of compliance" with their wishes and expectations (p. 169) or to a failure to follow their advice. Hostility that was hitherto "pressed into civilized forms" breaks out if neurotic persons do not succeed in having their own way (p. 174). Their bossing attitude and irritability may be due to their tendency to interpret seemingly innocuous situations as evidence that they are unwanted, excluded, or rejected (Horney, 1937).[5]

Grandiose claims are crippling in their effect. They make for "a chronic smoldering envy and discontent" (Horney, 1950, p. 47). Establishing "a title which exists in his mind only" and having "little, if any, consideration for the possibility of the fulfillment of his claims" (p. 47), the neurotic person is prone to experiencing repeated frustration. Feeling wronged, he becomes vindictive and insists on retribution (Figure 3-4). Vindictive elements are operating "when claims are made with reference to past frustration or suffering" (p. 51). When vindictive claims are made, "the injury done is stressed" (p. 55). Overemphasis on justice (appeals to justice), when making claims, may be "a camouflage for vindictiveness" (p. 55). The "search for glory", incentivised by an idealised self-image, is not necessarily vindictive but can take the form of a drive towards vindictive triumph. The vindictive element in a person's search

---

[5]Neurotic persons may differ quantitatively—not qualitatively, as advocated by Horney (1937)—from persons who are less insecure and more content in themselves; the main difference may lie in the readiness with which persons perceive a social situation as a threat to their position and to their access to others' approval or affection (and, hence, as a threat to their self).

for glory is usually hidden from consciousness (Horney, 1950), because it is socially unacceptable. Vindictiveness, when feeling wronged or when searching for glory, illustrates the territoriality of (neurotic) claims. Mechanisms regulating resident-intruder disputes between members of a territorial species likely operate "when the fulfillment of claims is felt as a triumph and their frustration as defeat" (p. 51). However, not only the neurotic "tries to make others accede to his claims" (p. 55), as Horney (1950) believed. Assertiveness is integral to the pursuit of socially acceptable goals and ambitions, and is likely to be equivalent to the vindictiveness employed in the search for glory.

> ... by and large the ways in which the neurotic tries to make others accede to his claims are intimately connected with the basis on which they are put. In short, he can try to impress others with his unique importance; he can please, charm, promise; he can put others under obligations and try to cash in by appealing to their sense of fairness or guilt; he can, by emphasizing his suffering, appeal to pity and guilt-feelings; he can, by stressing love for others, appeal to their yearning for love or to their vanity; he can intimidate with irritability and sullenness. The vindictive person, who may ruin others with insatiable claims, tries through hardhitting accusations to enforce their compliance. (Horney, 1950, p. 55)

### 3.5.3   Concealed hostility

Neurotic strivings for power, prestige, and possessions (and, probably the "normal" equivalents of these strivings) serve "as a channel through which repressed hostility can be discharged" (Horney, 1937, p. 166). When hostility is repressed, "the person has not the remotest idea that he is hostile" (p. 66). Neurotic striving for power "does not necessarily appear openly as hostility toward others", as it "may be disguised in socially valuable or humanistic

forms" (p. 174). Thus, "a certain amount of hostility may be discharged in a non-destructive way" (pp. 174–175). Insofar as hostility is concealed in socially constructive attitudes, such as "giving advice" or "taking the initiative or lead", "the other persons ... will feel it and react either with submissiveness or with opposition" (Horney, 1937, p. 174), much as—in analogy with the resident-intruder paradigm used in animal aggression research—intrusion into another animal's territory will elicit a submissive or offensive reaction from that animal.

There are other, less adaptive, channels for indirect expression of hostility. Neurotic persons may express hostility indirectly through an "appeal to justice" (Horney, 1937, p. 144). A neurotic person may use a personal traumatic experience or injury as a "basis for demands" for sympathetic treatment; and he "may arouse feelings of guilt or obligation in order that his own demands may seem just" (p. 144). His injury or illness may be used implicitly as an accusation, as "a kind of living reproach, intended to arouse guilt feeling" in others and to make them "willing to devote" all their attention to him (p. 144). Neurotic persons "may be willing to pay the price of suffering", "because in that way they are able to express accusations and demands without being aware of doing so, and hence are able to retain their feeling of righteousness" (Horney, 1937, pp. 145–146). A neurotic person may resort to more overt statements of "threats as a strategy for obtaining affection", threatening, for instance, to commit acts such as "ruining a reputation or doing some violence to another or to himself" (including threats of, or attempts at, suicide) (Horney, 1937, p. 146).

Despite their sensitivity to challenge and rejection, neurotic persons "often are incapable of defending themselves against attack" (Horney, 1937, p. 38) or of expressing anger directly in situations when this is warranted. The neurotic person, "knowing how hurt and vindictive he feels when humiliated, is instinctively afraid of similar reactions in others" (Horney, 1937, p. 179). Chronic repression of anger and hostility, maintained by repeated rejection and rebuff, may result in feelings of depression.

### 3.5.4   Self-hate

The neurotic person's pride "demands that he *should* be superior to everybody and everything" (Horney, 1950, p. 134). However, his grandiosity renders him liable to suffering humiliation. Humiliation, denigration, disparagement, or depreciation disrupts neurotic pride (and healthy self-esteem alike), inflicts pain (narcissistic injury), and, secondarily, causes rage, whereas frustration experienced in the process of self-actualisation (in compliance with one's "inner dictates") may cause anger more directly. Anger, experienced when one fails to measure up to (actualise) one's "idealised self", can be directed at a frustrating object or at one's self (Figure 4-2). Self-hate is anger directed at the actual self, the self as it actually is with all its limitations and shortcomings (as opposed to the idealised self). Self-hate "makes visible a rift in the personality that started with the creation of an idealized self" (Horney, 1950, p. 112). Hate directed towards the actual self—manifesting as "relentless demands on self, merciless self-accusations, self-contempt, self-frustrations, self-tormenting, and self-destruction" (p. 117)—readily arises whenever "we are driven to reach beyond ourselves" (p. 114) (that is, when we try to actualise the grandiose anticipation that is the "idealised self"). Self-accusations, stemming from neurotic pride, "express the discontent of the proud self with the individual's not measuring up to its requirements" (p. 131). Tormenting himself in imagination, the neurotic person engages "in endless and inconclusive inner dialogues, in which [he] tries to defend himself against his own self-accusations" (p. 145). In this process, the person may be "eaten up by self-doubts" (p. 145). In self-tormenting, the person "is always both the torturer and the tortured"; and "he derives satisfaction from being degraded as well as from degrading himself" (Horney, 1950, p. 148). In self-contempt, the person feels "inferior, worthless, or contemptible as a result of disparaging himself" (p. 132). Witnessing the superior skills or shining qualities of others, the person

"must call forth a self-destructive berating" (p. 134). As a result of self-disparagement (self-contempt), the neurotic person recoils from competition with others. At the same time, he may try to alleviate his self-contempt (or the anxiety with which his self-contempt is associated) by compulsively pursuing "*the attention, regard, appreciation, admiration, or love of others*" (Horney, 1950, p. 136).

> Self-contempt makes the neurotic hypersensitive to criticism and rejection. On little or no provocation he feels that others look down on him, do not take him seriously, do not care for his company, and in fact slight him. ... Being unable to accept himself as he is, he cannot possibly believe that others, knowing him with all his shortcomings, can accept him in a friendly or appreciative spirit. (Horney, 1950, p. 134)

### 3.5.5   Envy

In Western culture, power, prestige, and possessions "have to be acquired by ... competitive struggle with others" (Horney, 1937, p. 188). Hostility is inherent in competition "since the victory of one of the competitors implies the defeat of the other" (p. 192). The neurotic person, whose self-esteem or social position depends on his possessions or prestige, enters "a miserable state" (a state of anxiety) when "he fails to have the one advantage in which another person surpasses him" (p. 183). Similarly, the neurotic person feels humiliation "for having to give someone credit for something" (Horney, 1937, p. 196). This sense of failure or humiliation is related to the experience of rejection and, thus, incites hostility. In neurotic persons, in whom the striving for possessions is paramount, "hostility usually takes the form of a tendency to deprive others" (p. 180). Their tendency to deprive others, or their "impulse to defeat or frustrate the efforts of others" (p. 193), is "accompanied by an emotional attitude of begrudging envy", although most of us "will feel some envy if others have certain advantages we should like to have ourselves" (Horney, 1937, p. 182). The neurotic person also tends to underestimate "what he has himself", depriving himself of the ability "to enjoy and appreciate the possibilities for happiness that are available" (p. 183). Another consequence of his "tendency to deprive and exploit" others is "an anxiety that he will be cheated or exploited by others", that is, "a perpetual fear that someone will take advantage of him, that money or ideas will be stolen from him" (p. 185). Whenever he is actually cheated or deprived by others, a "disproportionate amount of anger is discharged", suggesting that there has been a projection of his "own abusing tendencies on others" (Horney, 1937, p. 186).

Thus, envy is the feeling of resentment or hostility towards the desirable qualities of another person. An aggressive impulse to spoil the desirable qualities of the other person is fundamental to envy (Joseph, 1986). In Kleinian theory, the infant first experiences envy in relation to the primary object, the mother. Envy seeks to spoil the object's creativity. Secondarily, envy is projected outward in the form of fears of persecution. Attribution of envy to the object leads to fears of envious attack and, later, feelings of guilt over one's own creativity (reviewed in Kernberg, 1980). Alternatively, the infant may first experience envy in relation to the father, for he has qualities that distract the mother's interest away ("penis envy"). From then on, envy arises in relation to any rival competing for the object's devotion. Envy may not only arise when there is a threat or potential threat to the exclusivity of our object relation, but also when others' qualities, being perceived to be more attractive than our own, prevent us from establishing such exclusive relation in the first place.

### Defences against envy

Envy it is typically defended against in a civilised context. Competitiveness can be seen as a defence against unacceptable feelings of envy. Through the acquisition of socially desirable qualities (in competition with others), the individual prevents intolerable feelings of envy towards others. Some envious people restrict contacts with others and avoid situations that can stimulate feelings of envy (Joseph, 1986). Other defences against envy are (i) denigration of the good qualities of the envied object, (ii) projection of envy so that others appear envious and destructive, (iii) idealisation of the envied object so that comparisons with oneself become irrelevant, (iv) identification with the envied object and introjection of the object's good qualities so that the envious person feels he possesses these good qualities, and (v) feelings of (omnipotent) hopelessness to prove the object on whom one depends worthless (Spillius, 1993). Projection of envy involves stirring up feelings of envy in other people by making them aware of one's own outstanding qualities. In masochism, the person seeks to devalue himself in an attempt to increase the gap between himself and the enviable person (Joseph, 1986). Similarly, regarding the enviable person as inferior or idealising him would render the object of one's envy as either not enviable after all or being on a pedestal and out of reach (Joseph, 1986). Freud (1921) thought that members of a group overcome their envious rivalry with one another in a common idealisation of the group leader.

### 3.6   Clinical aspects of violence

Aggression contributes in intricate ways to a great variety of normal and abnormal social behaviours. The omnipresence and critical contribution of aggression to social behaviour is impressively revealed under pathological conditions. The clinical context in which violence occurs provides insights into how aggressive impulses are regulated in normal social behaviour. The amygdala links social cues, such as those that communicate social threat or challenge, with affective behaviours, including defensive (affective) aggression. Increased neuronal excitability in the amygdala may result in excessive emotional reactions, such as outrage, to personal slights. Nondirected aggression, being the hallmark of "intermittent explosive disorder", is related to defensive (affective) aggression. Prefrontal functioning is important for keeping the expression of aggressive impulses that frequently arise in everyday social situations within bounds of social acceptability. Frontal lobe impairment may cause aggressiveness by increasing impulsivity and lowering the individual's coping skills and frustration tolerance. Aggressive behaviour may not only be a clinical symptom but can also constitute a criminal act, whereby organic or functional psychopathology may or may not contribute to criminal behaviour.

### 3.6.1    Criminal aggressiveness

> We have reasons to believe that in human life, activity and aggression alternate in cycles with passivity and submission. (Schilder, 1951, p. 209)

An important aim of activity and aggression is "to be the master of the fate of objects" (Schilder, 1951, p. 213). Schilder (1951) argued that "aggressive action takes place when the individual feels restricted in his power to achieve an adequate mastery of the situation" (p. 219). Inability to control objects or the situation—when the individual feels that a passive role has been forced upon him—may provoke a reaction of aggression and criminal behaviour. Schilder (1951) regarded the aggressive criminal act as "a protest against passivity and enforced submission" (p. 218). Acts of aggression ("especially with a gun") help the individual to restore his "threatened masculinity" (p. 214), that is, to assert his capacity to control his fate and environment. Through the criminal act, the "aggressive criminal restores his prestige" (Schilder, 1951, p. 218); or, at least, he unconsciously aims to restore his prestige. Inability to control one's fate or environment is mirrored in feelings of inferiority and insecurity. Feelings of inferiority and insecurity, which Schilder (1951) found to be present in all but one of the aggressive criminals he studied, may

increase dispositions to perceive a threat and/or to react to a threat with counteraggression. Aggressive criminals often explained their aggressive action with reference to "real or imaginary minor aggression of another"; or they often felt that their "action was a counteraction against the aggressiveness of others" (p. 215). Feelings of inferiority and a sense of enforced passivity can be seen as predisposing factors to criminal behaviour, insofar as an "aggressive impulse has a much greater chance of becoming criminal action when the criminal action can reckon with open or tacit approval of those social forces which play a part in the ego formation" (p. 217). Organic factors, too, play a role in the aetiology of criminal aggressiveness. Schilder (1951) found that many of his forensic patients "were unable to coordinate their impulses in a unified goal" (p. 216) (indicating executive dysfunction). An increase in motor impulses (increased impulsivity) was felt to be "merely one factor which may determine an aggressive action" (p. 216). Schilder (1951) observed a "primary increase in aggressiveness" only in patients "with an organic hyperkinesis" (p. 215).

> Criminal aggressiveness in our cases was almost invariably reactive in its nature. It was a reaction to an immediate situation and to a situation in childhood. Since cultural influences connect passivity and submission with femininity and activity and aggression with masculinity, the assault becomes a symbol for masculinity regained. (Schilder, 1951, p. 215)

### 3.6.2    Reaction to threat

Affective and non-directed forms of aggression can present in the context of mental illness or delirium. Schizophrenia, in particular, is associated with affective violence. Patients with schizophrenia are more sensitive to threat, whereby high sensitivity to threat may be a trait-related, rather than state-related, characteristic of schizophrenia (Scholten et al., 2006). Some men who are prone to domestic violence show increased heart rate during domestic conflict. Domestic violence perpetrated by these "type 2" men (Gottman *et al.*, 1995) and aggression occurring in the context of morbid jealousy or stalking are forms of affective aggression that can be understood as a response to a real or perceived threat of rejection or abandonment by a love object (McEllistrem, 2004). In children and adolescents, "reactive aggression" (which is to be distinguished from "proactive aggression") similarly arises in response to a perceived threat or provocation (Kempes, Matthys, de Vries & van Engeland, 2005). Children may interpret their peers' behaviour as intentionally harmful and deploy reactive aggression as a means of retaliation (Crick & Dodge, 1996). Affective violence is associated with low intelligence. In individuals with a history of affective violence, prefrontal functioning tends to be decreased, which is in keeping with the notion that affective offenders lack prefrontal control during their relatively unregulated aggression (reviewed in McEllistrem, 2004). Affective aggression can present as part of an organic aggressive disorder (characterised by relative absence of perceptual or mood disturbances) after brain injury (Cassidy, 1990).

## Episodic dyscontrol

Episodic dyscontrol syndrome ("intermittent explosive disorder") is characterised by sudden, unpredictable and often unprovoked outbursts of uncontrollable rage with severe physical aggression and destructiveness. Outbursts of episodic dyscontrol are short lived, accompanied by sympathetic arousal, poorly organised, and usually directed at the nearest available object or person. In some cases, aggression is more clearly directed against a source of antagonism; but it typically takes trivial degree of irritation, frustration, or provocation to elicit a disproportionately violent response. The patient feels powerless to stop these outbursts, although he may have a degree of control over the direction of aggression and divert the attack to an inanimate

object. Episodes of dyscontrol occur against a backdrop of generally normal affect and behaviour and are followed by feelings of regret and remorse on part of the patient. Alternatively, the patient is amnesic for the episode or has only vague dreamlike recollections (reviewed in Cassidy, 1990; Eames & Wood, 2003; Miller, 1994). Remorse and regret that follow an episode of dyscontrol suggest that superego functioning is preserved in these patients but that aggressive impulses are too powerful to be delayed and expressed in a culturally sanctioned and situationally appropriate way.

Episodic dyscontrol is associated with traumatic damage to the medial temporal lobe. Episodic dyscontrol can be caused by tumours of the temporal lobe or subarachnoid haemorrhage with damage to medial temporal structures, the amygdala in particular (reviewed in Eames & Wood, 2003). The relationship with epilepsy is unclear. Nondirected and unprovoked aggression occurs during temporal lobe partial complex seizures, however, in patients with temporal lobe epilepsy, interictal aggression characterised by intense affect in response to environmental triggers is more common (reviewed in Hollander *et al.*, 2002). It is thought that subconvulsive discharges can produce outbursts of nondirected aggression. Intrinsic activity in neuronal assemblies of the amygdala may be unstable due to local pathological processes, allowing electrical excitability to build up intermittently towards the spontaneous generation of discharges that produce emotional behaviour states such as rage or fear (Eames & Wood, 2003). Alternatively, repeated stimulation of the amygdala may produce a cumulative increase in excitability and a lowering of seizure threshold, so that subsequent minor stimuli can incite paroxysmal neuronal discharges that activate aggression-related structures in the hypothalamus and periaqueductal gray (Miller, 1994). At the outset of episodes of dyscontrol, the patient may be in a paranoid state with heightened perception of stimuli provoking fear, anger, or rage (McEllistrem, 2004). Traumatic temporal lobe damage can also lead to the development of an episodic mood syndrome characterised by abrupt changes in mood, or mood swings, that occur without apparent external trigger. Changes in mood may lower the patient's frustration tolerance and make him vulnerable to outbursts upon slight provocation, which, again, tend to be followed by remorse (Miller, 1994).[6]

### 3.6.3   Low frustration threshold

Aggressive outbursts by patients with frontal lobe damage follow the thwarting of approach to a goal or an interpersonal provocation; and, in contrast to episodic dyscontrol, the external trigger of aggression is usually apparent. Attacks are clearly directed at the source of the provocation. They tend to be less violent but more tantrum-like with verbal abuse, threatening gestures, and throwing of objects. Patients can be cajoled out of their aggressive state more easily, yet there is typically no remorse or regret over the outburst afterwards (reviewed in Miller, 1994). Acceleration-deceleration head trauma often affects the frontal lobes. Patients with frontal lobe damage find it difficult to carry through nonroutine tasks that would require a degree of cognitive flexibility and problems solving skills. Thus, they may be more easily frustrated in a nonstructured environment. Moreover, patients with frontal lobe damage experience problems with judgement and self-control, leaving them impaired in their ability to inhibit aggressive impulses and modulate the behavioural expression of changes in mood. Predictable routine, reducing the number of frustrating situations, and explicit and consistent external guidance ("surrogate frontal lobe") are key in the management of aggression in frontal lobe-injured patients (reviewed in Miller, 1994).[7]

There is a high incidence of sociopathic behaviour—characterised by impulsivity, stimulation seeking (including substance misuse), and antisocial cognitive style—preceding traumatic brain injury. Head injuries are more likely to affect those with impulsive and aggressive lifestyles, yet preexisting impulsive traits or behavioural difficulties often go unnoticed or are glossed over after the brain injury ("retrospective falsification"). Impulsively antisocial populations show an increased prevalence of frontal neuropsychological impairment (preexisting executive deficits), so that, as a result of brain injury, sometimes rudimentary adaptive skills, frustration tolerance, judgement, and abilities to self-restrain are further diminished. Patients may use their impairment as an excuse for continuing and even escalating antisocial behaviour, and treatment sometimes has to aim at habilitation rather than rehabilitation (reviewed in Miller, 1994).

### 3.6.4   Predatory or instrumental aggression

While "reactive aggression" in children and adolescents may constitute a response to a perceived threat to one's status in the peer group, "proactive aggression" may be aimed at advancing the individual's social status. Proactive, but not reactive, aggression in children and adolescents is related to expectation of positive outcomes (anticipation of reward) by the perpetrator (Kempes, Matthys, de Vries & van Engeland, 2005; Smithmyer, Hubbard & Simons, 2000). Children with proactive aggression have greater confidence in

---

[6] Treatment of episodic dyscontrol involves anticonvulsants, such as carbamazepine or sodium valproate or perhaps clonazepam, plus behaviour therapy in a structured environment (Cassidy, 1990). When episodic explosiveness is accompanied by high sympathetic and emotional arousal (Miller, 1994) or associated with features of attention deficit disorder (Eames & Wood, 2003), favourable results can be achieved with β blockers, such as propranolol, titrated to high doses.

[7] Psychostimulants may work in some cases where low attention span and drowsiness contribute to irritability (Miller, 1994). β Blockers or clonidine, an agonist at $\alpha2$ presynaptic autoreceptors, have been used in the treatment of "frontal aggression". Patients with affective aggression due to traumatic brain injury may benefit from serotonergic agents, such as trazodone or trazodone plus tryptophan (Cassidy, 1990).

their ability to perform violent acts than those who primarily use reactive aggression (Crick & Dodge, 1996). Proactive, but not reactive, aggression in children predicted later "externalising problems", such as delinquency and disruptive behaviours (i.e., oppositional defiant and conduct disorders) (Vitaro, Gendreau, Tremblay & Oligny, 1998).

Predatory violence in adults is associated with chronic underarousal, autonomic hyporeactivity, low emotional reactivity, proneness to boredom, sensation seeking, and a history of drug abuse. Chronic underarousal may be aversive and lead to seeking of stimulation and risk taking, thus predisposing to criminality. Psychopaths, in particular, who tend to display high levels of instrumental or predatory aggression, have low levels of anxiety, lower skin conductance activity, and lower resting heart rates. Psychopaths are callous and cold, yet can be rageful at times; they disregard the feelings of others and lack remorse or guilt (reviewed in McEllistrem, 2004), suggesting a deficit in superego function. Some men prone to domestic violence lower their heart rates at the beginning of domestic conflict. These "type 1" men tended to be more belligerent, contemptuous, and angry than those whose heart rate increased during domestic conflict ("type 2"). "Type 1" men were also more violent outside the marriage, had higher rates of sadistic characteristics, scored lower on dependency needs, and were more likely to be drug dependent (Gottman *et al.*, 1995). The lowering of heart rate at the beginning of marital conflict in "type 1" men is consistent with predatory aggression, which, in the context of marital conflict, may be aimed at manipulating the wife's response. In individuals prone to predatory aggression, prefrontal functioning tends to be normal (reviewed in McEllistrem, 2004). Predatory aggression in patients with antisocial traits may be exacerbated by brain injury; or it may arise *de novo* as a consequence of severe acceleration-deceleration brain injury. Such aggression is not accompanied by autonomic arousal and not associated with irritability; and it may manifest as biting and lunging at objects entering the patient's visual field (Cassidy, 1990).[8]

### 3.7  Summary

Appetitively seeking relatedness—and manipulating others in the process of seeking relatedness—manifests as transference, projective identification (Kernberg, 1992; Feldman, 1997), or imposition of role relationships (Sandler & Sandler, 1978). Social behaviours that manipulate others are forms of appetitive behaviour and are ultimately derived from navigational behaviours. Manipulative behaviour has an assertive or aggressive component—one that stems from the need to exert effort in behaviours instrumental to achieving a desired goal. Behaviour that transcends time—by sequentially achieving or creating a situation (an outcome) that is resourceful or otherwise favourable—has retained the assertive-aggressive component of appetitive (purposive, preparatory, or goal-directed) behaviour originally employed in the realm of navigation but has lost its locomotor component. Instrumental aggression, employed in the pursuit of resources, may overlap with territorial and offensive aggression, used in the defence of resources. Speech, to a large extent, is appetitive (manipulative) behaviour that transcends time (and is therefore evolutionarily relatedness to locomotion) insofar as speech is also, to some extent, an instrumentally or offensively aggressive behaviour. McDougall (1924), Hass (1968), and Blanchard and Blanchard (1989) are amongst those who have hinted at an evolutionary link between speech and aggression.

Failure by others to act in accordance with social norms awakens the aggressive drive (releases aggressive energy) within oneself. Why should this be so? Violations of social norms perpetrated by other individuals challenge the framework within which one's self (an abstract

---

[8]Benztropine has been tried for post-traumatic predatory aggression with varying success (Cassidy, 1990).

territory) is defined. A challenge to one's self elicits an offensively aggressive reaction, similarly to how others' intrusions into one's physical territory or property can bring about an angry reaction within oneself. By acting aggressively or assertively, one induces submission and normative behaviour in others. Conversely, others' normative and submissive behaviours inhibit one's potential for offensive aggression. Irritability may be seen as readiness with which others' failure to adhere to social conventions activates one's aggressive potential. Being at the receiving end of offensive aggression is painful and aversive. The aversiveness of being the target of others' offensive aggression is important for avoidance learning and the perpetuation of social norms. Normative and complying behaviours are acquired (through avoidance learning) to avoid repeated exposure to disapproval or criticism; they are forms of avoidance behaviour. The pain experienced when one is offensively attacked (insulted, criticised, disrespected) during territorial or dominance disputes facilitates defensive fight or flight behaviour (defensive aggression or withdrawal). It also promotes submissive behaviour, which is partly a form of ritualised withdrawal. Submissive behaviour has the effect, directly or indirectly, of terminating the opponent's offensive attack behaviour. Submissive behaviour may signal or imply that

one surrenders claims to disputed territory or dominance status; and, by surrendering these claims, one ceases to incite the opponent's aggression. Normative and complying behaviours, too, have an appeasing effect in that they reinstate the framework within which the opponent's self is defined and, thereby, remove the trigger for the opponent's offensive aggression (Figure 3-5).

Others' expression of interest in oneself, others' approval of oneself, and others' respect for oneself signal that their potential of aggression is inhibited. Conversely, a loss of relatedness to others is tantamount to an increased risk of becoming the target of others' offensive aggression, an increased risk that is signalled by anxiety. Being actually attacked or criticised by others is not only painful or aversive but also increases the risk of further exposure to attack or criticism, and, therefore, renders the immediate situation or relationship anxiogenic. Others' expressions of disapproval, disgust, or anger towards oneself all indirectly serve to increase anxiety and lower self-esteem (with the consequence that one prefers submissive over assertive behaviours in direct interactions). Anxiety is *not* a direct response to conspecific challenge or social punishment but merely reflects an increased likelihood of such harmful events. Similarly, safety—the state we reach by overcoming anxiety—indicates an increased likelihood of receiving attentive,

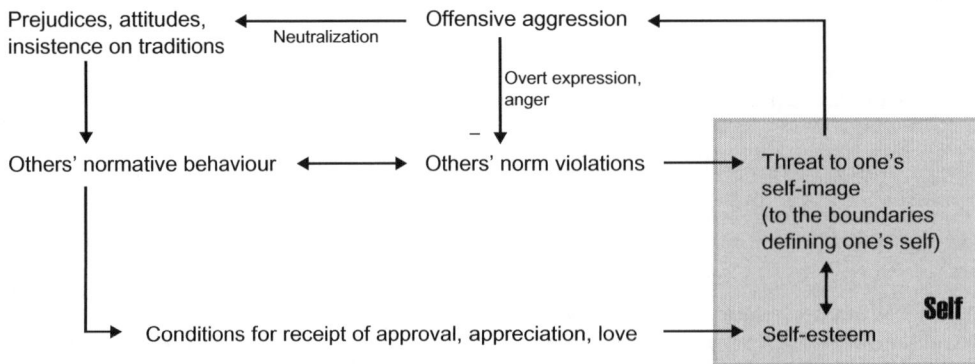

Figure 3-5.    A perceived threat to one's self-image and social position (corresponding, in territorial animals, to an intrusion into one's territory) causes reactive offensive hostility directed against those from whom the threat is seen to emanate.

respectful, or approving signals from otherwise ignorant or hostile conspecifics. Anxiety, whether it reflects a conditioned dangerousness of a situation or relationship (fear-conditioned context) or the fact that one has become acutely unrelated to the social environment (and, therefore, vulnerable to attack), engenders renewed efforts to withdraw to a safe situation and attain social or object relatedness. Anxiety is intricately linked with appreciation of the situational context; predictors of conspecific attack emanate from the evaluation of the context within which social interactions take place. Imagery of disapproval or criticism does not have the effect of exposure to disapproval or criticism but may affect behaviour, like the perception, in the immediate situation or relationship, of cues predictive of disapproval or criticism (fear-conditioned contexts) does affect behaviour. Exposure to a context associated with the possibility of forthcoming punishment may be as anxiogenic as anticipation, in imagination, of a socially punished outcome. In overcoming anxiety, appetitive safety-directed (escape) behaviour seeks to establish a situation in which affectionate behaviours remain unpunished and are likely to be reciprocated. Caring interactions and positive affective exchange are rewarding and render a situation or relationship safe (insofar as hostile interactions are inhibited). Anxiety reduction, especially when it is brought about coincidentally, reinforces contextually sensitive safety-directed behaviour, that is, behaviour that, in responding to the social context, reestablishes one's relatedness to one's object or wider social environment.

CHAPTER FOUR

# Submission and harm avoidance

Dominance and submission are reciprocally linked in social interactions. Displays of aggressive readiness or potential (dominance) automatically induce a disposition toward submissive displays in another individual, and displays of submission, in turn, tend to inhibit offensive aggression in those who are the recipient of submissive signals. In conversations, we automatically assume postures of submission when talking to somebody in authority, while our conversation partner unknowingly emits signals of dominance (reviewed in Ferguson & Bargh, 2004).[1] As already recognised by Burrow (1949), the "disposition of an individual to exercise projective control over others [is] coupled with a reciprocal subservience on the part of his listeners" (p. 4). It is possible that, especially in primates, submissive behavioural displays evolved into agreeable, polite, and attentive displays that served to reinforce relationships and political alliances. Thus, the dichotomy that Burrow identified in human social behaviour may define more generally a contrast between

offensively aggressive and dominant behaviours, on the one hand, and submissive and affiliative behaviours, on the other.

> By virtue of this authoritarian give-and-take that now characterizes man's interrelational level of behaviour, there is to-day early imbued in him—in us all—a dichotomous attitude of servile dependence upon other people on the one hand, and of vindictive repudiation of them on the other. The social fabric of human relations is now shot through with this dualistic factor of personal attraction and repulsion. This bipolar reaction is universal. Our mental world is divided between those towards whom we feel kindly disposed, and those towards whom we feel unkindly disposed. People with whom we agree, or who agree with us, are those for whom we feel affection, while people with whom we do not agree, or who do not agree with us, are those with whom we do not share our affections. (Burrow, 1949, pp. 4–5)

Burrow (1949) saw that, at the heart of all social interactions, individuals "approve and

---

[1]This is similar to flank marking dynamics in interacting dominant and subordinate hamsters (Ferris, Meenan, Axelson & Albers, 1986).

are approved of" and "disapprove and are disapproved of"; and that "society is composed exclusively of these two complemental reactions" (p. 5). However, Burrow also thought that this dichotomy in human interrelational behaviour is entirely socially conditioned, that it is acquired in childhood development as a result of exposure to parental and societal attitudes that have been reinforced in cultural evolution; whereas Lorenz (1963) saw culture and society themselves as emerging from large-scale interactions between phylogenetically evolved processes of intraspecific aggression and submission. In higher social animals, ritualised behaviour patterns "form a unitary integrated system", the rigidity and regulatory force of which "derives from the tension between opposing rituals, such as those of threatening and those of appeasement" (Lorenz, 1973, p. 213). Instinctive, that is, phylogenetically evolved, patterns of behaviour play an important part in human social behaviour. In addition, cultural ritualisation affects virtually all social conduct.[2] All means of verbal communication and displays of emotion in all cultures have traditional ritualised elements superimposed upon innate components (Lorenz, 1973). Language and language-based social behaviour draws on several motivational processes. Offensive aggression is expressed through language and gesture. Moreover, language and gesture are an important part of behaviour that aims to inhibit offensive aggression in conspecifics. Unless we actively inhibit others' potential for offensive aggression, we inevitably become the target of such aggression. For instance, failure to behave in accordance with social norms and the expression of ideas that, in a given social situation, are inappropriate will inevitably disinhibit others' hostility, the very hostility we habitually inhibit through our normative language- and gesture-based behaviour. Conversely, disturbances of social behaviour we notice in others elicit our negative valuation of them (Lorenz, 1973).

_____

[2] Instinctive actions that are not affected by cultural ritualisation are those that are socially taboo (Lorenz, 1973).

Many, perhaps most, disorders of social conduct, whether this conduct be innate or the product of cultural norms, induce in normal men strong feelings of aversion and rejection. (Lorenz, 1973, pp. 243–244)

### 4.1   Appeasement

The majority of fights between members of a species for territory or ranking position are ritualised tests of strengths; they are rarely lethal. The victor in agonistic interactions is usually satisfied with retreat or acceptance of subordinate status by the defeated animal. The defeated animal displays "appeasement gestures" (a "submissive attitude") to signal to its opponent that it concedes victory (Lorenz, 1963; Eibl-Eibesfeldt, 1970). Appeasement gestures (submissive attitudes) displayed by the weaker animal have the effect of inhibiting further attack from the victorious animal. Species-specific appeasement gestures produce active inhibition of aggression in members of the same species (Lorenz, 1963). Appeasement gestures often involve the turning away, from the victor, of the animal's natural weapons or the presentation, to the victor, of the animal's vulnerable part. Importantly, juvenile expression movements (infantilisms) can serve as appeasing gestures (Lorenz, 1963), pointing to a possible evolutionary link between active inhibition of others' aggression and the solicitation of care (care-inducing behaviour). Juvenile expression movements and care-inducing behaviours may *prevent* intraspecific aggression by inhibiting others' *potential* to become aggressive. Juvenile expression movements are not dissimilar from gestures that, when displayed during agonistic encounters, make the losing animal appear smaller (Eibl-Eibesfeldt, 1970). Lying flat on the belly in front of the victor—as can be seen, for instance, in marine iguanas—is designed to make the losing animal appear smaller, which actively inhibits the victor's aggression or removes the stimulus situation ("Reizsituation") that releases (and sustains) the victor's aggression. By contrast, gestures that enlarge the animal's physical stature are ritualised displays of aggressive intent that act to challenge or threaten a conspecific (Eibl-Eibesfeldt, 1970).

Social manners are appeasement gestures formed in the process of cultural evolution (Lorenz, 1963). Manners and mannerisms are "culturally ritualised exaggerations of submissive gestures most of which probably have their roots in phylogenetically ritualised motor patterns conveying the same meaning" (p. 77). In humans, social manners inhibit aggression by "permanently producing an effect of mutual conciliation between the members of a group" (Lorenz, 1963, p. 75).

> Everything that is called manners is, of course, strictly determined by cultural ritualisation. "Good" manners are by definition those characteristic of one's own group and we conform to their requirements constantly; they have become second nature to us. We do not, as a rule, realize either their function of inhibiting aggression or that of forming a bond. Yet it is they that effect what sociologists call 'group cohesion'. (Lorenz, 1963, p. 75)

Appeasement of aggression is an essential function of social rites, whether rites are phylogenetically evolved or culturally developed (Eibl-Eibesfeldt, 1970). In humans, most gestures of appeasement and submission are innate, and even those appeasement and submission gestures that are culturally developed have an innate element. Thus, one submits to another person by making oneself smaller, which culturally developed into bowing or kneeling or lying flat in front of the ruler (Eibl-Eibesfeldt, 1970). Bowing, as a culturally ritualised appeasement gesture, inhibits others' *potential* aggressiveness. Nodding is a ritualised bowing gesture and signals submission, too. When nodding towards a speaker, "we are submitting, as listeners, to the ideas of the speaker" (p. 169). Nodding is also gesture of affirmation (as well as a greeting gesture). If the speaker feels unsure of himself, he "will look enquiringly at his friends and wait for a sign of encouragement: a nod or a wink will suffice" (Eibl-Eibesfeldt, 1970, p. 177). Saying "yes" and nodding means that "one accepts the views, suggestions, or commands of another" (Hass, 1968, p. 147). The nod for "yes" may be "a curtailed inclination of the head—that is to say, a ritualised appeasement gesture" (p. 147), whereby ritualisation involved not only curtailment but also acceleration and reiteration of the movement. Correspondingly, our expression of "no" is a "curtailed, accelerated, and reiterated" (that is, ritualised) movement of aversion (Hass, 1968, p. 147).

### 4.1.1    Evolving complexity

Hostile and appeasing patterns of phylogenetically ritualised behaviour (displays) coevolved. Perceivers of hostile "messages"—contained in hostile displays and performances—"should come to behave as if they understood the hostile valence of the performance"; and "the performer should come to expect the reactions of the perceivers and react appropriately" (Moynihan, 1998, p. 101). Appeasement refers to "any behavior pattern that reduces an opponent's tendency to attack" (p. 51). Looking away is an effective signal. Removing face, eyes, and beak from the eyes of an opponent may terminate a hostile encounter between birds "by virtually hiding the releasing stimuli" (p. 44). Presenting to an opponent vulnerable parts of the body, and thereby exposing them to possible attack, also inhibits the opponent's aggression. The "advertisement of vulnerability", which is likely to be related to care-soliciting gestures of infants, is a common method (message) used to control intraspecific aggression (Moynihan, 1998, p. 44). Appeasement behaviours are often derivatives of infantile behaviours. Alloinfantile behaviour, which is "reminiscent of the behavior of young animals seeking comfort or protection from a parent", reduces the probability of fighting between partners and, at the same time, may help soliciting in sexual encounters (Moynihan, 1998,

p. 48). For instance, patterns that "are used by young birds to induce, even force, their parents to feed them" may be used, later in life, for the purpose of soliciting in sexual encounters (p. 51) or inhibiting intraspecific aggression. Alloparental behaviour in gregarious mammals and birds (in which one individual reacts to another as if it was it's own infant) similarly inhibits intraspecific aggression. Allopreening and allogrooming (preening or grooming another individual instead of oneself) in birds and mammals, respectively, are ritualised patterns that may be closely related to alloparental behaviour. Allopreening and allogrooming, which involve tactile contact, seem to *prevent* hostile encounters, rather than acutely reduce hostility, between partners. Tactile signals "are both particularly risky and perhaps unusually effective in reducing social tensions" (Moynihan, 1998, p. 98).

All of these performances have the "side effect … that different individuals become accustomed to one another" (Moynihan, 1998, p. 47). Familiarity itself reduces hostility between territorial rivals. Territorial rivals that have become familiar with one another fight less frequently and less vigorously with each other. Familiarity also reinforces the cohesion in family units, herds, flocks, groups, and dominance hierarchies (p. 14). Familiarity is based upon individual recognition. Animals from exceedingly diverse species can recognise each other, whereby the type of clues used for recognition ("probably usually olfactory or visual") "must differ in different cases" (Moynihan, 1998, p. 87). The complexity of appeasing patterns increases inasmuch as offensive patterns become more complex, too; and the increased complexity of ritualised behaviour patterns involved in the control of competition translates into a higher complexity of social organisation. Moynihan (1998) suggested that the progressive complication of interactions between aggressive patterns and appeasements should be compared with "the escalation of predatory and protective devices among marine animals" or "the race between mammalian ungulates and carnivores to develop better brains" (p. 107).

Greeting behaviours, observed in some species, "are ritualized forms of submission that confirm asymmetries of status between the participants or partners" (p. 50). Greetings are usually initiated by subordinate individuals. Formal expressions of status "often obviate the need for actual attacks or fighting" (p. 97). Punishment, or retaliatory aggression, is used to maintain dominance relationships and discipline offspring. Punishment also provides "a convenient outlet … for the residual aggressive tendencies that may be supposed to lurk underneath the placid surfaces of even the most friendly associations" (Moynihan, 1998, p. 54).

### 4.1.2    Infantilisms

Gestures of submission displayed in the course of an agonistic confrontation signal admission of defeat to the opponent and inhibit any further attack from the opponent (Eibl-Eibesfeldt, 1970). Infantile behaviour inhibiting an opponent's aggression is exemplified by the behaviour of lying on the back. A dog or wolf can break off a fight by rolling onto his back and urinating a little. This ritual replicates the behaviour of "a cub offering itself to its mother to be cleaned" (p. 65); it not only inhibits aggression but can elicit parental care behaviour in the opponent. The mother responds to infantilisms displayed by the young with care and by looking after the young (Eibl-Eibesfeldt, 1970). Appeasement rituals capitalise on this mechanism.

Begging for food and mutual feeding are common behaviours among social canids (Lorenz, 1973). Dogs and wolves may feed other animals in the pack with the prey they have caught. Begging behaviour can induce the mutual feeding response in a dog or wolf returning to the pack with prey or, insofar as domestic dogs are concerned, in a human master (Lorenz, 1973). For begging behaviour to be effective in this regard, it has to inhibit the conspecific's aggressive potential at the same time. In wolves and dogs, ritualised behaviour patterns that derived from the young animal's begging for food have an appeasing function. During a confrontation, the ritualistic display of begging to be fed arouses a friendly mood in the opponent (reviewed in Eibl-Eibesfeldt, 1970). Similarly, a dog can use "puppyish" behaviour to induce a friendly mood in the opponent. Human beings display helplessness, weakness, and infantile behaviours in order to arouse pity in an opponent and, thereby, inhibit or prevent the opponent's aggression (Eibl-Eibesfeld, 1970).

### 4.1.3    Greetings

The function of greeting rites in humans and animals is to appease aggressive feelings in conspecifics or inhibit their aggressive potential. Greetings also play a role in establishing and maintaining bonds (Eibl-Eibesfeld, 1970). In birds, the passing over of nesting material is a common greeting gesture with a clear appeasing function. In some species, the sight of a conspecific "releases strong aggressive feelings which can only be appeased by the offer of nesting material" (p. 105). Gifts have a similar function in humans. Gifts and food are offered in greeting to guests in the tradition of various peoples (Eibl-Eibesfeldt, 1970). Similarly to other species, the sight of a conspecific innately releases fear and aggression in humans, as best illustrated, perhaps, by the infant's fear of strangers. Familiarity effects a powerful inhibition of intraspecific aggression, but aggression is less inhibited with regard to strangers (Eibl-Eibesfeldt, 1970). The aggression-inhibiting effect of greeting gestures is especially relevant when meeting strangers or people with whom one is less familiar. In primitive peoples and some isolated communities, strangers "are rejected, often attacked, or at best tolerated with reserved curiosity" (p. 217). It is the function of greeting gestures and culturally augmented greeting rituals to prevent aggression towards or from strangers. Humans greet each other following a period of separation, often repeatedly during the day and after only a short separation. We feel an urge to greet as soon as "we step out of the anonymous crowd"

(Eibl-Eibesfeldt, 1970, p. 167). We greet a stranger "when we enter a shop or a strange house" or "if we meet him alone somewhere out in the open" (p. 167). If we fail to offer greetings in these situations, "we experience an unpleasant feeling of tension" (p. 167). Omission of a greeting releases others' aggression. Conversely, a greeting "can relax the tension in a situation" (p. 166). The return of a greeting "is generally a guarantee of security" (Eibl-Eibesfeldt, 1970, p. 166).

Many greetings in humans have an innate basis. In the "most differing peoples in the world", greeting takes the form of "a rapid raising and lowering of the eyebrows, accompanied by a smile and often also a nod" (Eibl-Eibesfeldt, 1970, p. 16). Greeting with the eyes is a phylogenetically ritualised expression of pleasant surprise. Ebil-Eibesfeldt thought that, in our phylogenesis, eyebrows have survived the otherwise widespread loss of facial hair because they evolved into "a means of emphasizing the optical greeting" (Hass, 1968, p. 116). It is not a coincidence that "girls spend so much time on their eyebrows", "painting them and tracing their outlines" (Hass, 1968, p. 116). Smiling, while greeting with the eyes, powerfully inhibits the other's aggressive potential or dissolves his anger ("smile disarms") (Eibl-Eibesfeldt, 1970). Nodding and bowing are gestures of submission used in greetings.[3] Nodding is more ritualised than bowing or falling to one's knees. In other vertebrates, too, making oneself small is a submissive gesture and "the precise opposite of threatening behaviour" (Eibl-Eibesfeldt, 1970, p. 172). Greetings are often culturally emphasised. Culturally developed greeting rites include the raising of a hand, the touch to the side of one's head, or the shaking of hands. The raising of the open hand in greeting demonstrates peaceful intent and "that one is not holding a weapon in the right hand" (p. 181). Finally, leave taking is a form of greeting behaviour in humans. When a person walks away from another person, he enters a dangerous

---

[3]They are also gestures of affirmation used in other social contexts.

situation (Eibl-Eibesfeldt, 1970), albeit insofar as he leaves the aggression-inhibiting context in which the interaction took place. One's interaction with the other could have been competitively motivated, in part, so that, when leaving the aggression-inhibiting context in which the interaction took place, one has to assure oneself of the other's peaceful intentions.

### 4.1.4   Smile

> The suspicious or surly face is an unmistakeable warning which arouses uneasiness in the person approaching—not only because of past experience but because of an innate recognitive reaction situated far deeper within us. (Hass, 1968, p. 123)

Hass (1968) spoke of an "instinctive tendency to remain aloof from members of the same species"—a tendency that "constitutes a disruptive factor" in processes of mating and bond formation (p. 121). Human smile, which expresses a friendly and accommodating attitude, became "an arrow which pierced these invisible barriers", fulfilling "the important function of bringing us aggressive creatures closer together" (Hass, 1968, p. 131). Smile became "a means of eliciting contact readiness in others and of conveying our own accessibility to contact" (p. 123).[4] Smile probably evolved as the "antithesis" (Darwin's term), that is, as the direct opposite, of threatening expressive movements ("Ausdrucksbewegungen"). This is to say that the facial expression communicating "friendliness and accessibility to contact" evolved to be as dissimilar as possible from expressive movements signalling an aggressive stance (p. 130). Smile is, thus, the opposite of "the human facial expression which conveys ill humour", the latter being characterised by "a mouth drawn downward at the corners, vertical furrows in the forehead, and a slight jutting of the lips" (Hass,

1968, p. 130). Smiling is fundamentally different from laughter, "both in significance and origin" (p. 126). Smiling, unlike laughter, does not involve the opening of the mouth or the emission of sounds. Both signals (smiling and laughter), however, possess "a strongly infectious quality" (Hass, 1968, p. 127).

> If we encounter a stranger and laugh at him on sight, he will probably interpret it as a sign of derision and disparagement rather than as a greeting. If we smile at him, all misunderstanding is precluded. (Hass, 1968, p. 127)

### 4.1.5   Bond formation

Children have an innate fear of strangers, perhaps of conspecifics in general. Importantly, adults never outgrow the fear of strangers (Eibl-Eibesfeldt, 1970). The "bond with the person the child is attached to" increases as the fear of strangers matures in the second year of life (p. 211). Bond formation specifically counteracts the innate aversiveness of the mother. In most mammals and birds, the mother's bond with her young is individualised. Mothers *recognise* their own offspring and "often drive strange youngsters away fiercely" (Eibl-Eibesfeldt, 1970, p. 121). Acquaintanceship has the function of inhibiting the mother's aggression towards her own offspring. Nevertheless, "aggression between mother and child is inevitable" (Storr, 1968, p. 41). The bond between partners in parental care, too, is based on acquaintanceship; their personal acquaintance has a similarly appeasing effect. Mere personal acquaintance can have an inhibitory effect on otherwise pervasive intraspecific aggression. In birds, at the beginning of bond formation, courtship ceremonies serve to inhibit aggression. As soon as the bond has been formed, and partners recognise each other, acquaintanceship takes over the function of inhibiting aggression between partners, so that appeasing behaviour may be required less frequently or not at all (Eibl-Eibesfeldt, 1970).

---

[4]Smile can be "embarrassed, shamefaced, or nervous", in which case "the friendship signal is superimposed upon the expression of fear or shame appropriate to the circumstances" (Hass, 1968, p. 128).

Lorenz (1963) proposed that personal bonds (partner bonds) evolved on the foundation of appeasement gestures. Appeasement gestures not only contribute to bond formation by inhibiting intraspecific aggression; appeasement gestures lie at the heart of the bond. Personal bonds are, in their nature, "aggression-inhibiting, appeasing behaviour mechanisms" (Lorenz, 1963, p. 133). The proposition that bonding behaviour is based on appeasement gestures implies that intraspecific "aggression was antecedent to brotherly love" (Storr, 1968, p. 35). Bond formation, established through appeasement gestures, was shown by Lorenz (1963) to be more prevalent in species with highly developed intraspecific aggression (even when a species' aggressiveness is heightened only under certain environmental conditions or at certain times, such as during breeding seasons). Formation of personal bonds is dependent on active intraspecific aggression since personal bonds tend to dissolve when animals lose their aggressiveness on a seasonal basis (e.g., during flock formation in storks) (Lorenz, 1963). Storr (1968) agreed that "it is only when intense aggressiveness exists between two individuals that love can arise" (p. 36).

"Appeasement ceremonies" foster bonds between animals taking part in these ceremonies; animals "recognise as friends those with whom they habitually perform these ceremonies" (Storr, 1968, p. 35). Ritualised appeasement ceremonies are bound to the individualities of participating partners, suggesting that, through them, a distinction arises between friend and stranger. In closed groups of social animals, personal bonds are "inseparably linked with the individualities of group members" (Lorenz, 1963, p. 161). Personal bonds between individuals self-organise into group structure. Appeasement gestures may contribute to the maintenance of a group's dominance hierarchy by confirming dominance relationships between individuals. As a consequence of suffering social defeat, an animal may become more submissive ("conditioned defeat") and, hence, more likely to display appeasement gestures in subsequent confrontations with other group members. However, the assignment of ranking positions to members of the group cannot depend on individuals' behaviour alone; instead, ranking positions have to be assigned to recognisable constellations of individual characteristics (individualities) that differentiate one member of the group from another.

Appeasement gestures foster the bond between mother and infant or between breeding partners by inhibiting mutual aggressive rejection, much as submissive gestures terminate aggression in agonistic confrontations. Mother-infant and partner bonds, maintained by appeasing gestures and acquaintanceship, may have become established in the course of evolution when selection pressures favoured modifications that improved the protection of offspring. The infant's attachment to its mother, in turn, could have paved the way for the evolution of care-soliciting and care-giving behaviours, whereby care-soliciting behaviours could have evolved from appeasement gestures (Figure 4-1). Care-soliciting and care-giving behaviours then became the substrate from which other ritualised appeasement behaviours used in pair bond formation evolved. It may appear that social mannerisms and greetings (appeasement gestures used in a social context) and the individualisation of members of a group are derived from interpersonal displays that originally evolved to maintain mother-infant and partner bonds in spite of the repulsive effect of intraspecific aggression.

## 4.2   Compliance

A child responds with "fear of punishment" to the parental threat of punishment, and it is this fear that "exerts a restraining influence upon his activities" (Rado, 1956, p. 224). The parental threat of punishment, to which the child responds with fear of punishment and behavioural inhibition, becomes an internalised threat that can act as an internal stimulus. In the process of avoidance learning, an aversive experience, such as a "violent attack of fear", becomes associated with "the *sensory context of*

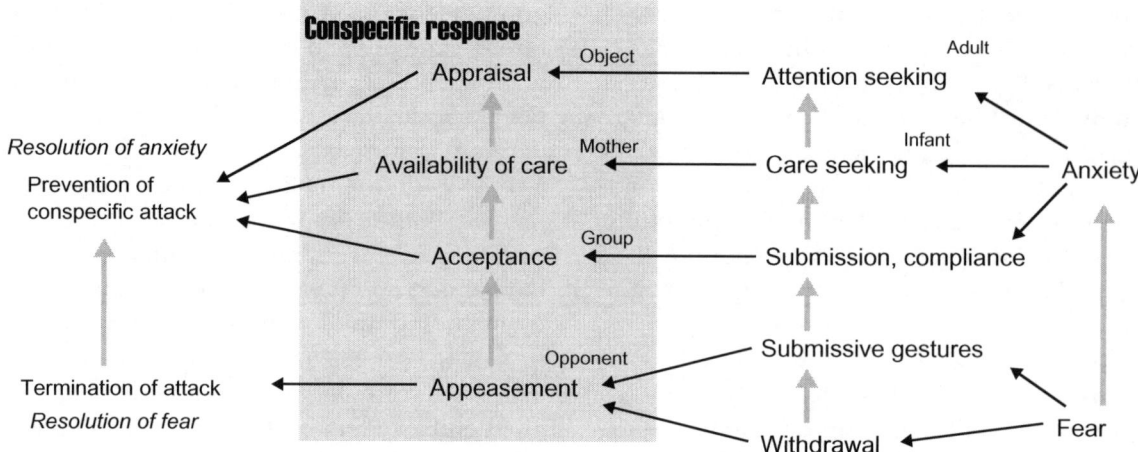

Figure 4-1.   Hypothetical evolutionary links between fear and anxiety, on the one hand, and submissive and care-seeking behaviours, on the other. Fear arises when conspecific attack is imminent, anxiety arises when circumstances indicate a potential for intraspecific aggression.

*its occurrence*", so that, henceforth, whenever the child's "memory stresses the visual picture", he will "be forced to avoid the situation branded by the crucial attack" (Rado, 1956, p. 229). The recollection of a memory of a punishing or threatening gesture or vocalisation made by parents on a previous occasion, which may involve "the inner reproduction of the original auditory experience" (a voice saying "don't do it!") (p. 226), may act as a contextual fear stimulus that has the effect of restraining the child's behaviour and defeating his temptation. With progressive "automatisation", the inescapable (because internalised) fear of punishment becomes the "fear of conscience". In a parallel process, parents "reward the child's obedience with loving care" (p. 224) and praise. With progressive "automatisation", parental reward becomes "the self-reward of self-respect and rising moral pride" (p. 225). These mechanisms, shaping obedience, continue to work into adulthood "as fear of social punishment, and as rising self-respect and pride in social recognition" (Rado, 1956, p. 224).

> The automated version of this fear of inescapable punishment must be recognized as the fear of conscience. The fear

of conscience is the most effective, and socially the most valuable mechanism of self-restraint we possess. (Rado, 1956, p. 225)

Fear of conscience elicits conscious restraint, or automatic repression of dangerous thought and desire, and automatic inhibition of dangerous action. Guilty fear, on the other hand, elicits the reparative pattern of expiatory behavior, a pattern often complicated by rage retroflexed and vented on the self. (Rado, 1956, p. 245)[5]

### 4.2.1   Avoidance learning

According to the principle of "hedonic self-regulation", "the organism moves towards the source of pleasure and away from the cause of pain" (Rado, 1956, p. 339). The more advanced organism also seeks "to repeat pleasurable experiences and to avoid painful ones" (p. 333). For a pleasurable experience to be repeated,

---

[5]Consistent with Horney's (1937) insights that feeling guilty is a defence against anxiety, and that expressions of guilt and the self-recriminations that accompany feelings of guilt are intended to invite positive reassurances from the object.

or a painful one to be avoided, learning has to take place. If "pleasure is the reward for successful performance", then "memory of pleasure invites repetition of the beneficial activity" (p. 291). Likewise, if pain is "punishment for failure", then "memory of pain deters the organism from repeating the self-harming activity" (Rado, 1956, p. 291).

> Nature has placed massive pleasure rewards on the operations which supply the organism's aboriginal needs; such as, intake of food, evacuation of waste and reproduction. The perennial problem of cultural development is to extend this system of pleasure rewards to the operations that will supply the organism's acculturated needs, i.e., where it will have adaptive utility, in a given culture. At the same time, pleasure-yielding yet socially undesirable activity must be vigorously combatted by the threat of punishment or, in other words, the infliction of pain. The reward and punishment system of society is based upon, and is but an extension of, the hedonic self-regulation of the biologic organism. (Rado, 1956, p. 291)

When a noxious stimulus (unconditioned stimulus) impinges upon an organism, the organism will engage in behaviour designed to eliminate that stimulus (unconditioned response) (Mowrer & Lamoreaux, 1946). In fear conditioning, an affectively neutral stimulus paired with a noxious stimulus (traumatic event) acquires the capacity to elicit fear. A stimulus that has acquired the capacity to elicit fear (and has thus become a fear-conditioned stimulus) serves as a warning signal with regard to the original traumatic event (unconditioned stimulus). Fear, not unlike pain, motivates the organism to engage in whatever behaviour is best calculated to remove this "painful emotion" (Mowrer & Lamoreaux, 1946). By removing fear, the organism averts reexposure to the traumatic (noxious) stimulus; although, it has to be said that the response required to

eliminate the fear-conditioned stimulus *and the attendant fear* is principally different from the response required to eliminate a noxious stimulus and the attendant pain (Mowrer & Lamoreaux, 1946). Mowrer and Lamoreaux (1946) proposed that reduction in fear (elimination of this "painful emotion") constitutes a rewarding state, which reinforces the link between fear (or, rather, the fear-conditioned stimulus or situation) and the *behaviour* that immediately preceded the reduction in fear. Similarly, Miller (1948) showed that fear reduction serves as a reinforcer to produce learning of the immediately preceding response. Thus, fear is not only learned but can also motivate new learning. Fear reduction, as Miller (1948) argued, plays a crucial role, similar to that of primary rewards, in the acquisition and maintenance of new habits. A new response is learned when it allows the animal to remove itself from a fear-producing cue (or to escape from a fear-inducing situation) or when it allows the animal to eliminate the fear-producing cue in other ways (e.g., by turning a wheel or pressing a bar) (Miller, 1948). Fear is an essential intermediate step ("intervening variable") in avoidance learning: a conditioned stimulus produces fear, which then elicits a fear-reducing response, which, once reinforced, becomes an avoidance response (Mowrer & Lamoreaux, 1946).[6]

### 4.2.2  Traditions and norms

> I did indeed say that man's fidelity to all his traditional customs is caused by creature habit and by animal fear at their infraction. I did indeed emphasise the fact that all human rituals have originated in a natural way, largely analogous to the

---

[6]Frustration, another aversive emotional state, may play a similar role in learning. Frustration is a state that results from nonreinforcement of a previously reinforced instrumental response or from the blocking, by an obstacle, of a previously reinforced instrumental sequence. Frustration may facilitate learning of aspects of behaviour that precede a reduction in frustration.

evolution of social instincts in animals and man. (Lorenz, 1963, p. 80)

Compliance with traditions and rites, which may be seen as a form of *submission* to culturally ritualised symbols and customs in which members of a group or society enshrine, and through which they communicate, their dominant status, protects against anxiety. In order to avoid anxiety, the subject may comply "with the potential wishes of all persons" and avoid "everything that might arouse resentment" (Horney, 1937, p. 97). Thus, one may comply with the desires of others in order to feel safe. Compliance not only protects against "basic anxiety" and engenders feelings of security; compliant and submissive attitudes and behaviours may also "serve the purpose of securing reassurance by affection" (p. 97). An attitude of compliance, which "may take the form of not daring to disagree with or to criticise the other person, of showing nothing but devotion, admiration and docility" (pp. 119–120), may be the price one has to pay for the procurement of other persons' affection or approval (Horney, 1937). This would be consistent with the notion that compliant and submissive behaviours are evolutionarily related to care- or attention-seeking behaviours and serve a similar function; both, submissive and care-seeking types of behaviour, if effective, generate security and prevent anxiety (Figure 4-1). The "complying attitude" is incompatible with, and behaviourally opposed to, an attitude of assertion or dominance; the "complying attitude" extinguishes, within oneself, "not only aggressive impulses but all tendencies toward self-assertion" (Horney, 1937, p. 120). In other words, one cannot—in one's interactions with others—be both, self-assertive or dominant and compliant or submissive, at least not to the same extent.

To emphasise, adherence to social norms and traditions has a twofold effect: the procurement of affection or approval and the avoidance of social punishment (in the form of criticism or hostility). With regards to the latter aspect, adherence to social norms can be regarded as culturally evolved and ontogenetically acquired *avoidance* behaviour. By behaving in accordance with social norms, we avoid becoming the target of others' offensive aggression. Conducting behaviour in accordance with social norms reduces the risk of exposure to punishment (conspecific attack) and, thereby, prevents the experience of anxiety and inner tension.

> Authoritative, even rigid, rules of many kinds are convenient for living. They make reflection unnecessary and save energy. They are not followed out of deep conviction, but out of vague acceptance, often not quite acceptance of their usefulness, but of their authority; it is inconvenient to consider them thoughtfully. One drives the way one has been taught to drive, and one's table manners are what they are supposed to be. Many rules— perhaps religious rules, various customs and traditions—we follow simply because it feels wrong or, again, would require inconvenient reflection to do otherwise. (Shapiro, 2000, pp. 51–52)

For the same reason, we adopt authoritative ideas and conventional opinions, although we may do so with varying degrees of readiness and conviction. In persons with hysterical or compulsive character pathology, there may be a greater "readiness to defer to authoritative opinion, to accept ideas and eventually 'believe' them, or rather to think that one believes them" (Shapiro, 2000, p. 41). In general, conventional ideas "are not genuinely believed, but they cannot be dismissed without great anxiety" (Shapiro, 2000, p. 41).

### 4.2.3 False self

One's failure to conform with social norms or traditions implicitly challenges others' position or dominance rank (i.e., in a sense, their territory) in the group and, hence, disinhibits their innate aggressiveness. According to Laing (1960), one's "false self" or "persona" is constructed from compliance with others' social expectations and is designed to keep in check one's fears of aggression. One's "false self" or "persona" is one's "identity-for-others" (or, rather, the identity given to the individual by others)—an identity that arises "in compliance with the intentions or expectations" put forward by one's social environment (Laing, 1960, p. 105). What Laing (1960) called "false self" corresponds to what Heidegger (1927) called the "they"-self, which—in an effort to "flee" existential anxiety—replaces our genuine sense of being. It is one's fear of being aggressed or hated, that is, one's fear of social punishment, rejection, or retaliation (and, with it, the emergence of existential anxiety) that permeates or accentuates one's sense of self.

> One of the aspects of the compliance of the false self that is most clear is the fear implied by this compliance. The fear in it is evident, for why else would anyone act, not according to his intentions, but according to another person's? Hatred is also necessarily present, for what else is the adequate object of hatred except that which endangers one's self? However the anxiety to which the self is subject precludes the possibility of a direct revelation of its hatred, except ... in psychosis. (Laing, 1960, p. 106)

The self is constructed from images that other persons have framed of oneself (James, 1890). Self-consciousness is "an awareness of oneself as an object of someone else's observation" (Laing, 1960, p. 113). Importantly, "the preoccupation with being seeable may be condensed with the idea of the mental self being penetrable, and vulnerable" (p. 113)—that is, vulnerable to intraspecific attack in the form of criticism or ridicule. One needs to be seen in order to belong; but the self-conscious person is "frightened that he will look a fool, or that other people will think he wants to show off" (Laing, 1960, p. 114). Frightening experiences of self-consciousness arise if tendencies

of excessive exhibitionism, for which one was punished in childhood, have not been curtailed or cannot be suppressed (Kohut, 1971). Giddens (1997) similarly recognised that "reflexive self-consciousness" is concerned with the evaluation of *risks* which, emanating from society, threaten to undermine one's sense of social belonging.

> In a world full of danger, to be a potentially seeable object is to be constantly exposed to danger. Self-consciousness, then, may be the apprehensive awareness of oneself as potentially exposed to danger by the simple fact of being visible to others. ... Indeed, considered biologically, the very fact of being visible exposes an animal to the risk of attack from its enemies, and no animal is without enemies. Being visible is therefore a basic biological risk; being invisible is a basic biological defence. We all employ some form of camouflage. (Laing, 1960, p. 117)

What better camouflage, what better way to avert attack, than our "false self" or "persona" representing our striving for conformity? Defences employed against the "many anxieties about being obvious, being out of the ordinary, being distinctive, drawing attention to oneself"—in essence representing fears of attack from others and rejection by the group—"so often consist in attempts to merge with the human landscape, to make it as difficult as possible for anyone to see in what way one differs from anyone else" (Laing 1960, p. 118).

### 4.2.4 Inner dictates

The neurotic person tries to assert exceptional rights for himself and makes unreasonable demands ("claims") on others in order to actualise an "idealised self" conjured up in imagination (Horney, 1950). At the same time, the neurotic person tries to become his idealised self by setting out "to work to mold himself into a supreme being" (p. 64). The neurotic person (and, to some extent, any person) tries to actualise his idealised self-image (and, thereby, achieve his social goals) by making demands on himself, by complying with "inner dictates" ("a complicated system of shoulds and taboos" (p. 25)). Compliance with inner dictates allows the person to gain access to resources of narcissistic supplies (affection from others, being wanted by others) and, thus, to escape anxiety and attain security (Figure 4-2). Inner dictates of the neurotic person are equivalent to moral standards and ideals that constitute the superego, however, where moral standards and ideals "have an obligating power over our lives", inner dictates of the neurotic person have a coercive character (p. 73). Where the healthy person tries to "fulfil" his ideals and "live up" to his standards, the neurotic person obeys his inner dictates at the cost of his "freedom" (Horney, 1950). The more the neurotic person is driven to actualize his idealized self, the more his inner dictates "become the sole motor force moving him, driving him, whipping him into action" (p. 84). Where "there are quick retributions if we do not measure up to expectations", the neurotic person responds to nonfulfilment of his ideals with "anxiety, despair, self-condemnation, and self-destructive impulses" (Horney, 1950, p. 74).

The origin of these emotional reactions to nonfulfilment of ideals and failure to obey superego demands lies partly in the anger that is experienced when appetitive striving is frustrated. Failure to measure up to expectations and standards also causes anxiety, insofar as the objective of security has not been reached (Figure 4-2). Anxiety reactions tend to be fleeting "because the customary defences against anxiety are set going instantaneously" (p. 74). Anxiety may also give rise to "an increased need for affection" (p. 74) and need to "feel wanted" (Horney, 1950, p. 75).

If the person realises that he cannot measure up to his inner dictates, he starts to hate and despise himself. Alternatively, failure to measure up to perfectionist standards may invoke feelings of inferiority (Horney, 1950). Attitudes towards the "tyranny" of inner dictates "range between the opposite poles of compliance and rebellion" (p. 75). Compliance takes the form of self-righteousness; rebellion is associated with guilt feelings. Externalising his self-righteousness and his compliance with his inner dictates, the person imposes "his standards upon others" and makes "relentless demands as to *their* perfection" (p. 78). Externalising his inner experience, the neurotic person tries to "make other people do the 'right' thing', and he often does so 'by force'" (pp. 84–85). Thus, self-criticism "becomes tenaciously externalized" (Horney, 1950, p. 79). Indeed, we enforce norms and laws insofar as these norms and laws help to define our self (and our ego ideal).

> The more he feels himself to be the measure of all things, the more he insists—not upon general perfection but upon his particular norms being measured up to. (Horney, 1950, p. 78)

### 4.3    Superego

In a first approximation, the superego can be regarded as an inner voice that exclaims "don't!" and, thereby, deters the child from libidinous or aggressive acts he wishes to carry out. In the developmental constellation of the Oedipus complex, the boy unconsciously sees his father as a competitor for the affection of his mother and so, out of fear of the father's aggression, has to suppress his libidinous impulses towards his mother. Freud (1923) considered the superego ("ego ideal") to be "the heir of the Oedipus complex" (p. 36). He argued that the superego arises when the boy identifies with his father in an attempt to resolve or repress the Oedipus complex. Dealing with an unconscious "dread of castration" by the father (fear of punishment for libidinal impulses), the boy takes his father as a model. Through this unconscious identification with his father, the boy preserves his object relation to his mother. A similar development occurs in girls. The repression of the Oedipus complex, that is, the repression of libidinal desires for the opposite-sex parent, is thought to be responsible for "the interruption of libidinal development by the latency period" (Freud, 1923, p. 35).

> The super-ego retains the character of the father, while the more powerful the Oedipus complex was and the more rapidly it succumbed to repression … the stricter will be the domination of the super-ego over the ego later on—in the form of conscience or perhaps of an unconscious sense of guilt. (Freud, 1923, pp. 34–35)
>
> It is easy to show that the ego ideal answers to everything that is expected of the higher nature of man. As a substitute for a longing for the father, it contains the germ from which all religions have evolved. (Freud, 1923, p. 37)

Irrespective of the significance of the Oedipus complex, Freud understood that the superego, or conscience, forms in the individual's early life through the internalisation of attitudes and standards of parents and other significant persons. The superego takes over the function of disapproval previously fulfilled by external authority figures (in accordance with their attitudes and standards) (Freud, 1930). The child's instinctive aggression against the "external authority" is in conflict with his need for its love, so that his aggression is inhibited by anticipation of punishment from this "external authority" (whereby parental disapproval or punishment is of an instinctively aggressive nature, too). Conscience (or the fear of conscience) can be conceptualised as internalised (and automatised) fear of disapproval (Rado, 1956). As a result of this fear, the child's aggression is not discharged against his objects but is said to be recoiled against his ego. Freud (1933) thought that "aggressiveness that has turned back from the external world is bound by the super-ego, and so used against the ego" (p. 141). The superego "is endowed with that part of the child's aggressiveness against its parents for which it can find no discharge outwards on account of its love-fixation and external difficulties" (Freud, 1933, p. 142). In melancholia,

an excessively strong superego "rages against the ego with merciless violence", illustrating how "the destructive component had entrenched itself in the super-ego and turned against the ego" (Freud, 1923, p. 53).

> It is remarkable that the more a man checks his aggressiveness towards the exterior, the more severe—that is aggressive—he becomes in his ego ideal. … the more a man controls his aggressiveness, the more intense becomes his ideal's inclination to aggressiveness against his ego. It is like a displacement, a turning around upon his ego. But even ordinary normal morality has a harshly restraining, cruelly prohibiting quality. It is from this, indeed, that the conception arises of a higher being who deals out punishment inexorably. (Freud, 1923, p. 54)

### 4.3.1   Fear of punishment

The superego essentially is a set of avoidance behaviours that were acquired owing to previous experiences of fear of punishment; they were acquired through the reinforcement of socially appropriate and normative behaviours that occasioned a reduction in this fear (Mowrer & Lamoreaux, 1946). When the timing, source, and severity of punishment are uncertain, the fear of punishment is experienced as anxiety. Abstract avoidance behaviours must be acquired through a reduction in anxiety; and the infraction of internalised social norms later in life has to be accompanied by a form of anxiety, rather than a concrete fear. The superego "manifests itself essentially as a sense of guilt (or rather, as criticism—for the sense of guilt is the perception in the ego answering to this criticism)" (Freud, 1923, p. 53). As Freud (1930) acknowledged, behind the sense of guilt, anxiety is at work. The sense of guilt is an indistinct fear of retribution (an anxiety) for having pursued or considered satisfaction of aggressive or libidinal drives outside the channels permitted by authority or sanctioned by society. In the course of development the fear of the "external authority" becomes a fear of the "internal authority" (or superego)—manifesting as guilt. The sense of guilt is "nothing other than a topical variety of anxiety; in its later phases it merges completely with *fear of the superego*" (Freud, 1930, p. 72).

Fear of punishment and anxious feelings of guilt inhibit one's actions, one's naturally arising aggressive and sexual impulses in particular. Freud (1930) considered the chronological sequence of "first, renunciation of the drives, resulting from fear of aggression from the external authority ..., then the setting up of the internal authority and the renunciation of the drives, resulting from fear of this authority, fear of conscience" (p. 64). The "internal authority" or superego ultimately merges with what Freud called the "cultural superego" of society. In society, the individual lives with a constant (albeit subliminal) fear of communal punishment, symbolised by the "cultural superego". The cultural superego makes "stern ideal demands" on the individual; and "failure to meet these demands is punished by 'fear of conscience'" (Freud, 1930, p. 78). The merger of the "individual superego" with the "cultural superego" emphasises that fear of intraspecific or social attack (punishment) lies at the heart of the superego, although the habitual performance, as opposed to acquisition, of parentally prescribed or socially normative behaviour would not be accompanied by either fear or anxiety. Fear of punishment and feelings of guilt are called forth by the inadvertent infraction of social demands and norms and act as spurs for further learning.

Anxiety and fear arising in social situations not only signal a risk of being aggressed (or criticised), they also signal inaccessibility of libidinal interactions, that is, of the exchange of care-soliciting and care-giving signals. Freud (1930) remarked that the fear of aggression from authority (social anxiety) amounts to "fear of the loss of love" (p. 64), consistent with the view that social anxiety attests to the individual's "helplessness and dependence on others" (p. 61). Freud (1930)

thought that an important role "in the emergence of conscience and the fateful inevitability of guilt" is played by the libidinal drive (p. 68). The individual renounces his aggressive drive against his authority not only because of a fear of authority—so as to *avoid* the emergence of social anxiety—but also "in order to avoid losing [the authority's] love" (Freud, 1930, p. 64).

### 4.3.2   Ego ideal

> The father is often experienced by the child as hampering or cutting off access to its mother at various times of day and night and, indeed, as imposing limitations on the kind of satisfactions the child can achieve with the mother, ... (Fink, 1997, pp. 91–92)

The father has a separating function, "refusing to allow the child to be no more than *an extension of the mother*" (Fink, 1997, p. 92). In the oedipal period, the father "gets in the way of the child's otherwise exclusive relationship with its mother" (Fink, 1997, p. 91). The function of the father is to bring about repression of the child's exclusive attachment to his mother. Demanding and prohibiting paternal functions ensure that the child's libidinal interactions with his mother are subordinated to culturally accepted norms. The father's prohibitions, separating the child from the primary source of satisfactions, create "desire"—desire that the child learns to express and pursue on the plane of "the symbolic" (Lacan, 1966). The child's desire can only be expressed and pursued on the symbolic plane, that is, in accordance with norms and conventions (the "law"). The father's prohibitions also cause anxiety (in association with desire). All "symbolic" relations are associated with "castration anxiety" (Lacan, 1966).

The child comes to see his actions as his parents see them, "judged as worthy of esteem or scorn as its parents would (the child believes) judge them" (Fink, 1997, p. 88). Moreover, the child comes to see *himself* as his parents do. The child judges himself in accordance with his parents' ideals and internalises those ideals (formation of the ego ideal). The ego ideal ties the child's sense of self to parental approval. The self, tied to the ego ideal, becomes the vehicle through which libidinal resources can be accessed in a culturally appropriate fashion—a vehicle that, due to its critical role in the pursuit of libidinal desire, is invested with libido. The superego (ego ideal), according to Lacan (1966), is actually a vehicle for gratification. We seek to ensure access to gratifying affectionate interactions with the mother by adhering to norms and rules laid down by the father, and we do so by identifying with the father, by taking on his attributes and traits. It is this identification that, after the resolution of the Oedipus complex, constitutes our sense of self. Following the oedipal period, we live our lives looking through the eyes of the metaphorical father (the third object), or rather through the eyes of the ego ideal representing the metaphorical father.

### 4.3.3   Procurement of narcissistic supplies

> Now a constant watchman has been instituted in the mind, who signals the approach of possible situations or behavior that might result in the loss of the mother's affection, or the approach of an occasion to earn the reward of the mother's affection. This watchman fulfills the essential function of the ego: to anticipate the probable reactions of the external world to one's behavior. (Fenichel, 1946, p. 102)

The superego is an aspect of a system that regulates the receipt of narcissistic supplies (in the form of praise and affection), which is to say that the superego is involved in the regulation of self-esteem (being a measure of the availability of narcissistic supplies). The superego is constituted in such a way that "self-esteem is dependent upon whether or not ideals are fulfilled" (Fenichel, 1946, p. 106). The superego signifies that social protection is provided on conditions of obedience and fulfilment of ideals.

The punitive function attributed to the superego may refer to nothing more than the subject's disposition to experience pain when attempts to actualise the ego ideal are frustrated, when rejection occurs, and when, thus, favourable conditions for the receipt of love (narcissistic supplies) are lost. Indeed, what is conceptualised as "inner punishment performed by the superego" is felt by the subject "as an extremely painful decrease in self-esteem and in extreme cases as a feeling of annihilation" (Fenichel, 1946, p. 105). If self-esteem is a measure of the availability of narcissistic supplies, then the "fear of being punished or abandoned by the superego" is actually a "fear of annihilation through lack of [narcissistic] supplies" (Fenichel, 1946, p. 105).

> This feeling of annihilation must be characterized as a cessation of the narcissistic supplies which were initially derived from the affection of some external person and later from the superego. (Fenichel, 1946, p. 135)

Fenichel (1946) emphasised the close relationship between superego and outside world. The superego is "the inner representative of a certain aspect of the external world", which is to say that "the superego is derived from the introjection of a piece of the external world" (p. 106). The aspect of the external world that is represented by the superego is the sphere of "threat and promise, of punishment and reward" (pp. 106–107). Introjection refers to a learning process. Once the demanding and prohibiting functions of authority figures have been "introjected" (acquired), superego functions can be "reprojected, that is, displaced onto newly appearing authority figures" (p. 107). Group formation and the belief in authority are based on the reprojection of the superego onto external persons (Fenichel, 1946).

### 4.3.4   Ego psychology

The child adopts the commanding and prohibiting attitudes of his parents, whenever he identifies with them. Gradually, all "ego states" associated with these identifications merge into the superego (Federn, 1952). Initially, a nucleus representing "psychically no more than the first inhibitions" is formed, which is then "enlarged by many identifications until a useful, often excessively strong, superego" is formed (p. 316). Although the superego derives from identification with commanding and prohibiting persons of childhood, representations of the original persons are repressed, as the superego develops, and "only the inhibiting and direction-giving power [remains] in consciousness" (p. 316). Federn (1952) thought that the superego has sharp boundaries towards the ego. These boundaries do not exist at first; "feelings of guilt exist much earlier, but only gradually and much later does the superego obtain its sharp boundaries toward the ego" (p. 339).[7] Superego functions have the ego as their object, whereby "in the process of self-supervision the ego might well feel itself to be the object of supervision by the superego" (p. 310). Strict supervision (executed by the superego) and fear of supervision (experienced by the ego) accentuate the boundary between ego and superego. Ego and superego are distinct states or "ego feelings"; they are not contiguous in consciousness. Federn (1952) argued that "ego feeling vacillates between ego and superego" and that "one cannot simultaneously be ego and superego"; one has to lose "the sensation of one's ego before one gains that of one's superego, and vice versa" (p. 314). Ego and superego "have an analogous distance from, and potential connection to, the object cathexes" and external "reality" (Federn, 1952, p. 315).

The object of self-reproach may not be the ego itself but rather a representation which one has formed of the ego (Federn, 1952). This representation of the ego is a form of ego feeling—one that is set apart from the superego. A similar constellation can be seen in narcissism.

One's inclination to think positively about one's ego (and be preoccupied with one's ego) is a manifestation of narcissism ("secondary narcissism", in particular). In narcissism (secondary narcissism), there is "a distinct libidinal relation of a subject to an object" (p. 311). Both, subject and object, "lie inside the ego but seem most frequently to be differentiated functions or parts of the ego" (Federn, 1952, p. 311).

### 4.3.5   Defences against superego cruelty

Bergler (1952) advanced the notion that the superego ("unconscious conscience") has two constituents: the "ego ideal" and what he called the "daimonion"—an accumulation of rebounding aggression within the superego. With regards to the ego ideal, this is an unconscious structure founded on (i) identification with the parents' prohibitions and (ii) infantile megalomania ("the child's boasting about what he can do and will do in the future" (Bergler, 1952, p. 13)). First, inner prohibitions, established by introjection, substitute the parents' external prohibitions and thereby save the child from repeated punishment (avoidance of punishment acquired through reinforcement learning). Introjected "precepts of the images of the parents" (p. 17) and introjected environmental taboos (all of which are unconscious and need to be distinguished from the individual's conscious set of moral precepts) provide the child with a way of *avoiding* external conflicts. Second, "the ego ideal contains a sector composed of the child's own narcissism" (p. 14). The ego ideal "enshrines all the grandiose ideas the child has built up in speculating about his own glorious future" (p. 257). The other constituent of the superego, the inner accumulation of self-directed aggression ("daimonion"), "metes out punishment by holding the ego ideal up to the ego" (p. 257). When the ego acts in accordance with the ego ideal, that is, when the ego achieves a "narcissistic victory" in form of "external success, acknowledgement, flattery" (p. 305), the "daimonion" is temporarily silenced. Conscious elation "represents the

---

[7]In severe psychoses, the superego dissolves in the ego (Federn, 1952).

unconscious ego's elation" at having silenced the "daimonion" (p. 305). The "daimonion" is also silenced whenever "a defense corresponds to one of the precepts enshrined in the ego ideal" (p. 257). In both cases, "the ego allies with the ego ideal to achieve temporary immobilization of the Daimonion sector of the superego" (Bergler, 1952, p. 258).

> By pointing to the unachievable ego ideal, Daimonion silences the ego, which then accepts punishment for the discrepancy. On the other hand, any defence instituted by the ego which corresponds to the ego ideal's precepts will silence Daimonion; ... (Bergler, 1952, p. 258)

Any discrepancy between the ego and the ego ideal ("between present reality and the bragging of the past" (Bergler, 1952, p. 18) or "between the grandiose promises of childhood and the realistic achievements of the adult" (p. 350)) causes dissatisfaction, guilt, and depression. Since such discrepancy is unavoidable, "guilt is unavoidable too" (p. 257). Bergler (1952) thought that the superego, or more precisely the "daimonion" within the superego, imposes a "sentence" ("exacts penance") on the ego in form of dissatisfaction, guilt, or depression. Moods, such as depression, but also elation, he argued, "are the outward reverberation of the dynamic fight between the different parts of the unconscious personality" and attest to the "superego's predominance in the formation of moods" (Bergler, 1952, p. 305). The ego counteracts the superego's cruelty by engaging in "psychic masochism", which, according to Bergler (1952), is reflected in an unconscious craving for injustice ("injustice collecting"). "Psychic masochism" describes the ego's "masochistic submission" to the superego's cruelty (submission that has become "secondarily libidinised"). "Psychic masochism", in turn, is defended against by "pseudo-aggressive behaviour"—a form of passive aggression that provokes external retaliation (external aggression) and, thereby, allows the subject to blame the "bad outer world" for the perceived injustice. However, the initial defence of "pseudo-aggression" ("pseudo-aggressive defence") is generally vetoed by the superego and replaced by a libidinous ("secondarily libidinised") defence (Bergler, 1952).

Lines of defence

Bergler (1952) regarded the superego not simply as a restrictive institution but as the "antihedonistic force" in the personality. Superego reproach wards off inner wishes (originating from the "id"). Confronted with an unconscious wish, the superego emits a stop signal—"a signal which is meant to be obeyed, and is obeyed" (p. 22). Repressed wishes ("driven back into the storehouse of the unconscious" (p. 22)) emerge "as raw material for dreams or as sublimations (after translation into socially approved functions)" (p. 22). The superego veto prompts the employment of defence mechanisms by the unconscious ego (the latter being "the factory of inner defenses" (p. 19)). The first line of defence is usually warded off by a second veto from the superego, leading to the employment of a secondary defence by the ego. The secondary defence "is chosen in such a way that it coincides, if only tangentially, with some precept enshrined in the ego ideal" (p. 259). It is only the secondary defence that "appeases" the superego. Thus, the superego "allows innuendos of unconscious pleasure" that "do not emerge directly" but are "screened against repressed wishes by a double defence mechanism" (p. 22). In other words, "the ego receives attenuated wish-fulfillments, camouflaged with double unconscious defences" (p. 22). Bergler (1952) argued that it is the secondary defence that produces the patient's neurotic symptom ("only the defense against the defense is shown in the neurotic symptom" (p. 264)). In neurotic patients, the superego allows gratification of inner wishes (insofar as they have been modified and attenuated by defence mechanisms) "in exchange for the bribe of depression, unhappiness and self-damage" (p. 23). Punishment by the superego can be anticipated.

In neurotic patients, anticipation of punishment by the superego causes the unconscious ego to produce depression beforehand ("preventive depression") (Bergler, 1952).

## 4.4   Masochism

> … in sadism and masochism we have two admirable examples of the fusion of the two kinds of instincts, Eros and aggressiveness, … (Freud, 1933, p. 135)

Sadism is a destructive or aggressive tendency directed outwards. Sadism is characterised by enjoyment of the victim's suffering and by an unconscious wish to "maintain the relationship with the hated object in an enactment of an object relationship between a sadistic agent and a paralyzed victim" (Kernberg, 1992, p. 24). Aggression may be "unable to find satisfaction in the external world, because it comes up against objective hindrances"; then, one's aggression may turn back on oneself, causing self-destructiveness within (Freud, 1933, p. 136).[8] "Masochism", referring to self-destructiveness in general, involves "introjection" of a hated or disappointing object into the self or ego. The self, identified with the hated object, is a "safer" target for intolerable aggressive impulses. Through introjection of the hated object, the person can redirect unacceptable and consciously disowned hostile impulses against himself. The self or ego, in other words, becomes the less hazardous scapegoat (Laughlin, 1970). Masochism, according to Freud, is a fusion of aggressive and libidinal instincts directed against the self. In masochism, intertwined libidinal and aggressive impulses are directed against the object identified with the ego. The libidinal aspect of masochism may relate to the unconscious wish to maintain the relationship with the hated object. Masserman (1968), doubting that a desire for pain or suffering lies at the heart of masochism, considered whether "patterns of conduct usually interpreted as 'masochistic' are essentially not 'self-punitive', but instead rooted in expectations of previously available rewards through temporarily strenuous or even hurtful behavior" (p. 206). These may be libidinal rewards in the form of the object's affection or interest or care.

### 4.4.1   Moral masochism

Superego functions acquired in childhood dispose the individual to develop an unconscious sense of guilt whenever unacceptable drives are activated (Kernberg, 1992). Behaviourally, this manifests in "a proneness to minor self-defeating behaviors", in "characterological inhibitions and self-imposed restrictions of a full enjoyment of life", or in a "tendency for realistic self-criticism to expand into a general depressive mood" (p. 36). These are minor manifestations of "moral masochism" and "an almost ubiquitous correlate of normal integration of superego functions" (Kernberg, 1992, p. 36). Patients who present a syndrome of "moral masochism" (or "depressive-masochistic personality disorder") seek out a position of victim (without any sexual pleasure involved) in order to appease their unconscious sense of guilt. Integration of cruel objects within the early (preoedipal) superego "leads to sadistic superego demands, depressive-masochistic psychopathology, and secondarily rationalized sadism correlated with the integration of cruel and sadistic ethical systems" (Kernberg, 1992, p. 29). A strong superego may be the cause of self-directed hatred in depression. In melancholic depression, when the self is identified with the betraying or lost object, suicide is the only way to destroy the hated object. Similarly, suicidal and self-mutilating behaviour in patients with severe personality disorder "typically reflects unconscious identification with a hateful and hated object" (p. 26). In patients with histrionic or borderline personality disorder, self-destructive behaviour, emerging at times of intense rage, "frequently represents an unconscious effort to reestablish control over the environment by evoking guilt feelings in others" (Kernberg, 1992, p. 40).

---

[8]Earlier, Freud (1920) thought that self-destructiveness (masochism) is a more primitive tendency that can be secondarily turned outwards in the form of sadism.

### 4.4.2   Submergence in misery

Masochism refers to a tendency to submerge one-self "in feelings of helplessness, unhappiness and unworthiness" (Horney, 1937, p. 264). A masochistic person "unconsciously exaggerates his weakness and he tenaciously insists on being weak" (p. 268). This submergence in misery is a strategy for coercing others to fulfil one's wishes. The masochistic person uses suffering and help-lessness as "means of obtaining affection, help, control" (pp. 263–264). Unconsciously, he wishes to "be completely taken care of" (p. 269). At the same time, his suffering and helplessness allow him to express "accusations against others in a disguised but effective way" and "to evade all demands others might make on him" (Horney, 1937, p. 264). Moreover, masochism is a strat-egy for alleviating the pain of loss or rejection. Neurotic persons cover up a "feeling of intrinsic weakness" ("a deep feeling of insignificance or rather of nothingness") (p. 267) with a grandi-ose and fragile façade or "persona"; hence, these persons are exceedingly sensitive to criticism. For neurotic persons, "even a minute disagree-ment is equivalent to a criticism" (p. 243). Incur-ring "a defeat in competition" or being criticised ("having to realize a definite weakness or short-coming") is "unbearable" for a person who has "high-flung notions of his uniqueness" (Horney, 1937, p. 265). Such "aggravating experience loses some of its reality" when the person submerges "himself in a general feeling of misery or unwor-thiness" (p. 265). Abandoning his "self to exces-sive suffering" narcotises the pain of rejection or loss (p. 265). In a sense, the neurotic person allevi-ates his pain "by acutely intensifying it" (p. 267). However, the aim of the masochistic person "is not suffering itself but a relinquishment of the self" (Horney, 1937, p. 280).

### 4.4.3   Drive towards oblivion
###         and devotion to a cause

It could be said that the masochistic attitude trans-forms deep feelings of insecurity and vulnerability into "a feeling of being in the power of others"

(Horney, 1937, p. 267). The common denominator in masochistic fantasies "is a feeling of being putty in the master's hand, of being devoid of all will, of all power, of being absolutely subjected to another's domination" (p. 274). Submergence in misery produces "satisfaction by losing the self in something greater, by dissolving the individu-ality, by getting rid of the self with its doubts" (Horney, 1937, p. 270). The dissolution of the self in the group may be satisfying because it is associ-ated with a suspension of anxiety. The satisfaction of breaking "through the shell of individuality" (p. 274) and losing oneself in something greater is evident in normal phenomena such as love and "enthusiasm for a cause" (p. 272). By sur-rendering our self to a cause, "we feel at one with a greater whole"; by losing our selves, we "can become at one with God or nature" (p. 273). By "dissolving the self in something greater, by becoming part of a greater entity", the individual overcomes his limitations and his sense of iso-lation (Horney, 1937, p. 273). Thus, in the inter-est of protection against anxiety, the self can be either abandoned or built up. In fact, masochistic strivings of self-dissolution are "are counter-acted by the neurotic's extreme emphasis on the uniqueness of his individuality" (p. 276). The "drive toward power and self-aggrandizement" is incompatible with the "drive toward obliv-ion", however both drives share the common aim of overcoming the "fears, limitations and isolations that are universal in human existence" (p. 276). Compromise solutions are possible, in that, for example, a neurotic person may "live in a helpless dependence and at the same time exert a tyranny over others by means of his weakness" (Horney, 1937, p. 277).

### 4.5   Summary

Many behaviour patterns communicating submission or asserting dominance are phy-logenetically ritualised facial and gestural expressions that may also involve vocalisations (prosodic aspects of language). Species-specific displays of offensive aggression (usually involv-ing vocalisations) act as punishment, making behaviours that precede the perception of these displays less likely to reoccur in similar situations. Social exclusion or rejection produce an aversive state, too (a derivative of the state of social isolation), and behaviour that precedes such state of affairs is similarly unlearned. Behaviour that is modified by aversive experience is goal-directed (appetitive) and *contextually guided*. Through aversive conditioning, the individual learns to maintain interpersonal and social conditions that are conducive to care-taking and care-giving (libidinal) interactions. Correspondingly, appetitive behaviour that, in responding to an interpersonal or social situation, is instrumental to overcoming the aversive state of social exclusion or unrelatedness (and creating a state of social or object relatedness) is reinforced. The sum of behaviours that move the individual from an anxiogenic situation (bearing the hallmarks of social exclusion or isolation) to secure conditions, in which one can readily engage another individual in libidinal (affectionate) dyadic interactions, is symbolised by the superego. Conditions or situations that are conducive to libidinal interactions refer to certain types of object relationships and, as the individual matures, certain types of relationships with the social world that capture the essence of secure object relationships. We enact role relationships with external objects that instate a derivative of our primary object relationship (Sandler, 1976; Feldman, 1997) and that, thereby, procure care and attention and overcome (or guard against) anxiety.

Superego function is mediated, to some extent, by imagery of disapproval or reprimand (punishment). As the superego develops, aversive experiences of being disapproved or reprimanded are memorised, so that they can be recalled (in imagination) in certain circumstances as *expectations* of disapproval or reprimand (punishment) (Rado, 1956). Expectation of punishment, that is, conscious imagery of punishment, may refer to an unconscious expectation of loss of conditions in which one can receive affection and care (and satisfy libidinal strivings) (Horney, 1937). Guilt (a form of anxiety) is specifically linked to the expectation of punishment or disapproval, rather than the experience of punishment or disapproval itself. Being associated with the experience of guilt or anxiety, expectation, in imagery, of disapproval (or punishment) discourages (inhibits) libidinal actions and, instead, facilitates defensive actions and behaviours that escape anxiety and that, thereby, reinstate conditions of interpersonal security.

If, according to Federn (1952), ego feeling or ego state were to refer to a state in which we fantasise the receipt of approval, then the superego state may be defined as that state in which we *imagine* disapproval. In other words, if, in the ego state, the receipt of approval is simulated and predicted, then superego state is that in which the receipt of disapproval is simulated and predicted. Behaviour guided by the superego state can become, through learning, habitual avoidance behaviour (which is not accompanied by anxiety), much like behaviour incentivised by ego states can become, through learning, habitual attention-seeking behaviour. Imagery associated with ego states, that is imagery of the "idealised self" (Horney, 1950), incentivises appetitive behaviour seeking to instate a favourable relationship or social situation (favourable, in that it enables the receipt of narcissistic supplies). We strive for approval and interpersonal security; and, as we do so, habitually or incentivised by idealising self-imagery, we are repeatedly frustrated and induced to offensively aggressive action by others striving for care and attention, too (and, hence, frustrating our pursuit of self-actualisation and infringing on securing interpersonal conditions we seek to maintain), as illustrated by the oedipal constellation. The task is to express offensive aggression (and to induce submission) so that our striving for conditions favourable to the receipt of approval is not undermined. The superego ensures that aggressive impulses are converted into actions that are consistent with our striving for security and approval (Bergler, 1952).

Our striving for approval and for interpersonal conditions or object relationships that favour the

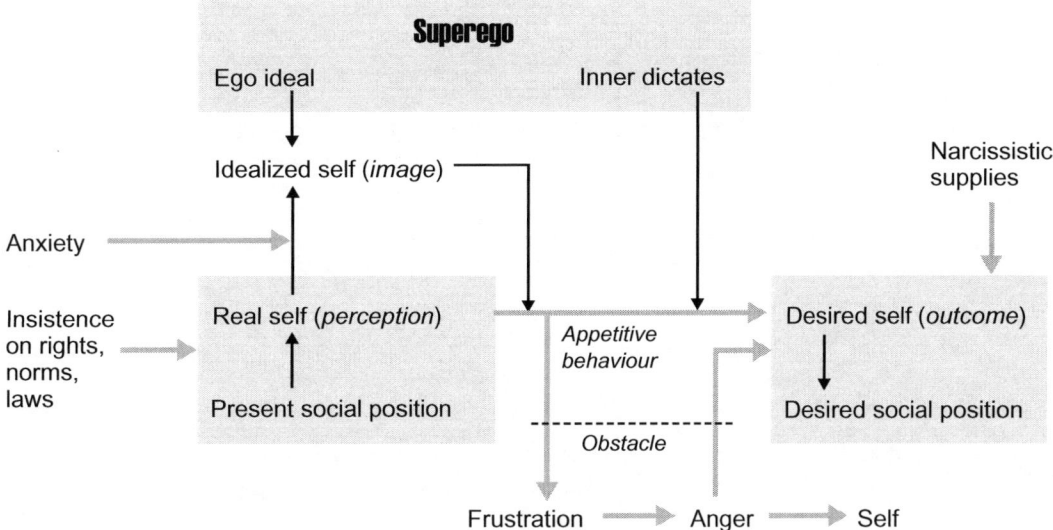

Figure 4-2. Imagination of the idealised self is an explication (incarnation) of the ego ideal and is, at the same time, connected to the experienced self that derives from (and thereby abstracts) the present social situation. The anticipatory image of the idealised self incentivises appetitive behaviour that, in accordance with inner dictates, actualises the idealised self and, thereby, creates a social situation (the desired outcome) in which the subject can be assured of narcissistic supplies and, hence, of protection and help from conspecifics. Frustration of appetitive self-actualisation could be due to excessive idealisation of the imagined self or self-deceptive perception of the real self. Frustration mobilises anger, which overcomes an obstacle on the path to self-actualisation or—if the situation reached prevents its externalisation onto an object—is directed against the self.

receipt of approval is linked to that part of the superego that is called ego ideal. The ego ideal is constituted from introjected objects with which the child identified in the oedipal period and beyond. If we consider the ego ideal to be an internal (unconscious) representation, then we can say that the "idealised self", which is experienced in imagination (Horney, 1950), is a reprojected ego ideal—"externalised" in imagery (Figure 4-2). The "idealised self" signifies a desired outcome in which narcissistic supplies are secure; and it serves—just like an incentive cue—to energise appetitive behaviour. Appetitive behaviour is concerned with turning the self—being a measure of the security of narcissistic supplies in the situation that the individual presently occupies—*into* the idealised (desired) self, thereby increasing the probability of libidinal interactions. To repeat, appetitive social behaviour is

concerned with "actualisation" or realisation of the person's idealised self. The starting point of self-actualisation can be a state of anxiety, in which the individual is deprived of narcissistic supplies and, hence, experiences a lack of protection and help (rendering the situation anxiogenic).[9] Appetitive behaviour, especially in its instrumental form, then transposes the individual from a state of anxiety to a situation in which the individual can receive not only protection and help but also affective signals meeting his narcissistic needs (Figure 4-2).

---

[9]The availability of narcissistic supplies, in the form of benevolent interest and affectionate signals expressed by conspecifics, is evolutionarily connected with the accessibility of help (help in meeting physiological needs) and protection (against predators and other sources of harm).

# CHAPTER FIVE

# Praise and acceptance

McDougall (1924) realised that several "instincts" contribute to social behaviour. The "mating instinct", leading to courtship and the act of union, is unlocked by the perception of sex characteristics in a member of the opposite sex. The "parental instinct" is most powerfully evoked by the cry of distress from the young, but can respond to the sight of any young and helpless creature. Emission of the cry of distress, in turn, is an expression of the "instinct of appeal" (McDougall, 1924). Approach to other members of the species may be brought about by the "gregarious instinct", the goal of which is "merely the near presence" of others (p. 154). Uneasiness and restlessness, and a craving to be back in the company of others, afflict the individual on his absence from the group (McDougall, 1924). According to Sullivan (1953), our recurrent "need for contact with others"—a need that is paralleled in gregarious animals—is often felt as "loneliness" and accompanied by a restlessness to bring about a situation that constitutes a relief from loneliness. The contact we seek, and actively solicit, is one that communicates to us a sense of relatedness, of being accepted. It is the desire for relatedness that is a major motivational force in human behaviour. Lack of relatedness to others and, earlier in development, absence or disappearance of the mother are sources of anxiety or distress—feelings that may be evolutionarily related to the anxiety that arises in places with an increased risk of predation or difficulty of detecting a predator. The infant uses proximity to the mother or relatedness to the mother as a secure "home base" to which he returns from exploratory ventures.

Kohut (1971) considered the child's need to be admired, a basic narcissistic need, as an important determinant of adult interpersonal interactions (a principle that is illustrated by the concept of "mirroring transference"). Positive attention (praise and appreciation) received from another individual is rewarding. We modulate another individual's attention and affective displays—through the *situationally appropriate* use of gesture and language—"in order to" attract reassuring or appraising eye contact, facial expressions, or vocalisations. Interaction between individuals by means of affectionate eye contact or facial expressions may correspond to mutual grooming (allogrooming) in other primates. Furthermore, gesture and language may be used to bring about a *situation* or atmosphere that *promotes* dyadic interactions by means of affectionate eye contact or gestural or tactile expressions. This is consistent with the notion that language may have evolved, in part, from vocalisations of separation distress. In social situations, we overcome anxiety due to unrelatedness or relative exclusion—essentially a form of separation distress—by creating a situation in which we *can* attract others' benevolent interest and caring attention. It is argued that, through language-based behaviour, the individual controls his social situation or position in order to escape social unrelatedness and move to a situation of interpersonal safety—equivalent to conditions under which the distressed (anxious) infant can receive again the mother's reassuring vocalisations and eye contact. Grooming interactions are actively sought, through language-based preparatory behaviour, when the subject operates from within a positive emotional state, whereas language-based safety-seeking behaviours are produced within, and would help to overcome, an aversive emotional state of social unrelatedness (which may be associated with anxiety). Although language-based solicitation of affectionate displays during dyadic interactions as well as language-based "escape" into the safety of social inclusion (relatedness) (Heidegger, 1927) can be regarded as forms of *preparatory* (appetitive) behaviour (and although the evolution of language may have accelerated due to the implication of language in context-sensitive preparatory behaviours, that is, in the seeking of positive attention or praise as well as the seeking of relatedness or acceptance), affectionate (grooming) interactions—representing forms of *consummatory* behaviour—may involve language, too.

Many social behaviours are automatically triggered by the perception of others' actions (Ferguson & Bargh, 2004). Verbal and gestural expressions are elicited more or less automatically by the perception of others' linguistic and affective motor patterns. Individuals involved in a conversation "prime" each others' linguistic representations, brining them close to the threshold at which they produce the encoded motor pattern, thus making it likely that "each

partner generates his utterances on the basis of what he has just heard from the other" (Garrod & Pickering, 2004, p. 9). Social behaviour during a conversation is concerned not only with priming each others' linguistic representations (and representations of affective expressions) but also with creating a situation in which affectively attuned interaction can take place. Conversation partners interactively align their "situation models", which are "multi-dimensional representations containing information about space, time, causality, intentionality and currently relevant individuals" (Garrod & Pickering, 2004, p. 8). Conversation partner may, for instance, align situation models derived from archaic parent-child interactions. Psychoanalysis posits that, when relating to each other, we recreate aspects of early object relations, especially with regard to the context they provided for the interplay of infantile care-soliciting and maternal care-giving signals. We solicit others' caring attitude and benevolent interest (without us being aware of this), and we replicate—in increasingly abstract forms—early conditions under which we securely received affectionate and soothing maternal signals. The unconscious striving to create and maintain conditions under which we receive praise and affection, or which assure us of our *potential* to receive praise and affection, is one of the principles that underpins social behaviour across the lifespan.

### 5.1  Infantile development

Social behaviour begins with the infant's affective attunement to the mother's (caregiver's) facial expressions. Face-to-face interactions emerge in the infant's development at approximately two months of age. Being disposed to gaze at faces, and especially at the eyes, the infant engages with his mother in periods of intense mutual gaze. In this process, infant and mother synchronise the intensity of their affective behaviour (Feldman, Greenbaum & Yirmiya, 1999). Mutually attuned, synchronised face-to-face interactions can be playful or exploratory; and, when the infant is anxious, they have a soothing effect.[1] An asynchrony in reciprocal facial communication, that is, the mother's failure to express appropriate soothing gestures in response to the infant's initially subtle distress signals, causes the infant to experience overt stress and anxiety—a state that is probably akin to separation distress in mammalian infants. While the mother's gaze at her infant is an aspect of her innate care-giving behaviour, the infant's striving to engage the mother in mutually attuned affective interactions is an early form of care-seeking behaviour. The infant tends to express his care-seeking behaviour especially at times of distress, pain, or anxiety; and it is the mother's affective response, evoked by the infant's care-seeking behaviour, that has the effect of soothing the infant's distress, pain, or anxiety (Bowlby, 1988).

The presence of the caregiver is experienced by the infant as soothing and her absence gives rise to anxiety. We are innately drawn to the primary caregiver's presence, and the same seems to be true for the caregiver's positive affective responsiveness. Similarly to the caregiver's presence, the caregiver's positive attitude and interest in her infant is evolutionarily linked to the satisfaction of the infant's physiological needs. Temporary unresponsiveness or disinterest of the caregiver can be a cause of anxiety, much as her absence can be anxiogenic. The infant learns to actively influence the caregiver's emotional state, similarly to how the infant learns to bring about the caregiver's presence through his appetitive behaviour. The child learns to control (through appetitive behaviour) the relationship with his primary object, and thus the conditions for the expression of instinctive behaviours and the satisfaction of physiological needs, on increasingly abstract levels, reflecting the inherent complexity of the social environment into which he is born. Our relationship with the primary caregiver remains the blueprint for our engagement with others and groups later in life. Not only do we employ appetitive behaviour to establish and maintain object relationships, that is, relationships in which we unconsciously seek to reexperience the object's devotion and availability, but we do so while fending off competitors for the object's attention, thereby reexperiencing the dilemmas of the Oedipus complex.

### 5.1.1   Perceptual propensities

The functional specialisation of the human brain for language and face perception does not arise from passive unfolding of an innate maturational sequence but requires a process of development that is critically shaped by postnatal experience. Attentional biases guide the way in which the infant's environment shapes functional brain development after birth (Johnson, 2001). Infants are born with a bias to preferentially track and fixate stimuli with face-like configurations (Johnson, Dziurawiec, Ellis & Morton, 1991; Valenza, Simion, Cassia & Umilta, 1996).[2] Although these stimuli initially lack meaning for the infant, innate perceptual propensities guide learning and ensure that the developing brain receives more input from social aspects of the environment (Johnson, 2001). Infants reveal their innate preference for complex and face-like stimuli by smiling at these stimuli. Reviewing the evidence available at the time, Schecter (1973) concluded that "the infant is equipped innately with the capacity for a smiling response, a capacity that is evoked by a set of key releaser stimulus configurations, such as the human face gestalt, which become effective at certain phases of development" (p. 22). Preferential orienting to face-like stimuli declines during

---

[1] With the emphasis in early development on affective attunement between mother and infant by way of gaze and facial expressions, it is not a surprise that the right hemisphere, which is specialised for the perception of visual and auditory (nonverbal) affective signals and for the facial and vocal expression of affective states (including prosody of voice), has an early developmental advantage.

[2] Neonates are also able to discriminate their mother's face from that of a stranger (Field, Cohen, Garcia & Greenberg, 1984).

the second month of life (Johnson, Dziurawiec, Ellis & Morton, 1991).

Four-months-old infants visually fixate smiling faces in preference to neutral or angry facial expressions (La Barbera, Izard, Vietze & Parisi, 1976). Humans have an innate capacity to recognise not only the basic layout of the face but also "the most fundamental and important facial movements" (Hass, 1968, p. 119). The raising or lowering of the corners of the mouth, for instance, is an innate "expressive movement" ("Ausdrucksbewegung") that acts "as an indication of mood" (Hass, 1968, p. 117)—an indication that, owing to innate perceptual schemas, is understood by conspecifics. Gergely (2001) suggested that, during the first three months of life, infants prefer to interact with objects that behave in a manner that is perfectly contingent on their actions (that is, they prefer perfectly response-contingent stimulation). Around three months of age, infants' exploration preference switches to objects that give imperfectly contingent responses (Gergely, 2001). These are essentially reactive social objects giving affective responses. Gergely (2001) hypothesised that the switching from one contingency preference to another does not take place in autism. Autistic children would continue to prefer perfectly response-contingent stimulation, while in normal children preference for imperfect response contingencies becomes a stepping stone for further social development.

### 5.1.2    Affect mirroring and synchronisation

Newborns are predisposed to express certain emotional states (affects) by facial expressions, vocalisations, and gestures (Izard, 1994). Affects, as stated by Kernberg (1996), "always include a cognitive component, a subjective experience of a highly pleasurable or unpleasurable nature, neurovegetative discharge phenomena, psychomotor activation, and, very crucially, a distinctive pattern of facial expression" (p. 127). Patterns of facial expression associated with affects originally served "a communicative function directed to the caregiver"

(p. 127). Affects have evolved (i) as a way for the mammalian infant to signal dependency and emergency needs to its mother and (ii) as a complementary way for the mammalian mother to respond to the infant's affective signals with appropriate nurturing and protective behaviours (Krause, 1988, as discussed in Kernberg, 1996). Communication is based on innate (that is, phylogenetically ritualised) expressive movements and coevolved innate recognition mechanisms (Lorenz, 1935; Moynihan, 1998). Perhaps, most social actions are constructed around innate expressive movements that have evolved to elicit states of mood in others. This would also form part of the basis on which language evolved.

> In conversation, the face of the listener often echoes what the other person is saying. If the latter says something serious, the listener grows serious; if he speaks of a surprise, the listener performs a facial movement conveying the same. (Hass, 1968, p. 118)

Short face-to-face interactions between mother and infant emerge around the age of two months. During face-to-face interactions, infant and mother attune to each other's affective expressions, that is, they synchronise their affective behaviour (Feldman, Greenbaum & Yirmiya, 1999). At times, the infant will be in distress and synchrony will be disrupted; however the mother usually reattunes her affective expressions to allow the infant to recover from distress. These synchronised interactions between maternal and infant affective states are crucial for the infant's further social development and emergence of self-control (Feldman et al., 1999). Schecter (1973) discussed evidence suggesting that "one can reinforce the infant's smiling response by responding to his smile with a smile or tend to extinguish the smile by failing to respond to it" (p. 23). Similarly, "an infant's vocalisations can be markedly increased by the adult's social responsiveness" (p. 23). The patterned social stimulations provided by a responsive mother or other significant person determine the development of the infant's social responsiveness.

> It is this responsiveness—reciprocal, sensitive, sometimes imitative, familiar in pattern, but sparked with novel variation—that characterizes human relatedness increasingly from the first months onwards. By six to seven months, the infant who is being enjoyed by his parents spends a good part of his day in social interactions involving mutual regard (sometimes with intense eye to eye contact), mutual smiling, and vocalisations, with or without tactile and kinaesthetic stimulations, modalities combined in various forms. (Schecter, 1973, p. 23)

An inborn tendency to imitate affective expressions would enable the infant to reexperience emotional states of the caregiver. Lier (1988) suggested that the infant's inborn capacity of imitation (affective mirroring) needs to be supported and patterned by his mother's affective responses. This allows the infant to develop a basic pattern of social relating by two to three months. If the mother does not support her infant's early attempts to imitate her affective responses, then, at this stage, the infant may fail to develop skills of social contact. Infants with simple social privation may not engage in vocal interaction and may avoid eye contact (Lier, 1988). Legerstee and Varghese (2001) confirmed that the infant's attention to his mother and his positive behaviours towards her, such as smiling and vocalisations, around the age of three months depend on the mother's responsiveness and degree of affect mirroring. Importantly, for the mother, eye-to-eye contact with her infant and reception of his smile are innately rewarding (Eibl-Eibesfeldt, 1970).

## Macaques

Machado and Bachevalier (2003) emphasised the similarities between macaques and humans in emotional and social development. In the first few postnatal weeks, macaque infants remain in close physical contact and establish frequent face-to-face interactions (mostly lip-smacking) with their mothers. In the first weeks, macaque infants spend considerable time watching other individuals interact at a distance. They quickly develop an appreciation of the meaning of social signals, such as direct eye contact. Already by the middle of the second postnatal week, infants show gaze aversion to another individual's direct stare. Between the fourth and sixths weeks, infants start to leave their mother's secure base for exploration of their physical and social environment. In the second month, infants begin to initiate grooming with their mother (reviewed in Machado & Bachevalier, 2003).

### 5.1.3   Intersubjective relatedness

Between the seventh and ninth months of life, human infants develop a sense of "subjective self" based on "intersubjective relatedness" between infant and mother. "Intersubjective relatedness" entails "the creation of mutually held mental states" ("the joining of subjective psychic experience") (Stern, 1985, p. 127)—a joining that is actively (appetitively) sought. Intersubjective relatedness between self and an other rests on capacities of (i) sharing a focus of attention with the other, (ii) sharing affective states, and (iii) attributing intentions and motives to the other (Stern, 1985). The sharing of affective states ("affect attunement") "is the most pervasive and clinically germaine feature of intersubjective relatedness" (p. 138). Affect attunement with their mother allows infants to recast their situation and shift the focus of attention to what is important. When infants encounter a novel or uncertain situation, "they look towards mother to read her face for its affective content, essentially to see what they should feel, to get a second appraisal to help resolve their uncertainty" (p. 132). Attunements "occur largely out of awareness and almost automatically" (p. 145). Affect attunement "is the performance of behaviors that express the quality of a shared affect state without imitating the exact behavioral expression of the inner state" (Stern, 1985, p. 142). Affect attunement may be mediated less by imitation and more by mutual induction of innate "expressive movements" (which act as releasing "stimulus situations" for the other's affective displays).

> For there to be an intersubjective exchange about affect, then, strict imitation alone won't do. In fact, several processes must take place. First, the parent must be able to read the infant's feeling state from the infant's overt behaviour. Second, the parent must perform some behavior that is not a strict imitation but nonetheless corresponds in some way to the infant's overt behavior. Third, the infant must be able to read this corresponding parental response as having to do with the infant's own original feeling experience and not just imitating the infant's behavior. (Stern, 1985, p. 139)

Affect attunement is a continuous process extending over some time; the experience of connectedness, of being in attunement with another, "feels like an unbroken line" (Stern, 1985, p. 157). Attunement, it could be added, unites interpersonal events and experiences under the umbrella of an interpersonal situation that extends along a temporal dimension. It therefore helps to generate the context within which instinctive expressions (displays) can be exchanged between partners.

### 5.1.4   Tenderness and play

Playfulness "constitutes a remarkably easy vehicle for the mutual exchange of affectionate and exuberant affects" (Schecter, 1973, p. 24). Social reciprocity in playful interactions allow the infant to learn that he can evoke a social response even at times when his physiological needs are satisfied. The infant's realisation that he can evoke playful patterns of response from significant others leads to the development of a "sense of social potency". The infant's confidence that he can produce a social response is internalised as self-esteem. It is this sense of social potency

or self-esteem that prepares the infant for separations from his mother without undue anxiety. The initially omnipotent sense of potency has to be frequently frustrated so that the child can acquire a "sense of the realistic limits of his powers" and learn about "the differentiation of his self and the other" (Schecter, 1973, p. 26).

> Toward the end of the first year and during the second year, the child develops the capacity to mentally ("internally") *represent* his mother when she is absent from the perceptual field and endows this representation with qualities of increasing permanence and objectivity. ... The toddler has made mere beginnings in recognizing that mother and others have feelings, wishes, and intentions that are separate and different from his own; for many of us this achievement may involve a lifetime struggle. (Schecter, 1973, p. 27)

Schecter (1973) argued that reciprocal social stimulation and responsiveness during early social play provides a basis for the formation of the infant's *emotional attachment* to his mother. Moreover, reciprocal social stimulation and responsiveness in early life has important consequences for the adult's capacity to form enduring, mutually satisfying relationships. Early reciprocal stimulation is one of "the precursors to all human communication"; mutual playfulness "prepares the individual and group for communication, language, and collaboration" (Schecter, 1973, p. 25). Tenderness (tender behaviour) between mother and child "facilitates mutual satisfaction" (Chrzanowski, 1973, p. 140). Mutual praise and displays of affection in adult dyadic encounters may be equally satisfying or rewarding. The "pursuit of satisfaction and security" is one of the "basic motivational forces in interpersonal situations" (p. 142). Although we are innately disposed to express tenderness or engage in tender or loving interactions, we can do so only in "a relatively anxiety-low atmosphere" (Chrzanowski, 1973, p. 140). If anxiety prevails, the motivational emphasis may shift from affectionate to defensive and safety-seeking behaviours ("security operations" (Sullivan, 1953))—behaviours that are designed to improve self-esteem (Figure 5-1).

## 5.1.5   Attention seeking

Infants of about two months of age react emotionally to attention directed to them. Eye contact elicits smile, but still-faced or noncontingent gaze directed at them causes distress in infants. By around four months of age, infants make attempts to attract others' attention to them (i.e., "calling" when attention is absent). After the middle of their first year of age, infants perform actions such as "showing off", "clever actions", "clowning", and "teasing" in order to attract others' positive attention (such as praise or laughter) (reviewed in Reddy, 2003). In infants from three months of age, attention can be cued to a peripheral object by the direction of eye gaze of an opposite face (reviewed in Johnson, 2001). Having become able to follow others' attention to objects or events in the world, infants from about the age of twelve to fourteen months attempt to actively direct others' attention to the world (reviewed in Reddy, 2003). Reddy (2003) concluded that "what appears to be developing is an awareness of the objects to which

other's attention can be directed: the first of these is the self, followed by what the self does, then what the self perceives, and then what the self remembers". Being an object of others' attention is what lies at the heart of one's self-awareness. Reddy (2003) pointed out that "before the infant has a conception of him or herself, he or she is aware of being an object to others".

James (1890) thought that instincts drive us not only to be in sight of our fellows but also to be recognised by them favourably. He noted, "we have an innate propensity to get ourselves noticed, and noticed favourably, by our kind" (p. 293). "Social self-seeking", which refers to behaviour patterns directed at attracting others' positive notice and inducing their admiration, is the "outcome of simple instinctive propensity" (James, 1890, p. 320). Being outside others' range of attention or not being regarded by them positively becomes a state imbued with anxiety. Our disposition to seek others' attention and positive regard reflects some kind of "place preference" for a class of situations in which basic drives that maintain our existence can expect to find satisfaction. With greater developmental maturity, anxiety-driven or habitual (affectively neutralised) behaviour may be concerned with creating more abstract replicas of the mother-

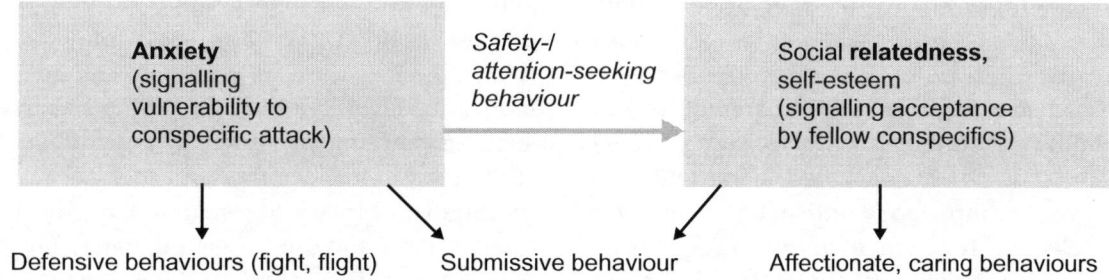

Figure 5-1.   Proposed relationship between anxiety and affectionate interactions: Ingratiating, infantile, affectionate behaviours, serving a communicative function, are more likely to be employed in an atmosphere of social relatedness or acceptance—an atmosphere that can be seen as essential characteristic of the situation towards which the individual learns to move in an appetitive (goal-directed) fashion. Defensive responses to external stimulus situations, by contrast, tend to occur under conditions of anxiety. Submissive patterns evolved as ritualized versions of flight behaviour but also contain aspects of care-soliciting behaviour, namely infantilisms.

infant relationship, providing the context within which affiliative and other drives are *reliably* satisfied. Our ability or confidence to engage in affiliative interactions depends on the absence of anxiety. The set of conditions we seek to impose on our social environment in an attempt to calm existential anxiety changes with personality development, inasmuch as the social context within which we attain and maintain a state of *predictable* satisfaction of needs becomes ever more complex.

### 5.1.6  Autism

Autistic children cannot recognise the emotional or contextual meaning of facial expressions, gestures, and nonverbal vocalisations, although they have no general problem with perception (Hobson, 1986). A specific problem in orienting towards human stimuli may be the primary behavioural manifestation of the pathological process in autism spectrum disorders (Maestro *et al.*, 2002). Retrospectively viewing home movies, Maestro *et al.* (2002) found that, during the first six months of life, behaviours such as looking at people, orienting towards people, smiling at people, and vocalising towards people were significantly reduced in children who were later diagnosed as autistic. These children were also less likely to seek contact, anticipate another person's aim, or engage in explorative activity. On the other hand, there was no difference between the autistic and control groups in behaviours such as orienting towards inanimate objects and smiling at such objects (Maestro *et al.*, 2002). Maestro *et al.* (2002) concluded that attention is not generally impaired in autism but is impaired as a selective function towards social stimuli. Other evidence shows that autistic children are slower in establishing a focus of visual attention (Harris *et al.*, 1999), show weaker gaze engagement with targets (van der Geest *et al.*, 2001), and make more frequent saccadic eye movements (in passive viewing tasks) (Kemner *et al.*, 1998). Structural abnormalities in the cerebellum reported in autistic patients (Couchesne *et al.*,

2001; Kemper & Bauman, 1998) have been associated with deficits in orienting to visual cues (Harries *et al.*, 1999; Townsend *et al.*, 1999). Autism has also been associated with a more part-orientated as opposed to gestalt-orientated bias in perception (that is, a fundamental deficit in the capacity of holistic processing of sensory information) (Frith & Happe, 1994; Shah & Frith, 1983). Abnormalities in visual attention or perception may cause social deficits by depriving infants of opportunities to learn about the relationship between their caregiver's emotional expressions and their own emotional states. Lack of imitative interaction, possibly secondary to constitutional deficits in infants' abilities to perceive facial expressions or orient towards faces (especially eyes), contributes to autistic development, as suggested by observations that systematic exposure to imitative interaction later in life can improve social deficits (Escalona, Field, Nadel & Lundy, 2002; Field, Sanders & Nadel, 2001).

Deficits in joint attention and pretend play in children with autism become apparent only after the age of twelve months. In a prospective study, Baron-Cohen, Allen, and Gillberg (1992) found that the presence of at least two of the following behavioural deficits at the age of eighteen months predicted a later diagnosis of autism (at reassessment at thirty months): deficits in joint attention, protodeclarative pointing, social interest, pretend play, and social play. Despite their abnormalities in social interaction and failure to develop attention-sharing behaviours such as pointing or showing, autistic children still attend to their mother and seek her proximity (Sigman, Mundy, Sherman & Ungerer, 1986). Their normal proximity-seeking behaviour suggested that autistic children do become attached to their mothers (Dissanayake & Crossley, 1996; Rogers, Ozonoff & Maslin-Cole, 1991). They may feel secure in the presence of their caregiver or even become positively attached to her. Autistic children still depend on their caregiver for satisfaction of their basic needs. They are, however, better at expressing their needs than at engaging in eye contact or sharing attention to other stimuli (Mundy, Kasari & Sigman, 1992).

## Theory of mind

"Theory of mind" refers to an individual's cognitive ability to understand or "represent" other peoples' states of mind, especially their beliefs and intentions. Lack in "theory of mind" is thought to be the core psychological deficit in autism (Baron-Cohen, Leslie & Frith, 1985). It would explain the failure by individuals with autism to appreciate social situations and understand social communications, in general. However, autistic children's difficulties in relating to others arise well before the development of cognitive abilities necessary to pass "theory of mind" tasks (Klin & Volkmar, 1993). Hobson (1986) thought that a difficulty in recognising others' emotional states is the primary psychological deficit in autism that explains the unfolding clinical picture. "Theory-of-mind" deficits may arise at a later stage and are therefore unlikely to be central to the psychopathology of childhood autism. The emerging consensus seems to be that "theory-of-mind" skills develop from infants' earlier abilities to attend to human faces and language and respond to affective expressions (Tager-Flusberg, Joseph & Folstein, 2001). Performance on "theory-of-mind" tasks also depends on verbal skills and general cognitive abilities (Meins *et al.*, 2002; Sparrevohn & Howie, 1995), and was shown to be influenced by the way in which mothers commented on their children's mental state at an earlier stage of development (at age six months) (Meins *et al.*, 2002). Thus, "theory-of-mind" tasks may be sensitive for autism but they are not specific, and may be progressively less so with increasing mental retardation.

### 5.1.7  Attachment

The infant is helpless and dependent on others for nourishment and protection. Hence, the infant has an innate need to maintain proximity to others, especially his mother (Bowlby, 1977,

1988). Emotional attachment to a caregiver allows the infant not only to obtain nourishment and protection but also to receive stimulation for further cognitive and social development (Bowlby, 1977, 1988). Anxiety increases the infant's need to maintain proximity and to elicit parental behaviours. Separation from the caregiver causes distress. Reunion with the caregiver after separation is reassuring, resolves anxiety, and invokes a pleasant affect. Emotional attachment to the mothering figure is evident when the infant, by the seventh or eighth month, shows "clear differential responses to mother as against others in being held or soothed, in being played with or simply approached" (Schecter, 1973, p. 25). The intensity of attachment can be measured by the infant's protest response (crying) to the mother's leaving (separation distress). By seven or eight months, the infant's protesting at the disappearance of social stimulation ceases to be related nonspecifically to any social partner but "appears to be related to a specific attachment to one or more persons" (p. 28). The constancy of the attachment to the mother is revealed by the fact "that she usually continues to be preferred and sought after though she may be a source of frustration, disappointment, and even cruelty" (Schecter, 1973, p. 26).

There are several aspects of parental behaviour that critically contribute to the infant's secure attachment and normal personality development. First, the mother is innately responsive to the infant's care-seeking behaviour and separation distress. The mother's attraction to her infant is "motivated by the parental care drive" (Eibl-Eibesfeldt, 1970, p. 120). Parental (care-giving) behaviour has evolved to be complementary to the child's care-seeking and attachment behaviour (Bowlby, 1977). Second, "a certain amount of hostile control", exerted by the caregiver, is required to "assure normal socialization" of the child (Benjamin, 1996, p. 188). Hostile control in the form of blaming or ignoring is highly aversive to the child, ensuring that the child learns to "behave in ways that will help avoid" experiences of being blamed or ignored (Benjamin, 1996,

p. 188). Third, the caregiver provides the child with a secure base from which to explore his environment. The child's innate exploratory behaviour alternates with attachment behaviour. The task of the caregiver is to permit or encourage the child's exploratory behaviour and to actively intervene whenever the child "heads for trouble" (Bowlby, 1977). The child has a need for independence that gets stronger as he gets older. Secure attachment to the caregiver is a prerequisite for the child's ability to periodically separate from the caregiver and find opportunities to develop his competence and independence. Anxiety (insecurity) causes renewed seeking of contact with the attachment object, which, if successful, renews the child's security (Benjamin, 1996). If attachment is not secure, the child tends to remain close to the attachment object, fearing that his attachment object will be lost and cannot be recovered. Thus, insecure attachment restricts the child's opportunities for acquiring independent coping skills and social competence.

### 5.1.8    Psychic proximity

The infant's propensity to form attachments "provides the organizing template for personality" (Benjamin, 1996, p. 213). Personality development involves the copying of attachment objects in order "to create internal working models of the attachment relationships" (p. 213). The child develops an "internal working model" or "internalised representation" of the primary caregiver (attachment object) in three different ways: (i) imitation of the caregiver's behaviour, (ii) recapitulation of the caregiver's behaviour when the caregiver is absent, and (iii) "introjection". "Introjection" is evident "when the child treats him/herself as did the attachment object" (Benjamin, 1996, p. 185). The "internalised representation" of the attachment object (or "internalised representation" of the attachment relationship) allows the child to establish "psychic proximity" to the attachment object at times of anxiety. Benjamin (1996) thought that the child, and later the

adult, can bring about "psychic proximity" by activating this "internalised representation", that is, by (i) acting like the internalised attachment object, (ii) acting as if the internalised attachment object were present, or (iii) treating the self as would the internalised attachment object. In other words, behaving "as you did with the attachment object" evokes "psychic proximity" (p. 214). Again, anxiety increases the need to seek or maintain "psychic proximity". Similarly to the effects of proximity after physical separation from the mother, "psychic proximity is reassuring and invokes pleasant affects and cognitions" (p. 189). Through "psychic proximity", the child, and later the adult, can simulate conditions for receiving love from derivatives of early attachment objects. Concurrently, whenever soliciting love in this way, the child, and later the adult, has to avoid rejection by, or attack from, the internalised representatives of early attachment objects (Benjamin, 1996). Avoidance of rejection or attack may be ensured precisely by reproduction of previously approved behaviour, that is, by activation of "internal working models".

## 5.2    Solicitation of approval

Persons obtain gratification by means of receiving love, praise, admiration, and approval from the "dominant other"—a symbolic representation of the primary love object (mother) (Arieti, 1973). The need for approval and love from the "dominant other" requires constant replenishing. Insofar as people *seek* to obtain gratification in the form of praise, admiration, or approval, the neurobiological mechanisms underpinning the performance and learning of these aspects of social behaviour ought to be related to mechanisms supporting other forms of appetitive (reward-seeking) behaviour and reinforcement learning. Appetitive striving for approval or affection (care-seeking behaviour) may take subtle forms; we control how persons around us perceive us by adjusting our gestures, our bodily postures, or our verbalisations (usually in accordance with social norms and expectations)—without necessarily interacting directly with those by whom we want to be approved. Approval- or attention seeking behaviours in adulthood are not randomly directed; not uncharacteristically, we seek to be "treated kindly by a person who is powerful and influential" (Horney, 1937, p. 110), although we tend to be unaware of such directedness. Arieti's (1973) notion of need for approval and praise from the "dominant other" is relevant to understanding the motivation of belonging to a social group. The need for approval may be transferred onto the leader of the group to which one belongs or onto an abstract leader of an abstract social constellation with which one identifies. We unconsciously equate the leader of a group with our primary love object, so that parts of social behaviour in adulthood are determined by efforts to reestablish, in unconscious phantasy, attachment to the primary object (as a prerequisite for receiving caring interest from the primary object). Burrow (1949) stated that "the infant organism's primary identification with the mother-organism" sets "a pattern that remains dominant throughout the development" of the individual, in that it "carries through life the biological impress of [the individual's] intraorganismic identity with the mother" (p. 321).

Individuals build up a set of mental representations (templates) of how their caregivers have responded to their care-seeking behaviour. These "internal working models" (Bowlby, 1988) or "internal representational models of experience in relationship" (Heard & Lake, 1986) can be used as predictors and guides for care-seeking behaviour. Past experiences in relationships and predictions concerning further enactments of care-seeking behaviour are coded within the self (McCluskey, 2002). The attention we believe we receive, or ought to receive, from significant others or social formations that have taken on the function of the primary love object importantly contribute to our self-image. As we are for "ever foraging for images of security that are purely fanciful" (Burrow, 1949, p. 217), we form "a sense of 'I'—the social image of separateness, of distinction, of private or personal importance" (p. 223). Bowlby

(1988) recognised that attachment behaviour continues throughout life, resurging especially under circumstances of anxiety, distress, fear, loss, or illness. If attachment behaviour, that is, care-seeking behaviour, fails to reach its objective, that is, if conditions conducive to the receipt of care and love cannot be induced, then pain or anxiety arises, which, in turn, may further energise care-seeking behaviours, especially anxious care-seeking behaviours ("attention-seeking behaviours"). The pain or distress experienced when care-seeking behaviours fail is likely related to infantile separation distress. Failure to effectively solicit care or "attention" not only produces distress and invigorates care-seeking behaviours but also promotes "self-defensive behaviours and interactions" (McCluskey, 2002).

> If the careseeker fails to have his or her careseeking needs met, the behavioral patterns that accompany careseeking cannot shut down and the system for careseeking is infiltrated by the activation of the personal defense system. In this way careseeking is then expressed by whatever behaviors have been found to evoke in the caregiver responses that assuage the pain of not reaching careseeking goals. (McCluskey, 2002, p. 133)

### 5.2.1  Infantilisms

> The cherishing behaviour patterns of parental care have their natural counterpart in the signals which release them, which have been taken over into the repertoire of contact-making and aggression-inhibiting behaviour patterns as "infantile appeals". (Eibl-Eibesfeldt, 1970, p. 148)

Infantile behaviours displayed by young animals are designed to elicit the mother's caring (cherishing) behaviour. In mammals and birds, "the young of the species transmit signals which release cherishing behaviour" (Eibl-Eibesfeldt, 1970, p. 120). Adult animals display infantile behaviour patterns "whenever the aim is to release appeasement and cherishing" behaviour in a conspecific (p. 113). Humans who seek to elicit affectionate behaviour "relapse quite involuntarily into the role of a small child" (Eibl-Eibesfeldt, 1970, p. 148). Culturally or phylogenetically ritualised displays of helplessness release the impulse to cherish the person displaying these patterns, much as an infant's display of genuine helplessness releases the mother's caregiving behaviour.

Most bond-establishing rites are derived from the field of parental care. In courtship, animals display phylogenetically ritualised behaviour patterns that are modified infantilisms and actions derived from parental cherishing behaviour (Eibl-Eibesfeldt, 1970). Parental cherishing behaviour includes protective behaviour towards the infant, such as the fetching back the infant if it goes too far away during its explorative forays. Coy behaviour is ritualised flight behaviour signalling an invitation to pursuit in the mating foreplay.[3] Young animals use contact calls to establish contact with their mothers; and it is again interesting to note that adult male hamsters and squirrels emit the contact call of the young when pursuing a female in courtship. Adult female deer do the same when attracting a buck (Eibl-Eibesfeldt, 1970). Begging behaviour of young animals elicits a feeding response from their parents. Begging behaviours of young animals have, in many species of birds, evolved into ritualised appeasement gestures and expressions of affection (Eibl-Eibesfeldt, 1970). Many courtship behaviours in birds are derived from the begging of the young animal. For instance, "fluttering of the young bird begging for food has been ritualized into a courtship movement" (p. 111). In anthropoid apes (gorilla, chimpanzee, orang-utan) and some human cultures, mothers feed their children with premasticated food. Ritualised feeding behaviour has an appeasing and bond-strengthening effect. Kissing is a

ritualised feeding gesture used by humans and chimpanzees during courtship or when greeting each other. Offerings of food or drink are ritualised feeding behaviours, too. They, too, have an appeasing and bond-strengthening effect. Sharing food and eating together forms part of many bond-forming cultural rituals (Eibl-Eibesfeldt, 1970).

> Even the individualized relationship— love—evolved primarily from the parental care relationship. ... The roots of love are not in sexuality, although love makes use of it for the secondary strengthening of the bond. (Eibl-Eibesfeldt, 1970, pp. 124–125)

Social grooming is derived from parental care behaviour. Caressing is a ritualised derivative of the mother's grooming of her infant (Eibl-Eibesfeldt, 1970). Like ritualised feeding behaviour, social grooming has an appeasing and bond-strengthening effect. Ritualised social grooming serves to maintain friendly relationships. In many cases, social grooming behaviours have been ritualised into pure gestures. Cover and protection offered by conspecifics is "one of the roots of the urge of contact" (p. 118). Seeking and granting contact have the function of seeking and granting reassurance, respectively. Extending our hand and placing it on a hand held out to us are gestures of seeking or granting contact that are derived from parent-child interactions (Eibl-Eibesfeldt, 1970). Other gestures of granting contact are patting and embracing. The embrace, originally a protective action on part of the mother towards her infant, has been ritualised into a social gesture of comforting and greeting. Gestures of feeding or granting contact can be expressed verbally in a highly ritualised form (such as the giving of good wishes or the declaration of interest and sympathy). Conversation provides an important medium for bond-forming rituals in humans. Stereotypes conveying protective assurances and soothing remarks are part of affectionate conversations (Eibl-Eibesfeldt, 1970).

---

[3]Embarrassment in humans is ritualised hiding movement (Eibl-Eibesfeldt, 1970).

### 5.2.2   Narcissistic needs

> The small child loses self-esteem when he loses love and attains it when he regains love. That is what makes children *educable*. They need supplies of affection so badly that they are ready to renounce other satisfactions if rewards of affection are promised or if withdrawal of affection is threatened. The promise of necessary narcissistic supplies of affection under the condition of obedience and the threat of withdrawal of these supplies if the conditions are not fulfilled are the weapons of any authority … (Fenichel, 1946, p. 41)

Narcissistic supplies are needed in order to maintain self-esteem (Fenichel, 1946). Narcissistic needs "compel the child to ask for affection" (p. 41). Children may procure essential narcissistic supplies, that is, supplies of affection and approval, "by force", or they seek to obtain them "by submissiveness and demonstration of suffering" (Fenichel, 1946, p. 41). Narcissistic supplies are accessible under certain conditions. The child learns to create and maintain these conditions; much of social behaviour can be understood in this way. The need to maintain conditions favourable to receiving narcissistic supplies leads to the differentiation of ego and superego. Fulfilment of ideals ("ego ideal"), that is, obedience, adherence to parental demands, and fulfilment of parental expectations, raises self-esteem insofar as it creates conditions conducive to receiving narcissistic supplies. Developing their superego, children become less dependent on narcissistic supplies "from the outside" (Fenichel, 1946, p. 41). To say that the superego provides narcissistic supplies to the ego internally is equivalent to stating that appetitive social behaviour has become *less obviously* or directly, but not less effectively, concerned with the attraction of narcissistic supplies (in the form of approval and affection). Through behaviour conceptualised as superego function, we move across time and space to a type of situation in which we are likely to receive praise and affection, even though we or others do not suspect that praise and affection are what motivates our behaviour.

> The superego is the heir of the parents not only as a source of threats and punishments but also as a source of protection and as a provider of reassuring love. Being on good or bad terms with one's superego becomes as important as being on good or bad terms with one's parents previously was. … Self-esteem is no longer regulated by approval or rejection by external objects, but rather by the feeling of having done or not having done the right thing. (Fenichel, 1946, pp. 105–106)

### 5.2.3   Selfobjects

> We would infer that I need something from the milieu around me, a response to me of a particular kind, in order to experience a sense of well-being. (Wolf, 1988, p. 14)

Self and identity "are not facts about people; they are technical ways of thinking about people; and they have become ways in which many people think about themselves"; they include "an idea one has about one's being, a way of organizing and giving more meaning to one's subjectivity, a conception of continuity based on recognition or familiarity" (Schafer, 1976, p. 189). The self is an ambiguous term; it fosters "illusions of natural, rightful, and conscious unity of being" (p. 190). Nevertheless, "many people use self to refer essentially to ideas they do not experience as threatening" (Schafer, 1976, p. 190). These ideas may include an awareness of the positive attentions or appraisals one attracts, or has the *potential* to attract, from others in the social environment. The self, according to Sullivan (1953), consists of reflected appraisals from significant others. The child sees himself, and feels about himself, as his parents see and feel about him. The child's self-esteem is "connected with his capacity to avoid doing what the parents do not want him to do" as well as "with his capacity to do what his parents want him to do" (Arieti, 1970, p. 21).

The self has been conceptualised as a narcissistic structure (Kohut, 1971). Interaction with important others (objects) provides so-called selfobject experiences that evoke and sustain the sense of self and enhance the individual's self-esteem. "Being heard and responded to" are such selfobject experiences "performed for the self by objects" (Wolf, 1988, p. 26). The template for all selfobject experiences is that of the infant "sensing the mother's active and benevolent interest in him or her" (pp. 14–15). Importantly, an individual's social role or possessions can perform a selfobject function (Wolf, 1988), possibly insofar as they enhance the *probability* of receiving approval or care from others. The self "feeds" on selfobject experiences, but it may do so in a self-deceiving manner. Self-deception is an important contributor to "resistance" in psychoanalytic therapy (Schafer, 1976). An emotional "state that is most unpleasant" arises if one feels "unresponded to, disconnected from one's surroundings" (Wolf, 1988, p. 27). High anxiety and imminent "self-fragmentation" may bring about desperate attempts to provoke the environment into supplying selfobject experiences, such as bragging or arrogance, which may lead to antagonistic reverberations that worsen the individual's anxiety and suffering (Wolf, 1988) (Figure 2-5).

> If a person is to feel well—to feel good about himself, with a secure sense of self, enjoying good self-esteem and functioning smoothly and harmoniously without undue anxiety and depression—he must experience himself consciously or unconsciously as surrounded by the responsiveness of others. The mode of this responsiveness varies from simple to complex and changes age-appropriately. Archaic modes are characterised by the need for the ministering physical presence of caregiving others; in maturely ripened modes, the needs for selfobject responsiveness are often highly complex and can be met by symbolic representatives supplied by and characteristic of the general culture. (Wolf, 1988, p. 39)

Kohut envisaged the self as a bipolar structure: from the "pole of ambitions" we seek "mirroring selfobject experiences" that meet our need to feel *recognised* and *accepted*, while from the "pole of values and ideals" we seek "idealising selfobject experiences" (reviewed in Wolf, 1988). With regard to the former, we cast others into the role of an accepting or admiring audience ("mirror transference"). We elicit "mirroring selfobject experiences" from those with whom we interact and, thereby, avoid the unpleasant emotional state associated with self-fragmentation, which, in essence, is a state of existential anxiety. We avoid anxiety for as long as we have no difficulty, in the present social framework, to elicit "mirroring self-object experiences", that is, to have experiences of being accepted, praised, or admired. With regard to the "pole of values and ideals", "idealising selfobject experiences" cater for one's desire to merge with an idealised object or organisation. The "psychological image" of the organisation one joins "can serve as an idealizable selfobject", which, similarly to an idealised parent, "provide[s] a self-confirming selfobject experience" (Wolf, 1988, pp. 47–48).

### 5.2.4   The self as measure of approvability

> Those images of me in the minds of other men are, it is true, things outside of me, whose changes I perceive just as I perceive any other outward change. … when I perceive my image in your mind to have changed for the worse, something in me … contracted, and collapsed. … Is not the condition of this thing inside of me the proper object of my egoistic concern, of my self-regard? (James, 1890, pp. 321–322)

"Social self-seeking" refers to emotional behaviour that controls "images other men have framed of me" (James, 1890, p. 321). The desire for admiring recognition can be seen to drive many aspects of social behaviour. A man's collection of property, for instance, insofar as it contributes to "the recognition which he gets from his mates" (p. 293), is motivated by social self-seeking. Even "the places and things I know enlarge my Self in a sort of metaphoric social way" (p. 308); and "much that commonly passes for spiritual self-seeking in this narrow sense is only material and social self-seeking beyond the grave" (James, 1890, p. 309).

> It is his image in the eyes of his own "set", which exalts or condemns him as he conforms or not to certain requirements that may not be made of one in another walk of life. (James, 1890, pp. 294–295)

The self reflects one's potential to access praise and positive attention from the social milieu. It also encapsulates one's vulnerability to conspecific attack. These aspects are related. The readiness with which we attract others' praise and benevolent interest is negatively correlated with the probability of being attacked offensively by conspecifics. In a state of high self-esteem, we are likely to be praised, approved, or respected; whereas in a state of social anxiety (which is the diametrically opposite state), we are likely to be condemned, criticised, or punished (Figure 2-5). The two probabilistic states are opposed to each other, much as conspecific signals of approval and signals of offensive aggression have opposite and mutually inhibitory effects. Receipt of signals of approval inhibits fear of a conspecific, and, similarly, contextual evidence for social approvability and worth inhibits anxiety and signals protection against conspecific attack. Receipt of signals of conspecific aggression arouses fear, and, similarly, contextual cues predictive of conspecific attack arouse anxiety. Contextually sensitive (and normative) social behaviour, modulating others attitudes towards us and the image others have framed of us, pursues a two-fold goal: to increase acceptability (relatedness) and reduce vulnerability (unrelatedness). Danziger (1997) discussed the self as an "object of social control"

and the "core of a monitoring mechanism". Individuals are constantly assessing their own worth, inasmuch as they are "actively engaged in maximising the flow of approval from others" (Danziger, 1997).

> … individuals learn how important the good opinion of others is to their welfare and therefore seek to influence the good opinion by appropriate conduct. (Danziger, 1997, p. 144)
> The objectified self that persons now harbour within them is above all an object of approval and disapproval, both by others and by the person herself. This self is always conceived as an object of variable worth, and therefore the desire to raise or maintain its worth comes to be regarded as an identifiable human motive. (Danziger, 1997, p. 145)

James (1890) noted that we evaluate ourselves differently in different social situations according to the different standards and expectations that characterise these situations, which led him to the conclusion that "a man has as many social selves as there are individuals who recognise him and carry an image of him in their mind" (p. 294). Gergen (1977), too, considered that "the stability of self-esteem is importantly dependent on the consistency of the social environment". Self-esteem is "inextricably linked to the social context" insofar as one's concept of self changes in accordance with varying "messages received from others concerning one's worth". Self-worth and the sense of personal identity are crucially dependent on the type of social milieu and the qualities of "those available for comparison" (Gergen, 1977). There can be no source in which to look for "true knowledge of self"; self-knowledge "is only constructed anew". Self-esteem does not derive from an "essential core level of self-evaluation" (Gergen, 1977), instead self-esteem is a measure of one's dynamic position in the competitive social structure to which one presently relates; it is, hence, a dynamic measure of one's protection against conspecific attack and of one's "rights" of access to resources of approval and affection.

> The longing or greed for good things can relate to any and every imaginable kind of good—material possessions, bodily or mental gifts, advantages and privileges; but, beside the actual gratification they may bring, in the depths of our minds they all ultimately signify one thing. They stand as proofs to us, if we get them, that we are ourselves good, and full of good, and so are worthy of love, or respect and honour, in return. Thus they serve as proofs and insurances against our fears of the emptiness inside ourselves, or of our evil impulses which make us feel bad and full of badness to ourselves and others. They also defend us against our fear of the retaliation, punishment or retribution which may be carried out against us by others, whether in material or in moral ways, or in our affections and love-relations. One great reason why a *loss* of any kind can be so painful is that unconsciously it represents the converse idea, that we are being exposed as *unworthy* of good things, and so our deepest fears are realized. (Riviere, 1937, p. 27)

### 5.2.5  *Significant and confirming others*

Disapprobation by others gives rise to anxiety, because it potentially removes us from the protection of the group. We seek approbation and appraisals of others inasmuch as we avoid, or escape from, anxiety. Our sense of self ("self-image") "at any given time is a reflection of the appraisals of others as modified by our previously developed self" (Gerth & Mills, 1954, p. 85). The person's sense of self is built "on the basis of a long sequence of previous appraisals and expectations which others have presented to him" (Gerth & Mills, 1954, p. 85). We automatically enhance or maintain our self-esteem (and thereby remain related to the group to which we

belong), much as we cannot but avoid, or escape from, dangerous situations, including situations of unrelatedness and loneliness. This tendency in the construction of our self is reflected in the selection of our relationships with others. The person tends to "to select and pay attention to those others who confirm this self-image, or who offer him a self-conception which is even more favorable and attractive than the one he possesses" (Gerth & Mills, 1954, p. 86). Gerth and Mills (1954) called significant others that are selected by the person for the purpose of confirming his self-esteem "confirming others". The person limits "his significant others to those who thus confirm his prized self-image" (Gerth & Mills, 1954, p. 86).

> This principle leads the person to ignore, if he can, others who do not appreciate his prized or aspired-to self-image, or who debunk his image or restrain the development of it. A circle of friends is typically made up of those who further, or who at least allow the other persons to retain, their respective self-images. … One avoids as best he can the enemies of the self-images one prizes. The cumulative selection of those persons who are significant for the self is thus in the direction of confirming persons, … (Gerth & Mills, 1954, p. 86)

We are what others think of us. There is also the image to which we aspire, which we seek to actualise by trying to have others accept or confirm this image. It is "our eagerness to be well thought of by those who matter to us most" that influences our behaviour towards them (Gerth & Mills, 1954, p. 91). Moreover, "we are also to some extent what we think others think of us" (p. 92). Disparity between "what we think others think of us and what they actually do think" is evidenced by other's flattery and our craving to be popular (Gerth & Mills, 1954, p. 92).

### Generalised other

> Significant others, as we have remarked, are those to whom the person pays attention

and whose appraisals are reflected in his self-appraisals; authoritative others are significant others whose appraisals sanction actions and desires. The generalized other is composed of an integration of appraisals and values of the significant, and especially the authoritative, others of the person. (Gerth & Mills, 1954, p. 95)

And some of those who have been significant others may not operate in the generalized other, but may have been excluded from awareness—a fact that is in line with the principle of selecting as significant those others who confirm the desired image of self. (p. 96)

The person can be appraised by "others who are not immediately present" (Gerth & Mills, 1954, p. 95). He may then "re-experience and use in evaluating his own self-image" past experiences of appraisals by significant others—past appraisals that have been deposited and integrated into the "generalised other" (p. 95). In the "generalised other", past appraisals of many significant others, including appraisals "of later others which are more appropriate to [the person's] adult roles", "are organised into a pattern" (p. 97). The content of the generalised other reflects normative attitudes of the group or society to which the person belongs, because only "these attitudes have been selected and refracted by those who have been and who are authoritatively significant to the person" (Gerth & Mills, 1954, p. 96).

As new appraisals are added to older ones, and older ones are dropped or excluded from awareness, the generalized other normally changes. (Gerth & Mills, 1954, p. 98)

The concept of generalised other overlaps with the Freudian concept of ego ideal, an aspect of the superego. The generalised other approves of the person, and enhances his self-esteem, when he performs an act or displays an attitude that is in line with expected norms and that, thereby, replicates an attribute of the ego ideal. A compli-

mentary aspect of the superego (called by Bergler (1952) the "daimonion") would be operative when, in the words of Gerth and Mills (1954), the person experiences "a general disapproval of his self" because he "performs an act that is out of line with the expected norms" (p. 97).

### 5.2.6   Companionable interactions

One's potential for attaining social support and approval dynamically depends on views and attitudes held by significant others. One monitors one's social environment for the availability of opportunities for supportive and companionable interactions (Heard & Lake, 1986). The environment one monitors for availability of opportunities for supportive and companionable interactions is constructed, in part, from memories of "contexts in which an individual has experienced harmonious forms of companionable and supportive interaction"—memories that "act as a vision of a secure environment" (p. 432). Companionable and supportive interactions with others take place over common goals or interests. Recognition by others, as ascertained by one's monitoring of one's potential and competence in the pursuit of common goals or interests, is associated with feelings of wellbeing and a sense of confidence and self-esteem. Companionable and supportive interactions are effective whenever "an individual construes from the emotive messages sent by companions, that they are taking interest in and showing appreciation of his contributions" (Heard & Lake, 1986, p. 431).

Distress arises "when a companion or support-giver fails to recognise or acknowledge a request for supportive or companionable interaction, or having recognised it, devalues or rejects it" (Heard & Lake, 1986, p. 435). A support-seeking individual may put the other, potentially support-giving, person "under painful pressure to accept" the supporting and validating role; and anger "in such situations is frequently an expression of the intensity with which an individual endeavours to force the other to comply with his wishes and beliefs" (Heard & Lake, 1986, p. 435). When external support cannot be elicited, the individual experiences anxiety, depending on the effectiveness of his defences. The individual engages in "anxious exploration" whenever he has "been exposed over long periods of time to the experience of ambivalent and/or highly conditional support with key figures" (p. 435). Then, "interests are pursued with anxiety" (p. 436). Loss in confidence to *manage one's external circumstances*—when the support-seeking individual "has few expectations of being able to gain realistic appreciation and/or recognition of his abilities and work" (p. 436)— causes reactivation of memories of earlier losses and failures, a sense of low self-esteem, and feelings of futility, helplessness, and hopelessness (Heard & Lake, 1986).

An individual's internal system for psychological support is derived from experiences of interactions with principle caregivers in infanthood and childhood. This "internal support system" is constructed from "internal representational models of experience in relationships", which capture past successes and failures in companionable and supportive interactions and allow predictions about how companionable and supportive interactions can be found and what can be expected to take place within each relationship (Heard & Lake, 1986). When an individual seeks support and approval, he automatically uses "internal representational models of experience in relationships" "to provide memories of analogous situations in which he has experienced effective support" (p. 432). Memories of successful interactions can be experienced consciously. Previous disassuaging experiences, on the other hand, "are partially or wholly segregated from conscious awareness" (p. 343), although "any current circumstances that seem similar to previous disassuaging events act as reminders of them" (p. 434). Heard and Lake (1986) pointed out that "glimpses into segregated events" elicit "defensive patterns of behaviour, seen e.g., in transference and countertransference phenomena" (p. 434), possibly mediated by the reexperience of distressing affects associated with disassuaging events.

Individuals devise "strategies to minimise each particular type of regularly repeated ineffective support" (Heard & Lake, 1986, p. 435). These strategies tend to become habitual and generalise "to analogous situations, so becoming a character trait" (p. 435). Some of these strategies "may be grossly maladaptive when used in contexts which only seem similar to the original" (p. 435). Individuals may exclude "from supportive interactions persons predicted to be more successful in claiming the attention of a support-giver" (sibling and other forms of rivalry); or they may stay "in contact with ambivalent support-givers by creating the illusion that they are effective, through selective exclusion of contrary information" (Heard & Lake, 1986, p. 435).

### 5.2.7   Controlling the social situation

The individual controls the conduct of others, especially their attitudes and behaviours towards himself; he gives them an "impression that will lead them to act in accordance with his own plan" (Goffman, 1959, p. 4). The individual expresses himself "in a given way solely in order to give the kind of impression to others that is likely to evoke from them a specific response he is concerned to obtain" (p. 6). This method of control involves expressions of "the more theatrical and contextual kind, the non-verbal, presumably unintentional kind, whether this communication is purposely engineered or not" (p. 4). In effect, the individual projects a "definition of the situation" that aims to present him in a favourable light (Goffman, 1959). The "plan" the individual envisages for his social encounters, unconsciously of course, or the situation he seeks to "project", is designed to provide him with a sense of relatedness, while avoiding social dissonance and exclusion. Others will "themselves effectively project a definition of the situation by virtue of their response to the individual", whereby "[o]rdinarily the definitions of the situation projected by several different participants are sufficiently attuned to one another" (Goffman, 1959, p. 9). "Together the participants contribute to a single over-all definition of the situation", which involves agreement "concerning the desirability of avoiding an open conflict of definitions of the situation" (pp. 9–10). Establishing a "working consensus", "participants must be careful to agree not to disagree on the proper tone of voice, vocabulary, and degree of seriousness in which all arguments are to be phrased" (Goffman, 1959, p. 10). As an individual "projects" a "definition of the situation", "disruptive events" may occur "which contradict, discredit, or otherwise throw doubt upon this projection". Then, "the individual whose presentation has been discredited may feel ashamed while the others present may feel hostile" (p. 12). Individuals usually employ "preventative practices" to protect their own projections and avoid "definitional disruptions". Anxieties that motivate "precautions taken to prevent disruption of projected definitions" find their catharsis in expressions of humour (Goffman, 1959, p. 14).

When adjusting the "definition of the situation" that we project onto the context in which social interaction takes place, we automatically pay attention to a multitude of cues including others' posture, speech patterns, facial expressions, and bodily gestures as well as cues related to other's "appearance" "which function at the time to tell us of the performer's social status" (Goffman, 1959, p. 24). Our theatrical "performance" or "role play" in social situations is aimed at winning others' favour or respect and gaining a sense of relatedness, while avoiding social exclusion or rejection. As Goffman (1959) noted, performers "offer their observers an impression that is idealized" (p. 35) partly in the interest of "upward mobility" in a social hierarchy. The "desire for a place close to the sacred center of the common values of the society" (p. 36) is acted upon by incorporating and exemplifying in one's performance "the officially accredited values of the society" (Goffman, 1959, p. 35). Thus, role performance and normative behaviour in social situations aim to create conditions under which one is likely to attract positive attention, the kind of attention one attracted from the primary

caregiver in infanthood. At the same time, such performance would be motivated by avoidance of others' hostility and by fears of disengagement from the social situation.

## 5.3 Characterological enhancement of approvability

Children (and especially those who become neurotic later in life) "try to identify the reasons for which their parents view them as lovable and worthy of attention" (Fink, 1997, p. 62). They "take on these reasons as their own", adopting desirable traits and characteristics, and, thereby, "come to see themselves as they believe their parents see them" (p. 62). Children's concern with discerning their parents' demands and wishes "is related to the formation of the ego ideal" (Fink, 1997, p. 62). Generally, by conforming to others' demands, values, and wishes (and adopting these demands, values, and wishes as our own), we seek to render ourselves lovable and worthy of others' attention and praise. In Lacanian terms, we express our "desire" (to be loved and appreciated by "the other") by conforming to the "law". "Desire" is subservient to the "law"; and the law brings desire into being (Lacan, 1966).[4] Characterological strategies to conform to social norms and traditions substantially overlap with defence mechanisms, both aiming to enhance our chance of being appreciated or loved (and reduce the risk of being punished for, or frustrated in, our libidinal and assertive actions), although the notion of defence mechanisms emphasises avoidance or reduction of *anxiety* (being a measure of our risk of being offensively aggressed, that is, socially punished). Some defence mechanisms avoid anxiety by increasing perception of cues in the social environment that signal approval and appreciation by others. Some of these defence

---

[4]Lacan (1966) situated our aspiration to conform to social ideals, and thereby become worthy of others' love and attention, on the "symbolic" axis (an axis that is perpendicular to the "imaginary" axis on which affective attunements take place).

mechanisms—balancing our need to express aggressive and libidinal or sexual instincts with our need for safety in an inherently hostile environment—play an important role in character formation. Defence mechanisms may prevent anxiety by (i) influencing others' behaviour and enhancing their appraisal of ourselves or (ii) restricting and shaping our conscious awareness of the social situation in a way that augments our perception of positive appraisal and filters out disapproval. Conscious awareness of the social situation (as it relates to probabilities of punishment and receiving approval) is intricately linked, and perhaps synonymous, with our sense of self; and both, consciousness and self, seem to be involved in the regulation of anxiety, that is, in the control of the "dangerousness" of the social situation we face.

### 5.3.1   Idealisation and identification

Freud and his followers have justly pointed to the fact that one often wants to take the place of an admired love object and may express such a wish, of which one is not aware, by assuming some characteristics of the other. This is called identification, which is an imitation that does not take place in the full light of consciousness. One may identify oneself with a person because one wishes to be like this person and potentially receive whatever the other person does. (Schilder, 1951, p. 273)

Idealisation refers to the emotional overestimation or aggrandisement of a person, group, or some other object. Unacceptable aspects of the object are "denied" in the process of idealisation (Laughlin, 1970). The individual seeks to accrue "emotional satisfaction" through libidinal attachment to the ideal he has created. In other words, the individual seeks to obtain "emotional supplies" (narcissistic supplies) from the idealised object. "Emotional supplies" or gratifications from an object that has been idealised are illusory (Laughlin, 1970). Idealisation as a defence mechanism may deal with a hidden dissatisfaction

with one's own ego. Formation and maintenance of an "unobtainable ideal" "aids in the preservation of defensively-intended distance" to the object and, thereby, guards against renewed loss or hurt (p. 127). In personality development, idealisation of parents fosters the child's identification with his parents and, thereby, importantly contributes to character formation. During the oedipal period, the child tends to identify with the parent of the same sex (based on idealisation of the same-sex parent), which leads to the resolution of the Oedipus complex (Laughlin, 1970).

It is during this phase that a child's subsequent sexual behavior is decisively influenced—indeed, determined. The child now shows a willingness to identify with its later sexual role and uses its parents as practice aids for subsequent partnership behavior. The boy becomes particularly clinging and affectionate toward his mother, modeling himself upon his father. The girl flirts with her father, thus assuming the mother's role. (Hass, 1968, p. 167)

Idealisation is an important prerequisite for identification, in general. Attributes of the idealised object are "attractive and appealing, and thus are far more readily emulated or taken over" (Laughlin, 1970, p. 130). In the process of identification, one takes over traits, mannerisms, goals, or attitudes of another person. Through identification with a socially more successful person or a person of higher social position or celebrity status, one unconsciously aims to gain acceptance, recognition, or approval, and, hence, safety or security. Identification with another person manifests an unconscious wish to be liked like the other person. In most instances, identification is "motivated by deep basic needs for acceptance, approval, and love" (p. 135), that is, by desires for "acceptance or love from the object" (Laughlin, 1970, p. 146). Not only admiration but also envy of another person can foster identification with that person and adoption or reproduction of his or her characteristics. Both, idealisation and identification, can be employed as defences against envy (Spillius, 1993).

## Superego

The primitive superego—a demanding and prohibitive primitive morality—forms by introjections of "bad objects" (persecutory objects) (Klein, 1940, 1952). This is to say that, early in life, the superego derives from identification with commanding and prohibiting aspects of one's parents. According to Kernberg (1996), superego functions can operate on an earlier, "persecutory level" or on a later, "idealising level". The first layer of the superego would consist of "all-bad, "internalized" object relations" (p. 113), while the second layer of the superego "is constituted by the ideal representations of self and others reflecting early childhood ideals that promise the assurance of love and dependency if the child lives up to them" (Kernberg, 1996, p. 113).[5] Earlier psychoanalysts, such as Freud (1923) and Bergler (1952), recognised that, during the oedipal period, identification with desirable aspects of the idealised same-sex parent provide a defence against the fear of persecution by this same-sex parent (that is, persecution for desiring the opposite-sex parent), and that this identification lays the foundation for superego development. Kernberg's structural and developmental model of a multilayered superego reconciles Kleinian and Freudian conceptualisations of the superego (which presume that superego development begins in the first year of life or the oedipal period, respectively).

### 5.3.2  Reaction formation

Two of man's basic, so-called instinctual impulses ultimately are preservative-hostile and sexual in nature. With reactive patterns of excessive kindness, fairness, morality, and idealism, humans seek to protect themselves against the dangers resulting if they were to follow their inner impulses of anger, sex, or rage. The goal is protective and defensive. One seeks to avert anxiety. In this way, through the use of the dynamism of Reaction Formation, their self-evaluation is maintained and enforced. (Laughlin, 1970, pp. 287–288)

Reaction formation can be defined "as the development of a pattern of attitudes and reactions" which hinders "the expression of contrary impulses" (Laughlin, 1970, p. 281). In the process of reaction formation, the individual develops socially acceptable and, hence, personally tolerable goals, attitudes, and character traits that can be regarded as the antithesis of goals and attitudes that had been relegated to the unconscious through their "repression". Reaction formation bolsters (establishes more securely) an established repression; reaction formation operates "in an attempt to keep repressed such inclinations as are consciously disowned" (p. 288). The "development of opposing attitudes and types of behavior" serves to prevent "certain painful or dangerous thoughts from entering consciousness" (p. 280). Outwardly acknowledged goals, feelings, or attitudes aid the concealment and control of socially unacceptable and, hence, personally undesirable goals, feelings, or attitudes—insofar as the former were formed as part an unconscious "reaction" to the latter. In other words, "the development of reversed outward attitudes and traits" guards against "awareness and potential expression of disowned and repressed emotions, drives, and complexes" (Laughlin, 1970, p. 280).[6]

---

[5] Kernberg (1996) spoke of a "third layer of the superego corresponding to the ego's stage of object constancy" (p. 114) (the stage during which all-bad and all-good aspects of objects are integrated into whole objects).

[6] Furthermore, reaction formation can be "rebelliously motivated" insofar as it can manifest "the nearly complete rejection and reversal of a given set of parental attitudes" (p. 285), that is, a complete turning away by the child "from his parents in certain major areas of their views, attitudes, and behavior" (Laughlin, 1970, p. 286).

Internal drives that require repression and reaction formation are "particularly those which are ultimately aggressive-hostile and sexual in nature" (Laughlin, 1970, p. 294). The development of character traits that secure the receipt by the individual of appraisal from his social environment may not exactly be the reverse or opposite to aggressive and sexual drives which he or she seeks to conceal or suppress. In fact, socially desirable attitudes and behaviours may have been acquired because they were differentially reinforced in early development, while alternative behaviours that involved expression of aggressive or sexual drives were differentially punished. Reaction formation, in cases where it has become clinically evident, may simply attest to a particularly effective learning process in which the child's reactions to ambiguous social situations were shaped by differential application of reward and punishment.

### 5.3.3   Compensation

Compensation is a characterological defence mechanism that is closely related to reaction formation. Through compensation, the individual seeks to offset, or make up for, actual or imagined deficiencies in his or her "physical, intellectual, or emotional endowment" (or to offset "almost any aspect of failure" in his or her "personal attributes or experiences") (Laughlin, 1970, p. 26). Strivings for power and prestige may be compensations for physical weakness or feelings of inferiority. Athletic skills or scholastic achievements may stem from compensatory endeavours in response to personal deficiencies. Alfred Adler (1965) introduced the notion of "inferiority complex" and highlighted the importance of compensation in personality development. According to Adler (1965), the infant's "basic feelings of inferiority" establish the striving for superiority as an enduring character trait. Compensation as an ego defence operates outside conscious awareness, although, in some cases, compensation is "achieved primarily through conscious efforts" (Laughlin, 1970, p. 24).

Compensation is motivated by "inner needs to secure ego reenforcement" (p. 18), that is, "inner needs for acceptance and love" (Laughlin, 1970, p. 25). Compensation reflects conscious and unconscious desires to attract others' attention and to procure "recognition, approval, acceptance, or love" from others (p. 18). Approval, acceptance, and love may be sought not only "externally in the social context from others" but also "from internal aspects of oneself" (p. 18). Endeavours "to secure recognition, attention, or self-esteem" through compensation "may be the result of actual inferiorities, deficiencies, and losses, or it may follow purely subjective and even quite unrealistic feelings of this nature" (p. 25). Pathological overcompensation, such as in form of grandiose delusions, may be a consequence of chronic physical illness or loss of ability. Confabulation in Korsakoff's syndrome (the filling-in of memory gaps by imaginary experiences that are relayed as though they are factual) can be regarded, in part, as a compensatory phenomenon, and, in part, as a type of rationalisation (Laughlin, 1970).

### 5.3.4   Sublimation

The concept of sublimation ("rechannelisation") is based on the assumption that inner drives "press for recognition that would prove unacceptable" or "for action that would be destructive" (Laughlin, 1970, p. 297). Sublimation establishes "ways for securing gratification of otherwise unacceptable unconscious desires and wishes" (p. 300). Intolerable instinctive drives "secure disguised outward expression and constructive utilisation through their unconscious diversion into approved and useful pathways" (p. 297). Aims substituted through sublimation "must of necessity have the acceptance of society" (p. 313); that is, ways in which instinctual drives are expressed "must be ways which are acceptable socially" (Laughlin, 1970, p. 314). Utilising socially more acceptable avenues, instinctive drives secure a "welcome and constructive external expression" (p. 298). The idea is that "inner libidinal energy becomes outwardly expressed as nonlibidinal", and that "the energy of aggression … becomes expressed in outwardly nonaggressive terms" (p. 299). It is supposed that, through sublimation, nonsexual activities secure the satisfaction of the sexual instinct, while nonaggressive activities secure the gratification of the aggressive drive. The classical psychoanalytic notion that, in the process of sublimation, a drive is "deflected and redirected" and "discharged through its new outlet" (Laughlin, 1970, p. 303) may be criticised as being overly mechanistic (Schafer, 1976; Shapiro, 2000). Nevertheless, sexual symbolism helps to elegantly explain vocational choices and other forms of sublimation. The concept of sublimation casts an instructive light into the "relationship of character formation to oral, anal, and genital function in infancy and early childhood" (Laughlin, 1970, p. 314).

Socially acceptable channels for outward expression of drives are gradually formed at a time (between ages 5 and 10) "when the superego is being concurrently established" (Laughlin, 1970, p. 317). Sublimation "contributes to character and personality development" and "plays a major role in the amelioration and resolution of emotional conflict, in the prevention of anxiety, and in the maintenance of emotional health" (p. 297). Sublimation aims to avert conflict and anxiety. Although it has been emphasised that, in the process of sublimation, intolerable instinctive drives are "diverted" so as to secure their disguised external expression and utilisation in socially acceptable channels (Laughlin, 1970), in essence, sublimation may be concerned more with the prevention of anxiety, generally through the maintenance of conditions that allow the induction of care-giving behaviour in others. Sublimation "may be viewed as the diverting of purely instinctual energy and purpose toward aims which society looks upon with greater favor, and which are therefore also more acceptable to the ego or self" (Laughlin, 1970, p. 312). Although it is recognised that, through sublimation, we acquire behaviours of which society *approves*, it should be emphasised that, through sublimation, we *establish and maintain social approvability* (acceptability) as we progressively extend the scope of social perception and interaction (in personality development). Through sublimation, we learn to manipulate our the social environment (and influence the way in which we are perceived by others) in highly sophisticated ways, so as to create and maintain conditions under which we can receive love and care (in the form of praise, benevolent interest, or appreciation). Thus, in some sense, "rechannelisation" of libidinal energy (libidinal investment) does play a central role in sublimation after all.

### 5.3.5   Regression

Regression refers to unconscious reactivation of an earlier era of personality development and reversal back to behaviour modes characterising this era (Laughlin, 1970). The individual adopts emotional reactions, coping behaviours, and patterns of thinking that are characteristic of an earlier level of adjustment. In other words, the ego reverts "to an earlier and less mature level of adjustment and development" (p. 320). By contrast, "fixation" refers to an arrest or cessation of personality development (Laughlin, 1970). Regression is a personality defence that may be employed at times of physical or emotional illness or in response to overwhelming stress, when the individual's attempts to cope with his or her environment consistently fail. Regression is a "response to overwhelming unconscious needs for safety and security" (p. 322). An "individual weakness of ego organization" is a precondition for regression (p. 334). Retreating from "danger, anxiety, stress, and responsibility", the ego "stabilizes itself on an earlier, simpler level" of functioning (p. 322) (representing a safer, more favourable or satisfying era). In many severe cases ("major regression"), the ego comprehensively reverts to the infantile level of functioning. The position towards which the ego retreats is one of greater dependence and safety—"a more protected and less exposed position" (Laughlin, 1970, p. 322).

The essence is that the individual seeks to obtain "acceptance, love, and security" by adopting an earlier, often infantile mode of gratification (Laughlin, 1970, p. 322). The individual reverts "to the position in development which is "remembered" (unconsciously of course) as providing him the most gratification" (p. 331). This is often a passive position. Through regression, "dependency needs" seek gratification (regression "as a dependency-seeking process" (p. 338)). Overt "attention-seeking behaviours", which are frequently seen in patients with mental illness, represent regressive attempts to satisfy dependency needs. Depressive and other mental illness may provide a "secondary gain". This means that, through their symptoms and illness-related behaviours, patients can attain "attention, sympathy, love, solace, affection, and protection" (p. 342). Fatigue states and neurasthenia may be manifestations of regression, too. Regression may be facilitated by psychogenic recapitulation (unconscious readoption) of symptoms that were associated with a serious or prolonged illness in early life (Laughlin, 1970).

> At times there is psychic reversion to a childhood period which was significant because of illness. This can represent an important era of gratification because of the extra care, attention, and love received at such times. Parental worry and concern over health also come to be valued by the child, especially when acceptance or love are lacking. (Laughlin, 1970, pp. 331–332)

## 5.4   Neurotic dependence on approval

Dependence on others' approval or affection is excessive in neurotic persons (Horney, 1937). The striving to be loved or approved of may take the form of "an indiscriminate hunger for appreciation or affection" (p. 36). The neurotic person may "feel entitled to demand special attention" (p. 143). He may try to obtain approval or affection by bribery, "by appealing to pity", "by a dramatic demonstration of his complaints",

or "by involving himself in a disastrous situation which compels our assistance" (p. 141). Similarly, children "may either want to be consoled for some complaint or may try to extort attention by unconsciously developing a situation terrifying to the parents, such as an inability to eat or to urinate" (Horney, 1937, p. 142). Excessive dependence on approval may manifest in form of constant requests for company, an incapacity to be alone, and a tendency to cling to significant others. Our security depends on being liked and approved of. Excessive dependence on others' approval attests to an inner insecurity. Excessive dependence on approval or affection is associated with feelings of inferiority. Feelings of inferiority "may be covered up by compensating needs for self-aggrandizement, by a compulsive propensity to show off, to impress others and one's self with all sorts of attributes that lend prestige in our culture" (Horney, 1937, p. 37).

There is, thus, a close link between one's security and the approval or appreciation one receives from others. Perhaps, one's security and self-esteem reflects one's *potential* to procure others' approval or affection. The search for others' approval or affection and also one's willingness to provide others with care or affection, or to approve of others, are superimposed on an unconscious network of hostile interactions within the social formation to which one belongs. The risk of becoming the target of others' hostility and disapproval (disrespect) gives rise to anxiety. By attaining others' approval or affection, we not only suppress our own hostility but inhibit others' innate hostility, too, and, thereby, overcome anxiety and render our position or situation safe. Social situations or positions that have been experienced as safe are those towards which anxiety-related escape behaviour (safety-directed behaviour) henceforth strives. Discussing the structure of neurotic personality, Horney (1937) referred to "the dilemma of feeling at once basically hostile toward people and nevertheless wanting their affection" (p. 111). Even though the dilemma is most evident in neurotic persons, it may pervade, as a fundamental principle, social behaviour, in general. The receipt of affection or approval (or awareness of contextual cues indicating one's capacity to attain affection or approval) may inhibit one's hostility, much as deficits in this regard would bring one's hostility back to the surface. Hostility, in turn, may be employed in an effort to solicit affection or approval from others—approval, which, then, may be forthcoming partly in form of other's submission.

### 5.4.1  Insecurity

A distinction may have to be drawn between the need for love and the neurotic need for approval. However, assuming that both are, in part, derivatives of infantile care-seeking behaviour, their emotional accompaniments, underlying motivations, and behavioural manifestations likely overlap. Both may represent, in more or less abstract form, a longing for reunion with the primary object. Alternatively, we may consider that the need for love is attributable to a libidinal drive, whereas the neurotic need for approval is related to infantile attachment behaviour. Horney (1937) argued that the distinction "lies in the fact that in love the feeling of affection is primary, whereas in the case of the neurotic the primary feeling is the need for reassurance" (p. 109). Neurotic persons are afflicted by an incapacity for love, perhaps insofar as they cannot *give* care or affection to others, for they "may become extremely afraid of incurring obligations" (Horney, 1937, p. 143). At the same time, the neurotic person "reaches out desperately for any kind of affection for the sake of reassurance"; he "needs another's affection for the sake of reassurance against anxiety" (p. 109). The neurotic person's *search* for affection or approval aims to resolve "basic anxiety"—a state in which "one feels fundamentally helpless toward a world which is invariably menacing and hostile" (p. 106). Feeling fundamentally helpless, the neurotic person finds himself unable to be alone; he insists on another person's presence (or clings to the other person). Then, reassurance would be "supplied

by the fact that the other is available" (Horney, 1937, p. 118).

The search, by an anxious or neurotic person, for affection or approval impresses as lacking in spontaneity or flexibility (Horney, 1937). The greater the anxiety, the greater is one's incapacity to be alone, and the more desperate or random are one's attention- or reassurance-seeking behaviours. Feelings of anxiety signal that one's prospects of receiving approval or affection from others and giving love in return are low (while one's vulnerability is high). Anxiety prompts the person to withdraw to, or create, a safe situation or relationship (if this is available or conceivable), suggesting that attention- or reassurance-seeking behaviour is a form of defensive behaviour (rather than libidinally motivated behaviour). If anxiety is high, attention- and reassurance-seeking behaviour is more erratic, and the outcome of such safety-directed behaviour is less certain. Horney (1937) thought that the striving to be approved of or loved not only helps to overcome "basic anxiety" but also represents an attempt to *protect* oneself against "basic anxiety"; she stated that receiving others' affection or reassurance serves "as a powerful protection against anxiety" (p. 96).

### 5.4.2  Rebuff

Neurotic persons (and nonneurotic persons, too) feel hurt when the attention they try to elicit is not forthcoming. Persons with a neurotic disposition may experience an "inordinately sharp sting of disappointment" when their secret expectation of a return for favours or generosity shown to others is *frustrated* (Horney, 1937, p. 143). A rebuff "not only throws them back on their basic anxiety", it also "arouses a tremendous rage" (Horney, 1937, p. 135). While anxiety signals that one's security has been undermined, the pain of rejection arises when one's efforts to attain or maintain a safe position have been frustrated or when one's safety has been undermined by a sudden loss (albeit a perceived loss) of social relatedness, position, or status. The acute loss of social relatedness or position, which is registered by the person as narcissistic pain and an acute loss of self-esteem, engenders anger and offensive aggression (or, if pain is intense, defensive aggression). Especially in persons with neurotic personality, a rebuff "may stimulate outbreaks of hostility or result in a complete withdrawal of all feelings, so that they are cold and unresponsive" (p. 136). Hostility may manifest as irritability, spitefulness, or vindictiveness. In most instances, "rebuff may have been so slight as to escape conscious awareness", and, therefore, "the connection between feeling rebuffed and feeling irritated remains unconscious", too (Horney, 1937, p. 136).

### 5.4.3   Search for glory

What underpins the neurotic person's ambition is the "drive towards external success" and the "search for glory" (Horney, 1950). The neurotic person's "search for glory" (that is, for glorifying praise and recognition) "springs from the need to actualize the idealized self" (p. 38). Horney (1950) thought that drives aiming for the actualisation of the idealised self "are by necessity compulsive" (p. 38). It could be argued that even the healthy person's striving for recognition and approval reflects a state of being *driven*—one that is similarly guided by an image of the self that represents a social position that is desirable to the person and that renders the person attractive to others. Horney (1950) admitted that neurotic ambition and healthy strivings are similar, "because they have a common root in specific human potentialities" (p. 37), however, for the most part, she emphasised that the "search for glory" is neurotic and qualitatively different from "the live forces of the real self" that "urge one toward self-realization" (p. 38). The healthy person, too, can be ambitious in his strivings for praise and recognition (representing essential narcissistic supplies), however—and here lies a difference—the neurotic person's "glow of elation over the favourable reception of some work done, over a victory won, over any sign

of recognition or admiration ... does not last" (p. 30). The neurotic person's "relentless chase after more prestige, more money, ... keeps going, with hardly any satisfaction or respite" (Horney, 1950, p. 30).

The capacity of imagination is at the service of the search for glory (Horney, 1950). The search for glory can be conceived of as an appetitive behaviour that transposes the person from his current social position—as captured abstractly by the person's sense of self in the here-and-now—to a desired position represented by (or linked to) his idealised self (Figure 4-2). The problem of the neurotic person is that he misperceives his current social situation—the very situation that inspires his self-idealising imagination. In other words, he misconstrues his actual self—the very self to which his idealised self-image is linked (via an abstract path through time and space). Appetitive social behaviour that sets out from a misperceived position is likely to fail. This is one of the ways in which *"checks on imagination"* can malfunction in the search for glory (Horney, 1950, p. 35). As Horney (1950) recognised, actualisation of the idealised self by the neurotic person (but not by the healthy person) involves falsification of reality. The neurotic person "is aversive to checking with evidence when it comes to his particular illusions about himself"; "he disregards evidence which he does not choose to see" in a great number of ways (p. 36). It could be argued that fantastic self-glorification in imagery, as it is characteristic for neurosis, can only derive from a self-deceptive representation of the person's social reality and, hence, an illusionary representation of his present self abstracted from the immediate social situation. Alternatively, the link between the person's appreciation of his present social situation (in the form of his actual sense of self) and the image of a desired outcome (in the form of an idealised self) may be loosened. In either case, the person fails "to recognize limitations to what he expects of himself and believes is possible to attain" (Horney, 1950, p. 36).

The person may "shove aside the checks" on imagination because the "need to actualize his idealized image is so imperative" (Horney, 1950, p. 36). This raises another problem, namely that the neurotic person's drive for glory is excessively intense or is invoked all too readily (possibly on a background of insecurity and anxiety). The neurotic person *must* search for glory and must actualise his idealised self "lest he incur anxiety, feel torn by conflicts, be overwhelmed by guilt feelings, feel rejected by others" (p. 29). The search for glory can be "a most powerful drive"; it can be "like a demoniacal obsession" (p. 31). The search for glory and attempts to actualise the idealised self-fantasy are compulsive in the neurotic person (Horney, 1950), however even the healthy person could be seen as being appetitively *driven* in his pursuit of access to resources of narcissistic supplies (in the form of approval and perhaps glory).

> He *must* come out victorious in any argument, regardless of where the truth lies. … The compulsiveness of the neurotic person's need for indiscriminate supremacy makes him indifferent to truth, whether concerning himself, others, or facts. (Horney, 1950, p. 30)

### 5.4.4   Pride

The neurotic person has an imperative "need to be proud of himself" (Horney, 1950, p. 93). He "feels at bottom unwanted, is easily hurt, and needs incessant confirmation of his value" (p. 86). Any "lack of genuine warmth and interest" gives him "the feeling of being unloved and unworthy—or at any rate of not being worth anything unless he is something he is not" (p. 87). If he "wields power and influence and is supported by praise and deference", he "may feel strong and significant" (p. 86). However, "in a strange environment", where "this support is lacking", his "feelings of elation collapse easily" (Horney, 1950, p. 86). The neurotic person's imagination of an idealised self is "an attempt to remedy the damage done by lifting himself in his mind above the crude reality of himself

and others" (p. 87). If his idealised self cannot be actualised, "he gets all the glory in imagination" (p. 87). Excessive dependence on external narcissistic supplies (the availability of which inherently fluctuates) and on imagination is characteristic for "neurotic pride", which Horney (1950) contrasted with healthy self-confidence or self-esteem.

Neurotic pride "rests on the attributes which a person arrogates to himself in his imagination, on all those belonging to his particular idealized image" (Horney, 1950, p. 90). Neurotic pride may become less fleeting, and elation may become more sustained, if the "glorified version of oneself" (pp. 88–89) can be actualised through accumulation of power, prestige, and possessions. Neurotic pride can also rest on compulsive compliance with external standards (reflective of "inner dictates"), allowing the person to "feel that he is a moral wonder to be proud of" (Horney, 1950, p. 93). The neurotic person's pride can thus be invested outside of himself, while, at the same time, "work of intellect and imagination" goes into "maintaining the private fictitious world through rationalisations, justifications, externalisations, reconciling irreconcilables—in short, through finding ways to make things appear different from what they are" (p. 91). Shame arises if this discrepancy comes to light, if the neurotic person "is caught in a lie" (p. 97). Work of intellect and imagination is also required to transform virtues of the idealised self into assets which the neurotic person can be proud of (Horney, 1950). Similarly, self-imagery, in accordance with the person's ego ideal, guides normal ambitions and strivings for success along a path that is socially acceptable and constructive (Figure 4-2).

### 5.5   Narcissism

There are two forms of libido investment (Federn, 1952). First, "object libido" is invested in representations of objects (significant persons). External objects that are cathected with "object libido" are experienced as *pleasant*. In the second form of libido investment, the ego is cathected with "ego libido" ("narcissistic cathexis") (Federn, 1952). "Narcissism" means investment of libido in the ego (Freud, 1920). Freud thought that, as a result of such investment, the ego becomes a "reservoir of libido". Federn (1952) proposed that the pleasure achieved by "narcissistic cathexis" does not constitute full satisfaction; nevertheless, a *pleasurable* "ego feeling" shows that narcissistic cathexis is at work. Perhaps, narcissism could be conceived simply as dependence or overdependence on external supplies of praise and admiration. Praise attracted from others provides some pleasure, while confidence in one's potential to attract praise guards against anxiety. Horney (1937) thought that the narcissistic person, who "is constantly preoccupied with inflating his ego", "does it not primarily for the sake of self-love, but for the sake of protecting himself against a feeling of insignificance and humiliation, or, in positive terms, for the sake of repairing a crushed self-esteem" (Horney, 1937, p. 172). For the neurotic person, every "shortcoming, whether recognized as such or only felt dimly, is considered a humiliation" (p. 172). In order to defend himself against the resulting anxiety, the neurotic person needs "to be infallible and wonderful in his own eyes" (p. 172). Internalisation of his quest for prestige and self-aggrandizement presupposes that the neurotic person remains distant in his relations with other persons (Horney, 1937).

Patients with a narcissistic personality disturbance are handicapped by an "inability to regulate self-esteem and to maintain it at normal levels" (Kohut, 1971, p. 20). Narcissistic patients have an "intense hunger for a powerful external supplier of self-esteem and other forms of emotional sustenance in the narcissistic realm" (p. 17). Narcissistic patients tend to be "vain, boastful, and intemperately assertive with regard to their grandiose claims" (p. 178). Their narcissistic displays are designed to elicit "narcissistic sustenance" from others in the form of their approving, mirroring, and echoing responses (Kohut, 1971). When forming a relationship (such as in the process of psychoanalysis), the narcissistic patient engages the object only insofar as it satisfies his needs in the area of "narcissistic

requirements"; the patient "acknowledges the object only as a source of approval, praise, and empathic participation" (p. 174). The narcissistic patient experiences "a chronic sense of dullness and passivity"; however, "in consequence of having received external praise or of having had the benefit of interest from the environment", he "feels suddenly alive and happy" and, for a short period of time, "has a sense of deep and lively participation in the world" (Kohut, 1971, p. 17). Unavoidable "narcissistic injury' in the form of a "rebuff, the absence of expected approval, the environment's lack of interest in the patient, and the like, will soon bring about the former state of depletion" (p. 17). In view of any sign of disapproval of him or loss of interest in him, the narcissistic patient may "become first enraged and then cold, haughty, and isolated" (p. 58) (Figure 2-5). Furthermore, any revelation of his persistent infantile grandiosity and exhibitionism can provoke shame and anxiety. Narcissistic persons may cover up their extreme neediness in the area of "narcissistic requirements" "by a display of independence and self-sufficiency" (Kohut, 1971, p. 293).

### 5.5.1   Primary and secondary narcissism

Investment of "ego libido" in the ego or parts of the ego is called "secondary narcissism" (Federn, 1952). "Secondary narcissism" is of an object-libidinal nature. The object in secondary narcissism is the ego or a part of the ego, not the external world. All secondary narcissism has as its object the ego or what has been incorporated into the ego (Federn, 1952). Cathexis of the ego as an object of narcissism ("narcissistic cathexis") is the result of, first, establishment of a true object cathexis (libido invested in an external object) and, second, identification with the object thus cathected. The transformation of object cathexes into secondary narcissistic cathexes is "the result of the expansion of the ego feeling to cover object representations" (p. 319). Thus, secondary narcissism is a turning back to the ego "of a quantity of libido which has previously been turned toward an external object"

(Federn, 1952, p. 319). Freud (1914) previously observed how libido can be withdrawn from the object and directed onto the ego (in a process of "introversion"). A similar process of "turning round of the instinct upon the subject's own ego" is responsible for masochism; in masochism, a synergy of aggressive and libidinal instincts (which in sadism is directed towards an external object) "has been turned round upon the subject's own ego" (Freud, 1920, p. 54). Unlike Freud, Federn conceived the ego as an experiential phenomenon related to self-awareness (akin to Kohut's concept of self). Hartmann (1964) saw narcissism "as the libidinal cathexis not of the ego but of the self" (p. 127). Libido can be withdrawn onto the self, and libidinal object cathexis can be replaced by self-love. In schizophrenia, for instance, there would be "withdrawal of libido from the objects and its subsequent investment in the self" (p. 193). Not only libidinal but also aggressive cathexes can be "turned back from the objects upon the self and in part upon the ego" (Hartmann, 1964, p. 130).

One can be narcissistic without object cathexis. There is a kind of narcissism that has nothing to do with objects. "Primary narcissism", which stems from autoerotism, is objectless (Federn, 1952). Primary narcissism ("psychic autoerotism") is experienced as well-being in the ego; it is "the source which feeds the ego feeling in the form of objectless, but always object-ready, libidinal striving" (p. 318). In primary narcissism (psychic autoerotism), "we recognize only the sensation of craving for pleasure and its satisfaction in one's own person, not yet a *directing* of the libido toward oneself" (one's self) (p. 312). As soon as the ego becomes an object of narcissism, we speak of secondary narcissism (Federn, 1952). Fairbairn (1952), by contrast, defined "primary narcissism" as identification with *the* object in a state of infantile dependence, whereas "secondary narcissism" refers to a state of identification with an object that has been internalised. Thus, narcissism, in general, would be "a state in which the ego is identified with objects" (Fairbairn 1952, p. 83). The concept of secondary narcissism is valuable when trying to understand the nature

and function of the self and its relationship with the world of objects.

### 5.5.2   Child development

Consistently with Mahler's (1968) developmental scheme, according to which an initial phase of unrelatedness to the object ("autism") is followed by a phase of union with the object ("symbiosis") and, then, a phase of autonomy from the object ("individuation"), Kohut (1971) conceived personality development as proceeding from primary narcissism (autoerotism) to "the two branches of narcissism itself" (p. 219). The two "archaic narcissistic configurations" that establish themselves in early childhood are: the "grandiose self" and the "idealized parent imago". These archaic configurations of "narcissistic libido", aiming to maintain union with the object, "are comprehensible, adaptive, and valuable within the context of the total stage of personality development of which they form a part" (p. 229). Having been exposed to unavoidable disturbances in "the psychological equilibrium of primary narcissism", the child assigns "all bliss and power" to the object and attempts "to maintain a continuous union with it" (Kohut, 1971, p. 37).

> The equilibrium of primary narcissism is disturbed by the unavoidable shortcomings of maternal care, but the child replaces the previous perfection (a) by establishing a grandiose and exhibitionistic image of the self: *the grandiose self*; and (b) by giving over the previous perfection to an admired, omnipotent (transitional) self-object: *the idealized parent imago*. (Kohut, 1971, p. 25)

The "grandiose self" has "subject quality", whereas the "idealised parent imago" is an archaic selfobject (Kohut, 1971, p. 33). Both, "grandiose self" (the narcissistic subject) and "idealised parent imago" (the narcissistic object), are cathected with "narcissistic libido" (in form of "grandiose-exhibitionistic libido" and "idealizing libido", respectively). It is important to distinguish "narcissistic libido" from "object libido". "Object love" is the antithesis of narcissism. The phase of "individuation" entails the cathexis of "object love", which, according to Kohut (1971), does not arise secondarily to narcissism but develops in parallel with narcissism from archaic to higher levels.

## Grandiose self

The child's exhibitionism and grandiosity derive from his "undisguised pleasure in being admired" by others (Kohut, 1971, p. 25). As the child develops, "having to recognize that the claims of the grandiose self are unrealistic" (p. 229), "the exhibitionism and grandiosity of the archaic grandiose self are gradually tamed" (p. 27). Tamed exhibitionism and grandiosity become the "instinctual fuel for our ego-syntonic ambitions and purposes" in adult life (p. 27), while the pleasure in being admired becomes a "nonerotic satisfaction" with ourselves or our achievements (Kohut, 1971). Self-esteem carries "the earmark of the original narcissism" (p. 108). The original narcissism, which pervades early childhood, "infuses into the central purposes of our life and into our healthy self-esteem that absoluteness of persistence and of conviction of the right to success" (p. 108). The child's "need for omnipotent certainty concerning the results of his efforts and for unlimited success and acclaim" is transformed into "ego-syntonic attitudes of persistence, optimism, and reliable self-esteem" (p. 151). "Optimal maternal acceptance" is a precondition for the transformation of the child's "crude exhibitionism and grandiosity into adaptively useful self-esteem and self-enjoyment" (Kohut, 1971, p. 284).

## Idealised parent imago

When, in a parallel process, the child has to "recognize that the idealized self-object is unavailable or imperfect" (Kohut, 1971, p. 229), the "idealised parent imago" (idealised selfobject), being the counterpart of the "grandiose self",

becomes integrated into the personality. The "idealised parent imago" and its cognitive elaborations later in life (including "its therapeutic amalgamation with the psychic representation of the analyst") are "objects that are experienced narcissistically" (p. 33); they are not "objects" in the strict psychoanalytic sense, since they are cathected with "narcissistic libido" (as opposed to "object libido"). Objects in the strict psychoanalytic sense are those "childhood images" that are invested with object-instinctual cathexes, namely love ("object love" or "object libido") and hate. Under optimal developmental conditions, the child's idealisations, which retain their narcissistic character, will coexist and become integrated with object-instinctual cathexes. "Idealizing narcissistic libido" (which is invested in selfobjects) "plays a significant role in mature object relationships, where it is amalgamated with true object libido" (Kohut, 1971, p. 40). The normal state of being in love not only involves investment of "object libido" but also has a narcissistic component, which "does not detach itself from the object cathexes but remains subordinated to them" (p. 76). Similarly, in the "transference neuroses", the narcissistic investment in the analyst "always remains subordinated to the object cathexes" (Kohut, 1971, p. 55).

## Idealisation of the superego

The child's archaic idealisation of his parent (the "idealised parent imago") is developmentally continuous with "idealisation of the parental objects of the late preoedipal and of the oedipal periods" (Kohut, 1971, p. 40). As a result of "oedipal disappointment in the parent" (p. 41), the superego is "invested with narcissistic instinctual cathexes" (p. 40). The "idealised superego", which, unlike Klein's primitive "persecutory superego", is formed during the oedipal period, represents a "the massively introjected internal replica of the oedipal object" (p. 47). The oedipal object's "loving-approving and angry-frustrating aspects" are internalised and "become the approving functions and positive goals of the superego, on the one hand, and its puni-tive functions and prohibitions, on the other" (pp. 47–48). Kohut (1971) thought that one of the functions of the superego is to sustain the per-son's self-esteem independently of selfobjects. If idealisation of the superego remains incom-plete, the person "will forever search for exter-nal ideal figures from whom he wants to obtain the approval and the leadership which his insuf-ficiently idealised superego cannot provide" (Kohut, 1971, p. 49).

### Early fixation

A developmentally earlier "inexpressible disap-pointment in the idealised mother which may have been due to the unreliability of her empathy" may similarly render the person liable to later reactivations of the need for archaic, narcissisti-cally experienced selfobjects (Kohut, 1971, p. 53). Kohut (1971) thought that "early disturbances in the mother-child relationship (due to emotional coldness of the mother, the absence of consistent contact with the mother, the baby's congenital emotional coldness, the mother's withdrawal from an unresponsive baby, etc.)" lead to "a fail-ure in the establishment of an idealised parent imago" and a fixation on "the primitive stages of the (autoerotic) body self and on the archaic (pre) stages of the grandiose self" (p. 301). Further development would be "stunted by the child's lack of the needed admiring responses from his mother" (Kohut, 1971, p. 301).

### 5.5.3    Ego feeling

Objects (significant others) are represented in two different ways, since they can be cathected with one of two types of libido (narcissistic or ego libido and object libido). An object representation cathected with object libido can be distinguished from a narcissistically cathected representation of the object (Federn, 1952). Narcissistic repre-sentations of objects may encode our potential to attract signals of approval or benevolent interest (care-giving signals) from these objects.

Narcissistic object representations underpin the individual's sense of social *attractiveness* and, hence, bolster the individual's protection against anxiety (consistent with Horney's (1937) under-standing of narcissism). Libidinal representa-tions of objects (i.e., objects cathected with "object libido" or "objects in the strict psychoanalytic sense" (Kohut, 1971)), by contrast, encode our *attractedness* to these objects. Objects cathected with object libido (or simply, "libidinal objects") are those that attract (or have the potential to attract) our care-giving behaviour. We approach libidinal objects (or control the situation of which they are a part, using appetitive, goal-directed behaviour) in order to obtain a stimulus situation that releases our innate care-giving signals. As it turns out, narcissistic object cathexes, but not libidinal object cathexes, strengthen the ego feeling (i.e., the sense of self) (Federn, 1952). Our sense of self is constructed from those aspects of the social milieu that signal one's worth in the eyes of others and one's potential to attract their approval or admiring recognition (James, 1890; Danziger, 1997). Indeed, Federn (1952) thought that the ego is built up by narcissistic libido; "the unitary ego feeling is maintained through a contiguous narcissistic cathexis" (p. 319). In a sense, ego feeling is synonymous with narcissistic libido.

### Identification

"Symptomatic mannerisms", which are charac-teristic of increased narcissism, reveal what or who the narcissistic person wants to represent (Federn, 1952). They point to a process of iden-tification with an object that possesses desirable attributes. Ego feeling may accrue through such identifications. In the process of identification ("secondary identification"), as Federn (1952) saw it, objects are cathected with "ego feeling" (narcissistic libido or "ego libido") and are, thus, absorbed into the ego. Identification with an object means that "ego feeling" permanently pervades the representation of the object. Gradually, "ego libido" (narcissistic libido) encompasses more and more object representations (Federn, 1952). Ego feeling invested in an object representation fuses with the libido ("object libido") invested in the same object. Fusion of ego feeling with object libido—as a result of identification—causes enlargement of the "ego boundary" (Federn, 1952). Rather than direct narcissistic cathexis of the ego, it seems that "the narcissistic cathexis has taken a detour via the identification by means of the ego expansion" (p. 359). Federn (1952) proposed that, in every psychic occurrence, "the object representation, with its libido cathexis, unites with the narcissistically cathected representations of the same object which pertain permanently to the ego" (p. 305). Fantasies of love, greatness, and ambition "always unite contents and goals that are clearly narcissistic and those that are directed toward the object" (p. 358). Unions of ego libido and object libido achieve "incomplete satisfaction" (Federn, 1952).

### 5.5.4   Idealising transference

The "idealised parent imago" (omnipotent object) is "an archaic, rudimentary (transitional) self-object" that is formed in an early phase of psychic development (Kohut, 1971). Revival of the "idealised parent imago" in the context of a relationship later in life is called "idealising transference". In a setting of psychoanalytic therapy, narcissistic patients reactivate "the need for an archaic, narcissistically experienced self-object" (p. 46). The transference formed by a patient with narcissistic personality disturbance elaborates "a narcissistically cathected omnipotent and omniscient, admired and idealised, emotionally sustaining parent imago" (Kohut, 1971, p. 8). The idealising transference, thus, manifests a yearning for the idealised object. In essence, the narcissistic patient attempts to regulate his self-esteem by attaching himself to a strong and admired figure (a replica of the archaic "idealised parent imago") whose acceptance he craves and by whom he needs to feel supported (p. 62). The narcissistic patient, wanting to attach himself to an omnipotent archaic object, seeks to derive "narcissistic sustenance" "from the aggrandized

object that he has created in fantasy" (Kohut, 1971, p. 111). So long as his "self experience includes the idealized analyst whom he feels he controls and possesses", the patient "feels whole, safe, powerful, good, attractive, active" (p. 90). A disturbance in the transference—any "event that disrupts his narcissistic control over the archaic parent imago, the analyst"—causes the narcissistic analysand to respond with rage ("narcissistic rage") and despondency (p. 90). The analyst, in turn, experiences "painful narcissistic tensions", which he defensively tries to fend off, "when the repressed fantasies of his grandiose self are stimulated by the patient's idealisation" (Kohut, 1971, p. 262).

An "idealising transference" (*archaic type*) can arise on a developmental background of disappointments in the idealised mother that occurred at a "period when the idealized mother imago is still completely merged with that of the self" (Kohut, 1971, p. 55). An "idealising transference" (*oedipal type*) can also establish itself as a consequence of a developmental "fixation" on a period prior to the ultimate internalisation of the idealised object, "i.e., before the consolidation of the idealisation of the superego" (p. 54). If there had been a "fixation on the narcissistic aspects of the preoedipal or oedipal idealized object" and an "insufficient idealisation of the superego", then the person is "forever attempting to achieve a union with the idealized object" (Kohut, 1971, p. 55). Due to insufficient idealisation of the superego during the oedipal period, the patient's "narcissistic equilibrium is safeguarded only through the interest, the responses, and the approval of present-day (i.e., currently active) replicas of the traumatically lost self-object" (p. 55). The "idealising transference", due to a structural deficit of the superego (*oedipal type*), needs to be distinguished from "the well known idealisations of the analyst which occur in consequence of superego projections" (p. 78). Unlike transference manifestations associated with the classical "transference neuroses", which involve investment of the analyst with "object libido", "the   apparent   transference   manifestations in the idealizing transference are due to the mobilization of narcissistic cathexes" (Kohut, 1971, p. 204).

### 5.5.5   Mirror transference

Mobilisation, in a psychoanalytic setting, of the other archaic narcissistic configuration, namely the "grandiose self", gives rise to one of three forms of "mirror transference" (Kohut, 1971). In the most archaic form of "mirror transference", the patient "merges" with the analyst who is "experienced as an extension of the grandiose self" (p. 114). The patient tries to reestablish an ancient identity with the object. For as long as the analyst is a part or extension of the patient's self, the patient "expects unquestioned dominance over him" (p. 115). The analyst "experiences this relationship in general as oppressive and he tends to rebel against the unquestioning abso-lutarianism and tyranny with which the patient expects to control him" (Kohut, 1971, p. 115). In a less archaic form of mirror transference (called "alter-ego transference" or "twinship"), the patient assumes that the analyst is like him; that is, the analyst (a "narcissistically cathected object") "is experienced as being like the gran-diose self" (p. 115). Thus, in the merger and the twinship transferences, "the analysand confines the analyst to the more or less anonymous exist-ence either of being included in the system of his grandiose self or of being its faithful replica" (Kohut, 1971, p. 175).

> In the twinship (alter-ego) and merger varieties of the remobilization of the gran-diose self, ... the analyst as an independ-ent individual tends to be blotted out altogether from the patient's associations. (Kohut, 1971, p. 271)

## Mirror transference in the narrower sense

In the most common and most mature form of mirror transference ("mirror transference in the narrower sense"), the analyst is seen as "an object which is important only insofar as it is invited to participate in the [patient's] narcissistic pleasure and thus to confirm it" (Kohut, 1971, p. 116). The analyst "is reacted to only insofar as [he] con-tributes to (or interferes with) the analysand's narcissistic homeostasis" (p. 122). The mirror transference ("in the narrower sense") "concerns the patient's revelation of his infantile fantasies of exhibitionistic grandeur" (p. 148). The patient *demands* from the analyst "an echo and a con-firmation of his greatness and an approving response to his exhibitionism" (p. 123). The ana-lyst is *coerced* by the patient into making echoing, approving, and confirming gestures and remarks. Thus, in the mirror transference ("in the narrower sense"), the patient assigns to the analyst "the performance of only one function: to reflect and echo his grandiosity and exhibitionism" (Kohut, 1971, p. 175).

> ... the analyst, though cognitively acknowledged as separate and autono-mous, is nevertheless important only within the context of the analysand's nar-cissistic needs and is appealed to and oth-erwise reacted to only insofar as he is felt to fulfill or to frustrate the patient's demands for an echo, approval, and confirmation of his grandiosity and exhibitionism. (Kohut, 1971, p. 204)

The "mirror transference in the narrower sense" derives developmentally from "the gleam in the mother's eye" and other maternal expressions of approval or interest in response to the child's exhibitionistic displays—maternal expressions that function to "confirm the child's self-esteem" (Kohut, 1971, p. 116). Mobilisation of the "gran-diose self" in the mirror transference means that the patient can "cathect a reactivated grandiose self with narcissistic libido" (p. 128). In essence, the "listening, perceiving, and echoing-mirroring presence of the analyst" serves to maintain the cohesiveness of the self (self image) of the analysand (Kohut, 1971, p. 125). When a mirror transference has been established, the patient elaborates recurrent themes of being special, being unique, or being precious—themes which appear "to be the nodal point of a host of frightening, shameful, and isolating narcissistic fantasies" (Kohut, 1971, p. 150). Lies, in this context, serve to "ascribe some great achievements to the self of the liar" (Kohut, 1971, p. 110). Lying, as a symptom of narcissistic personality disturbance, "may be due to the pressure of the grandiose self" (pp. 109–110). Moreover, "the persistent demand of the grandiose self" may force the ego "to respond with unusual performance" (p. 112). Narcissistic persons may struggle "valiantly to live up to the assertions of the grandiose self concept on which they have become fixated" (Kohut, 1971, p. 112).

### 5.5.6   Fantasy

Narcissistic ego exaltation is one of the goals of daydreaming (the pursuit of object libidinal gratification being another goal) (Federn, 1952). Daydreaming also provides a sense of invulnerability. The daydreamer experiences himself (an image of his self) in his daydreams or fantasies, whereby "the ego figure of these phantasies has arisen through identification with persons in whom the desired claims are fulfilled" (Federn, 1952, p. 358). In conscious fantasies of love, greatness, and ambition, narcissistic goals are satisfied, albeit transiently. Narcissistic fantasy may indulge in self-flattery and, thus, provide partial satisfaction. Such satisfaction may derive from a transient sense of social relatedness and attractiveness (approvability), and, hence, safety (invulnerability). Full satisfaction of narcissistic fantasies depends upon the receipt of care-giving signals from real objects (or the realisation of one's potential to attract such signals). In healthy narcissism, the satisfaction gained from narcissistic fantasies is conditional on object libidinal discharges (Federn, 1952). Conversely, healthy narcissism can be employed in support of object strivings, whereby "satisfaction of the object libido is often conditional upon the simultaneous satisfaction of the preformed narcissistic phantasies" (p. 359). When narcissistic fantasies are "slanted more and more toward real tasks, interests, relations, desires, and activities" (p. 358), they can "turn into useful planning and pondering endowed with a normal narcissistic component" (Federn, 1952, p. 359).

Unhealthy narcissism "indulges in timeless sham events, actually substituting for the present" (p. 360). Unhealthy narcissism "consumes libido which should benefit reality adjustment and the objects; it prevents relationships with other persons" (Federn, 1952, p. 342). Instead of being invested in selfobjects (that is, in the ego via selfobjects), "narcissistic libido" may be "tied to the unrealistic unconscious or disavowed grandiose fantasies and to the crude exhibitionism of the split-off and/or repressed grandiose self" (Kohut, 1971, p. 144). The "damming up of primitive forms of narcissistic-exhibitionistic libido" lowers "the capacity for healthy self-esteem" (supplied by "real" selfobjects) and, instead, produces a "heightened tendency to hypochondriacal preoccupation, self-consciousness, shame, and embarrassment" (Kohut, 1971, p. 144). Awareness of a discrepancy between the self-image of one's fantasy and the reality of one's relatedness to, and position in, the social world—or failure to overcome this discrepancy (through self-actualisation)—can be profoundly injurious ("narcissistic injury"). If the narcissistic balance can only be maintained by an imaginary idealised object or by the grandiose self, contact with external objects has to be avoided. Indeed, excessive narcissism renders the establishment of a transference neurosis in psychoanalytic therapy impossible.

### 5.6   Summary

The animal ascertains information about the risk of exposure to conspecific attack or about an infringement into its territory (and, implicitly, a challenge to its access to recourses) from the environmental, and particularly social, context. First, with regards to the risk of conspecific attack, contextual information highlighting novelty, unpredictability, or fluidity of a social situation (instability of patterns of relatedness) gives rise to anxiety. Second, a challenge to one's established territory, which gives rise to anger, is the evolutionary precursor of a challenge to one's social rank or position and injury to self-esteem, which, too, are states of affair that can be discerned only from social contextual information, processed presumably by the hippocampus. Either, appreciation of the risk of conspecific attack or realisation of infringement upon one's territory, leads to arousal—manifesting as anxiety or anger, respectively—and reduces the activation threshold for defensive or offensive (offensively aggressive) behaviours, respectively. In addition, defensive or offensively aggressive arousal, that is, anxiety or anger, would *drive* appetitive behaviour seeking to create conditions that match an innate "stimulus situation" that can "release" submissive (fearful) or aggressive displays in dyadic interactions (Figure 2-4). The important point is that affective arousal both increases the probability of certain types of instinctive displays or actions and energises appetitive behaviour. Appetitive drive manifests as more or less random general-purpose agitation and restlessness or as habitual and seemingly goal-directed instrumental behaviour.

Expressive movements ("Ausdrucksbewegungen" or affective displays) are phylogenetically ritualised, instinctive motor patterns that serve intraspecific communication. Instinctive (consummatory) behaviour is often preceded by an epoch of appetitive (preparatory or goal-directed) behaviour. Lorenz (1935, 1937, 1939) and Tinbergen (1951) recognised that appetitive behaviour serves to obtain an innate "stimulus situation" ("Reizsituation"), which, in turn, releases an instinctive motor pattern, such as an "expressive movement". Lorenz and Tinbergen (1938) also pointed out that appetitive behaviour is composed of orienting movements (such as head direction adjustments) and locomotor behaviour. Orienting movements and epochs of locomotor behaviour have the effect of changing the animal's "view" (spatial contextual information) ahead of itself and its situational context around itself, respectively. Obtaining an innate stimulus

situation alone may not be sufficient to release an instinctive behaviour pattern. Thresholds for instinctive motor patterns are regulated by the organism's emotional appreciation of its environmental and physiological context. The preferential release of instinctive behaviour patterns under specific environmental and physiological conditions would be of obvious evolutionary advantage. Emotional feelings merely *reflect* a preparedness to enact certain instinctive motor patterns. Emotional feelings play a role in the acquisition of situationally appropriate appetitive behaviour, but they, in themselves, do not make instinctive responses more or less likely to occur. Instead, the lowering of the threshold for enactment of certain instinctive patterns is part of an unconscious emotional state (emotional behaviour mode) that has been activated in response to the situation that the animal faces. For as long as the animal's behavioural state is one of anxiety, and for as long as the animal's situational context is, therefore, "coloured" by feelings of anxiety, stimulus constellations being perceived outside consciousness can, if they match an innate stimulus situation, elicit innate motor patterns of fight or flight (Figure 5-1). Moreover, in an emotional state of anxiety, when instinctive defensive responding is facilitated, behaviour is acquired (learned) that instates (arrives at) a secure situation, a situation that is associated with a reduction in the emotional feeling of anxiety.

Apart from increasing defensive preparedness and facilitating the search for targets of fight or flight behaviour, anxiety promotes the identification of routes of escape (based on spatial contextual information) and the more or less targeted search for places of safety. Safety-seeking behaviour is evidently appetitive in nature. Responding to the situational context appetitively (in accordance with previous reinforcement learning), the animal moves from a dangerous situation to one that is safe. Once the animal is in a safe situation, a different set of instinctive interactions with conspecifics is promoted. Attaining a state of social relatedness, the animal becomes able to respond to certain constellations of external sensory stimuli with instinctive displays involved in affiliative interaction or concerned with the induction and provision of parental care. We can argue that safety-seeking behaviour (anxiety-related appetitive behaviour) aims to create a situational context in which innate "stimulus situations" (processed independently of awareness) can release affective displays used in care-inducing and care-giving interactions. Much of what we regard as attention-, approval-, or care-seeking behaviour has as its goal the creation of emotional conditions favourable to affective interaction. The condition (situational context) the individual seeks to create through his social appetitive behaviour is characterised by his relatedness to the social environment and acceptance by his fellow conspecifics. By creating such context, as reflected in a reduction in anxiety and an increase in self-esteem (Figure 2-5), the individual escapes a situational context—marked by anxiety—in which he is vulnerable to conspecific attack.

Social behaviour can directly influence another person, or it elaborates and furnishes the self, persona, or defensive screen that one maintains in or around oneself. Direct interaction with another person contains both appetitive and consummatory elements. During interaction between two persons, affective displays of one person can create a releasing stimulus situation for affective displays of the other. Specifically, assertive or dominant displays induce submissive displays in the partner (Ferguson & Bargh, 2004), while care-inducing displays (infantilisms) elicit reciprocal care-giving displays (affective attunement), in accordance with two main patterns of dyadic interactions (McCluskey, 2002). Contextual aspects of a dyadic interaction, including the general direction in which a conversation proceeds, determine the prevailing pattern of the dyadic exchange. Much of our social behaviour is concerned with changing the social context within which we operate (Goffman, 1959). In social situations, we are always attentive to others (unless we withdraw into a dissociative state); and, even when we are not engaged in direct interaction with another person, we

monitor others' behaviour with regard to its significance to our self-assessment, and we consider the impact that our seemingly nonsocial behaviour has on others and others' perception of ourselves (Heard & Lake, 1986). Self-esteem is inextricably linked with the social context encoding information concerning one's worth and others' appreciation of oneself (Gergen, 1977; James, 1890). The self can be seen as part of a mechanism that controls behaviour directed at changing the present social situation in a goal-directed fashion. Goal-directed (appetitive) efforts to change the situation may come to a conclusion as soon as anxiety is no longer supported by contextual information (Figure 5-2). Successful achievement of a secure situation may or may not be mediated by the actual receipt of positive attention from others. Both, affectionate affective interaction (e.g., Eibl-Eibesfeldt, 1970) and anxiety reduction (e.g., Young, 1959), are rewarding and may retrospectively reinforce emotional and spatial dimensions of a preceding epoch of appetitive behaviour.[7]

In a social situation, the individual may "unconsciously" predict or expect that his apparently nonsocial behaviour, in which he happens to be engaged, has the effect of enhancing his social visibility or increasing his worth or acceptance in the eyes of others (Heard & Lake, 1986; James, 1890). These are social goals of behaviour that is not directly social in nature, highlighting the social goal-directedness of kinds of behaviour that are seemingly more concerned with coincidental tasks or oneself than with others. Through actions unknowingly carried out for the purpose of adjusting our image in the eyes of others, we control the probability of receiving approving signals from others. The signal that mediates or accompanies this effect would

---

[7]To say that behaviour that overcomes an aversive emotional state, such as the state signalling social unrelatedness or exclusion, is "rewarded", means that the link between the aversive situation and the subsequent, more or less randomly chosen combination of locomotor and orienting behaviour is reinforced.

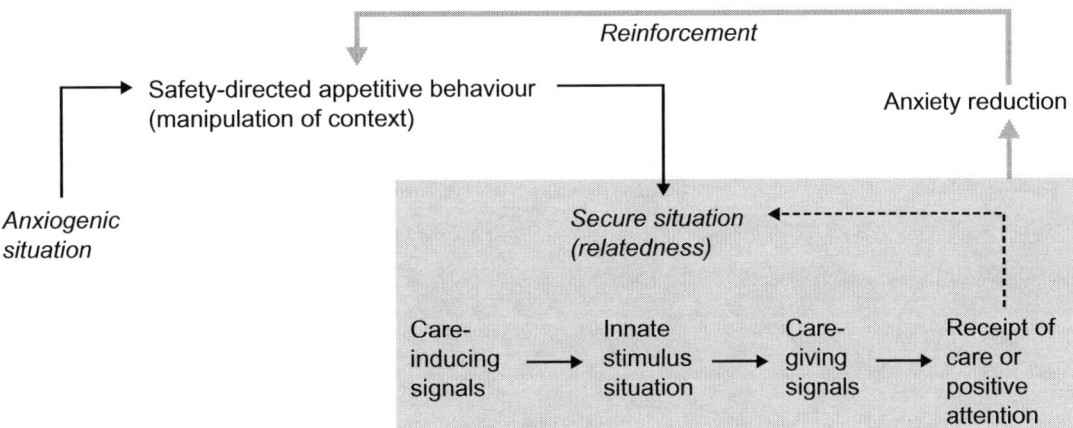

Figure 5-2.   Safety-directed (attention-seeking) behaviour, borne out of anxiety, may be reinforced by the achievement of a situation that is judged by the organism to be secure. A situation is secure if it allows the induction of care-giving signals (positive attention) in other individuals or if care-giving signals are actually received. The *receipt* of care-giving signals, or appreciation of the potential to receive care-giving signals, may mark an ambiguous situation as secure, indicating a reduced risk of becoming the target of intraspecific aggression.

be a change in the character of the situation from greater to lesser anxiogenicity. Frank anxiety is not necessarily present when we seek attention or adjust our public persona in a social situation (or ruminate about ourselves even outside social situations) but neither is hunger always present when we obtain, store, or prepare food, or plan to do so. Habitual social behaviour responds to contextual social information by automatically steering us away from (and thereby avoiding) anxiogenic situations. Frank anxiety may suggest that attention-seeking and self-concerned behaviour has become more random or exploratory and less certain in its effects, so that any coincidental reduction in anxiety reinforces social behaviour, just like a coincidental reduction in hunger reinforces food-seeking behaviour (Young, 1959). Once the individual has entered or created a *secure* situation (marked by an absence of anxiety), he is likely to respond to an innate releasing stimulus situation with an appropriate display of care-inducing or care-giving behaviour (Figure 5-2). Affective attunement, supporting intersubjective relatedness (Stern, 1985), transference, and projective identification

are interpersonal processes that maintain an anxiety-free situation, that is, a relationship, in which care-inducing and care-giving (libidinal) signals can be exchanged.[8]

_____

[8]The concept of narcissism may be closely related to appetitive care-soliciting behaviour, especially insofar as such behaviour has become automatic or habitual through reinforcement learning. Narcissistic behaviours solicit praise and affection, or they maintain or establish social relatedness and access to affectionate and care-related signals and, coincidentally, keep us away, or remove us, from situations of unrelatedness and anxiety. Thus, narcissism may describe behaviour strategies or personality habits that seek to procure approval directly or that, on a higher level of abstraction, promote the individual's social acceptability, albeit sometimes in a maladaptive fashion.

# CHAPTER SIX

# Anxiety

"Anxiety" describes a particular state of expecting the danger or preparing for it, even though it may be an unknown one. "Fear" requires a definite object of which to be afraid. "Fright", however, is the name we give to the state a person gets into when he has run into danger ... (Freud, 1920, p. 12)

Anxiety is the ego's response to perceiving a danger situation and anticipating a repetition of a remembered early infantile traumatic situation (Freud, 1923, 1933). In the early years of childhood, anxiety is caused by the danger of loss of object or, indeed, by object loss itself. Anxiety *signals* when a traumatic factor threatens to recur, however it may also be "the direct effect of a traumatic factor" (Freud, 1933, p. 123). Separation from the mother causes the "most painful feelings of tension"—feelings that are not dissimilar from the anxiety experienced by the baby at birth (representing the original separation from the mother) (p. 115). It was Otto Rank who first understood that "birth anxiety" is the prototype of all later danger situations. At later developmental stages, anxiety is caused, according to Freud (1933), by "fear of castration", and, finally, by "fear of the superego". Early

separation distress is evolutionarily related to the risk of attack by predators. Anxiety may have evolved as the emotional response to a *situation* in which there is an increased risk of this kind. Castration anxiety and "fear of the superego", on the other hand, may be related to the evolutionarily more recent risk of being aggressed by a conspecific in a social situation. The latter type of anxiety is latent but pervasive. Sullivan (1953) recognised that "anxiety appertains to the infant's, as also to the mother's, communal existence" (p. 42). He also understood that "the relaxation of the tension of anxiety ... is the experience, not of satisfaction, but of interpersonal *security*" (Sullivan, 1953, p. 42).

> We all underestimate, I think, the extent to which we are constantly haunted by anxiety and equally long for security. (Lorenz, 1973, p. 200)

Anxiety may arise in interpersonal situations that we encounter or create as we seek to satisfy physiological needs or express instinctive behaviour patterns. Sullivan (1953) argued that "anxiety always interferes with any other tensions with which it coincides", particularly tensions deriving from the satisfaction of physiological needs. Anxiety opposes "tensions of needs" and the satisfaction of these needs. Anxiety would also inhibit the expression of affiliative behaviour. Anxiety and related aversive feelings (guilt, shame, disgust) oppose the discharge of "instinctual drives"; they "tend toward withdrawal from the world", while an instinctual drive that concurrently seeks discharge "tends toward the world" (Fenichel, 1946, p. 140). Anxiety and related aversive states are counterforces that "seem to be governed by a striving to avoid objects", while the drive pressing for discharge is "governed by its hunger for objects" (p. 140). These conflicts play a role in neurotic symptom formation (Fenichel, 1946). By avoiding anxiety, we maintain conditions favourable to the satisfaction of physiological needs and to the release of consummatory instinctive motor patterns. Circumventing situations that may cause anxiety (while remaining in contact with others), we "long-circuit" (sublimate) the resolution of needs in a socially acceptable manner.

> Simple performances which would relax the tension of some needs have to be made more complicated in order that one may avoid becoming more anxious. Before he is very many months of age, the child will be showing full-fledged *sublimation*, in the sense of quite unwittingly having adopted some pattern of activity in the partial, and somewhat incomplete, satisfaction of a need which, however, avoids anxiety that stands in the way of the simplest completely satisfying activity. (Sullivan, 1953, p. 154)

Anxiety cuts off foresight employed as a means of advancing appetitive behaviour. As Sullivan (1953) saw it, "the more anxious one is, the less the distinguished function of foresight is free to work effectively in the choice, as we call it, of action appropriate to the tensions that one is experiencing" (p. 44). Sullivan (1953) thought that, unlike stimuli that induce fear, "the

circumstances conducive to anxiety cannot be removed, nor destroyed, nor escaped" (p. 53). This may be true when anxiety is severe and foresight is cut off. When anxiety is not associated with overwhelming stress, the individual uses appetitive behaviour to move away from anxiogenic circumstances, by approaching or creating secure circumstances. Anxiety, signalling the presence of a danger *situation*, prompts the engagement of protective or defensive mechanisms (Freud, 1933).

> The more the development of anxiety can be restricted to a mere signal, the more the ego can make use of defensive acts, which amount to a mental binding of the repressed, and the more the process approximates to the standard of a normal modification of the impulse, without of course ever reaching it. (Freud, 1933, p. 119)

Anxiety, as an emotional state, constrains behaviours in such a way that the individual's security, or sense of security, is likely reestablished. The situation giving rise to anxiety may be novel, uncertain, and unpredictable, so that security-seeking behaviour is generated more or less randomly. Security-seeking behaviour is reinforced as it succeeds in removing the individual from an anxiogenic situation or reducing the anxiogenicity of that situation. Reinforcement and acquisition of defensive behaviour would be linked to a reduction in the signal that anxiety represents. The individual faced with an anxiogenic situation may employ defensive behaviours habitually without experiencing feelings of anxiety. Although anxiety is involved in the formation of defensive behaviour patterns, anxiety (as an "output phenomenon") may not continue to be part of the generation of these patterns; defences would be automatised and characterological (Breger, 1968).

> What sense, then, does the traditional explanation of defenses as means to avoid

anxiety have, when there is not necessarily even any anxiety present? Again, it only makes sense if we conceptualize "anxiety" as an output phenomenon of a process that involves perception, organization, transformation, and output. Although anxiety, anger, sexual arousal, and the like *may be* involved at earlier periods in the development of a particular perceptual-memory system, it is the *structuring of the systems* that determines present output, and not the affect or anxiety. (Breger, 1968, pp. 60–61)

## 6.1   Developmental lines

… much of the sophisticated superstructure of cognitive and feeling processes characteristic of Western man in the realm of fear is intelligible only in terms of the primitive genetically biased groundwork that evolved in a different environment and that we share with other primate species. … Not only is the behaviour of every human adult influenced by these primitive processes but so also are his most sophisticated cognitive structures and his most sensitive ways of feeling. (Bowlby, 1973, p. 140)

Bowlby (1973) confirmed that separation, or the threat of separation, from loved figures is a principle source of anxiety, although anxiety can be aroused under many different conditions; "missing someone who is loved and longed for" is only one of them (p. 31). Other conditions that elicit alarm and retreat are "mere strangeness", noise, "objects that rapidly expand or approach", darkness, and isolation (p. 85). All of these conditions are "statistically associated with an increased risk of danger" (Bowlby, 1973, p. 85). Under any of these conditions, animals "behave in fact as though danger were actually present" (p. 85). Animals may take avoiding action, run away, cower, hide in a shelter, or seek others' company. They also display "a preparedness to meet

real dangers" (p. 86) (defensive preparedness). Behaviours indicative of anxiety include "wary watching combined with inhibition of action" and "a frightened facial expression accompanied perhaps by trembling or crying" (p. 88). "Freezing" refers to "behaviour that results in immobility" (Bowlby, 1973, p. 90). The "biological function" of all of these behaviours is the protection against potential danger. Different types of anxiogenic, that is, potentially dangerous, conditions may activate different and somewhat separate anxiety-related "systems of behaviour", such as freezing or withdrawal, which "may even be mutually inhibiting" (p. 88). Other types of behaviour act in concert, such as running away from a dangerous situation and running towards cover or company. An animal or person may, not infrequently, try "simultaneously to escape from one situation" and "gain proximity to another" (p. 95). Behaviour that increases the distance to a situation of relative isolation and, at the same time, reduces the distance to a person that provides protection "is nothing other than attachment behaviour" (Bowlby, 1973, p. 89) (Figure 6-1).

### 6.1.1   Distress vocalisations

Separation distress is likely an evolutionarily derivative of pain (Panksepp, 2003). Distress vocalisations that are emitted by the infant when separated from the mother would correspond to pain vocalisations. Many young mammals emit cries when having lost contact with their mother or fallen out of their nest. A newborn child frequently cries—and only "calms down when it is caressed, picked up or spoken to" (Eibl-Eibesfeldt, 1970, p. 206). Human infants tend to cry when they are put down, and not when they are carried.

> This is a natural and probably innate reaction which has its roots in our remote past. If the child of primitive man lost contact with its mother, it was exposed to attack by predators. Cries, which functioned as a request to the mother to reestablish

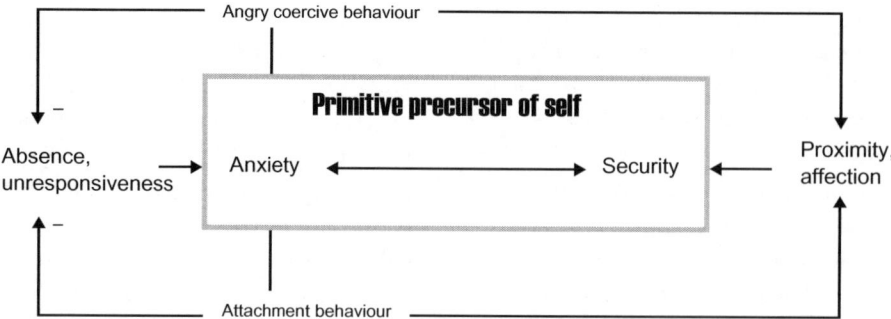

Figure 6-1.   Anxious attachment behaviour or angry coercive behaviour are engaged when the infant is anxious due to the object's inaccessibility (separation anxiety) or emotional unresponsiveness, much as flight or attack behaviour is engaged in response to pain. Anger assists in overcoming obstacles to reunion or reengagement with the attachment object, but also promotes avoidance learning *by the object*, and, hence, increases control over the object (Bowlby, 1973).

contact, were thus of species-preserving importance. (Hass, 1968, p. 164)

Mammals are "equipped with appetitive behaviour for restoring contact—to begin with by crying out and later through active seeking" (Eibl-Eibesfeldt, 1970, p. 205). The mother's responding to the infant's cries aids the development of a bond with the mother. With the advent of active seeking behaviour, the mother becomes the "goal-in-flight" for the infant. Appetitive behaviour for contact "is the true root of the bond between mother and child" (Eibl-Eibesfeldt, 1970, p. 205). As the child develops, he seeks and restores contact in increasingly abstract ways, whereby "contact" may be defined as accessibility (availability), within the present social context, of approving signals emitted by maternal cherishing displays.

> ... to hold the hypothesis that fear behaviour in a situation of maternal inaccessibility is instinctive in no way rules out the possibility that learning of some kind is necessary for its development. All that such a view requires is that, when an individual is reared in the species's environment of evolutionary adaptedness, opportunity for the necessary learning is always present. (Bowlby, 1973, p. 179)

### 6.1.2   Proximity seeking

Being alone and separated from the mother "carries an increased risk of danger" (Bowlby, 1973, p. 178). Bowlby (1973) argued that separation anxiety is "an instinctive response to one of the naturally occurring clues to an increased danger" (p. 86). Separation anxiety occurs when "either mother leaves child or child is removed more or less unwillingly from mother" (p. 32), not when the child takes the initiative. Upon separation from his mother, the infant "is likely to take action aimed at detaining her or finding her; and he is anxious until he has achieved this goal" (p. 31). Attachment behaviour, not only in humans but also in other species, serves to "maintain a younger or weaker individual in more or less close proximity to another discriminated and stronger individual" (Bowlby, 1973, p. 148). Attachment behaviour is "directed as least as much to regaining the familiar figure as it is to escaping from the strange people and situation" (p. 96) (Figure 6-1). During the latter half of the first year, the infant's "attachment to a mother figure is becoming steadily better organized", and so is his "withdrawal from a fear-arousing situation" (p. 122). By twelve months of age, the infant "has become able so to organize his behaviour that he moves simultaneously both away from one type of situation and towards another type" (p. 122). Attachment behaviour remains evident throughout life. Regardless of age, "separation anxiety" and attachment behaviour serve to "maintain the whole individual within a defined part of the environment" (Bowlby, 1973, p. 149). Thus, anxiety that arises upon separation from the primary love object or, later in life, from a derivative of the primary love object, prompts the individual to reestablish proximity to the object or, later in life, to a familiar and safe situation—a situation providing what Sullivan (1953) called "interpersonal security". One of Freud's most enduring contributions to understanding motivated behaviour is "the idea that present motivated activity is a transformation of earlier patterns" (Breger, 1968, p. 51).

> Neurotic phenomena (such as symptoms, life styles, choice of partners, forms of sexuality and of aggression) are essentially later symbolic transformations of early acquired patterns. (Breger, 1968, p. 61)
>
> … because models of attachment figures and expectations about their behaviour are built up during the years of childhood and tend thenceforward to remain unchanged, the behaviour of a person today may be explicable in terms, not of his present situation, but of his experiences many years earlier. (Bowlby, 1973, p. 256)

### 6.1.3   Stranger anxiety and neophobia

Separation enhances the infant's responding with fear or anxiety to the emergence of a threatening stimulus or another dangerous situation. In the mother's absence, the infant not only becomes distressed but also "responds to all sorts of slightly strange and unexpected situations with acute alarm" (Bowlby, 1973, p. 31). Heightened responsiveness to strange situations may indicate that "separation anxiety" (separation distress) contains the developmental beginnings of infantile "stranger anxiety". At the age of one year, the infant's response to a stranger ranges from mild apprehension and wide-eyed staring to "outright terrified screaming and

panic behaviour" (Schecter, 1973, p. 29). Often, the infant's response consists in "a freezing (inhibition) of motor and expressive behaviour" (Schecter, 1973, p. 29). As the fear of strangers matures in the second year of life, the "bond with the person the child is attached to" increases (Eibl-Eibesfeldt, 1970, p. 211). Adults never outgrow the fear of strangers. In primitive peoples or isolated communities, strangers "are rejected, often attacked, or at best tolerated with reserved curiosity" (Eibl-Eibesfeldt, 1970, p. 217).

Schecter (1973) distinguished three forms of infantile anxiety. Separation anxiety, evident at around eight months of age, was suggested to have its dynamic root in the "fear of object loss", whereas stranger anxiety *in addition* derives from the infant's general "fear of the strange" (Schecter, 1973). Any unfamiliar configuration of stimuli that conflicts with an anticipated pattern can provoke this fear (neophobia). The fear of the strange can also arise in a social situation that contains strange elements in conjunction with familiar elements. Schecter (1973) thought that stranger anxiety, in turn, contributes to the third form of infantile anxiety: the anxiety that is induced in the infant by anxiety of the mother (anxiety as a contagion, "empathetically induced anxiety"). Automatic imitation of the mother's fearful expressions may contribute to the experience of this type of anxiety. Importantly, "the mother has the power to neutralize certain forms of anxiety in her infant, if she is not too anxious, by familiar and now symbolically reassuring behavior, such as the playful interchange, the calm smile or embrace" (p. 32). By calming the infant's anxiety, the mother can render that which is strange into that which is engagingly novel (Schecter, 1973).

> Once anxiety becomes a prominent experience in the infant's life, the need to avoid experiencing it, and later the related propensities to shame and guilt, become society's most effective vehicle by which it values and structure are maintained. (Schecter, 1973, p. 34)

### 6.1.4   Fear over loss of love

> Fear is felt … lest there be a loss of certain pleasurable feelings, such as well-being, protection, and security, which were hitherto present. This feared loss may be characterized as a loss of self-esteem, the most extreme degree of which is a feeling of annihilation. (Fenichel, 1946, p. 134)

Fenichel (1946) recognised that "all anxiety is a fear of experiencing a traumatic state" (p. 133). The infant's fundamental anxiety is a "fear over loss of love" and a fear over "loss of help and protection" (p. 44). Evolutionarily, the availability of narcissistic supplies (love) is linked to the availability of help and protection. The availability of narcissistic supplies, experienced by the subject as intact self-esteem, may be the antithesis of the state of anxiety, which signals an increased probability of exposure to harm (due to lack of help and protection) (Figure 6-1). Anxiety, reflecting a loss of help and protection, is equivalent to a loss of self-esteem, "so that a loss of help and protection means also a loss of self-esteem" (Fenichel, 1946, p. 44). Anxiety arises "out of loss of narcissistic supplies" (p. 136). Anxiety, being a warning signal, may also indicate "that there is a danger of a cessation of essential narcissistic supplies"; the behavioural effect of this signal "must be to influence objects to furnish these supplies" (pp. 135–136). Early self-esteem depends on external narcissistic supplies (affection and praise). With the resolution of the Oedipus complex, "the anticipating ego begins to guard against any action on its part that might result in a loss of the necessary parental love" (Fenichel, 1946, p. 136).

> With anticipatory imagination and the resultant planning of suitable later actions, the idea of danger comes into being. The judging ego declares that a situation that is not yet traumatic might become so. This judgement obviously sets up conditions that are similar to those created by the traumatic situation

itself, but much less intense. This, too, is experienced by the ego as anxiety. (Fenichel, 1946, p. 43)

### 6.1.5   Shame

The infant's need for proximity to his mother may be developmentally continuous with his need to be acknowledged by the mother. Maternal proximity and acknowledgement are reassuring to the infant, whereby the former signals protection against predatory attack and the latter signals that intraspecific attack, including attack by the mother herself, is unlikely. The mother's acknowledgement and acceptance of her infant becomes the blueprint for individual's relatedness to his social environment later in life. Infantile strivings for acknowledgement would be the evolutionary precursor for all the complexity of human behaviour directed at eliciting acknowledgement and reassurance from increasingly abstract representations of the primary love object. Behaviours aimed at soliciting the mother's acknowledgement and, later in life, an acknowledging response from the social milieu, at large, are exhibitionistic in their essence.

Shame is rooted in an "archaic physiological reflex pattern" that counteracts exhibitionism (Fenichel, 1946, p. 139). Shame arises when one does not want to be looked at or seen, since being looked at, in certain situations, "is automatically equated with being despised" (Fenichel, 1946, p. 139).[1] In narcissistic patients, situations that normally arouse anxiety, apprehension, and worry elicit immoderate and intense upset and "temporary paralysis of psychic functions" (Kohut, 1971, p. 230). The narcissistic patient is "flooded with shame and anxiety" when he recalls a situation in which he "told a joke which turned out to be out of place" or "talked too much about himself in company" (p. 230). He, then, experiences "painful embarrassment"

---

[1]Disgust, like shame, is an archaic physiological reflex pattern. Shame, guilt, and disgust are "motives of defence", as much as anxiety is a motive of defence (Fenichel, 1946).

and "anger that the act that has been committed cannot be undone" (Kohut, 1971, p. 231).

> The narcissistic patient tends to react to the memory of a *faux pas* with excessive shame and self-rejection. His mind returns again and again to the painful moment, in an attempt to eradicate the reality of the incident by magical means, i.e., to undo it. Simultaneously the patient may angrily wish to do away with himself in order to wipe out the tormenting memory in this fashion. (Kohut, 1971, p. 231)

Kohut (1971) observed that patients' grandiose and exhibitionistic tendencies (their "old grandiosity and exhibitionism") are at "the center of these reactions" (p. 232). Anxiety associated with narcissistic disturbances relates to patients' awareness of their vulnerability to "narcissistic injury" and their assessment that they have lost contact with their social environment despite (and because of) their exhibitionistic efforts. Anxiety encountered in the analysis of narcissistic personality disorders represents a "fear of loss of contact with reality and fear of permanent isolation through the experience of unrealistic grandiosity"; or it may reflect "frightening experiences of shame and self-consciousness through the intrusion of exhibitionistic libido" (Kohut, 1971, p. 153). In essence, the anxiety underlying narcissistic disturbances may stem from a loss of relatedness to others and a fear of being ostracised for one's grandiose and exhibitionistic tendencies.

### 6.1.6   Fear of punishment

Shame is related to guilt feelings (Fenichel, 1946). Guilt is a sense of deserving or expecting punishment from the internalised authority figure (superego), which is formed during the oedipal phase of development (Freud, 1923). Although narcissistic patients are readily "overwhelmed by shame", they are not easily "swayed by guilt feelings (they are not inclined to react unduly to the pressure exerted by their

idealized superego)" (Kohut, 1971, p. 232). Neurotic anxiety ("castration anxiety") reflects retribution fears arising as a consequence of "competition with superior rivals" (p. 154). "Castration anxiety" is a fear, originating in the oedipal developmental phase, "of being killed or mutilated by a circumscribed adversary of superior strength" (Kohut, 1971, p. 153). In what is called "castration anxiety" (compared to narcissistic anxiety), there is "a greater degree of elaboration of the source of the danger (a personal adversary)" and "a greater elaboration of the nature of the danger (i.e., the punishment)" (pp. 153–154). Anxieties encountered in the analyses of "transference neuroses" may be concerned not only with the possibility of "punishment by an object which is cathected with object-instinctual energies" but also with "the possibility of a lonely longing for an absent object" (p. 21). Self-esteem decreases only secondarily in cases of "castration anxiety" or anxiety related to the longing for an absent object (Kohut, 1971, p. 21).

### 6.1.7   Pain of rejection

A perceived lack of reassurance from the mother and, especially, unresponsiveness of the mother to the child's presence or actions cause him to feel anxious. Maternal disapproval is another source of the child's anxiety. As Sullivan (1953) pointed out, when the mother is approving, the child is content; when the mother is disapproving, the child is anxious. Maternal disapproval also causes pain. Maternal disapproval, in this regard, has the same effect as, later in life, offensive attack from conspecifics with whom the individual competes in his efforts to procure reassuring acknowledgement. Pain, as an acute emotional response, may arise when the child's behaviour is met with disapproval (hostility), when *expected* reassurance is not forthcoming, or when his *seeking* of reassurance is met with rejection. Attachment and reassurance-seeking behaviours are modified, during the child's development, by experiences of pain due to rejection ("narcissistic injury") or disapproval (punishment)—similarly to the role of physical pain and injury in other forms of avoidance learning (Figure 6-2). Recurrent experience of pain due to rejection or disapproval in childhood is a major factor in establishing enduring patterns of interpersonal behaviour.

Pain of rejection remains a potent factor throughout life. Persons with *schizoid* personality disturbance are easily hurt by a perceived rejection. As a consequence, schizoid persons retreat from human closeness; they have "learned to distance themselves from others in order to avoid the specific danger of exposing themselves to a narcissistic injury" (Kohut, 1971, p. 12). Their distancing is a consequence of "the correct assessment of their narcissistic vulnerability" (p. 12). Similarly, patients with *narcissistic* personality disturbance—due to a fixation on childhood grandiosity and exhibitionism—are easily hurt and offended. Expecting "to shine" in a social situation and "anticipating acclaim in his fantasies", the narcissistic patient readily experiences pain when he feels that a rejection has occurred (Kohut, 1971, p. 230). This may escalate to intense rage and self-rejection. Thus, pain is experienced not only in response to aversive displays of

offensive aggression (including expressions of disapproval) but also when behaviour soliciting praise is *frustrated* or when expected and *desired* acclaim remains elusive, whereas anxiety reflects an assessment of an increased likelihood, in a particular situation, of incurring painful social stimulation in the form of disapproval or rejection (Figure 2-5).

### 6.2   Social relatedness

> We have feelings of affection, anger, suspicion, so fleeting that they scarcely invade awareness, and so transitory that we forget them. These feelings may really be irrelevant and transitory; but they may just as well have behind them a great dynamic force. … Concerning anxiety this means not only that we may have anxiety without knowing it, but that anxiety may be the determining factor in our lives without our being conscious of it. (Horney, 1937, pp. 45–46)

Sullivan (1953) emphasised the infant's need not only for contact but also for "tenderness".

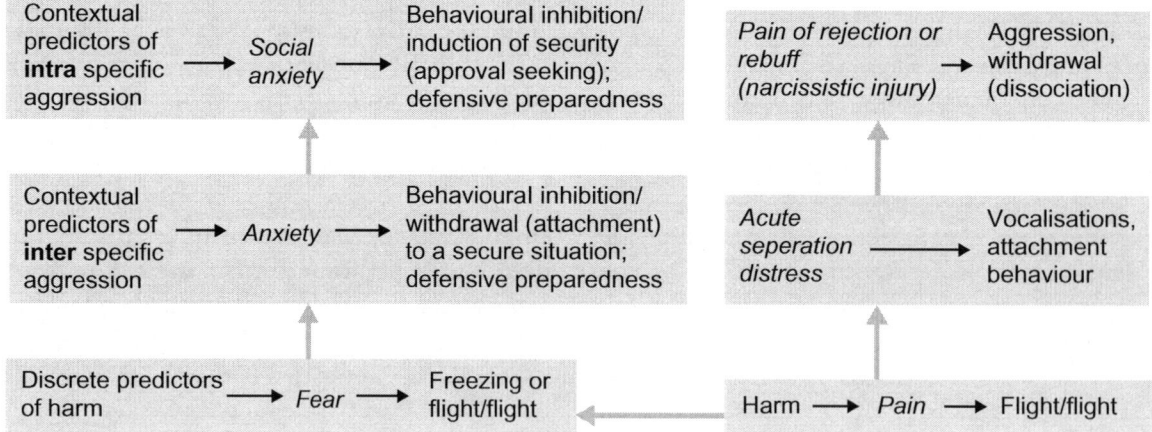

Figure 6-2.   Proposed evolution of social anxiety ("castration anxiety") and "narcissistic injury" from pain. Contextual predictors of *interspecific* aggression include novel situations, bright and open or dark places (species-specific), and social separation or isolation. Contextual predictors of intraspecific aggression include unresponsiveness of the object and unrelatedness to (ignorance by) the social environment. Pain of rejection arises when attachment behaviour (appetitive) is frustrated and anticipated narcissistic supplies are not forthcoming.

The human infant engages in affectionate (tender) interactions with his mother from an early age. Affectionate interactions are likely to be evolutionarily derived from instinctive behaviours involved in the provision and solicitation of parental ministrations. Culturally or phylogenetically ritualised displays of helplessness, for instance, release in others the impulse to cherish (Eibl-Eibesfeld, 1970). The awakening, in others, of the impulse to cherish inhibits their aggressiveness (and thereby prevents the subject's anxiety and renders the situation safe). An individual solicits, through infantile appeals, others' ritualised gestures of feeding or granting contact, which, in humans, can be expressed *verbally* in a highly ritualised form. Stereotypes conveying protective assurances and soothing remarks are often part of conversations (Eibl-Eibesfeld, 1970). Instinctive motor patterns ("expressive movements") involved in affectionate and caring interactions can be released under conditions of maternal proximity and responsiveness or, later in life, under conditions of proximity and responsiveness of a derivative of the primary object or under conditions of social acceptance and group relatedness. Social relatedness can be seen as an envelope (a general situational context) around a channel of instinctive communication between two individuals—a consciously experienced umbrella under which ritualised affectionate and care-related interactions can take place (unconsciously).

Human infants have an innate need for social relatedness. Early relatedness to the mother is a goal in itself; it is a need that exists for its own sake (Fairbairn, 1952; Sullivan, 1953). Early relatedness is not secondary to more primary physiological goals; it does not depend on the satisfaction of physiological needs (Bowlby, 1973; Stern, 1985). With further development, the need arises "for human-group-psychic-membership—that is, inclusion into the human group as a member with potentially sharable subjective experiences" (Stern, 1985, p. 136). Similarly to maternal proximity and responsiveness, social acceptance and relatedness provide a protective context within which the exchange of instinctive caregiving and care-inducing interactions can take place and within which physiological needs can be met.

Stern (1985) suggested that nature has "provided the ways and means for any intermeshings of individuals that would add survival value" (p. 137). Seeking protection (safety) is an old and powerful motive for association with conspecifics (Eibl-Eibesfeldt, 1970). However, in group-living species, association with conspecifics is in itself anxiogenic. Being acknowledged and accepted by others in a group reduces the risk of intraspecific aggression and counters social anxiety. It seems that attachment behaviour, which, in humans, includes behaviours aiming to establish and maintain maternal responsiveness (intersubjective relatedness between infant and mother), is developmentally continuous with behaviours that aim to establish the individual's relatedness to his social milieu. Contact seeking is motivated by loneliness (Sullivan, 1953) (or anxiety associated with being separated or being in an unpredictable or strange location), whereas behaviour aiming to establish interpersonal or social relatedness may be "motivated" by, or, rather, acquired through, interpersonal or social anxiety, which is to say that anxiety experienced *vis-à-vis* another individual's (such as the mother's) unresponsiveness or when the individual is not accepted by, or included in, a group plays a role in the acquisition of such behaviour. "Intersubjective relatedness" between infant and mother is *reinforcing* (Stern, 1985), perhaps insofar as intersubjective relatedness, when it is achieved, reduces anxiety. It is the achievement of "*security* needs" or "attachment goals" that reinforces the infant's behaviour towards the mother. Stern (1985) found that "intersubjective successes can result in feelings of enhanced security", whereas "minor failures in intersubjectivity can be interpreted, experienced, and acted upon as total ruptures in a relationship" (Stern, 1985, p. 136). Failed attachment behaviour, that is, the frustration of behaviour instrumental to achieving intersubjective relatedness, leads to the experience of pain and distress (narcissistic injury). The pain of rejection and separation distress may be more closely related to the experience of frustration than to anxiety, although frustration (and punishment, in general) and anxiety reduction may play equally important roles in the shaping of attachment behaviour.

### 6.2.1   Reinforcement learning

If an originally neutral stimulus is paired with a pain-arousing stimulus, the former stimulus (the conditioned stimulus) acquires the capacity to evoke an "anticipatory form of the pain reaction", namely a *fear* reaction (if the conditioned stimulus is discrete) or a state of *anxiety* (if the conditioned stimulus is vague or obscure, i.e., contextual) (Miller, 1948; Mowrer & Lamoreaux, 1946).[2] In personality development, conditioned stimuli or contexts signifying a lack of affection, a lack of prestige, or a lack of possessions acquire the capacity to arouse anxiety. Anxiety, when aroused, energises "whatever behaviour is directed toward goal objects by stimuli" (Brown, 1953). The "drive property" (energising function) of anxiety is responsible for activating latent "reaction tendencies" attached to stimulus cues that are perceived in a state of anxiety (Brown, 1953).

Similarly to how a reduction in fear reinforces behaviour that precedes the fear reduction (Miller, 1948; Mowrer & Lamoreaux, 1946), a reduction in anxiety following the achievement of a "goal object" would powerfully reinforce the behaviour that, in responding to an external stimulus or stimulus configuration, has been instrumental in achieving the goal and that has, thereby, reduced anxiety (Brown, 1953). For instance, if not having money is a cue for anxiety, then behaviour that is followed by the receipt of money (the goal object) removes or obliterates this anxiety-arousing cue and, hence, reduces

anxiety. The behaviour that incidentally secured access to money is powerfully reinforced by the reduction in anxiety attending the receipt of money (Brown, 1953).

A similar interpretation applies to human strivings for affection, prestige, or eminence. The "drive property" of anxiety is integral to all of them (Brown, 1953). Attention-seeking, approval-seeking, and prestige-seeking behaviours are reinforced by the decline in anxiety associated with receipt of attention, receipt of approval, and attainment of prestige or eminence, respectively. Once acquired, habitual behaviours that secure attention or approval or attain prestige or eminence would be engaged whenever anxiety is about to arise (in response to cues signifying a lack of approval or prestige, etc., whereby these behaviours serve to eliminate anxiety-arousing cues) (Brown, 1953). Whether we seek attention, approval, prestige, or money depends on our developmental stage and the type of social situation that gives rise to anxiety. All of these behaviours are not unlike attachment behaviours of infants (where a successful proximity-seeking response to an anxiogenic situation of isolation is reinforced by the decline in anxiety attending the reestablishment of maternal proximity); and they are not unlike flock- or herd-formation in gregarious animals (in which case a successful proximity-seeking response to an anxiety-provoking absence of surrounding conspecifics is reinforced by the decline in anxiety attending the reestablishment of proximity to the herd or flock).

### 6.2.2   Existential analysis

"Existential anxiety" drives us into social relatedness. As Heidegger (1927) saw it, there is a tendency to turn away form one's authentic "being in the world" and "fall" into the "they" (the "subject of everydayness") and the world of one's "concern". Heidegger thought that anxiety, which is at the core of one's existence in the world ("Dasein"), causes one's "thrownness" into the world (and projection into others), thus

---

[2] Although a discrete conditioned stimulus can elicit fear, fear is sometimes an acquired response to the situation of which the conditioned stimulus forms a part.

turning one's authentic being-in-the-world into the "they"-self. The "they"-self—which is what says "I"—thus replaces authentic existence (Heidegger, 1927).

> What expresses itself in the "I" is that Self which, proximally and for the most part, I am not authentically. ... one *is* that with which one concerns oneself. In the 'natural' ontical way in which the "I" talks, the phenomenal content of the Dasein which one has in view in the "I" gets overlooked. (Heidegger, 1927, p. 368)

Absorption in everydayness is *tranquilising* (anxiolytic). The "everyday publicness of the 'they' ... brings tranquillized self-assurance ... into the average everydayness of Dasein" (Heidegger, 1927, p. 233). For the most part, one is lost in the "they"-self, which is an existential modification of the authentic self; but even in this tranquillised being-in-the-world, anxiety is always latent. Emotion, or mood, according to Heidegger (1927), provides the existential background into which the perceived reality is immersed. Anxiety, like other moods, contributes to the emergence of the world as "always already" meaningful. Anxiety is inherent in human existence; and it is our constant "fleeing" form it that organises the everyday world in particular ways. Anxiety, when felt acutely, brings "Dasein" back from our absorption in the everyday distractions of the world, and reveals to us the nothingness at the core of existence (Heidegger, 1927), that is, the meaninglessness of objects and people (derealisation). Transience and fragility of social networks lead to chronic frustration of the individual's efforts to "flee" anxiety. Loss of traditions and lack of stable relatedness in modern society increase insecurity and make the search for transient resolutions of existential anxiety ever more desperate.

### 6.2.3  Interpersonal theory

Interpersonal theory, developed by Sullivan (1953), posits that the individual's personal responses to others (interpersonal patterns) are directly related to encounters with significant people in early development. This is to say that early object relations form the blueprint for interpersonal behaviour in later childhood and adulthood. Sullivan (1953) contended that we have a need for more or less continuous interpersonal contact. Isolation is tantamount to mental illness, although "a conspicuous indifference to other people's approbation constitutes a disorder in itself" (Chrzanowski, 1973, p. 142). Individuals' needs for contact and also tenderness are mutually resolved (or aggravated) in interpersonal relations. Denial of "tenderness" in this reciprocal process can bring about "frank anxiety, which aggravates the need for tenderness" (Sullivan, 1953, p. 198). Similarly, the "foresight of rebuff", that is, the anticipation of "forbidding gestures", can induce anxiety (p. 198). Anxiety that arises in an interpersonal context may be distinguishable from the feeling that accompanies social isolation. The felt component of the need for interpersonal contact, according to Sullivan (1953), is "loneliness". The experience of loneliness is integral to the need for compeers in the juvenile era and the need for acceptance, which arises in the later phases of juvenility. Loneliness also accompanies the need for intimate exchange in adolescence. Intense anxiety does not distract the person from trying to overcome loneliness and seeking companionship, which means that "loneliness in itself is more terrible than anxiety" (Sullivan, 1953, p. 262). Anxiety does not stop the person from "stumbling out of restlessness into situations which constitute, in some measure, a relief from loneliness" (Sullivan, 1953, p. 262).[3]

### Self-system

The essential undesirability of being anxious corresponds to the essential desirability of being acceptable to others (of being "good-me")

---

[3] The restless person's performance is hampered by "a primary lack of experience which is needed for the correct appraisal of the situation" (Sullivan, 1953, p. 262).

(Sullivan, 1953). The self is closely related to the experience of anxiety as well as to the receipt, or lack of receipt, of external appraisals. The "self-system" is formed "on the basis of reflected appraisals from others and the learning of roles which one undertook to live" (Sullivan, 1953, p. 17). The self-system constitutes "all the defenses that are built to cope with these appraisals and their distortions" (Arieti, 1973, p. 126). The way in which one sees oneself "is controlled by the self-system, since it manipulates the content of consciousness depending on the prevailing level of anxiety" (Chrzanowski, 1973, p. 143). The self is but "the content of consciousness within the framework of a person's socialisation, acculturation, and his formative relational patterning" (p. 133); it is "more or less coterminous with the information directly available to the individual" (Chrzanowski, 1973, p. 134). The self-system is engaged during the pursuit of "every general need that a person has" (Sullivan, 1953, p. 166).

> The origin of the self-system can be said to rest on the irrational character of culture or, more specifically, society. Were it not for the fact that a great many prescribed ways of doing things have to be lived up to, in order that one shall maintain workable, profitable, satisfactory relations with his fellows; or, were the prescriptions for the types of behavior in carrying on relations with one's fellows perfectly rational—then, for all I know, there would not be evolved, in the course of becoming a person, anything like the sort of self-system that we always encounter. (Sullivan, 1953, p. 168)

The self-system acts as a "vigilant guardian against the experience of crippling anxiety" (Chrzanowski, 1973, p. 142). Interpersonal experiences that deprive the person of appraisals and lower the his self-esteem give rise to anxiety; and lowered self-esteem precipitates "security operations", some of which are self-defeating. In interpersonal theory, "security operations" are regarded as activities of the "self-system" (Sullivan, 1953). The "self-system" and its "security operations" resemble the classical notions of ego and its defences. The self-system responds to, or prevents reexposure to, interpersonal situations that provoke anxiety, including situations that remind the person of the mother's "forbidding gestures" earlier in life. If the person goes "through a whole series of consistent failures of what we call security operations", "self-system activity will come in *more* readily at the faint hint of anxiety-provoking situations" (Sullivan, 1953, p. 191).

### 6.2.4   Ego interests

The ego, according to Hartmann (1964), "is defined by its functions" (p. 114). Ego development proceeds "in the direction of an ever closer adjustment to reality" (p. 82); and, accordingly, "ego functions" centre around the organism's relation to reality. Ego functions are manifold. First, the ego organises "perception of the outer world but probably also of the self" (Hartmann, 1964, p. 114). Second, ego defences (defence mechanisms) are ego functions that, in their ontogenesis, stem from "reflectory defenses against unpleasant stimuli" (p. 170). Defences may retain "an element (fight) that allows of their description as being mostly fed by one mode of aggressive energy" (p. 232). In addition, ego defences are "a specific expression of [the ego's] inhibiting nature" (p. 115); they often have "a definitely inhibitory aspect so far as the discharge of instinctual energy is concerned" (Hartmann, 1964, p. 124).

Third, many ego functions, such as strivings for wealth or social prestige, work with "neutralised" instinctual energy (derived from "id tendencies") (Hartmann, 1964). Some "ego tendencies" have aims that "center around values (ethical values, values of truth, religious values, etc.)" (p. 136). "Ego interests" are "a special set of tendencies", having aims that "center around one's own person (self)" (Hartmann, 1964, p. 136). "Ego interests", representing "only one set of ego functions" (p. 138), are "concerned with social status, influence, professional success, wealth, comfort, and so forth" (p. 64). Unlike mechanism of defence, "ego interests are hardly ever unconscious in the technical sense" (p. 136). Hartmann (1964) recognised that ego interests have a "defensive character"; they are "an attempt to deny inner conflicts and to protect oneself from fear" (p. 65). Fenichel (1946) thought that "ego interests and libidinal drives … have evolved from a common source", although ego interests and libidinal drives "later certainly are often in conflict with each other" (p. 58).

## Anxiety versus libido

Freud hypothesised that the ego is "the only seat of anxiety" (Hartmann, 1964, p. 292). Hartmann (1964) saw parallels between the "anticipating activities of the ego" and "the anxiety signal, which from a certain level of development on is used by the individual in danger situations" (p. 40). He regarded anxiety as a "special form of anticipation"—one that is "paramount among those forms of anticipation that make organized action possible" (p. 40). The capacity for anticipation, as exemplified by the organism's response to a danger *signal*, was thought to be "one of the most important" features and "a very general feature of the ego" (Hartmann, 1964, p. 292). The ego develops in consequence of conflicts between instinctual drives and reality. How does anxiety come into this? The cardinal conflict is between so-called instinctual desires and the child's "reality"-oriented strivings to be valued and accepted by others—strivings that forego anxiety. Hartmann (1964) realised that "the ego may be more—and very likely is more—than a developmental by-product of the influence of reality on instinctual drives" (p. 119). What is of key importance here is the insight that, in the process of ego formation, instinctual drives are deflected "from instinctual aims to aims which are socially or culturally more *acceptable* or *valued*" (Hartmann, 1964, p. 217, own italics). Social acceptance and approval have their origin in parental acceptance and approval, which are solicited from parents by the child in an attempt to escape or avoid anxiety. Acceptance and approval are sought-after resources in their own right. Indeed, Hartmann (1964) noted that "the child renouncing an instinctual desire expects, and often gets, a recompense in the form of *love* or *approval* by the parents" (pp. 251–252, own italics). Man's "highest achievements" (art, science, religion) can be considered to "have their origin in libidinal tendencies" (Hartmann, 1964, p. 217) insofar as the concept of "libidinal tendencies" can be extended to include behaviours aimed at inducing objects to provide security through acceptance, approval, and other selfobject experiences.

### 6.2.5   Object relations

The principle task of the ego "is to master the pressure of anxiety it is under" (Klein, 1932, p. 245). Much of this pressure of anxiety can be ascribed symbolically to "threats of a cruel superego" (Klein, 1932, p. 245), but it may be nothing more than an uncertain expectation of punishment or reprimand potentially exerted by the individual's objects and authority figures—punishment that will somehow be exerted unless the individual behaves in a socially normative and approved way. Anxiety stimulates ego development (Klein, 1932). The success of the process "by means of which the ego attempts to master his infantile anxiety-situations" is of "fundamental importance for the development of his ego" (p. 265). The individual's "reassurance against his anxiety … derives from his activities and from his social relations" (Klein, 1932, pp. 265–266).

The ultimate cause of the small child's anxiety, including its "fear of internal dangers", is the absence of the loved object, consistent with the profound dependence of the immature human infant on his mother. Trying to master anxiety, "the child summons to its assistance its relations to its objects and to reality" (Klein, 1932, p. 249). The child's "fear of internal dangers strengthens its fixation upon its mother and increases its need for love and help" (p. 248). The presence of and love from the child's real objects "help to lessen the small child's fear of its introjected objects and its sense of guilt", that is, they counter superego anxiety (p. 248). Approval from its objects is "a guarantee of safety and a safeguard against destruction from without and from within" (p. 231), that is, against punishment or threats from identifiable objects and from an abstract, unspecified authority (or, later, the group). Narcissism, that is, the extraction of love and approval from objects, plays an important role in the mastery of anxiety. Individuals "extract from their love-relations a tranquillization of their anxiety" (Klein, 1932, p. 264). Maintenance of object relations is equivalent to avoidance of anxiety.

> The conditions under which he can master anxiety are as specific as the conditions under which he can love, and are, as far as can be seen, very intimately bound up with them. (Klein, 1932, p. 264)

## Ego-syntonic pursuits

Klein (1932) showed that "all the activities, interests and sublimations of the individual also serve to master his anxiety and allay his guilt" (p. 264). The games played by children help them to achieve mastery of their anxiety. When playing games, "every wish-fulfilling mechanism" is employed by the ego "for the purpose of mastering anxiety" (p. 254). *Latent* anxiety, the latent "fear of internal dangers", "makes itself felt as a continual impulsion to play"; but as soon as anxiety becomes *manifest*, "it puts a stop to their game" (Klein, 1932, p. 254). This is in keeping with the "normal impulse to obtain pleasure from the overcoming of anxiety-situations that are associated with not too much and not too direct (and therefore better apportioned) anxiety" (p. 264). In the latency period, the child finds allayment of his anxiety "in the successful pursuit of his activities in so far as they are made ego-syntonic by the approval of his environment" (Klein, 1932, p. 262). Ego-syntonicity of activities denotes their capacity to be approved and recognised by the child's objects (and their potential to live up to the requirements of his super-ego). Mastering anxiety,

the child links his interests and achievements to his endeavours to win recognition and approval from his objects or the group.

> If the child's interests and achievements and other gratifications are too completely devoted to its endeavours to win love and recognition from its objects, if, that is, its object-relations are the pre-eminent means of mastering its anxiety and allaying its sense of guilt, its mental health in future years is not planted in firm soil. If it is less dependent on its objects and if the interests and achievements by means of which it masters its anxiety and allays its sense of guilt are done for their own sake and afford it interest and pleasure in themselves, its anxiety will undergo a better modification and a wider distribution—will be levelled down as it were. (Klein, 1932, p. 259)

In the period of puberty, allayment of the individual's anxiety and his sense of guilt must "to a much greater extent come from the value which his performances and achievements have for him in themselves" (Klein, 1932, p. 262). In puberty, "the child will no longer be able to master its anxiety if its chief means of doing so is its dependence upon its objects" (p. 260). For this reason, Klein (1932) thought, that "psychotic illnesses usually do not break out till later childhood, during or after the age of puberty" (Klein, 1932, p. 260).

> I think that my theory of the modification of anxiety helps us to understand by what means the normal person gets away from his anxiety-situations and modifies the conditions under which he feels anxiety. For that even a wide removal from his anxiety-situations such as the normal individual achieves does not amount to a relinquishment of them, analytic observation strongly inclines me to believe. To all intents and purposes those anxiety-situations, it is true, have

no direct effects upon him; but in certain circumstances such effects will reappear. If a normal person is put under a severe internal or external strain, or if he falls ill or fails in some other way, we may observe in him the full and complete operation of his deepest anxiety-situations. Since, then, every healthy person *may* succumb to a neurotic illness, it follows that he can never have entirely given up his old anxiety-situations. (Klein, 1932, p. 266)

## 6.3   Ego defences

Man seeks to avoid anxiety in every possible way. One major avenue for this defensively-intended avoidance is via the unconscious evolution of various of the ego defenses. Their hypertrophy, misdirection, inadequacy or failure contributes to psychopathology. This is a central formulation in our conceptions of the origin of the emotional illnesses, whether these are neuroses, character neuroses, or functional psychoses. (Laughlin, 1970, p. 211)

The defence against anxiety is one of the key functions of the ego (Hartmann, 1964). Defence mechanisms, according to Arieti (1970), are "devices to protect the self or the self-image" (p. 25). They are "cognitive configurations that lead the patient to feelings, ideas, and strategic forms of behavior that make the self-image acceptable or at least less unacceptable" (Arieti, 1970, p. 25). Laughlin (1970), too, thought that defence mechanisms serve the "preservation and enhancement of self-esteem" (p. 214). Defence mechanisms foster "ego integration"; and this effect may be mediated by neutralisation of "the disruptive effects of anxiety, conflict, and stress" (Laughlin, 1970, p. 213). It is usually understood that defence mechanisms are means predominately of *avoiding* anxiety; "defense processes consist of general, characteristic anxiety-forestalling attitudes and modes", which "do not involve only the individual's internal relationship with himself, but invariably involve, at the same time, his relationship with external reality" (Shapiro, 2000, p. 110). Defence mechanisms also act to *reduce* anxiety. Ego defences are unconscious attempts to deal with anxiety arising in response to "unconscious dangers" or from "conflicts which would otherwise prove intolerable" (Laughlin, 1970, p. 211). Emotional conflict arises, for instance, when intolerable and consciously disowned (repressed) memories are about to undergo "derepression". Defence mechanisms may eliminate an unconscious danger or resolve an emotional conflict and, thereby, reduce anxiety and produce an "increase of personal security" (Laughlin, 1970, p. 214).

Benjamin (1996) considered that some defences operate by distorting incoming information (as may be the case in projection, splitting, idealisation, devaluation) or blocking awareness of information (repression, somatisation, denial, intellectualisation, dissociation), while other defences operate by controlling "the choice of situation where the response is given" (displacement, acting out, sublimation) or altering "the pattern of behaviour that is chosen" (compensation, regression, undoing) (p. 194). Defence mechanisms maintain or reinforce "repressions" (Laughlin, 1970), eliminating factors or elements from the perceived social situation that could be construed as threatening to the ego or self and that would, if they remained in place, cause anxiety. Revision of the situation, as a result of the operation of defence mechanisms, may reduce or eliminate "the apparent dangerousness of the agent's situation; thereby they make it possible for the person to act, even act emotionally, without risking such intolerable real or imagined consequences as utter loss of love or castration" (Schafer, 1976, p. 323).

… defense is to be viewed partly as the agent's arranging things so that the dangerous actions and modes that would be performed under other circumstances are not performed and instead remain in the conditional mode, that is, as that which the agent would do under other circumstances. (Schafer, 1976, p. 323)

## 6.3.1   Repression

Through repression, "ideas, impulses, and emotional feelings which are consciously repugnant and thereby intolerable" are excluded from conscious awareness and assigned to the Freudian "unconscious" (Laughlin, 1970, p. 358). The unconscious can be considered as a "repository for much that is painful in fantasy, ideation, or experience" (p. 358).[4] Material that requires repression (exclusion from consciousness and relegation into the unconscious) is material that is "painful". Through repression, the ego seeks to avoid pain associated with some wishes, thoughts, and urges (Laughlin, 1970). Apart from pain, anxiety has been implicated in the motivation of repression. Freud (1933) held that anxiety is the motive force that causes the repression of instinctive impulses (p. 113). Laughlin (1970) thought that it is anxiety or the "threat of anxiety" that brings about repression. Repression prevents anxiety; and the need to circumvent anxiety ensures continued repression. When "derepression" threatens, acute anxiety ensues (Laughlin, 1970). One has to wonder whether pain and anxiety make differential contributions to the motivation of repression, unless, of course, anxiety can be regarded as an "intense psychic kind of pain" (Laughlin, 1970, p. 372), meaning that pain and anxiety are synonymous or indistinguishable in some situations. Consistent with the role of anxiety in repression, "interpersonal and social pressures" make "important contributions" (Laughlin, 1970, p. 364), perhaps by causing us to feel vulnerable (and, hence, anxious), within our social environment or an imaginary social context, for as long as we entertain in consciousness certain wishes, thoughts, and urges.

The *internalised* context that, by being replicated in form of an external or imaginary social context, exerts social pressures and causes anxiety is what we call the superego. "Superego" refers to internalised fear of punishment. One could argue that it is the fear of punishment—be it punishment by external agents or by the superego—that causes the repression of ideas or impulses liable to be punished. It is an *uncertain* expectation of punishment in a social context that motivates defensive repression (or, alternatively, gives rise to anxiety).

Having been assigned to the "deep layer of the psyche", the repressed material is inaccessible to conscious recall but remains an active and potent determinant of social behaviour, especially of forms of behaviour that manifest the operation of defence mechanisms. Often, another defence is required to reinforce a repression and prevent its "derepression" (Bergler, 1952; Laughlin, 1970). Anxiety acts as a signal indicating that the repressed material is about to become accessible to consciousness. Derepression, or the threat thereof, calls into operation defence mechanisms as reinforcements of the repression (Laughlin, 1970). The repressed material continues to seek expression in indirect ways through behaviour or ideation (Freud, 1920). Not infrequently, a second line of defence (a defence that modifies the defence that aids repression) is required to deal with intolerable aspects of ideation or behaviour (constituting a first line of defence) that attempt to express the repressed material indirectly (Bergler, 1952). Repression is a basic process that is a "prerequisite to the elaboration of the other ego defenses" (Laughlin, 1970, p. 359), including projection, "reaction formation", and sublimation. Reaction formation, "which the ego acquires, first in making its repressions", is a major contributor to character formation (Freud, 1933, p. 119), as is sublimation.

> What appears in a minority of human individuals as an untiring impulse towards further perfection can easily be understood as a result of the instinctual repression upon which is based all that is most precious in human civilisation.

---

[4]The unconscious, according to Freud, contains only those elements that have the potential to become conscious—and that, in the past, were part of consciousness—but that are now suppressed (repressed) by social influences. The Freudian unconscious does not include *mechanisms* that we deem to be unconscious.

The repressed instinct never ceases to strive for complete satisfaction, which would consist in the repetition of a primary experience of satisfaction. No substitutive or reactive formations and no sublimations will suffice to remove the repressed instinct's persisting tension; and it is the difference in amount between the pleasure of satisfaction which is *demanded* and that which is actually *achieved* that provides the driving factor which will permit of no halting at any position attained, … (Freud, 1920, p. 42)

### 6.3.2 Psychotaxis

Whenever it is possible for us to avoid or escape an unpleasant situation, we experience a strong tendency to do so. … In some, this tendency may be obscured by ideals of conduct, … (Moore, 1926, p. 211)

Unpleasant situations evoke an impulse to escape. We may be prevented from escaping an unpleasant (and implicitly dangerous) situation by experiencing a conflicting impulse, such as a fear of social punishment for escaping the dangerous situation. Anxiety may arise only insofar as we cannot give in to the impulse to escape an unpleasant situation. Moore (1926) thought that the "conflict of incompatible desires … is the main factor in producing a state of anxiety" (p. 209). Perhaps, defence mechanisms are not so much concerned with escaping an anxiety-provoking situation as they are concerned with escaping an *unpleasant* situation. Defence mechanisms primarily seek to escape or avoid unpleasant situations; secondarily they would avoid reexposure to anxiety, too (Figure 6-3).

The fundamental condition which calls forth a defense reaction is an unpleasant situation. (Moore, 1926, p. 231)

Moore (1926) conceived defence reactions as "spontaneous tendencies to get out of an unpleasant situation" or to avoid it (p. 230). Human beings have "very strong innate tendencies" to make use of, and enjoy, "all pleasant situations, and to get out of or avoid to the uttermost all unpleasant ones" (p. 183). These tendencies—called positive and negative "psychotaxes", respectively—"are almost reflex in character" (p. 183). Defence reactions are, therefore, "negative psychotaxes" (Moore, 1926).

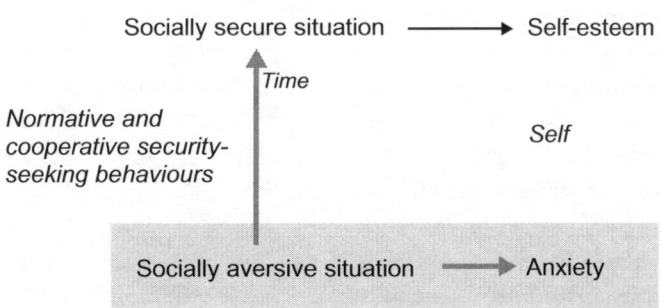

Figure 6-3. Psychotaxis denotes an automatically engendered decrease in the aversiveness of a situation, a form of appetitive behaviour transposing the organism from an aversive situation to a secure situation (automatically in accordance with previous reinforcement learning). Social (defensive) behaviour effects escape typically across time, rather than in the domain of space. The self may be an epiphenomenon of a process that moves the organism automatically from a socially aversive situation (unrelatedness or exclusion) to a safe and predictable one. Socially aversive situations are associated with anxiety—persisting for as long as escape cannot be effected.

We all dislike to remember certain unpleasant situations of the past, and to consider various disagreeable eventualities of the future. ... Most men have a spontaneous tendency to put this eventuality out of mind, and they just as spontaneously avoid anything that brings it up. Natural and spontaneous tendencies to make use of any ability in our mind to avoid an unpleasant thing, or a disagreeable situation, have every right to be considered impulses; and because they are impulses which have to do with the problems which arise in unpleasant situations, they belong to that group of mental reactions that we have termed the psychotaxes or parataxes. (pp. 230–231)

The mode of avoidance is indeed mental, but it is no less impulsive than the motor impulses that one experiences to get out of a cold bath, or to get in out of the rain, or to go from the sun to the shade on a hot day, etc. (Moore, 1926, p. 230)

## Self-esteem

Defence reactions effect repression and skew the content of conscious experience and, thereby, regulate self-esteem. Consciously, persons tend to overestimate themselves. A person's overestimation "tends to stay at the conscious level", while "the underestimation, because of its unfavourable character, is readily repressed to the depth of the unconscious" (Moore, 1926, p. 175). It is the "system of defense reactions" that guards "against the realization of our own defects" (p. 174). Self-awareness and self-esteem (including neurotic pride) are intricately liked with repression. We have "an instinctive tendency … to keep others from talking about anything in our life which we look upon as shameful or disgraceful" and "we do not like to think about such incidents ourselves" (p. 211). Events, "especially those involving wounded pride", "are at once glossed over with excuses" (Moore, 1926, p. 211).

With some, their personal self-esteem is so hedged in with a system of defense reactions that nothing seems capable of disturbing it. Their ignorant blunders, imperfections, sins, are promptly excused and all blame shifted on to the shoulders of others. Murmurings of a self-accusation are promptly suppressed and securely confined in the dungeons of the subconscious. With others, the least shadow of failure or disappointment brings on a depression, deprives them of all self-confidence, robs them of energy, takes away their desire and hope to do and accomplish. (Moore, 1926, p. 174)

If repression fails, self-esteem is momentarily undermined and an *unpleasant* state of narcissistic injury or pain arises, which, if it persists or cannot be escaped, enlists anxiety secondarily. Failure of repression has the same effect as a breakdown in self-deception.

A transitory success, often in something of a trivial nature, sends us soaring in our own personal estimation. But a momentary display of weakness or ignorance, which perhaps is made light of, or passes unnoticed by others, brings on a tremendous bear movement in our stock market—a veritable panic as we are brought face to face with the fact that we are not at all what we want to be and still pretend we are. (Moore, 1926, p. 174)

### 6.3.3   Conditional actions and counteractions

Schafer (1976) defined "impulse" as a "would-be or conditional action". An impulse "is an action a person would do were he or she not effectively refraining from it"; it "is an action that is not being carried out, and its not being carried out may be due to other actions one has engaged in to that very end" (Schafer, 1976, p. 137). In other words, we refrain from "acting on impulse" by engaging in a refraining action. Defences are actions that are taken to refrain from acting on impulse, that is, actions taken to "repress" an inappropriate and, hence, dangerous action or thought. Defences are "counteractions" to infantile psychosexual or aggressive impulses (would-be actions). A major part of the "dynamic unconscious" consists of "actions in which one *would be* engaged were one not refraining from doing so by engaging in counteractions" (p. 241). When engaging in counteractions, "one is remaining ignorant of actions one would do were one not engaged in effective counteractions of some sort" (p. 243). Conditional actions can take the form of a would-be *action mode* (an emotional way of acting). One *would* act in an infantile emotion mode, "without acknowledging that fact", were one not refraining from doing so by engaging in some effective counteraction (Schafer, 1976, p. 242).

> The emotions we successfully resist attending to may exist only in the conditional mode, that is, as some emotion-action we *would* perform or some emotional way of acting in which we *would* engage were it not for some circumstances, consequences, or objectives that we regard as being more important, such as dangers of loosing gratification and security. ... The conditional mode is psychologically real in its cognitive aspect, that is, in connection with the person's preconsciously or consciously *anticipating* situations, such as the prototypical danger situations. (Schafer, 1976, pp. 309–310)

## Thought

Thinking something may be a way of making sure that what one *would do* remains unconscious (Schafer, 1976). Thinking something, as a counteraction, may effect repression of an inappropriate and dangerous action. At other times, we may think "consciously of the action" that we "wished to perform and would have performed" had we "not deemed it too dangerous to do so" (Schafer, 1976, p. 206). A disturbing thought, concerned with a situation or outcome that is *dangerous*

for the self, may betray a conflict between "id" and "ego", between an instinctive drive and the fear of punishment or persecution for expressing this drive. Such conflict causes "behavioural inhibition", an inhibition that may be paralleled by engagement of the brain's default-mode network, which supports self-reflective thought or observation (internal or external monitoring) as an alternative to action. If, in this process, a thought or an idea arises that entails reward rather than punishment, behavioural inhibition may be terminated and a "refraining" action (counteraction) can be carried out. The process that links a disturbing thought through an alternative more acceptable idea with the refraining action is "unconscious" in the sense that it is not readily acknowledged by the patient to himself or the analyst.

### 6.3.4 Denial

Denial is a primitive defence mechanism that is closely related to repression. Denial concerns consciously intolerable facts, usually facts about oneself. What is denied is often an element of, or the basis for, an emotional conflict (Laughlin, 1970). Denial as a defence mechanism avoids emotional conflict and, hence, anxiety. Denial endeavours "to prevent anxiety, to ward off disapproval, to avoid hurt, to combat insecurity, and to preserve the ego" (p. 59). Denial serves to maintain or enhance one's self-image and to gloss over low self-confidence. As a consequence of denial, one sees one's self and "one's behaviour and standards as compatible with those of society" (Laughlin, 1970, p. 65).

One may deny the presence of terminal illness, emotional problems, alcoholism and its effects, drug addiction, physical handicap, as well as age and the effects of aging (Laughlin, 1970). One may deny these facts about oneself "because of personal embarrassment or self-critical attitudes, or because of unpleasant social connotations" (p. 69). Denial spares the individual from experiencing discomfort and fosters his or her unconscious sense of invulnerability.

The possibility of death is often denied, as is the possibility of external danger. Denial of external danger seems to magically avoid one's exposure to danger itself (Laughlin, 1970). Moreover, one's dependence on others can be denied, as is characteristically the case in mania. In essence, what tends to be denied, here, is one's vulnerability (and what tends to be avoided is awareness of one's vulnerability). One's longing for, and care about, others can be denied, too. Denial of the loss of one's love object is part of the mourning process. The defence mechanism of projection, when it is operative, usually involves denial, too. Denial operates in the service of idealisation; and rationalisation can operate in the service of denial (Laughlin, 1970).

### 6.3.5   Displacement

Emotional feelings, such as anxiety, fear, or anger, can be transferred onto an external object, which provides a safer and more "convenient" target for these feelings (Laughlin, 1970). Displacement often concerns painful feelings towards, or about, the self. As a result of displacement, the individual prevents painful awareness "of an internal threat" (p. 90) or "of the basic and internal source of the conflict" (p. 86), so that some instance of repression or denial can be maintained. The external object onto which painful feelings are displaced is perceived to be the source of threat. Anger can be displaced. Displacement of anger or frustration entails the "reassignment of anger, hostility, or resentment toward a different object" (p. 87). The object toward which anger is displaced, the scapegoat, provides a "safer and therefore less threatening or dangerous" target for one's angry feelings (p. 87). In phobias ("phobic displacement"), an "internal anxious threat and danger" is assigned "to a new and safer external object", which becomes a "convenient" target for anxious feelings (Laughlin, 1970).

### 6.3.6   Rationalisation

Socially unacceptable motives or wishes are consciously repugnant and intolerable and have to be "repressed" or hidden. Alternatively, the ego attempts to justify or modify socially unacceptable impulses, needs, feelings, or motives. Through rationalisation, one justifies one's behaviour to oneself and others (Laughlin, 1970). Rationalisation illustrates one's "dependence on others' opinion for one's self-esteem" (p. 264). While socially unacceptable and consciously intolerable motives are repressed, more tolerable motives are devised through rationalisation, leading to "increased acceptance, primarily from oneself, but also by others" (pp. 251–252). Rationalisation obscures injury and self-defeat that would result from the pursuit of socially unacceptable impulses, behaviours, motives, or wishes. We use rationalisation "to save face" and "to avoid being forced to make ego-deflating admissions" (p. 273). Envy, for instance, "is often personally and socially disapproved and therefore must be "covered over" or concealed" (Laughlin, 1970, p. 254). Given that "people tend to look down on feelings of envy", there "are often considerable pressures toward disowning this feeling" (p. 254). Rationalisation devises an explanation for one's behaviour that "is likely more socially and personally acceptable" (p. 254). Furthermore, we seek social approval through the pursuit of socially valuable goals. Failure to reach such goal causes injury to self esteem and produces anxiety, unless we "make that goal seem less worthwhile and attractive" (p. 259). Devaluation of an unobtained or unobtainable goal is a major function of rationalisation. Similarly, we use rationalisation to devalue material possessions that are beyond reach (Laughlin, 1970).

> Rationalisation is an unconscious endeavor to provide the ego with plausible, acceptable, and rational reasons for actions and motives. In this way, appeasement of the conscience or superego and society is sought. Rationalisation is often employed to maintain or enhance one's self-esteem. (Laughlin, 1970, p. 259)

By finding "extenuating circumstances for one's own lapses, failures, weaknesses, failings, or unacceptable behavior" or "supplying an acceptable motive in place of one which would ordinarily appear irrational or unacceptable" (Laughlin, 1970, p. 274), one seeks to maintain and build up one's self-esteem, whereby rationalisation "tends to modify one's realistic self-evaluation" (p. 264) and can lead to self-deception. Rationalisation is closely related to defence mechanisms of "denial" and "compensation". Confabulation can be regarded as a form of rationalisation (Laughlin, 1970). All of these mechanisms help us to maintain self-esteem, counter our sense of vulnerability, and, hence, ward off anxiety. They allow us to construe our social environment in a way that reduces our vulnerability to social disapproval and criticism (offensive attack) and that ensures ongoing receipt of approval and affection.

## 6.4   Neurotic behaviour

An important source of anxiety is "a fear of retaliation for the ruthless pursuit of ambition" (Horney, 1937, p. 207). In a competitive environment, power, prestige, or possessions can be acquired only at the cost of defeat of competitors. A person's anxiety reflects, in part, a fear that others "will want just as intensely to defeat him" (p. 207). The neurotic person, in particular, is "anxious about hurting others", since he "automatically assumes that others will feel just as much hurt and vindictive after a defeat as he does himself" (p. 196). He feels that "once he has shown an interest in success he is surrounded by a horde of persecuting enemies, who lie in wait to crush him at every sign of weakness or failure" (p. 211). He fears that "others will gloat over a failure" (p. 211) and that he becomes "the object of disrespect or ridicule" (Horney, 1937, p. 224). Anxiety is a feeling of being exposed to such dangers; it is also a feeling of helplessness. Anxiety "concurs with a feeling of intrinsic weakness of the self" (p. 96). This intrinsic weakness causes "a desire to put all responsibility upon others, to be protected and taken care of" (p. 96). The neurotic person's "fear of the begrudging envy of others" is linked to his fear "of the loss of their affection"

(p. 214). The less a person can rely on others' affection, the more vulnerable he is to their attack, and the more likely his assertive actions are met with their hostility. The more intense his anxiety, the greater have to be his efforts to control his environment by means of assertive or appeasing behaviours—including displays of dominance or infantilisms signalling helplessness. The neurotic person is caught, as Horney (1937) saw it, in a conflict between "an excessive desire to be loved by everyone", on the one hand, and "an aggressive striving for a 'no one but I' dominance", on the other hand (p. 208).

> If the outside world is felt to be hostile, if one feels helpless toward it, then taking any risk of annoying people seems sheer recklessness. For the neurotic the danger appears all the greater, and the more his feeling of safety is based on the affection of others the more he is afraid of losing that affection. … Hence he feels that annoying them involves the danger of a final break; he expects to be dropped altogether, to be definitely spurned or hated. (Horney, 1937, p. 252)
>
> … a child represses his hostility against his parents because he is afraid that any expression of it would spoil his relationship to the parents. He is motivated by plain fear that these powerful giants would desert him, withdraw their reassuring benevolence or turn against him. (Horney, 1937, pp. 86–87).

### 6.4.1   Modesty and withdrawal

Neurotic persons are often modest and avoid conspicuousness "by sticking to conventional standards, staying out of the limelight, being no different from others" (Horney, 1937, p. 213). Neurotic persons "have inhibitions about expressing their wishes or asking for something, about doing something in their own interest, expressing an opinion or warranted criticism, ordering someone, selecting the people they wish to associate with, making contacts with people" (pp. 37–38).

Orders "will be given in an apologetic, ineffectual manner" (p. 57). Their "anxiety concerning the hostility of others" renders them "afraid of success" (p. 214) and prevents them from pursing their demands and ambitions. Anxiety, insofar as it is a fear of retaliation, engenders an inhibition towards competition; the neurotic person "recoils" from competition (Horney, 1937). Alternatively, anxiety, reflecting feelings of insignificance, helplessness, and insecurity, may push the person "into enhanced efforts to be more successful and more invincible" (p. 208). His anxiety may impel him "to strive for and attain more and more strength and power in order to be safe" (p. 268). There are, according to Horney (1937), "four principle ways in which a person tries to protect himself against "basic anxiety": affection, submissiveness, power, withdrawal" (p. 96). Withdrawing from the world means achieving independence from it. One may attempt to achieve independence by becoming "emotionally detached from people so that nothing will hurt or disappoint one" (p. 99). Emotional withdrawal is also a means of gaining security. Feeling rebuffed or rejected may arouse acute anxiety and "result in a complete withdrawal of all feelings", manifesting in an attitude of coldness and unresponsiveness (Horney, 1937, p. 136).

### 6.4.2   Hostility and its inhibition

If a person's efforts to obtain other's approval or affection are rejected, he may become hostile towards them (Horney, 1937). If a neurotic person "feels that he will be rejected in any case, regardless of his behaviour", "if his special efforts to be kind and considerate are not returned right away or are rejected", then he may "in a single crises thrust upon others all he has ever held against them", "with the secrete hope, however, that they will realize the depth of his despair and therefore condone him" (p. 253). In this instance, he "feels himself in an emergency and makes a counter-attack, like an animal which is apprehensive by nature and strikes out when in danger" (Horney, 1937, p. 254). Such attacks on others

"are borne out of a sheer feeling of the need to ward off an immediate danger" (Horney, 1937, p. 254). Hostile reactions occur in response not only to a rejection "but also to the anticipation of a rejection" (p. 136). The expression of animosity is inhibited by "consideration of the circumstances as they are in a given situation" (p. 67). Circumstances show the individual "what he can and what he cannot do toward an enemy or alleged enemy" (p. 67). In most instances, hostility towards others, arising in response to rebuff, needs to be repressed because of a fear of further loss of others' approval or affection. In these cases, indirect ways of expressing hostility may be engaged, "which allow the neurotic to express his resentment without being aware that he does" (Horney, 1937, p. 255).

On the one hand, anxiety, "when based on a feeling of being menaced, easily provokes a reactive hostility in defence" (Horney, 1937, p. 74). On the other hand, anxiety is "the promoting factor behind inhibitions" (Horney, 1937, p. 59). Not only anxiety, or fear of rejection, but also the pain of rejection (signifying a failure to attain or maintain social relatedness) may promote avoidance learning, that is, the learning of "inhibitions". Cues predictive of rejection or punishment gradually cease to elicit a fear or anxiety reaction, and, instead, come to elicit habitual avoiding actions that effect, on a habitual basis, an inhibition of situationally inappropriate responses to social incentive stimuli. Inhibitions serve "to avoid the anxiety which would arise if the person attempted to do, feel or think those things" (p. 53). There is no awareness of anxiety during the operation of an inhibition; "and no capacity for overcoming the inhibition by conscious effort" (Horney, 1937, p. 54). The fear of rejection or rebuff "may lead to a series of severe inhibitions falling in the category of timidity" (Horney, 1937, p. 137).

> The fear of rebuff is thus a grave handicap to the wish for affection, because it prevents a person from letting others feel or know that he would like to have some attention. Moreover the hostility provoked

by a feeling of being rebuffed contributes a great deal toward keeping the anxiety alert or even reinforcing it. It is an important factor in establishing a "vicious circle" which is difficult to escape from. (Horney, 1937, p. 137)

Horney (1937) thought that hostile impulses are the main source of anxiety, and that the "repression of hostility leads with inexorable logic to the generation of anxiety" (p. 72), however it may be objected that the repression of hostile impulses actually prevents anxiety. Hostile impulses cause anxiety when acting on these impulses exposes the subject to external danger. Enactment of hostile impulses may cause anxiety and, thereby, undermine "the purpose of the self" (p. 63) only insofar as hostility, if expressed, renders the subject vulnerable to counterattack and rejection. Horney (1937) accepted that "an imperative impulse, *if yielded to*, would mean a catastrophe for the self" (p. 64, own italics) and bring about anxiety.

### 6.4.3   Deceit and self-deception

Sometimes the speaker looks directly and searchingly at the listener's eyes. The response he sees, or thinks he sees, in the listener's eyes has a special importance to him; he is remarkable sensitive to it. A confirming response from the listener produces visible relief, while the slightest hesitation is quite discomforting and often prompts the speaker to renewed efforts. Despite his apparent concentration on the listener, however, the speaker, here, is actually addressing and listening to himself. His concentration on the listener's expression is misleading; he is watching the listener in a way one looks carefully in a mirror for signs of a blemish, losing awareness of the mirror itself. He is addressing himself through the listener. (Shapiro, 2000, p. 37)

Neurotic persons often give the impression of artificiality or ungenuineness in their speech.

Such artificial and exaggerated speech has been described as "self-deceptive", insofar as it illustrates a suspension of "the normal relationship with external reality" (Shapiro, 2000). However, maintaining a relationships with, and communicating about, external reality are not the primary functions of speech. Speech has a defensive function, in that it serves to manipulate others' attitudes towards oneself (and even deceive others about oneself) in an attempt to render oneself more worthy of others' appraisals and, thereby, counteract one's anxiety, that is, one's fear of disapproval and rejection.

Human beings have developed and use language to spare themselves from all manner of arousal, pain, anxiety, guilt, loss, and destructiveness. They allude to what they are passing over as they pass over it. This allusiveness is part of what we call unconscious communication. It makes up a large part of what the analyst listens for. (Schafer, 1976, p. 145)

Neurotic speech demonstrates the motivational conflict between one's grandiosity and exhibitionism, aiming to attract others' "attention" and interest, on the one hand, and a fear of ridicule or rejection, manifesting as anxiety, on the other. Creating an air that facilitates or provokes others' expressions of praise and admiration, and sometimes deceiving others in the process, the individual has to be sensitive to signs of disapproval and rejection, and he has to be concerned that others will see through his façade and see in his communications the desperation, exhibitionism, and deceitfulness that drive him. He has to be concerned that his vulnerability—awareness of which he resists (represses)—becomes apparent to himself and, thus, to others, so that attacks from others upon himself cannot but follow.

In casual conversation, too, there is the talk that is interlarded with frequent laughter or giggling, too rapid speech or too slow, speech interspersed with affectations or unconscious imitation, speech that is impaired with affect-mannerisms, in which self-importance or an air of superiority obstructs the speaker's natural delivery. Then, last but not least, there is the prevalent disposition to excessive talk … And, in envisaging man's interpersonal disorders of speech, we may not overlook the compulsive tendency among people to interrupt one another. Like stammering, all these behavioural oddities are symptoms of social hesitation in communication. (Burrow, 1949, p. 303)

For stammering, as other impediments of speech, is a species of lying—a socially enforced concealment that causes a powerful impaction of tensions concomitant to an artificially enlarged personality-prerogative. … the stammerer is choked with fear and conflict because of his recourse to surreptitious part-reactions—his inveterate habits of evasion—… (Burrow, 1949, p. 304)

Expression of grandiosity—the attempt to actualise one's grandiose self-image—entails unconscious identification with an ideal (in form of another person or the "ego ideal") and reproduction of the ideal's speech and gesture. Seeking approval and reassurance, one manipulates others' attitudes towards oneself; and, in the process of this manipulation, one may lie, that is, deceive others about one's virtues and achievements. One's exaggerated efforts to manipulate the behaviour and attitudes of others—so as to make them reflect upon oneself more favourably—can be regarded as indirect self-deception (self-deception through deception of others). Alternatively, one may deceive oneself about others' attitudes towards oneself directly. Self-deception, as a distorted way of inferring one's self-image from the behaviour and attitudes of others, is a form of repression or denial. Finally, one deceives oneself—inasmuch as one deceives others—about the purpose or motives of one's own behaviours. For instance, histrionic

behaviour, characterised by pretentiousness, self-dramatisation, and insincerity, allows the agent to defensively ingratiate himself with others "in order not to realize that he believes himself to be unlovable" (Schafer, 1976, p. 327).

In addition to, or instead of, knowingly deceiving others by pretending, one may deceive oneself as to one's own emotion-actions and emotion-modes. … Unlike deception of others, which may be done consciously, self-deception can only be accomplished unconsciously. … One may pretend to oneself, more or less successfully, that one does not care or does care, does not hurt or does hurt, does not rejoice or does rejoice, and so on. (Schafer, 1976, pp. 327–328)

## 6.5    Guilt

It is as difficult to copy only the essentials in the behaviour of a man whom one reveres and strives to emulate as it is impossible to regard a man as a model in some respects while despising him in others. The powerful urge to emulate a teacher only takes effect if one is able to revere him in every respect, but particularly with regard to his ethical standards. What one inherits from such a model are mainly norms of social behaviour, or moral attitudes. The guilt one feels at any infraction of these norms is closely akin to the embarrassment one would feel if one were caught in the reprehensible act by the "father figure" in question. His mild disapproval, even in matters of skill and not ethics, can have the effect of a punishment. (Lorenz, 1973, pp. 203–204)

The possibility of identifying with a father figure and realizing that one is obeying the moral commandments of a super-ego, gives us an inner security that we cannot do without. (Lorenz, 1973, p. 205)

The superego, developing from idealisation of the parents and identification with them, "accounts for the fact that moral conflict and guilt feelings become a natural and fundamental aspect of human behavior" (Hartmann, 1964, p. 325). Guilt, according to Freud, is an idea or a feeling of deserving or expecting punishment from the internalised authority figure (superego). Guilt "is the expression of a condemnation of the ego by its critical agency" (Freud, 1923, p. 51). The sense of guilt signifies a "tension between the demands of conscience and the actual performances of the ego" (p. 37), that is, a "tension between the ego and the ego ideal" (Freud, 1923, p. 51). Guilt is not dissimilar from anxiety. Anxiety is a fear of punishment; "anxiety means anxiety about future punishment", whereas "guilt feeling means the unpleasant feeling of *deserving* punishment, irrespective whether the punishment is actualized or not" (Ariety, 1973, p. 123, own italics).

Schafer (1971) conceptualised guilt as an "emotion-mode", which entails "behaving as though one expects some deserved and perhaps severe punishment"—an emotion-mode in which one "thinks of oneself as an immoral wretch, and in many instances either consciously or unconsciously tries to bring about a "punishing" by some person or agency in one's environment or else punishes oneself through self-imposed deprivation, humiliation, pain, or injury" (p. 284). Freud (1923) distinguished between conscious sense of guilt (conscience) and unconscious guilt. Unconscious guilt may express itself "as a resistance to recovery" (p. 50); or it may manifest in criminal actions that seem to allow a fastening of "this unconscious sense of guilt on to something real and immediate" (Freud, 1923, p. 52).

The conscious sense of guilt is pronounced in melancholia and obsessive neurosis, in which "the ego ideal displays particular severity and often rages against the ego in a cruel fashion" (Freud, 1923, p. 51). In obsessional neurosis, but not in melancholia, "the patient's ego rebels against the imputation of guilt", because, in obsessional neurosis, "objectionable impulses" that deserve punishment remain outside the ego, "while in melancholia the object to which the super-ego's wrath applies has been taken into the ego through identification" (Freud, 1923, p. 51). Kernberg (1996) thought that patients with "depressive-masochistic personality disorder" have an extremely punitive superego, which predisposes them to self-defeating behaviour. The superego in these patients "reflects an unconscious need to suffer as an expiation for guilt feelings" (Kernberg, 1996, p. 126).

> The excessive dependency and easy sense of frustration of these patients go hand in hand with their "faulty metabolism" of aggression, where depression ensues when an aggressive response would have been appropriate, and an excessive aggressive response to the frustration of their dependency needs may rapidly turn into a renewed depressive response as a consequence of excessive guilt feelings. (Kernberg, 1996, p. 126)

### 6.5.1   Longing for forgiveness

> After the experience that punishment may be a means of achieving forgiveness, a need for punishment actually may develop. The punishment longed for is a means of achieving forgiveness; the individuals in question certainly would prefer it if they could achieve forgiveness without first undergoing punishment. (Fenichel, 1946, p. 138)

The fear of conscience, as Rado (1956) saw it, "is a fear of inescapable punishment" (p. 225). It serves to inhibit dangerous or disobedient action or thought. Developmentally, expectation of parental punishment for disobedience becomes an expectation of punishment that is inescapable but not administered by any particular agent (or is symbolically administered by the internalised parent or superego). Having been punished by his parents for disobedient behaviour, the child shows remorse or asks for forgiveness (expiatory behaviour), which prompts his parents "to take him back into their loving care" (Rado, 1956, p. 226). According to Fenichel (1946), normal guilt feelings contain an "impulsive demand for a chance to make good" (p. 103). Punishment becomes a prerequisite for forgiveness; "the pain of punishment is accepted or even provoked in the hope that after the punishment" the object's affection and forgiveness will be forthcoming (Fenichel, 1946, p. 103). Punishment, which—in the absence of a suitable external authority—may take the form of *self-punishment*, terminates guilt and allows for forgiveness by a symbolic representation of the parent, that is, by the internalised parent (superego). As Rado (1956) suggested, the child seeks relief from feelings of guilt ("guilty fear") by self-punishment "for the sake of forgiveness, and the recapturing of the love of the parents, which it entails" (p. 226).

> The crucial component of guilty fear is retroflexed rage; it is the component which humbles the self most. If this rage becomes once again environment-directed and defiant, the self turns from self-reproach to reproaching the very person he guiltily fears, from expiation to attack: "You are to be blamed (not I)." The self then believes it is acting purely in "self-defence". Actually, this is a mechanism of miscarried repair; we call it rage of over guilty fear, or guilty rage. (Rado, 1956, p. 226)

### 6.5.2   Sensitivity to disapproval

A person prone to feelings of guilt has a "tendency to seek and find fault within himself" (Horney, 1937, p. 249). Horney (1937) argued that guilt feelings "and their accompanying self-recriminations" (p. 241) are an expression of a *defence* against anxiety. Neurotic persons, in particular, are inclined to "cover up anxiety with guilt feelings" (p. 235). Anxiety is, in part, a feeling of "impending punishment, retaliation, desertion"; it is a "fear of disapproval" (p. 235). This means that the neurotic person is "excessively afraid

of or hypersensitive to being disapproved of, criticized, accused, found out" (p. 235); "he cannot help believing that others will despise him … if they find out about his weaknesses" (Horney, 1937, p. 240). The neurotic person "builds up a façade of strength" ("persona") in order to "hide how weak and insecure and helpless he feels" (p. 240). He must keep up his pretences, "because they represent the bulwark that protects him from his lurking anxiety" (Horney, 1937, p. 239). These pretences become ineffective when he is "found out". Acute loss of self-esteem, due to disapproval or rejection, causes a resurgence of "basic anxiety", which implies a loss of protection against, and an increase in vulnerability to, conspecific attack (punishment, retaliation). The neurotic person's feelings of guilt are related to, but not identical with, his "haunting fear of being found out or of being disapproved of" (Horney, 1937, p. 231). Unlike guilt, the fear of disapproval, when a person feels "honestly regretful or ashamed of something", is painful; and it is "more painful still to express" this fear to someone else (p. 233). Guilt feelings, by contrast, are expressed "very readily" (Horney, 1937, p. 233).

### 6.5.3   Self-recriminations

Horney (1937) thought guilt feelings are a result of, and a defence against, the fear of disapproval. The neurotic person "feels guilty because, as a result of his anxieties, he is even more than others dependent on public opinion" (p. 236). Guilt invites reassurance. Self-recriminations that accompany feelings of guilt "invite positive reassurance, by provoking reassuring statements to the contrary" (p. 242). In other words, the expression of guilt is a form of reassurance-seeking (care-seeking) behaviour. Moreover, self-recriminations, even "when no outside person is involved", enhance the neurotic person's "self-respect, for they imply that he has such a keen moral judgment that he reproaches himself for faults which others overlook" (p. 242). Self-recriminations "leave a secrete door open for a belief that he is not so bad after all" (p. 242). Guilt also serves as "a defense against making accusations" (Horney, 1937, p. 257). Self-recriminations "ward off the danger of accusing others, for it may appear the safer way to take guilt on one's own shoulders" (p. 247). Inhibitions, characteristic of neurotic persons, "toward criticising and accusing others" thus reinforce "tendencies to accuse one's self" (p. 247). In other words, "difficulties in criticizing and making accusations" (or "the fear of expressing resentment"), that is, a "lack of spontaneous self-assertion", contribute to "the inclination to transform accusations into self-accusations" (Horney, 1937, p. 250).

Further defence against disapproval is afforded by "a feeling of being victimized", "by feeling miserably neglected" or abused (masochism) (Horney, 1937, p. 245). This strategy "enables the neurotic not only to ward off accusations but at the same time to put the blame on others" (p. 246). Thus, he expresses his accusations of others indirectly through "the medium of suffering" (p. 255); "suffering makes accusations appear warranted" (Horney, 1937, p. 256).

## 6.6    Neurotic thinking

Organisms monitor their environment for opportunities. Such monitoring has to entail temporary behavioural inhibition, that is, the prevention of impulsive responding to one of several cues representing different aspects of the environment. Anxiety is an emotional state in which the environment is monitored not only for opportunities but also for threats, while the organism's readiness to respond to an emerging threat stimulus with flight or fight is increased. Anxiety arises when there is a conflict between motivational imperatives to remain in a dangerous situation (in order to potentially access a source of reward or avoid an otherwise certain punishment) and to escape from that situation (approach-avoidance and avoidance-avoidance conflicts) (McNaughton, 2006; McNaughton & Corr, 2004; McNaughton & Wickens, 2003). Social situations are complex and conflicting and often call for simultaneous engagement of competing

or incompatible behaviour modes. Anxiety is closely related to indecisiveness and ambivalence in decision making. Inability to resolve a conflict by weighing the significance of conflicting external cues may engage a mode of internal cognition in which future outcomes are simulated ("default mode") (reviewed in Behrendt, 2011). Anxiety contains "an impulse to consider over and over again unpleasant possibilities" (p. 198) "in all sorts of difficult situations" (Moore, 1926, p. 209). Anxiety is associated with a tendency to go "over and over again the possibility that the worst will some day come true" (p. 199), a "tendency to picture the anticipated evil", "*to bring up again and again to the mind the anticipated evil*" (Moore, 1926, p. 198).

> The normal psychotaxis of anxiety is nothing but an impulse to use the ability to think over a situation and its dangers. It may be called forth by the apprehension of the possibility of any painful event whatsoever. (Moore, 1926, p. 207)

Psychoanalysis understands *intellectualisation*, which refers to an excessive disposition to thought, as a "defence mechanism", in that it serves to minimise or overcome anxiety. Thought (internal cognition) may be a process that, in essence, allows the resolution of motivational conflict and the overcoming of behavioural inhibition (associated with anxiety) by generating determinants for action (cues) in a space that is distinct from the one representing the immediate environment or situation (but that is, nevertheless, linked, through learning, with the present environment or situation). Thought, which, in extreme cases, amounts to ongoing ruminations or fruitless preoccupations, may have evolved from goal imagery, on the one hand, and high-level decision-making capabilities (used in complex situations, including social situations, that require monitoring and invite various, contradictory behavioural responses), on the other. What we do when simulating future outcomes in the process of thought is to position ourselves in a situation that, acting as a stimulus, has the potential to launch a behavioural trajectory towards receiving approval and positive attention while avoiding hostility and exclusion. We may simulate several such outcomes until a behaviour mode (drawing on components of withdrawal from conspecifics, submission to conspecifics, induction of submission in conspecifics, and/or attraction of their attention) is selected that offers the greatest probability of reward (such as in the form of libidinal interactions), while exposing us to the lowest risk of punishment (such as in the form of conspecific attack). However, rather than embarking upon any of the trajectories linked, via imagery of a future outcome, to the present social situation, we may remain in a prolonged state of *indecision* and behavioural inhibition.

### 6.6.1    Conflict and hesitation

Masserman (1968) found that "when two or more urgent motivations are in sufficiently serious opposition so that the adaptive patterns attendant to each become mutually exclusive, the organism experiences a mounting internal tension ("anxiety"), develops increasingly intense and generalised ("symbolic") inhibitions and aversions ("phobias"), limited ritualizations of conduct ("compulsions")", as well as psychosomatic dysfunctions and deviated social interactions (p. 203). In experimental studies of conflict between hunger and fear, wherein animals trying to reach a normally safely obtainable food reward were faced with a fear-inducing stimulus (based on exposure to aversive stimulation in preceding trials), pervasive anxiety "was indicated by a low threshold of startle with persistent hyperirritability, muscular tension, crouched body postures" as well as autonomic and physiological alterations (Masserman, 1968, p. 211). Inhibitions of feeding were seen "even outside the experimental apparatus to the point of self-starvation and serious cachexia" (p. 211). Behaviours emerging in the experimental conflict paradigm that were "persistently ambivalent, ineffectively substitutive, and poorly adaptive" were considered

as "neurotic" (p. 203). As part of the neurosis engendered by the hunger-fear conflict, animals reverted to the more passively dependent behaviours characteristic of their infancy ("regressive behaviours") (Masserman, 1968).

> ... as in the animal, the conditioning of the hominid has also been marked by the presentation of two or more stimuli that are mutually opposed to one another. (Burrow, 1949, p. 137)
>
> With man, therefore, as with the experimental animal, there are the stimuli which in inducing a part-interest or response promote certain definite actions and, contrariwise, there are the interest-inducing stimuli which contravene these same actions. (p. 137)
>
> ... in man the opposed alternatives in his behaviour-conflict or neurosis are reactions to a complex constellation of differential affect stimuli—affect-stimuli which in each separate organism ... have become systematized into the spurious entity we called the "I"-persona. (Burrow, 1949, p. 235)

### Social imagery

The conflict is usually between approach (social engagement) and avoidance. The objective of approach (engagement), that is, the "cherished prize" we try to obtain, is the "security based upon mother-love or sympathy" (Burrow, 1949, p. 148). The seeking of security in group situations is offset by fear of the group, that is, fear of exposure to conspecific attack,—a conflict that is particularly evident in patients with mental or nervous illness. Such conflict and attempts to resolve it involve transient behavioural inhibition and the simulation, in mental imagery, of alternative social scenarios reflecting desired outcomes. Social imagery may become circular or ruminative and not be translated into goal-directed or instrumental action, so that, in severe cases, social withdrawal, dissociation, or catatonic stupor ensue. A "barrier of ambivalent mental images" may constitute an "impediment to the organism's natural goals" and an obstruction to the "natural approach to the environment" (Burrow, 1949, p. 130).

> Those of us who have devoted ourselves to the analysis of patients with mental or nervous illness know the extent to which these individuals are a prey to the nostalgic lures of a purely fantastic security, to the subtle enticements of the mother-image. We know that in their regression towards this fanciful basis of behaviour these personalities are invariably confronted with a two-way policy of action. Because of the reversal of their interest towards mere symbolic images of motivation in place of the organism's primary kinesthetic pattern of action, the capacity of these patients is not applied naturally or with balanced ease to the environmental object or situation. Beneath the outer manifestations of these personalities the wish is father to the thought, and ambivalent mental images obstruct a free passage to the task or incident before him. Fair is foul, and foul is fair. They earnestly want to do "right", but they are as earnestly prone to do "wrong". This behavioural dichotomy is inherent in the very concept "mental conflict" first introduced by Freud—a concept with which the formulations of psychiatry are in essential agreement to-day. (Burrow, 1949, pp. 128–129)

> In his dichotomous images of self-satisfaction the neurotic wavers between the affectively approved and the affectively disapproved response, between the comfort of parental protection and the hazards of parental rejection. Thus in his alternative conditioning the neurotic, no less than the experimentally dissociated animal, is faced with a critical choice between the issues of gain and denial, between "right" and "wrong"; and

> from the point of view of his ambivalent images he feels no permanent security as to the direction in which his advantage lies. (Burrow, 1949, p. 148)

However, "the socially "normal" individual is equally at a loss to distinguish between an advantageous and a disadvantageous behaviour-response, between the "right" and the "wrong" choice"; the individual's advantage or satisfaction "must be weighed in the balance against his disadvantage or dissatisfaction" (Burrow, 1949, p. 148). Such decision making involves imagery or simulation of alternative outcomes—"images of social assurance" and images "of social disfavour" (Burrow, 1949, p. 148)—images that, when experienced, may replicate the ability of the actually experienced social situation to induce, or dispose towards, a situationally appropriate behaviour mode. Imagery and social decision making may be too fleeting to come to our awareness, and motivational conflict between grandiosity and fear would manifest in all but slight hesitation.

### 6.6.2   Intellectualisation

Thinking is a means of making emotional contacts with others. Attempts to solve emotional problems intellectually "are meant in the first instance to pave the way for adaptive behaviour in relation to external objects" (Fairbairn, 1952, p. 20). Intellectualisation is a manifestation of preoccupation with the inner world. Preoccupation with the inner world and overvaluation of thought are related to difficulties experienced by schizoid individuals in expressing their feelings naturally towards other people and making emotional contact with them. Individuals with a schizoid tendency substitute intellectual solutions of their emotional problems for "attempts to achieve a practical solution" within the sphere of "relationships with others in the outer world" (p. 20). Individuals with a schizoid tendency "are often more inclined to construct intellectual systems of an elaborate kind than to develop emotional relationships with others on a human basis" (Fairbairn, 1952, p. 21). The "divorce between thought and feeling" in schizoid individuals "must accordingly be construed as the reflection of a split between (1) a more superficial part of the ego representing its higher levels and including the conscious, and (2) a deeper part of the ego", that is, a "more highly libidinal part of the ego" (p. 21). The more superficial part of the ego, "in which thought processes are more highly developed", would repress the deeper, more libidinal part of the ego (Fairbairn, 1952, p. 21).

### 6.6.3   Obsessionality

Shapiro (2000) hinted at the decision-making nature of ruminations in obsessive people. Decision making in obsessive people can become a protracted state of indecision.

> The anxiety of making a personal choice … drives the obsessive person to review the alternatives, even after the decision has been made. … The missed chance will be recalled with a rueful and unforgiving bias. Only those elements whose loss might be regretted will be recalled, and a picture will be constructed of someone or something now painfully desired. (p. 38)
>
> The opportunity missed becomes glorious in retrospect; its retrospective value is determined not by its personal appeal but by the scrupulousness of the regret. Much the same process is involved in obsessive indecision. Whichever alternative is about to be forgone must be reexamined against the possibility of error and immediately becomes attractive. (Shapiro, 2000, p. 121)

Obsessive people are preoccupied with an "anxious concern that a choice should not be made, if at all, without careful review of any possibility of a mistake; and a possible mistake should not pass without remorse and unpunished" (Shapiro, 2000, p. 38). Adverse outcomes are considered and weighed against favourable outcomes in a decision-making mode that is all too readily engaged.

> No possibility of personal error or fault that comes to this obsessive person's mind can be dismissed, no matter how remote or even preposterous it may be, and however little the individual himself may be convinced of its reality. Actually, an obsessive conscientiousness often goes further. Even when no such possibility of fault presents itself spontaneously, it must be sought; the mind must be searched for it. (p. 111)
>
> The obsessively dutiful person will feel obliged in general to pay special respect to the disturbing possibility, the possibility of trouble or calamity, while temptation to credit the less troublesome possibility will be disdained as foolish and irresponsible … Consequently he will assume the worst. (Shapiro, 2000, p. 112)

The brain's default mode is probably engaged during such ruminative, protracted, and often futile decision making. In consciousness, we experience this as fluctuating outcome imagery with transient simulation of alternative future situations. While the brain is presumably engaged in this mode, the obsessive person's disposition to action "fluctuates with the moment-to-moment internal dynamic situation" (Shapiro, 2000, p. 113), until his attitude eventually translates into action.

> At one moment the dynamics of his character require him to suspend the ordinary act of judgement in favour of the possibilities of personal fault, error, or misfortune. At another moment, or perhaps even the same moment, the presence of a simpler, more genuine judgement of reality may reveal itself in action or even, perhaps faintly, in consciousness. (Shapiro, 2000, p. 113)

### 6.6.4  Paranoia

> For people who feel vulnerable, an error of underestimating the possibility of threat is far more serious than its overestimation. Hence their bias toward an assumption of threat. But the suspicious person, like the obsessive, is not necessarily convinced of the realistic justification of his concern. He is convinced only that he must not neglect or underestimate its possibility, that he must not allow himself to be caught off guard, and therefore that he must not allow himself to believe he is safe. (Shapiro, 2000, p. 114)

Anxiety entails behavioural inhibition, risk assessment, monitoring of the external environment and related internal situations for threats, and scanning of the external environment and internal situations for access to safety. In obsessive-compulsive disorder, anxiety manifests in a proclivity to simulate and risk-assess internal situations, whereas paranoid states are associated with anxious monitoring predominantly of the external environment. Individuals with a paranoid character structure "are highly sensitive to slights, or disrespect, alert to the possibility of humiliation" (Shapiro, 2000, p. 86). Paranoid delusion is similar to obsessive worrying, in that both involve an increased alertness to the possibility of threat.

> Even the paranoid delusion in its general quality as an anxious preoccupying idea stripped of realistic proportion may be said to resemble an extreme form of obsession. (Shapiro, 2000, p. 85)

Schizophrenia is associated with "a loss of volitional cognitive control" and a loss of affect (Shapiro, 2000, p. 142). Perhaps, patients with schizophrenia find it difficult to translate either volitional or emotional experience into an action mode. As Shapiro (2000) understood, severe obsessive conditions can be a precursor for the development of paranoid or catatonic schizophrenia. In the case of catatonic schizophrenia, obsessive doubts and indecision may be so severe that the patient finds himself immobilised when faced with a decision; "catatonic stupor, in fact, seems in important respects to be a direct continuation and intensification of certain kinds of obsessive experience" (Shapiro, 2000, p. 149).

> The catatonic immobilization seems specifically to reflect a radically exaggerated obsessional hesitancy, indecision, and precautionary concern. (Shapiro, 2000, p. 149)

What may paralyse patients with catatonic schizophrenia is an overwhelming fear of choosing the wrong action, a fear that is part of an overpowering anxiety. "Behavioural inhibition", like risk assessment, is an aspect of anxiety; and, in catatonic schizophrenia, as conceived by Shapiro (2000), anxious inhibition may generalise to all volitional actions. By contrast, in obsessive persons, "indecision and its inhibition of action are usually limited to particular occasions when consciousness of personal choice is unavoidable and the accompanying self-conscious experience of agency is therefore acute" (Shapiro, 2000, p. 151).

### 6.7  Summary

Anxiety promotes risk assessment behaviour, defensive readiness, and appetitive safety-directed behaviour. Anxiety increases attention to threats and facilitates the perception of cues of danger, that is, of stimulus situations that release instinctive fear-related or defensively aggressive behaviours. Anxiety also facilitates the perception of escape cues or routes to safety, although perception of routes to safety and subsequent escape to safety may be more directly related to the aversiveness of the situation (psychotaxis). Escape cues are approached or otherwise manipulated in an appetitive manner. Escape cues include the sight of the distal mother, herd, flock, or group. Escape may be achieved by establishing proximity to the mother or group, however proximity to conspecifics can, in itself, be anxiogenic. Anxiety reflects the probability, in any given situation, of predatory (*inter*specific) attack or, as a more recent evolutionary achievement, of attack from conspecifics. Evolutionarily more recent social anxiety reflects an increased risk (as assessed by the individual) of being subjected to *intra*specific aggression from others. When others' behaviour indicates that their innate aggressiveness is inhibited in the direction of the individual, we can say that the individual is accepted by others or related to the group or social situation. Social anxiety arises when the individual is insufficiently accepted by, or related to, the group (lack of relatedness), which would be the case especially when the situation can be characterised as novel, fluid, or uncertain. From an evolutionary perspective, social anxiety (*intra*specific anxiety) may have evolved from the more primitive anxiety arising in situations of social separation or isolation (*inter*specific anxiety), much as *intra*specific aggression stems from more primitive *inter*specific aggression. Developmentally, social (within-group) anxiety is related to infantile fear of strangers, whereas isolation anxiety would be related to infantile separation distress. The pain or anxiety that accompanies experiences of social rejection or exclusion (pain of rejection, "narcissistic injury") may be related, in part, to infantile separation distress, whereas novel social situations in which relationship are fluid entail a reactivation of infantile stranger anxiety.

Escape or safety-directed behaviour, originally concerned with the establishment of proximity to the mother, herd, flock, or group (attachment behaviour), later became concerned with the attainment of a secure social situation, creating conditions for the engagement of another individual in an affective interaction that resembles affective attunement between mother and infant. Such engagement has an appeasing (aggression-inhibiting) effect, thereby reducing the risk of conspecific attack and relieving

anxiety. Safety-directed behaviours may also aim to create a situation that allows the individual to induce others to display dominant or submissive signals. We overcome or avoid within-group anxiety by assertive behaviour, adoption of a dominant position, and induction of appeasing and submissive displays in those who are subordinate, or, alternatively, by submissive displays and induction of signals of approval in those who are dominant. Appetitive behaviours, enlisted by the individual in a socially anxiogenic (but not necessarily anxiety-producing) context, would seek to create a situation in which the individual receives, or is likely to receive, positive attention in the form of submissive, respectful, approving, or praising signals from others. These signals communicate acceptance or recognition by others and relatedness to the group; and they imply a reduction in the risk of becoming the victim of intraspecific aggression.

It may be useful to distinguish between two dimensions of social behaviour: social context-guided (contextually responsive) behaviour and the mutual induction of instinctive displays. With regards to the former, the context to which appetitive behaviour is responsive may be a group context or the dyadic interpersonal context (i.e., a relationship). Social context-guided behaviour aims to establish and maintain one's relatedness to an object (in a dyadic relationship) or one's security within, or relatedness to, a group. The immediate social situation is experienced as secure or safe when one is attuned to one's object or when one feels accepted, respected, or recognised by the group to which one belongs. Behaviour that is responsive to, and directed at, the group context controls one's acceptance and recognition by the social milieu, that is, one's potential to attract positive attention from other individuals. Acceptance, respect, and recognition by the group can be gained and accumulated by means of normative and cooperative behaviours as well as by means of behaviours designed to increase one's status (as symbolised by one's possessions, profession, prestige, *etc.*). Safety-seeking behaviour that is guided by and directed at the social context is acquired through coincidental reductions in anxiety (and enhancements of self-esteem) that are brought about by inhibition of others' aggressive potential or by the receipt of signals of acceptance and recognition from the social milieu. Anxiety reductions are effected by more or less random (but nevertheless contextually sensitive) implementations of safety-seeking behaviour, implementations that have succeeded not only in eliciting approval from other individuals in the group but also in precipitating contextual information (reflecting others' behaviours and attitudes and the cultural context in which they occur) that confirms the inhibition of others' aggressiveness. The self, being the part of consciousness that is involved in the regulation of appetitive social behaviour, is constructed on the basis of one's acceptability to (or acceptedness by) others and the appraisals one is in a position to receive from others (Chrzanowski, 1973; Sullivan, 1953). The self, integrating this type of contextual information (and repressing unfavourable information), is the antithesis of social anxiety (which reflects one's vulnerability in the group) (Figure 6-4). Self and anxiety are intricately linked with each other and with context-guided behaviour that creates or maintains conditions of

social security. Freud (1923, 1933) thought that the ego is the seat of anxiety, however others have argued that the self is a derivative of approving and reassuring social information and evidence for a protective mechanism against anxiety (e.g., Heidegger, 1927; Sullivan, 1953).

The goal situation implemented by context-guided (contextually sensitive) safety-seeking behaviour allows the individual to express signals of care, dominance, or subordination in direct interactions with others, and also allows him to engage in subordinate appetitive behaviours that, through the medium of dyadic interaction, seek to obtain a "stimulus situation" ("Reizsituation") that can release an innate "expressive movement" ("Ausdrucksbewegung"), whereby the attainment of a stimulus situation and the release of an instinctive expressive movement can be rewarding and can reinforce a preceding epoch of appetitive (locomotor and orienting) behaviour (Lorenz, 1937, 1952). Thus, safety-seeking behaviour that is responsive to the wider social context may instate a secure situation in which interpersonal interactions can evolve—via a subordinate appetitive phase (in which one person exerts unconscious pressure on the other)—towards consummatory interactions that are derived

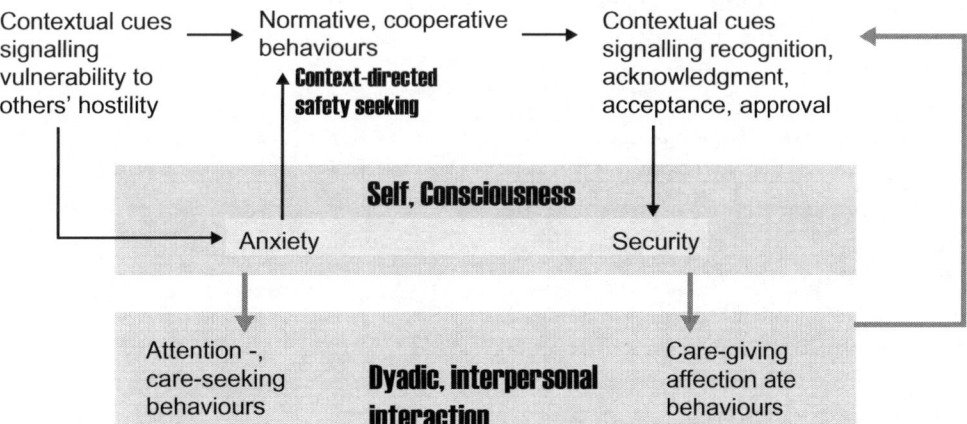

Figure 6-4.   Appetitive safety-seeking behaviour changes the situation from an anxiogenic to a secure one. Normative and cooperative behaviours that control the social context are perhaps derived from submissive and appeasement behaviours originally used in a dyadic interpersonal context. The self would have evolved as a mechanism controlling contextual aspects of social behaviour.

from mother-infant interactions, namely inter-actions that consist of instinctive care-giving or approving behaviours, which, under appropriate circumstances, create a stimulus situation for the release, in the other individual, of recipro-cal care-giving or approving behaviours. Similar considerations may apply to mutually reassuring dominant-submissive interactions occurring in a dyadic context, especially, perhaps, insofar as they replicate aspects of the mother-infant rela-tionship. Others' show of interest, approval, or affection renders the immediate situation secure; it obliterates anxiety and calms the safety-seeking (or relatedness-seeking) drive that is associated with anxiety (Figure 6-4). Others' approval or interest is rewarding because it eliminates anx-iogenic contextual cues, because it satisfies the *drive* behind attention- or care-seeking behaviour (narcissistic striving), or because it releases one's own *instinctive* expressive movements ("Aus-drucksbewegungen") of approval or interest, in return (libidinal signals directed at others).

To emphasise and conclude, the individual overcomes the inherent aversiveness of a novel or uncertain social situation by seeking to ensure that he is recognised, accepted, and respected by others, and that, thereby, others' aggressive-ness is inhibited. If attention-seeking or norma-tive and cooperative behaviours, engaged to this end, prove to be successful, the individual can be said to have "fled" anxiety into social relat-edness (Heidegger, 1927), that is, into a social or interpersonal situation in which he feels recog-nised and accepted by others and in which he can become the target of others' cherishing (libidinal) displays. Appetitive behaviour, reinforced by affiliative (libidinal) reward or a reduction in anxiety, can become habitual in its pursuit of social relatedness, which then prevents the recur-rence of social anxiety. Habitual behaviours that control others' interest in, and attitudes towards, oneself are integral to the individual's personality or defensive constitution. Strategies of appetitive behaviours that, in most situations, more or less habitually inhibit others' potential for aggression and maintain the prospect of receiving approval

and affection from significant others may break down or become ineffective in novel situations, leading to a resurgence of anxiety. Anxiety (due to loss of others' appreciation or respect) or the aversiveness of being in a situation of social unre-latedness (a form of loneliness) energises efforts towards obtaining others' appreciation, interest, or appraisal and towards appeasing their aggres-siveness. In other words, anxiety—arising in a situation in which we are not recognised and in which we are *unlikely* to obtain others' apprecia-tion or approval—or the aversiveness of being in such a situation increases efforts towards creating a situation in which others' aggressive potential is inhibited and in which we can obtain others approval and become the object of their benevo-lent interest, whereby such efforts may involve frank attention- and care-seeking behaviours directed at (and manipulative towards) signifi-cant others.[5]

---

[5]Approval- or attention-seeking behaviour is appetitive. Insofar as approval or attention is consciously sought and experienced, we are dealing with appetitive behaviour and its reinforcement. Approval as an instinctive expression (an affective display or "expressive movement") or as stimulus constellation that matches an innate releasing mechanism (received approval) is unconscious.

# CHAPTER SEVEN

# Object relations theory

Infants in many species seek proximity of their primary caregiver in response to external threats or when nutritional needs are unmet. The infant is biologically programmed to respond to separation from his caregiver with anxiety and searching behaviours (Bowlby, 1988). Anxiety related to the physical absence of the caregiver plays an important role in psychological development of the infant. The infant develops behaviours aimed at keeping the mother accessible or in sight, thereby reducing anxiety. Human infants will have formed a clear attachment to their caregiver by the age of eight months. Being attached, they become upset when their caregiver leaves, seek her comfort when feeling threatened, and become fearful in the presence of strangers (reviewed in Holmes, 2000; Yule, 2000). By the age of two to three years, children become less dependent on the physical presence of their attachment figure who can now be trusted to provide care and protection when needed. Secure and predictable satisfaction of the infant's instinctive needs requires not only the physical presence and accessibility of the caregiver but also her active interest in and devotion to the infant. The infant learns to exert subtle pressures on the caregiver to force her to adopt a positive and caring attitude towards himself (Cashdan, 1988).[1] If the caregiver remains unresponsive or disinterested, the infant or child remains anxious, similarly to how an infant at an earlier developmental stage would remain anxious in the absence of the caregiver. Object relations are concerned, to a large extent, with issues of personal desirability, lovability, and acceptability. The individual maintains a state of relatedness to the world, and thereby overcome his existential anxiety, by ensuring that he receives affectively positive responses from others: first from the mother, then from peers, and then, in ever more abstract ways, from ever more complex social configurations. Frustration of the individual's attempts to induce care-giving behaviours in the object is linked to anger, similarly to the frustration of needs in general. Riviere (1937) described this interplay of the infant's existential anxiety and aggression.

---

[1] Infantile attachment behaviour is an appetitive form of behaviour (Eibl-Eibesfeldt, 1970), and the same may be true for behaviour that establishes or maintains affective attunement with the caregiver or relatedness to the group.

But what happens if these expectations and wants are not fulfilled? In a certain degree the baby becomes aware of his dependence; he discovers that he cannot supply all his own wants— and he cries and screams. He becomes aggressive. ... This situation which we all were in as babies has enormous psychological consequences for our lives. It is our first experience of something like death, a recognition of the non-existence of something, of an overwhelming loss ... The immediate reaction to this painful state of things is that he tries to regain, and also then to preserve, some measure of blissful security he experienced before he felt the lack and his destructive impulses arose. Thus our great need develops for security and safety against these terrible risks and intolerable experiences of privation, insecurity and aggressions within and without. ... The hate and aggression, envy, jealousy and greed felt and expressed by grown-up people are all derivatives, and usually extremely complicated derivatives, both of this primary experience and of the necessity to master it if we are to survive and secure any pleasure at all in life. (Riviere, 1937, pp. 8–10)

Secure attachment arises from responsive and sensitive parenting and leads to the formation of "internal working models" of a responsive caregiver and a secure self (Bowlby, 1988). The caregiver's responses to the infant form the core of an emerging sense of self. The caregiver's empathic responsiveness is the origin of self-esteem (Cashdan, 1988; Holmes, 2000; Kohut, 1971; Yule, 2000). "Internal working models" of caregiver and self are intertwined, according to Bowlby (1988), so that, for instance, a model of the caregiver as rejecting is coupled with a model of the self as unworthy. Failure by the caregiver to respond to the child's care-seeking behaviours and to reinvigorate his sense of relatedness is internalised by the child as a sense of

undesirability, that is, a "bad self" (Cashdan, 1988).

## 7.1  Object-ego differentiation

Frustration of needs and absence of the mother are spurs for the development of object representations in infanthood. First, the infant expects automatic satisfaction and anticipation of all his wishes; and he wants his mother to always care for him with joy and complete devotion. The infant *cannot bear* having his needs not satisfied and *reproaches* his mother for her failure to meet his needs. The infant also needs more love than can be given. The impossibility of constant devotion and caring leads to frequent *pain* about not being loved, on the one hand, and a *longing to be at one* with the "ideal object", on the other. The mother as "ideal object" is expected to be at one with the infant and to have no other concerns (Balint, 1952). Second, the infant experiences *apprehension* when the mother disappears. The infant suffers in the absence of his mother as if he has lost a part of himself (Balint, 1952). Anxiety in the object's absence contributes to the development of a relationship with the object. The establishment of a sustaining relationship, which goes beyond the mere presence of the object and spans times of her absence, is paralleled by the creation of a "good" internal object (O'Shaughnessy, 1964). When the infant realises that his starvation and frustration are due to the absence of the object, he thinks about her as "bad". In the infant's fantasy, the object is attacked for her selfishness and neglect.

The first stable mental representation of the mother forms after the infant is five or six months old. An "inner maternal *presence*" becomes established by three years of age. When, by the age of three, the child becomes able to spontaneously evoke an imaginary (essentially iconic) representation of the mother, the mother's absence becomes less traumatic. "Transitional objects" (Winnicott, 1971), that is, inanimate objects, such as blankets and teddies, mitigate against feelings of abandonment and provide the child with a sense of comfort and security, smooth the transition from the mother as external object to mother as an inner presence (reviewed in Cashdan, 1988).

> By conjuring up a mental picture of the mother, the child internally "captures her" and in so doing invests her with a psychic permanence of sorts. The inner image acts as a substitute while the mother is gone and mitigates the panicky feelings her absence might otherwise produce. Much of the child's attempts to "preserve" the mother are wrapped up in efforts to create an inner maternal presence. (Cashdan, 1988, p. 40)

### 7.1.1   Affective understanding

The object excites the infant's curiosity. Satisfying his curiosity, the infant employs "projective identification" to explore his object (Bion, 1959). As a consequence of such explorations, the infant internalises (forms a representation of) the devoted and loving object. The unreceptive object will appear as hostile to curiosity. In the context of anxiety, exploration of the object, by way of projective identification, allows the infant to evacuate his anxiety. The object, in turn, picks up ("introjects") the infant's anxiety by way of "primary identification". Successful projective identification at times of anxiety allows the infant to reintroject and internalise (form a representation of) the tolerating and reassuring object. The infant's projective identifications and the object's capacity to accept (introject) projective identifications, that is, to tolerate and metabolise the infant's projections, are prerequisites to establishing a link between infant and object (Bion, 1959). The object's receptiveness, that is, her capacity to introject the infant's anxiety, will vary. If the object is receptive to, and reexperiences, the infant's anxiety, then she may either "retain a balanced outlook" or become a "prey to the anxiety" (Bion, 1959). If the object tolerates the introjected anxiety, then the infant will experience a reduction in his own anxiety. If, however, the object is not receptive to the subject's anxiety, then the subject's attempts at projective identification can become excessive and more violent. Hatred arises from frustrated efforts of evacuating one's anxiety; and such hatred and may be accompanied by envy for the object's ability to remain unaffected (Bion, 1959).

Bion (1962) described how the mother acts as a "container" for the infant's bad projections. The distressed infant needs to feel that the mother understands and can make sense of his experiences. The mother's reverie (*vis-à-vis* the infant) allows the infant to transform his distress, which is accompanied by an urge to act out, into a sense of being understood and of knowing himself. If the mother has a capacity for reverie, then she can make sense of the infant's distress by means of "correlation". The infant, experiencing the tolerating mother, reintrojects a sense of being understood, which allows him to integrate his anxieties and give them meaning. The infant receives "its frightened personality back again, but in a form that it can tolerate" (Bion, 1962). If the mother's capacity for reverie breaks down and she does not accept the infant's projections, the infant cannot gain an understanding of himself and his distress and is left with "nameless dread" (Bion, 1962).

Thus, experiencing the tolerating and understanding mother, the child develops an understanding of himself. Similarly, by experiencing the tolerating analyst, the analysand becomes able to gradually introject the tolerating analyst and thereby reshape his self-image, leading to the "patient's discovery of aspects of himself" (Carpy, 1989). The analyst's interpretation may amount for the patient to a refusal to accept his, the patient's, projective identifications, which could lead to a more violent and desperate use of projective identification by the patient. Bion (1959) compared this to the dutiful attendance of a mother to the crying infant without her taking in and experiencing the infant's fear.

### 7.1.2   Mirror stage

In the "mirror stage", the child is first presented with an image of his own unity and coherence, an image that is reflected back to the child by his parents (Lacan, 1966). The "mirror image", reflected back to the child, consists of the parents' approving gestures, their recognition and acknowledgement of the child. The mirror image is invested with libido and internalised (acquired as an unconscious representation); it thus becomes the core of the child's ego and sense of self (Lacan, 1966; reviewed in Fink, 1997). Although "ego" and "self" are often treated synonymously, it may be useful to distinguish between the ego as an unconscious representation and the self as a consciously experienced striving for recognition and acknowledgment (a striving towards libidinal resources)—a striving that is an explication of potentialities encoded within the ego. Alternatively, the self can be regarded a conscious instantiation (enactment) of the ego or, more precisely, of the ego ideal—an instantiation that is equivalent to an incarnation of the ego or ego ideal (even though the self, insofar as it can be regarded as an object, is experienced as part of the *inner* world). From this perspective, awareness of the self (self-consciousness) may not be different from awareness of objects; "consciousness may adopt it as an object to be observed like any other object" (Fink, 1997, p. 86). The self (or conscious aspect of the ego) can be regarded "as an external view or image of the subject which is internalized" (Fink, 1997, p. 86). If the self (conscious incarnation of the ego) is an object, then it can be cathected (invested) with libido and internalised like any other object. Freud (1923) considered the ego, that is, the self, to be an object; and he thought that the ego is a precipitate of abandoned object cathexes, that is, of former identifications with objects.

### 7.1.3   *Primary identification*

Libido, according to Fairbairn (1952), is inherently object-seeking (rather than pleasure-seeking, as Freud had thought). The real libidinal aim, as Fairbairn (1952) saw it, is to establish a satisfactory relationship with an object. The first object relationship, in the early oral phase of development, is one of "primary identification" with the object. "Primary identification" means libidinal "cathexis of an object which has not yet been differentiated (or has been only partly differentiated) from" the infant (Fairbairn, 1952, p. 145). The libidinally cathected object with which the infant is identified is, at first, a part object, and it is "equivalent to an incorporated object" (p. 42). The prominent feature of the infant's relationship with his mother is his extreme dependence on her ("infantile dependence"), which, at first, takes the form of an "oral dependence" on the object, with the breast of the mother (a part object) being the original object. Fairbairn (1952) concluded that the state of "infantile dependence" "is chiefly manifested in an attitude of oral incorporation towards, and an attitude of primary emotional identification with the object" (p. 145). For as long as the state of "infantile dependence" persists, "identification remains the most characteristic feature of the individual's relationship with his object" (Fairbairn, 1952, p. 47). In the state of infantile dependence, "separation from the object becomes the child's greatest source of anxiety" (p. 145). Primary identification (in the form of psychic incorporation) alleviates this anxiety over separation (Fairbairn, 1952).

The transition from the early oral phase to the late oral phase of infantile development is "marked by the substitution of a whole object (or person) for a part-object" (Fairbairn, 1952, p. 48). The infant establishes a more mature relationship characterised by *identification with an object that is differentiated from himself*. Progressive differentiation of the object is accompanied by a decrease in (primary) identification with the object. While, in the case of an infant, the more mature object relationship is focused on a single, albeit differentiated, object (namely the mother differentiated from the infant), in the case of an adult, "the object-relationship has a considerable spread" (Fairbairn, 1952, p. 47). As the child develops, the original object with which the infant had formed a relationship is progressively replaced by, and represented in, a multitude of concrete and abstract objects.

### 7.1.4   Failure to outgrow infantile dependence

Frustration of the child's "desire to be loved as a person and to have his love accepted is the greatest trauma that a child can experience" (Fairbairn, 1952, pp. 39–40). In order to successfully emerge from the state of infantile dependence, the child needs to obtain conclusive assurance that he is genuinely loved by his parents. Such assurance enables the child "to depend safely upon his real objects" (p. 39). If reassurance that the child is genuinely loved by his parents is not forthcoming, he will not be able "gradually to renounce infantile dependence without misgiving" (Fairbairn, 1952, p. 39). As a consequence of partial fixation in the state of infantile dependence, "the inherent libidinal drive towards the object leads to the establishment of aberrant relationships" (Fairbairn, 1952, p. 40). The individual will be compelled to maintain relationships with internalised objects, instead of relationships with objects in the outer world, given that his relationship with external objects would be "fraught with too much *anxiety over separation*" (p. 39). The individual with a schizoid tendency, in particular, "becomes afraid to love; and therefore he erects barriers between his objects and himself" (p. 50). As his libido is withdrawn from external objects, "it is directed towards internalized objects", so that it is in his "inner reality that the values of the schizoid individual are to be found" (p. 50). Excessive libidinisation of internalised objects leads to narcissism; "and such narcissism is specially characteristic of the schizoid individual" (Fairbairn, 1952, p. 50).

### Schizoid and depressive states

Failure to outgrow the early oral phase of dependence renders the child vulnerable to experience, henceforth, a "schizoid state". The schizoid state "is associated with an unsatisfactory object-relationship during the early oral phase" (Fairbairn, 1952, p. 55). The "depressive state", by contrast, has its root in an unsatisfactory object relationship during the late oral phase. Both, schizoid and depressive, states depend upon "a regressive reactivation, during subsequent childhood, of situations arising respectively during the early and late oral phases" (p. 55). Traumatic situations that cause schizoid or depressive states are those "in which the child feels that he is not really loved as a person, and that his own love is not accepted" (p. 55). This is consistent with the notion that loss of object, or any frustration in object relationships, is the essential trauma that provokes a depressive reaction. Fairbairn (1952) thought that "the schizoid and the depressive states represent two fundamental psychopathological conditions, in relation to which all other psychopathological developments are secondary" (p. 57).

## 7.2   Paranoid-schizoid position

Melanie Klein observed that, from the beginning of his life, the infant experiences love and hate towards the breast (a "part object"), which is seen as either all good or all bad. The mother, or a part of her, is experienced as "bad" whenever she rejects the infant's advances and frustrates his desires. The good object "embodies the comforting and rewarding aspects of the mother" and "is responsible for the child's feeling desirable and loved" (Cashdan, 1988, p. 10). For Melanie Klein, the introjection of good objects and bad objects is the result of fantasies of oral incorporation. Fantasies of orally incorporating objects establish internal objects and perpetuate the inner world. Mental life of the child, according to Kleinian theory, consists of "a constant interplay between the introjection of external objects and the projection of internalized objects" (Fairbairn, 1952, p. 154). Driven by anxiety, bad internal objects (part objects) are projected, while good objects (part objects)—when learning to avoid anxiety—are introjected. The central anxiety in the paranoid-schizoid position is the infant's fear of abandonment or loss of contact.[2] By dividing the mother into good and bad parts, the infant

---

[2]When abandonment is experienced or threatened, the infant responds with more intense expression of neediness or rage.

avoids the pain of abandonment and "is able to maintain his dependent ties without constantly feeling threatened" (Cashdan, 1988, p. 10). The paranoid-schizoid position extends over the first three to four or five months of life, followed by the depressive position which extends over most of the remaining months of the first year.

### 7.2.1   Persecutory fear

The infant's fear of persecution by an external object can arise in one of two hypothetical ways. First, the infant's fear of annihilation (existential anxiety) is externalised and, thereby, transformed into a fear of persecution. Transformation into a fear of persecution requires perception of an external persecutor, that is, a "bad object". Externalisation of danger is one of the earliest methods of defence against anxiety (Klein, 1940; Laughlin, 1970).

> In general, the organism prefers to feel dangers as threats coming from without rather than from within. Certain mechanisms of protection against unwelcome or overly intense stimuli can be set in motion only against external stimuli. (Laughlin, 1970, p. 223)

Second, inevitable frustration of the infant's needs is externalised into *hatred* of the "bad breast". The frustrating "bad breast" becomes the target of the infant's destructive impulses. Aggressive fantasies about attacks on the frustrating breast lead to fears of counterattack and fears of being punished for having these fantasies (paranoid fear). Paranoia ensues if fear of the external persecutor outweighs hatred. Persecutory fears create a constant need to monitor bad objects (Klein, 1940). The "bad breast" is not simply a feared persecutor but is seen as having taken on the infant's aggressive intentions. "Projection" allows the infant to attribute his destructive impulses to an external object and, thereby, experience these impulses as alien to himself. The stronger the infant's hostile feelings, the greater is the extent of paranoid fear

(Rosenfeld, 1965). The bad breast becomes the prototype for all later persecuting objects. Fears of counterattack and punishment for fantasising about attacks on the frustrating bad breast contribute to the formation of the "primitive superego" (Klein, 1940).

### 7.2.2   Splitting

"Part objects" are characteristic of the paranoid-schizoid position. The concept of "part object" not only refers to part of a person (such as the breast) but also designates the distorted perception of a person as either all good (ideal) or all bad (persecutory). Such distorted perception points to a cathexis of pure libido or pure aggression. It implies the presence of a splitting mechanism that separates libido from aggression and keeps the all-good part object separate from the all-bad part object. Experiences of the frustrating breast ("bad breast"), that is, projected feelings of frustration, form the prototype of a bad object. The "good breast", as the recipient of the infant's libidinal impulses, is kept separate from the "bad breast". Melanie Klein thought that the infant needs to protect his "good" internal object representation by splitting off and projecting hostile feelings that arise against the real object into a persecutory object representation that is all "bad" (reviewed in Bell, 2001; Kernberg, 1980).

The state in which libidinal and destructive impulses become confused is "associated with extreme anxiety" (Rosenfeld, 1965, p. 53), emphasising the defensive nature of splitting and projection. Rosenfeld (1965) thought that "aggressive energy is expended in keeping up the splitting processes" and whenever splitting processes lessen, through analysis or spontaneously, "aggressive energy is released and may temporarily be excessive" (p. 58). The primary purpose of projection and splitting may be to replace unfocused anxiety with a defensive response that can be targeted. After all, it is the purpose of anxiety to enable risk assessment and preparation for defensive responding. The primary developmental benefit of projection may not be to protect the "goodness" of the object. Instead, aggression that can be focused on the bad part object (or bad object) may be utilised for the purpose of control. The infant's overt anger directed at the caregiver's "badness" may allow him to learn ways of controlling the object in accordance with his needs. This would concord with the notion of "projective identification".

### 7.2.3   Aggressive control

Splitting protects the ego from anxiety ("paranoid anxiety") by means of destruction of internalised object relations (Kernberg, 1980). Splitting of objects (into good and bad part objects) and projection of one's destructive impulses (onto the bad part object) ensure the transformation of overwhelming anxiety ("paranoid anxiety") into a more concrete fear of persecution. The individual may try and flee from the external persecutor—created by splitting and projection—by increasing his dependency on an idealised *external* object. Moreover, by projecting intolerable (hostile) feelings onto the object (turning it into a bad part object), these feelings can be controlled effectively by use of justifiable outrage and aggression directed at the object (bad part object) (reviewed in Bell, 2001; Kernberg, 1980). In "projective identification", bad parts of the ego (or parts of bad internal objects) that have been split off are projected onto an external object with the aim of forcing the object to acquire these bad (unacceptable) characteristics. "Projective identification" involves forceful control of the external object. The object altered by projective identification is experienced as aggressive (bad) and, hence, needs to be controlled. Thus, an external object can be turned (manipulated) into a target for justified aggression. Stifling of emotions protects the ego from realising its own aggressiveness (reviewed in Kernberg, 1980).

### 7.2.4   Idealisation

Splitting ensures that good external or internal objects can be idealised. Idealisation is a defence mechanism that seeks to preserve all-good external or internal objects. By idealising the mother, the child represses the bad parts of the mother and reifies the good parts, transforming the mother into an all-good human being (Cashdan, 1988). Splitting ensures that, while bad part objects can be totally projected, all-good part objects can be totally introjected. Experiences of the gratifying breast are introjected to form the prototype of a good internal object. Fantasies about the good breast are at the core of ego identification (reviewed in Kernberg, 1980). Identification of the ego with an idealised object is particularly evident in narcissistic patients. Narcissistic patients have omnipotently introjected an all-good part object. As a consequence, patients with narcissistic object relations have a highly idealised self-image. As a result of omnipotent introjection, narcissistic patients deny any separateness from the object, avoiding recognition of any difference between object and self. Hence, they can deny any need for dependency on an external object. Any dependency on an external object would lead to intolerable envy of the object's desirable qualities and to intolerable aggressive feelings caused by frustration. External objects are used only for projections of undesirable parts of the patient (reviewed in Kernberg, 1980).

## 7.3   Depressive position

> Being lonely without the loved or longed-for person, experiencing a loss of love or a loss of object as a danger, being frightened of being in the dark alone or with an unknown person—all these things are, I have found, modified forms of early anxiety-situations, that is, of the small child's fear of dangerous internalized and external objects. At a somewhat later stage of development there is added to this fear of the object a fear *on behalf* of it; and the child now fears that its mother will die in consequence of its imaginary attacks upon her and that it will be left all alone in its helpless state. (Klein, 1932, p. 248)

Developmentally, the second half of the first year of life is dominated by the depressive position. Paranoid anxiety and splitting of objects diminish as the infant moves from the paranoid-schizoid to the depressive position. Inasmuch as splitting reduces, "libidinal and aggressive impulses can be brought closer together" (Rosenfeld, 1965, p. 62), and the infant realises that his love and hate are directed at the same object. The infant becomes aware of the good aspects of the external object towards whom his aggression and destructive fantasies are directed. Once love and hate are less split up, feelings of guilt and depression can emerge. The fear that the self will be destroyed by persecutory bad objects diminishes, and the predominant fear becomes that of harming the internal and external objects on whom the infant depends. The fear characteristic of the depressive position is that the object on whom the infant depends will be lost or destroyed as a result of the infant's own destructive impulses (Rosenfeld, 1965). This fear constitutes "depressive anxiety", as opposed to "paranoid anxiety" characteristic of the paranoid-schizoid position. The fear of harming good internal and external objects (depressive anxiety) amounts to, or importantly contributes to, feelings of guilt. Guilt may also stem from bad objects that have been introjected and that, due to reduced splitting, can no longer be projected outward. Internal bad objects, which constitute the primitive superego, set standards and make demands; and they attack the ego with guilt feelings (as evidenced by self-reproaches) (reviewed in Kernberg, 1980).

Guilt and depression, while difficult to bear, contribute to better integration of good and bad objects. The realisation that love and hate are directed at the same object enhances the infant's capacity to "introject" a good object more securely (Rosenfeld, 1965). External reality in form of close and happy relationships has to prove the groundlessness of the infant's insecurities; eventually, his fear of losing his mother diminishes and she is established (introjected) more securely internally (Klein, 1940), indicating that the depressive position has been "worked through". If external reality cannot provide proof for the groundlessness of the child's insecurities and worries

about his internal world, the ego is not capable of working through the depressive position. The fear of losing the loved object, characteristic of the depressive position, is merely superimposed on the fear of persecution by bad objects characteristic of the paranoid-schizoid position. Failure to work through the depressive position leads to a regression to the paranoid-schizoid position. During such regression, the child's harsh superego is projected back outside, so that excessive guilt can be avoided at the expense of reemerging early persecutory fears. These persecutory fears, in turn, justify the deflection of aggressive impulses out onto persecutory bad objects (Klein, 1940, 1952; Rosenfeld, 1965; Kernberg, 1980).

## 7.3.1   Defences against guilt

Idealisation of the good object can be used as a defence against guilt feelings arising in the depressive position. Idealisation in the depressive position is not based on splitting, unlike idealisation in the paranoid-schizoid position. Alternatively, depressive guilt can be denied by identification with the superego. Identification with the superego, which is a defence mechanism that plays a central role in mania, involves depreciation or hatred of external objects instead of the self. Omnipotence, enabling the denial of one's need for external objects, is based on identification with a powerful and idealised object. Omnipotence also involves a tendency to exert control over external objects. Control over external objects ensures that these objects are not dangerous (reviewed in Kernberg, 1980). Omnipotent control over objects manifests as dominant behaviour, and the neutralisation of others' dangerousness is achieved by inducing in them the display of submissive behaviours. Objects that are targeted by one's dominance behaviours are induced to display submissive behaviours towards oneself.

## 7.3.2   Trust and gratitude

Inner pleasurable states, reflecting the satisfaction of libidinal and other life instincts, are externalised onto objects, which are then introjected as good internal objects. A good *internal* object, formed as a result of gratifying experiences, can be projected onto new objects. This projection lies at the heart of basic trust. New gratifying experiences reinforce basic trust. New gratifying objects are reintrojected as good internal objects. Cycles of projection, gratification, and reintrojection promote "ego synthesis" (reviewed in Kernberg, 1980). By analogy, there is a tendency to externalise inner aversive states, reflecting the frustration of libidinal and other drives, onto external objects (transforming them into bad objects) and, then, to attack these objects. Once the infant becomes aware, in the depressive position, that the gratifying (good) object and frustrating (bad) external object are identical, he experiences guilt over attacking the object. The depressive position is "worked through" when guilt feelings over having attacked the good object are reduced by consistent expressions of love and gratitude towards the object ("reparation"). Gratitude, based on secure gratification of needs, is directed at the *external* good object. As a result of reparation (involving expressions of gratitude), good and bad part objects are synthesised into a whole object, which is then reintrojected as an internal good object. Guilt reinforces gratitude; and gratitude strengthens the infants love for the object. Authentic gratitude decreases greed. Gratitude, when it is not authentic, can be a defence against envy, in which case expressions of gratitude leave the individual to experience "feelings of being robbed" (reviewed in Kernberg, 1980).

### 7.3.3   Reactivation of depressive anxiety

Infantile developmental positions, during which the earliest object relations are played out, determine the expression of anxiety, aggression, and love in later object relations ("transference"). Anxiety situations that arise later in life, after the paranoid-schizoid position has been resolved and the depressive position has been worked through, will reactivate paranoid or depressive anxieties, and hence reinstate the object relation dynamics

of these infantile developmental positions. In normal mourning, processes belonging to the depressive position are repeated and guilt characteristic of the depressive position is reactivated. The mourner has to work through the depressive position again. Patients with manic-depressive illness have in infancy not been able to work through the depressive position. They have never established securely a good inner object and remain vulnerable to experiencing depressive anxiety or engaging in excessive and maladaptive defences to suppress this anxiety (reviewed in Kernberg, 1980).

### 7.4   Superego development

The primitive superego, according to Klein (1940, 1952), emerges in the second half of the first year of life, deriving from reintrojected bad objects (which are objects that were previously split off and projected outside). Klein (1932) contended that the formation of the superego and the early stages of the Oedipus complex extend from the middle of the first year to the third year of the child's life. Controversially, she thought that, at these early stages, the child "is already beginning to feel ... genital desires for the parent of the opposite sex and jealousy and hatred of the parent of the same sex" (p. 191). Feelings of hatred that arise in the early oedipal situation draw the child away from the parent of the same sex, although this reaction is partly applied to the fantasy object corresponding to the same-sex parent. Klein (1932) argued that these "destructive impulses and the anxiety they arouse" govern the early stages in the formation of the superego (p. 195); "it is chiefly impulses of hate which bring on the Oedipus complex and the formation of the super-ego and which govern the earliest and most decisive stages of both" (p. 193).

Superego pressures express unconscious morality and perfectionistic demands. The early superego is especially severe; "and, normally speaking, in no period of life is the opposition between ego and super-ego so strong as in early childhood" (Klein, 1932, p. 198). Klein (1932) thought that, in the early stage of the child's development, "anxiety proceeds from the pressure of the super-ego" (p. 202). The pressure of the superego, exerted on the child's destructive tendencies, arouses anxiety. The superego, being "formed in the earliest stages of the child's life", is "first felt by the ego as anxiety and then, as the early anal-sadistic stage gradually comes to a close, as a sense of guilt" (Klein, 1932, p. 229). Perhaps, the early superego symbolises nothing more than an *uncertain* expectation of reprimand and punishment for socially unacceptable behaviour—an uncertain expectation that is experienced as anxiety or guilt. The child's fear (or, rather, his uncertain expectation) that attacks may be made against him by his external and internal objects constitutes one of "the deepest causes of the child's feelings of anxiety and guilt" (Klein, 1932, p. 230). The primitive superego plays a central role in processes belonging to the depressive infantile developmental position—processes as a result of which the splitting of objects into good and bad is overcome (reviewed in Kernberg, 1980). From the depressive position on, prohibitive and demanding aspects of objects are introjected into the superego, while libidinal aspects of objects are introjected into the ego. The superego regulates ego function by raising depressive anxieties that represent fears over dangers to good internal objects or guilt over harm caused to good internal objects (Kernberg, 1980)—good internal objects that are integral to the ego.

### 7.4.1   Reciprocal introjection and projection

The child introjects its objects, that is, he forms a mnemonic representation of them. Internal (introjected) objects can be ejected and projected into the outer world, meaning that external replicas are formed of these objects (so that these objects are consciously perceived). Mechanisms of ejection and projection play an important role in superego formation (Klein, 1932). Having introjected the superego, the small child is in position to eject (project) "his terrifying superego" into the outer world, whereby "his act of ejection is a means of defence employed by his

fear-ridden ego against his super-ego" (p. 200). Anxiety, that is, the child's uncertain expectation of punishment by his external objects (conceptualised as pressure from the superego or as fear of introjected objects), promotes the ejection and projection of bad (persecutory) internal objects. Klein (1932) thought that "the child's fear of its introjected objects urges it to displace that fear into the external world" (p. 207). When, in states of anxiety, bad (persecutory) internal objects are projected into the outer world, anxiety is turned into a fear of persecution (a more certain expectation to be attacked by defined persecutors), enabling the targeted release of aggressive ("sadistic") impulses. Alternatively, the child's bad internal objects are projected into the world of imagination, so that he "protects himself from his fear of his violent object, both introjected and external, by redoubling his own destructive attacks upon it in his imagination" (Klein, 1932, p. 203). Projection is followed by reintrojection, that is, by further elaboration of representations of inner objects, including elaboration of the superego. The child's urge "to project his terrifying identifications on to his objects results, it would seem, in an increased impulse to repeat the process of introjection again and again" (p. 203). The "reciprocal action between projection and introjection" is "of fundamental importance not only for the formation of [the child's] superego but for the development of his object-relations to persons and his adaptation to reality" (p. 203). Real objects, reintrojected by the child, may have abstained from retaliation or may have been recognised by the child as objects with whom he also has libidinal relations. Libidinal relations to external objects counteract the child's fears of his internal and external enemies (Klein, 1932).

> In this way the interaction between super-ego formation and object-relation, based on an interaction between projection and introjection, profoundly influences his development. In the early stages the projection of his terrifying imagos into the external world turns that world into a place

of danger and his objects into enemies; while the simultaneous introjection of real objects who are in fact well disposed to him works in the opposite direction and lessens the force of his fear of the terrifying imagos. Viewed in this light, super-ego formation, object-relations and adaptation to reality are the result of an interaction between the projection of the individual's sadistic impulses and the introjection of his objects. (Klein, 1932, p. 209)

In consequence of the interaction of introjection and projection … the child finds a refutation of its fears in the outer world, and at the same time allays its anxiety by introjecting its real, "good" objects. (Klein, 1932, p. 248)

### 7.4.2   Mastering superego pressures

Ejecting the superego and attacking an external object that is a replica of the superego is a primitive mechanism by which the child tries to overcome anxiety resulting from superego pressure. Once the child has developed a more conscious fear of suffering retribution at the hand of his object, he "may turn *away* from it, on account of his fear of it as a source of danger and also in order to shield it from his own sadistic impulses" (Klein, 1932, p. 215). As a sign of ego development, the child's hatred of his dangerous object, experienced at times of anxiety, may not lead to a turning away from his object but give way to an acknowledgment of "the power of the object in addition to submitting to, and accepting the prohibitions of, a severe super-ego" (pp. 214–215). If the child reaches this developmental step, the ego overcomes anxiety principally by trying "to satisfy both external and internalized objects" (Klein, 1932, p. 215), that is, by submitting to them.

Splitting of objects into good and bad ones is another method of mastering the threats of the superego (overcoming the pressure exerted by the superego). Splitting up his "mother imago into a good and a bad one", allows the child to turn away from one external replica of his object, while turning towards another replica of the object "with greater positive feeling" (Klein, 1932, p. 215). The child's ambivalence towards his objects allows him to overcome "his fear of his superego by distributing it, after having directed it outwards, over a number of objects, so that certain ones stand for the object which he has attacked and which therefore threatens him with danger, and others, especially his mother, signify the kindly protecting person" (p. 215). The "mechanism of distributing the imagos" allows the ego to turn away from the dangerous object, while "it tries to make good on the friendly one the imaginary injuries it has done" (p. 216). When, with further ego development, splitting decreases and good and bad objects are integrated, "the hitherto overpowering threats of the super-ego become toned down into admonitions and reproaches", and the ego can find support against these threats in a positive object relationship (Klein, 1932, pp. 215–216).

As the libidinal impulses of children grow stronger and their destructive ones weaker, qualitative changes continually take place in their super-ego, so that it makes itself more and more felt by the ego as an admonitory influence. (Klein, 1932, pp. 243–244)

### 7.4.3   Ego ideal

Anxiety is objectless, but this does not imply that anxiety is a response to "internal dangers", the superego in particular, unless we recognise the superego as a metaphor and an abstract concept. When speaking of a displacement of internal anxiety to objects in the outer world, what we mean is a focusing of diffuse anxiety onto discernable, more certain threats. Anxiety, experienced in relation to an actual social situation, is generated internally only insofar as it depends on a growing body of *internalised* (acquired) experience relating to the dangerousness of classes of social situations. Destructive impulses are activated in relation to objects that are, as a result of "displacement" of anxiety into the outer world, experienced as threatening and dangerous (Klein, 1932). Objects are, and will be, experienced as "a source of danger to the child, and yet, in so far as they are felt to be kindly, they also represent a refuge from anxiety" (p. 247). The child's "relations to its objects and its various activities and sublimations" are "points of support against its fear of its super-ego and its destructive impulses" (p. 249). The child's efforts to master anxiety are "of fundamental importance for the child's adaptation to reality and for the development of its ego" (Klein, 1932, p. 249).

The superego can be regarded, again, as an inner (mnemonic) representation of an abstract hostile object (the reprimanding, persecutory authority). Klein (1932) thought that the superego overlaps, but is not identical, with the object that is the reprimanding or frustrating parent. The commands and prohibitions of the small child's superego "are by no means identical with the commands that come from its real objects" (p. 199). In consequence of this discrepancy between superego and object, the ego makes efforts "to make his real objects interchangeable with his imagos of them" (p. 217). The small child is burdened with the difference between its superego, "composed as it is of quite different imagos that have been formed in the course of development", on the one hand, and "the standards of its real objects", on the other (p. 250). The small child is "continually endeavouring" to make its superego and object "interchangeable, partly so as to lessen its fear of its super-ego, partly so as to better comply with the requirements of its real objects" (Klein, 1932, p. 249). In the latency period, when, according to Klein (1932), the development of the superego has reached completion, the "strengthened ego joins with the super-ego in setting up a common standard", the ego-ideal, which "is the well-behaved, 'good' child that satisfies its parents and teachers" (p. 250). The ego-ideal "takes into account the demands of reality" and denotes that "an adjustment is reached by the ego and super-ego agreeing upon a common standard" (Klein, 1932, p. 252).

The general process of stabilization which occurs in the child during the latency period is effected, I think, not by any actual alteration of its super-ego but by the fact that its ego and super-ego are pursuing the common aim of achieving an adaptation to its environment and adopting ego-ideals belonging to that environment. (Klein, 1932, p. 252)

For its ego only feels equal to the task of keeping down the id and opposing forbidden impulses so long as its elders assist its efforts. The child needs to receive prohibitions from without, since these, as we know, lend support to prohibitions from within. It needs, in other words, to have representatives of its superego in the outer world. This dependence upon objects in order to be able to master anxiety is much stronger in the latency period than in any other phase of development. Indeed it seems to me to be a definite prerequisite for a successful transition into the latency period that the child's mastery of anxiety should rest upon its object-relations and adaptation to reality. (Klein, 1932, p. 259)

### 7.5   Oedipus complex

In the paranoid-schizoid position, the infant deals with disturbing feelings and destructive impulses by projecting them into a split-off aspect of the object. The mother receives the infant's projections and alleviates the infant's underlying anxieties through her reactions towards him, especially her emotional "understanding" of him. As a result, the infant introjects an object that can contain and modify his distress (Bion, 1959, 1962). Introjection of a containing object, in turn, leads to the development of the infant's own ability to contain and work through his distress. Once the infant recognises that the object on which he depends is a *whole* object, destructive impulses against the object are not split off and projected anymore. Along with the integration of the ego, the infant develops concern for the object and a fear that his destructive impulses could destroy the object (depressive anxiety). This is as far as the depressive position takes us. Even though the infant overcomes paranoid-schizoid mechanisms of defence, these mechanisms remain latent and can reemerge at times of heightened "depressive anxiety" concerned with dependence on a whole object. The Oedipus complex implies that the child's development has reached a stage at which he can acknowledge his mother as a whole object on which he depends (Segal, 1997). Recognition of the mother as a whole object in the depressive position may be accompanied by a reluctance to accept that the object has a life of her own, including a relationship with the father (Segal, 1997).

### 7.5.1    Tolerating the third object

In the oedipal scenario, witnessing the mother in close relationship with a third party arouses unbearable feelings of exclusion and inferiority. Jealousy, experienced in view of the mother's relationship with the father, is an emotional characteristic of the depressive position (Segal, 1997).[3] Jealousy constitutes heightened "depressive anxiety" in the context of which aspects (especially defences) of the latent paranoid-schizoid position can reemerge. Segal (1997) argued that the triangular situation characteristic of the Oedipus complex is similar to the triangular situation that arises in the paranoid-schizoid position from the splitting off of unwanted aspects of the self onto a third object, usually a part object. Upon leaving the paranoid-schizoid position, the infant learns to sublimate destructive impulses directed against the bad breast (part object), whereas the developmental task in the oedipal scenario is to learn and tolerate destructive impulses against the father-mother relationship (Segal, 1997). Successful working-through of the Oedipus complex leads to the introjection of an object that is not only recognised as a whole object

but also allowed to have a life of her own. Such introjection, manifesting in an ability to observe others in their relationship without hostility and be benevolent towards them, represents further ego development. While progression from the paranoid-schizoid to the depressive position depends on the mother being able to contain the infant's distress and destructive impulses, successful working-through of the Oedipus complex depends on the benevolence of the parents *vis-à-vis* the infant's attacks on their relationship (Segal, 1997). If the Oedipus complex has not been worked through successfully, the return or presence of a third object will continue to arouse paranoid-schizoid anxieties.

### 7.5.2    Identification with the third object

The ability to think and symbolise, which, in the depressive position, has helped the infant to come to terms with the insight that the mother is a whole object on whom he depends, undergoes further development in the working-through of the Oedipus complex. Thinking is a means of modifying unacceptable (often destructive) impulses; thinking is incompatible with "acting out" of destructive impulses, but once paranoid-schizoid anxieties return, the capacity to think will be lost (Segal, 1997). In Lacan's (1966) system, the *dyadic* bond with the perceived "other" structures "the imaginary" plane. *Triadic* relations unfold on the plane of "the symbolic", that is, the plane on which social exchange is mediated by language. Lacan (1966) related the triadic character of "the symbolic" order to the triangular constellation of the Oedipus complex. The oedipal crisis ensues when the child realises that the mother's desire aims at an object other than himself (the father). Rivalry with the father sets in motion a transition from "the imaginary" to "the symbolic" mode of functioning. Through resolution of the Oedipus complex, the child accedes the symbolic mode of functioning. Insertion of the subject into the symbolic plane provides access to the process of "desire" (which Lacan distinguished from "drives"). The child's "desire" comes to be expressed through the "signifying system" of

---

[3]Jealousy of the mother's relationship with the father, as it occurs in the oedipal scenario, may be developmentally related to the more primitive situation in which the infant is envious of the mother's qualities or possessions, which may include the father (Segal, 1997).

the symbolic. In other words, the child becomes able to rely on language for *guidance* (implying goal-directedness) of thought and action (Lacan, 1966).

Accession to the symbolic plane in the oedipal period involves a transition from primary to "secondary identification" (Lacan, 1966). Secondary identification makes possible the formation of an "ego ideal" that is a composite of adopted and borrowed traits. After the oedipal crisis, the child is no longer bound to assume the properties of the object as a whole (primary identification) but can adopt or borrow particular traits of an other (the father). The father serves, in the oedipal period, to unite the child's "desire" with the laws of language and the norms and customs of the community to which the child belongs (Lacan, 1966). The superego is located on the plane of symbolic function. Formation of the superego stabilises the accession of the subject from the imaginary to the symbolic order (Lacan, 1966).[4] Through oedipal (secondary) identification, "the subject transcends the aggressivity that is constitutive of the primary subjective individuation" (p. 25) (on "the imaginary" plane). Failure of adequate "symbolic" mediation unleashes destructive forces on the level of the imaginary (Lacan, 1966). Narcissistic aggressiveness is a strategy used defensively when the loss of an ideal threatens the unity of the self on the symbolic plane.

The superego encapsulates the fact that "persons remain influenced in their behavior and self-esteem not only by what they consider correct themselves but also by the consideration of what others may think" (Fenichel, 1946, p. 107). As a result of identification with the third object in the oedipal period, self and other become, to some extent, interchangeable notions. Relationships formed with others later in life are often formed between the self-identified-with-another and a derivative of the primary love object. Fenichel (1946) saw that object relationships are coupled with identifications that are based on an earlier identification "with the objects of the Oedipus complex" (p. 109). Many object relationships are "interwoven with identifications", especially identifications in which objects are used "as ideal models to be imitated or as bad examples to be avoided" (Fenichel, 1946, p. 87).

### 7.5.3   Symbolic relations

Lacan's (1966) "imaginary relations" can be seen as affective attunements or dyadic communications. Attunements or communications can be libidinal (referring to the induction, giving, and receipt of care) or aggressive in nature. Imaginary relations taking place in the context of psychoanalytic therapy are often dominated by competition and rivalry (Fink, 1997). The analyst's countertransference reactions to the analysand are situated on the plane of the imaginary. The analyst, when acting out in accordance with his countertransference, and the analysand are caught up in a game of comparing themselves to one another, in mutual attempts to establish who is dominant and who is submissive (power struggles) (Fink, 1997). "Symbolic relations" are one's relations to social norms and the law, as laid down by one's parents and, later in life, by teachers and increasingly abstract representations of the paternal other (one's religion, one's country). One adopts these norms and laws with respect to social ideals (ideal objects) designated by one's parents and teachers. Symbolic relations are dominated by concerns with ideals, authority figures, and personal achievement (Lacan, 1966; reviewed in Fink, 1997).

On plane of "the symbolic", one's self is identified with an ideal object (the Freudian ego ideal); and it is on this plane that one seeks to attain a particular goal, usually in form of a situation or relationship conducive to affectionate (libidinal) interactions. On the symbolic plane (i.e., along the symbolic dimension or axis), the self (the speaking subject who says "I") establishes or maintains a relationship with a derivative of the primary love object (the "symbolic other", in Lacan's terms).

---

[4]At the same time, anxiety is transformed into guilt, whereby guilt is not only a form of anxiety but also a defence against anxiety.

The father is an object of the mother's desire that lies beyond the child-mother axis. Through triangulation in the oedipal period, the child becomes able to constitute himself as the object of the mother's desire. Positions (stances) we adopt *vis-à-vis* the "symbolic other" are defined by social norms and "the law"; we desire (along the symbolic axis) in accordance with the law (Lacan, 1966). "Imaginary relations" are subordinated to symbolic relations. The relationship between ego ideal (or self) and the "symbolic other" provides a context within which affectionate interactions with the derivative of the primary love object can take place (i.e., can be repeated in accordance with early childhood experiences), interactions that in themselves unfold along Lacan's imaginary dimension or axis.

### 7.6  Imaginary relationships

One of the mother's functions is to fail and disillusion the infant. Frustration of the infant's somatic needs due to the mother's temporary absence is an essential condition for the development of internal object relationships, but also represents a spur for the development of thought and reality testing. At times of hunger and frustration of his somatic needs, the infant learns to cope with the absence of the mother by "thinking" of her and activating an internal representation (O'Shaughnessy, 1964). In the absence of the mother, infants can hold on to a internal representation of their mother and anticipate the mother's return. As infants form an internal object relation by introjecting a representation of their mother, they become able to tolerate frustration. They can reevoke the internal object in order to comfort themselves at times of distress and sooth themselves in the object's absence (Balint, 1952). For this process to succeed, the mother has to be "good-enough", not ideal.

Bion (1962) argued that the development of thought reflects the infant's growing realisation that the external world is different from his wishes, consistent with Freud's reality principle. The ability to think helps the infant to "bridge the gulf of frustration between the moment when a want is felt and the moment when action appropriate to satisfying the want culminates in its satisfaction". Thoughts "diminish the sense of frustration intrinsic to appreciation of the gap between wish and fulfilment" (Bion, 1962). Thus, the ability to tolerate frustration is linked to the ability to think; thoughts modify frustration and enable delayed gratification. If the capacity to tolerate frustration is inadequate, the infant's preference is to project frustration rather than to modify it. Incapacity to tolerate frustration leads to "hypertrophic development of the apparatus of projective identification". Instead of a thought, frustration produces a "bad object, indistinguishable from a thing-in-itself, fit only for evacuation" (Bion, 1962). The absence of the gratifying object can be tolerated by projection of hostile and persecutory qualities into the object and by launching destructive attacks against it. Bion (1962) suggested that if the capacity to tolerate frustration is low, but not too low, then the infant may develop omnipotence as a mechanism of tolerating frustration. In his phantasy, the omnipotent infant is self-sufficient and independent; the infant feels he does not need the object.

### 7.6.1  Talking to oneself

Initially, the infant depends on the mother's physical presence for security. The development of a stable inner representation of the mother allows the infant to tolerate the mother's absence for periods of time. Having internalised the mother, the child is able to invoke a stable inner vision of her in her absence. As the child increasingly relies on language to engage the mother, he becomes able to engage the mother in inner conversations ("inner dialogue") when she is absent. Inner dialogue not only holds the mother in place and keeps her engaged, it also attracts, in imagination, her benevolent interest and approval. As the child's interpersonal world expands, "inner dialogues extend beyond the mother to include conversations with a whole host of others" (Cashdan, 1988, p. 45). Conversations with "invisible friends" or "talking to oneself" are outer manifestations of this "inner world dialogue"—manifestations that are "frowned upon" in social situations and that are, over time, increasingly suppressed ("driven inward"). The inner presences of childhood are transformed, according to Cashdan (1988), into a sense of self, so that, instead of talking to imaginary objects, children start talking to their selves (to themselves). As life goes on, more and more interpersonal relationships are internalised and, thus, accrued into a sense of self. The self, therefore, "is a complex configuration of multiple object relations which make up people's inner sense of who they are" (p. 47). Relationships that people establish with one another "are instrumental in maintaining a viable sense of self" (p. 55). People's notions of self-esteem, self-worth, and self-regard "describe how they feel about who they are and how they relate to others" (Cashdan, 1988, p. 47).

> When a person says, "I don't like myself", he may not realize it, but he is indicating that there are figures in his inner world who put him down and actively disparage him.
>
> In the last analysis the self is the linguistic derivative of internalized relationships that have their beginnings in childhood. (Cashdan, 1988, p. 48)

### 7.6.2   Anticipation of approval

Kernberg (1982) suggested that interpersonal relationships are enacted in accordance with internal templates of "self-other experiences". These interactional templates, along with the ways in which we perceive others in interpersonal situations, have been ascribed by Kernberg to "bipolar intrapsychic representations", which consist of an image of the self, an image of the other, and an affective colouring. "Bipolar intrapsychic representations" form the foundations of personality and are the "building blocks of the mind". Bipolar intrapsychic representations are synthesised into an integrated

sense of self, whereby the self, as the total sum of self images contained in bipolar intrapsychic representations, remains intimately connected with the total sum of object representations (reviewed in Cashdan, 1988). The self, based on bipolar representations of interpersonal relationships, becomes a security device for the child (Cashdan, 1988), much as interpersonal relationships themselves are concerned with the attainment of security. Relationships in the here-and-now are established and maintained through direct or indirect care- or approval-seeking behaviour—behaviour that is evolutionarily related to the seeking of proximity to the mother (attachment behaviour). Imagery of the self and conversations with inner presences (simulated or imaginary objects) may fulfil a function that is related to the anticipation of parental approval and care, or the anticipation of disapproval and the withholding of care. When an action is contemplated by the self or "I", the action (or its outcome) is "subjected to an imaginary audience" (Cashdan, 1988, p. 50). The self may function as a security device insofar as self-imagery, effectively being an imagery of a relationship with an audience, provides access to substitute approval. Internal generation of substitute approval (which is developmentally related to imagery of the absent mother) has taken on functions of major importance in the organisation of voluntary, "self"-directed, or goal-directed behaviour.

### 7.6.3   Splitting of the ego

Fairbairn (1952) argued that "the internalization of objects is the direct expression of libidinal needs of an object-seeking ego in the face of the vicissitudes of its early object-relationships" (p. 160). The child internalises his "bad objects" because "he seeks to control them" and "because he *needs* them" (p. 67). Bad objects are internalised because they are "desired as well as felt to be bad" (p. 111). "Badness" of objects, according to Fairbairn (1952), "consists precisely in the fact that it combines allurement with frustration" (p. 111). In particular, if the libidinal drive (need for affection) is frustrated, the infant seeks to coerce (control) the unsatisfying object (the bad object) by means of internalisation. It is *not* the satisfying (good) object that the infant seeks to coerce. According to the bad object's simultaneously alluring and frustrating qualities, the internalised bad object is split into two objects: the needed or "exciting object" and the frustrating or "rejecting object". Fairbairn (1952) contended that *exciting* and *frustrating* elements that have been split off an essentially *ambivalent* object are repressed, that is, excluded from consciousness. Parts of the ego "cathecting" the "exciting object" and the "rejecting object" are repressed, too, namely by the "central ego". These repressed parts of the ego are called the "libidinal ego" and "internal saboteur", whereby the "libidinal ego" is paired with the libidinally "exciting object", and the "internal saboteur" is paired with the "rejecting object". Fairbairn (1952) pointed out that each of the three egos ("central ego", "libidinal ego", and "internal saboteur") "naturally lends itself to being paired off with a special object" (p. 102), assuming that the central ego retains a relationship with the remainder of the bad object (the essentially ambivalent object). As already stated, "libidinal ego" and "internal saboteur" are both repressed. Fairbairn (1952) argued that "the dynamic of repression is aggression" (p. 108). The "libidinal ego" and the "internal saboteur" are both rejected or *attacked* by the "central ego". The splitting of the ego, that is, "the severance of the subsidiary egos from the central ego", observed in the schizoid position, "is due to the operation of a certain volume of aggression which remains at the disposal of the central ego" (Fairbairn, 1952, p. 108).

Relationships with objects that have been internalised "give rise to relationships between the various parts into which the original ego becomes split" (Fairbairn, 1952, p. 160). Relationships with internal objects are regulated by "defensive techniques".[5] There are "risks involved in the expression of libidinal and aggressive affect

---

[5]Defensive techniques for regulating relationships with internal objects are established during the transition from "infantile dependence" to "adult dependence" (Fairbairn, 1952).

towards his mother as a rejecting object" (p. 114). In order to "circumvent the dangers of expressing both libidinal and aggressive affect towards his object", the infant uses aggression to subdue his libidinal need. The suppression of libidinal need by means of aggression "resolves itself into an attack by the internal saboteur upon the libidinal ego" (Fairbairn, 1952, p. 115). Anxiety arises whenever the attack by the "internal saboteur" upon the "libidinal ego" fails to subdue libidinal need sufficiently. Moreover, attachment of the "libidinal ego" to the "exciting object" (libidinal object) "comes to absorb a considerable volume of libido" (p. 116). Fairbairn (1952) proposed that "the attack delivered by the internal saboteur is only secondarily directed against the libidinal ego and is primarily directed against the libidinal object which alternates with this ego" (p. 103).

## Dreams and fantasies

Situations depicted in dreams or waking fantasies are dramatisations of "situations existing in inner reality", whereby figures appearing in dreams or waking fantasies "represent either parts of the 'ego' or internalized objects" (Fairbairn, 1952, p. 99). In conformity with the schizoid position, the dreamer's ego "is split into three separate egos—a central ego and two other subsidiary egos" (p. 101). One of the subsidiary egos (the "attacked ego") "is the object of aggression on the part of the other" (the "attacking ego") (p. 101). The central ego corresponds to the observing "I" of the dream; the "attacking ego" ("persecutory ego") is the "internal saboteur"; and the "attacked ego" is the "libidinal ego". The "internal saboteur" partly corresponds to Freud's superego. The "aggressive attitude adopted by the internal saboteur towards the libidinal ego" corresponds, in Freudian terms, to "the attitude of the superego towards id impulses" (p. 116). The aggressive attitude adopted by the internal saboteur towards the "exciting object" corresponds to Freud's observation "that the self-reproaches of the melancholic are ultimately reproaches directed against the loved object" (Fairbairn, 1952, p. 116).

## Superego

The superego is essentially a good object to the ego (Fairbairn, 1952). The superego "must be regarded as essentially an internalised object, with which the ego has a relationship" (p. 61). This is a relationship based on identification—an "identification of the ego with the super-ego" (p. 61). The existence of the superego "provides evidence that a schizoid position has been established" (Fairbairn, 1952, p. 9). The nucleus of the internal *ambivalent object*, "which remains cathected by the central ego after the repression of the exciting and rejecting objects", is "the nucleus round which the super-ego is eventually built up" (p. 136). Fairbairn (1952) thought that "beneath the level at which the central ego finds itself confronted with the super-ego as an internal object of moral significance lies a level at which parts of the ego find themselves confronted with internal objects which are, not simply devoid of moral significance, but unconditionally bad from the libidinal standpoint of the central ego" (p. 93).

### 7.7   Role relationships and transference

Motivational underpinnings of interpersonal interaction and communication are unconscious. Consciously experienced language and behaviour are mere vehicles for unconscious communications between interacting persons. Partners in a relationship unconsciously assign roles to each other and induce each other to respond in certain ways (Sandler & Sandler, 1978). Moreover, interpersonal behaviour is constrained by, and appropriate to, the social situation and its emotional interpretation. Affective responses employed in the course of interpersonal interactions have autonomic, behavioural, *communicative*, and *cognitive* components (Kernberg, 1992). The *communicative* function of affects refers to the ability of affective displays to *induce* a situationally appropriate emotional (affective) response in the other person. Affects may have evolved, at first, to allow communication of the infant's needs to the social environment, especially to

the mother (reviewed in Kernberg, 1992). This conjecture about the evolutionary origin of affects partly elucidates the nature of interpersonal communication and the function of transference relationships. With regard to the *cognitive* component of affective responses, this component "always reflects the relationship between a self representation and an object representation" (Kernberg, 1996, p. 127). In the context of aggressive or sexual affect, for instance, the subject experiences "an image or representation of the self relating to an image or representation of another person" (Kernberg, 1992, p. 7). Behaviourally, the subject projects his self representation or object representation onto a significant other person, such as a therapist, "while enacting the reciprocal object or self representation" (Kernberg, 1996, p. 127). Thus, affect states, that is, their cognitive components, are translated into object relationships that can be analysed in terms of transference of early object relationships (Kernberg, 1996).

> The affects we observe in the psychoanalytic situation not only always have cognitive content but—and that is, I think, a crucial finding—always have an object relations aspect as well; that is, they express a relation between an aspect of the patient's self and an aspect of one or another of his object representations. Furthermore, affect in the psychoanalytic situation either reflects or complements a reactivated internal object relation. In the transference, an affect state recapitulates the patient's significant past object relation. Indeed, all actualizations of an object relation in the transference contain a certain affect state as well. (Kernberg, 1992, p. 11)

Early object relations provide the unconscious matrix for all object relationships in later life. Freud described this as the revival of the past in the present. All object relations from childhood on represent attempts at repeating an early object relation; and object relations in adulthood may be formed precisely for this reason: to seek the security experienced in an object relation in early childhood. In early life, "role relationships" develop as a vehicle to gratify instinctual needs and wishes; thus, even the simplest instinctual wish becomes a wish to impose and experience a particular role relationship (Sandler, 1976). In other words, role relationships develop as contexts within which needs can be satisfied (Figure 7-1). In role relationships established later in life, the other person is manipulated into behaving in a particular way that is determined by the early object relation. If the manipulation is successful, the other person takes on a "transference role" and acts accordingly (Sandler, 1976). Transference manipulations or provocations may be accepted by the other person if he or she is disposed in that direction ("role responsiveness"). Sandler (1976) argued that such manipulations are an important part of object relationships. Imposition of a role relationship is assisted by concealed aggression and threats; however, the motivational force behind the reenactment of early object relations in later life may be related to anxiety and its avoidance. What is enacted in object relations, from childhood on, are not only infantile role relationships but also the "defensive role relationships" constructed onto them after infancy (Sandler, 1976).

### 7.7.1  Projective identification

The notion of "projective identification" illustrates an important principle: we interact with significant others in order to induce in them certain responses or attitudes directed towards us. Normal variations of projective identification are used by us to ensure that significant figures in our life remain bound to us (Cashdan, 1988). Projective identification "involves the behavioral and emotional manipulation of others" (p. 56). The recipient is forced to respond to the individual's "projective fantasies", being pressured to think, feel, and act in a way that conforms with "ejected feelings". "Projective fantasy" refers to attempts to place a part of oneself in another human being. The person engaging in projective identification aims "to get the recipient to actually experience the feelings associated with the fantasy—to become submissive, dominant, sexually aroused or whatever—and behave accordingly" (Cashdan, 1988, p. 57). The behaviour induced in the recipient serves to enhance the projector's sense of self. The projector, too, allows himself to be "used" in turn. The term "projective identification" is often reserved for pathological forms of manipulative interaction, in which "there is usually only one person who reaps the benefits so that ultimately the other party feels used" (p. 58). The recipient may resist the induction and respond with anger or withdrawal, which would

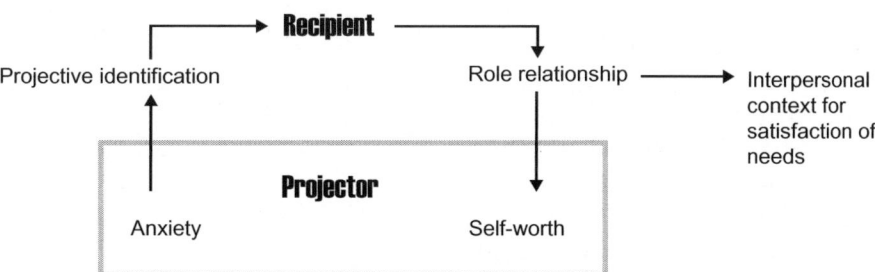

Figure 7-1.  The subject (projector) imposes a role relationship on his interaction with another person (replicating a pattern of interaction established in early childhood) and, thereby, (i) creates a context conducive to the satisfaction of needs (including needs for praise and affection) and (ii) enhances his self-esteem.

reinforce beliefs in the projector that he is bad or undesirable. The projector, in turn, may, and in pathological instances generally does, employ hidden or covert threats designed to keep the recipient in the relationship (Cashdan, 1988).

> A key dynamic in projective identification is the *induction* that underlies it. Individuals who rely on projective identification engage in subtle but nonetheless powerful manipulations to induce those about them to behave in prescribed ways. It is as if one individual forces another to play a role in the enactment of that person's internal drama—one involving early object relationships. The target of the manipulation is induced to engage in an *identification* with a disowned aspect of the person doing the *projection*—hence the term "projective identification". (Cashdan, 1988, p. 56)

Different forms of projective identification are associated with different patterns of communication and metacommunication. First, in the "projective identification of dependency", the projector, signalling helplessness, displays help-seeking or submissive behaviours. "Projective identification of dependency" induces care-taking behaviour in the recipient of the projection (investing the target of the projection with care-taking powers) and, if successful, recreates a caretaker-child relationship. Statements of suicidal intent may be used as threats that coerce the recipient of the projective identification into the adoption of care-taking and helping behaviours. If the recipient does not respond in the prescribed way, the projector may become despondent or depressed or resort to temper tantrums or hysterical crying fits (Cashdan, 1988). Second, in the "projective identification of power", the recipient is forced to take a subservient role. The projector makes efforts "to convince the target that he or she needs to be cared for and looked after" (p. 66). Projective identification of power is, therefore, the inverse of projective identification of dependency. A person prone to using projective identification of power may have learned in childhood that "feelings of competence and self-worth can be achieved only if he controls what takes place about him" (p. 68). Inducing others to feel incompetent or inadequate ensures that the person will not be abandoned by them. Third, in the "projective identification of ingratiation", the projector makes sacrifices, thereby provoking others to be grateful or appreciative. The projector makes self-sacrifices but expects something from the target of the projection in return. The target of the projection finds himself or herself in a situation in which he or she is forced to be thankful or appreciative and made to feel that he or she owes something to the projector. A person prone to using projective identification of ingratiation may have learned in childhood that his intrinsic worth lies in his ability to be useful to his caretakers; he may have learned that he needs to do things for those who care for him in order to be loved and *appreciated*. Whether projective identification of dependency, projective identification of power, or projective identification of ingratiation is used, the projector induces others into behaving in ways that ultimately enhance his *sense of self* and reduce *anxiety* (Cashdan, 1988) (Figure 7-1).

> We all want to believe that we are worthwhile human beings and to know that those closest to us feel we are worth being with. Persons who relate through projective identification of ingratiation have little faith that this is the way the world works. They do not really believe that other human beings, even their own family members, really love them for what they are. They are convinced that they need to ingratiate themselves to ensure that they will be wanted. And to make sure this happens, they establish relationships in such a way that others feel indebted to them. (Cashdan, 1988, p. 76)

### 7.7.2   Countertransference in the analytic process

The fundamental derivation of interpersonal relationships from primary object relations is illustrated by transference and countertransference phenomena arising in the process of psychoanalytic therapy. Sandler (1976) saw transference in the analytic process as an interactional phenomenon. What is being transferred in therapy from the patient onto the analyst is the "role relationship" of early object relations, that is, aspects of the patient's relationship towards his primary caregiver. The transferred role relationship consists of a role in which the patient casts himself and a complimentary role for the therapist (Sandler, 1976). Interaction between patient and therapist is not only determined by the internal role relationship that the patient seeks to impose on their relationship (i.e., transference), but also the therapist's response to this imposition (i.e., countertransference) and, to some extent, the therapist's unconscious attempts to impose his own role relationship on the interaction. The therapist's actions and responses to the patient are a compromise between his own behavioural tendencies and his acceptance of the role into which he has been manoeuvred by the patient. Again, transference entails unconscious attempts to *manipulate* the other person with the aim of reenacting early object relationships (Sandler, 1976). The patient's conscious speech and behaviour is a vehicle for his unconscious attempts to impose a role on the analyst. The analyst feels unconsciously compelled to cooperate with the splitting and projection that the patient depends upon, that is, he is compelled to use, rather than analyse, the transference (Caper, 1995). The patient uses the analyst as an object into which he can project split-off uncomfortable aspects of his personality. The feelings evoked in the analyst represent the patient's unconscious material. The analyst has to recognise the patient's contribution to his emotions and behaviour in the sessions. A "mutative interpretation" derived from the analyst's understanding of his countertransference towards the patient can help the patient to see the analyst as a real external object and recognise the feelings and responses evoked in the analyst as belonging to himself (Caper, 1995). Segal (1977) stressed that countertransference is to a large part an unconscious

phenomenon; the analyst becomes aware only of its conscious derivatives. The meaning and function of the conscious manifestations of his countertransference reaction, that is, the meaning of his conscious "acting out" and feelings towards the patient, remain unconscious in the first instance but can be subjected to insight.

### 7.7.3  Projective identification in the analytic process

> If an individual who employs projective identification targets an individual whose idiosyncratic needs conform to the projective identification, no problems need necessarily arise. A person who engages in a projective identification of dependency may be fortunate enough to stumble across someone whose life desire is to take care of people. If, on the other hand, the target offers resistance, the projector may experience anxiety, depression, rage, and other "symptoms" attesting to what amounts to projective failure. These are the people who most often end up seeking help. (Cashdan, 1988, p. 77)

According to Klein's original notion of "projective identification", the subject splits off parts of his self and projects them into an object. The subject projects and expels undesirable or threatening qualities of himself into the object. The object, as a result, is seen as possessing these qualities and is, thus, transformed in the subject's mind (Feldman, 1997). In psychoanalysis, the patient is said to use "projective identification" when he induces in the analyst a state of mind that is similar to the one he, the patient, attempts to eliminate in himself (Carpy, 1989). Countertransference can be understood as arising through the patient's projective identification. Importantly, projective identification is intended to produce a reaction in the analyst, since the analyst will be *compelled* by the feelings induced in him to "act out". "Acting out" by the analyst can manifest in subtle ways such as the wording, tone, and content of interpretations given to the patient (Carpy, 1989).

Impingement on the analyst's feeling, thinking, and acting is essential to the patient's use of projective identification in the analytic situation (Feldman, 1997). The analyst is induced by the patient's unconscious verbal and nonverbal manoeuvres into playing a particular role. As Feldman (1997) put it, the analyst's behaviour and attitude induced by the patient's verbal and nonverbal communication gratifies the patient's drive to reexperience "archaic object relations". If there is no correspondence between the object's representation in fantasy and the object's actual mental state and behaviour, the patient uses projective identification to *control* the analyst. Any discrepancy between the patient's unconscious fantasy concerning his archaic object relationship and the reality of the relationship in the therapy causes distress and drives the patient to exert conscious and unconscious pressure on the analyst to try and make him enact elements of archaic object relationships (Feldman, 1997). As Feldman pointed out, the patient does not relent until he has evidence that the analyst's experience and behaviour corresponds to his fantasy.

> The disturbance in either the patient, or the analyst, arises from the discrepancy between the pre-existing phantasies that partly reassure or gratify, and those with which each is confronted in the analytical situation, which are potentially threatening. … this unwelcome discrepancy drives each to deploy either projective mechanisms or some variety of enactment in an attempt to create a greater correspondence between the pre-existing unconscious phantasies and what they experience in the analytic encounter. (Feldman, 1997)
>
> … it seems to serve a reassuring function if what is enacted in the external world corresponds in some measure with an object relationship that is unconsciously present. The alternative, when [the patient] is confronted with the discrepancy between the two, is painful and threatening. (Feldman, 1997)

Behaviour aiming to reinstate archaic object relations is appetitive and instrumental, in that it would have been rewarded or "gratified" (and, thereby, reinforced) by the "blissful security" (Riviere, 1937) afforded by the mother's presence and caring attention (or its later developmental derivatives). Sandler (1990), too, understood that the patient's attempts to actualise his unconscious fantasies serve a gratifying function. The analyst's enactment, if it is congruent with the projected fantasy, would *gratify* the patient's drive to reexperience an early object relationship. This may be a mutual process and, in their collusion, both the patient and analyst would feel safe and comfortable, impeding the progress of analytic work (Feldman, 1997). If the analyst is not receptive to, or resists, the patient's projective identification, then the patient experiences greater distress and resorts to a more *violent* use of projective identification (Feldman, 1997). Pressure exerted on the analyst may have its motivational origin in anxiety (and separation distress); but pressure also implies the use of aggression as a tool of appetitive behaviour. Not surprisingly, overt anger arises in the psychoanalytic session if the analyst cannot be manipulated in accordance with the patient's unconscious expectation.

> … the recurrent pressure on the analyst to join the patient in the partial enactment of archaic, often disturbed and disturbing object relationships is one of the most interesting and puzzling phenomena we encounter. (Feldman, 1997)

### 7.7.4   Recurrent primary identification

A person who observes another person is drawn to imitate the other's verbal and nonverbal behaviour and reexperience the other's emotional state. The observer finds himself automatically behaving and feeling like the person whom he observes. Sandler (1993) called this process "recurrent primary identification". He noted that the act of imitation is below the threshold of overt expression and not consciously experienced.

The ability to experience others' emotional states is of evolutionary importance in that it allows individuals in group-forming species to synchronise their affective behaviour. When observing the expressions and behaviour of a child in distress, for example, the mother may experience the distress herself and act accordingly (Bion, 1962). Human infants, who show evidence for imitative capacities from the first months of their life, may use imitation of their mothers' expressions as a way of acquiring information about their situation. Recurrent primary identification, as conceived by Sandler (1993), has to be distinguished from projective identification and behaviours designed to impose role relationships. When one *engages* in dyadic interaction with another person (as opposed to observing and imitating the other person), one tries to induce in the other person a particular role; and the other person thrusts a role upon oneself. Instead of observing, imitating, and empathising, one finds oneself instinctively (affectively) responding to the other person and appetitively manipulating the relationship with the other person. Engagement in interpersonal interaction automatically gravitates towards enactment of a "role relationship" (Sandler, 1976; Sandler & Sandler, 1978), that is, towards reenactment of an "archaic object relation" (Feldman, 1997), similarly to how detached observation of another individual, and primary identification with him, automatically induces subthreshold imitative behaviour in the observer.

## Self-boundary

One's self-boundary (i.e., the boundary between others and one's self) may depend on whether one is the subject of others' role-inductive behaviours. When becoming the target of other's role-inductive behaviours, one automatically erects ego defences and discerns self-evaluative references from others' behaviour. Sandler (1993) thought that recurrent primary identification is associated with the relaxation of self-boundaries. Once self-boundaries are reerected,

"disidentification" occurs. In the analytic situation, imitative mirroring of the patient's feelings may only occur when the analyst is "not on the guard" (Sandler, 1993), that is, when his defences are low and his self-boundary is relaxed. As long as the analyst can let his attention float freely and keep his self-boundaries relaxed, he can automatically duplicate what the patient expresses by verbal and nonverbal means. Sandler (1993) suggested that recurrent primary identification gives way to conflict and activation of the analyst's defences if the patient's feelings and thoughts, as experienced by the analyst, do not fit with the analyst's own unconscious wishes or expectations. Alternatively, it could be stated that the patient's expressed feelings and thoughts disturb the analyst's observational stance (and disrupt the analyst's state of primary identification) whenever they are directed at the analyst in an attempt to induce in him a role. The analyst stops to *identify* and changes his stance from an observational one to an interactional one in accordance with his countertransference reaction. While "listening" to and understanding our countertransference reaction to the patient is a useful source of information about the patient's interactional style, we should also be able to lower our defences—or regress in a controlled way as Sandler (1993) put it—in order to directly listen to the patient's unconscious communication and be "at one with the patient's unconscious".

Primary identification and projective identification can be seen as mutually exclusive processes. In contrast to recurrent primary identification, where the patient's unconscious intention is irrelevant, projective identification is an interactive process in which the analyst is pressured by unconscious verbal and nonverbal manoeuvres into playing a particular role. Instead of automatic mirroring, there is automatic responding. Nevertheless, the two processes may interact. Sandler (1993) thought that the effectiveness of projective identification depends on recurrent primary identification. The ability to induce a certain mental state in another person may depend on one' ability to accurately perceive the other's mental state in the first place (and to ascertain the other's "role responsiveness").

## 7.8  Summary

Man's interest in (attention to) his companions is attributable, in part, to their ability to act as sources of approval. Their resourcefulness in this regard is encoded in the form of internal objects. The subject's unconscious expectations concerning the approving or disapproving functions of his internal objects—expectations that were initially formed in early childhood but that continue to be modified throughout life—are projected onto, and thus perceived in, persons occupying the subject's present social space (which may be a virtual or fantasised one). External objects (persons who we observe or with whom we interact) are but *instances* or embodiments of internal objects; other persons do not exist independently of the subject's experience, much as the spatially and temporally extending phenomenal world, as a whole, is a fundamentally subjective (private) creation and does not exist independently of the subject (Schopenhauer, 1844; reviewed in Behrendt, 2007). It is important to emphasise that internal objects are representations of the subject's *relationships* with significant others—representations that have arisen and are continually modified in the subject's history of exposure to others' approvals and disapprovals. Internal objects are not just representations of significant others; they are templates of *interpersonal* experience. Kernberg (1982) considered that interpersonal relationships are enacted in accordance with internal templates of "self-other experiences" ("bipolar intrapsychic representations")—templates that contain images of both self and object. Templates of interpersonal experience, which ontogenetically derive from, and continue to encapsulate, "archaic object relations" (Feldman, 1997), are enacted—in the form of "role relationships" (Sandler, 1976)—by exerting subtle pressures on the object (in a process called "projective identification"). In this process, a part of oneself (encoded as an internal object

or, rather, as an internal object relationship) is "projected" onto an external object, forcing the object to assume a role in accordance with the subject's past experience and unconscious expectation—a role for the object that complements the subject's need to overcome anxiety and attain security (Cashdan, 1988). The external object is then reintrojected—that is, the relevant template of interpersonal experience ("bipolar intrapsychic representations") is modified—as a function of the outcome (rewarding or punishing) of the subject's interaction with the object.

Ego and object are defined by their relationship with each other and may, as such, not be clearly distinguishable. The inextricable link between ego and internal objects may be explicable as a developmental consequence of the infant's "primary narcissism", in which ego and "ideal object" are *united* (Balint, 1952). The infant learns to tolerate the mother's absence by differentiating between himself and his mother and investing the image of the mother with libidinal and narcissistic significance ("secondary narcissism"). As the ego matures and differentiates its functions, more and more objects are cathected with narcissistic and object libido. To say, in terms of object relations theory, that libidinal aspects of objects are introjected into the ego (Kernberg, 1980) is equivalent to saying that the self is constructed from reflected *appraisals* of others (Sullivan, 1953) or that others fulfil narcissistic selfobject functions with regards to the self (Kohut, 1971).

Some of the time, man uses projective identification to transform his interactions with others into role relationships (projecting his definition on the context within which the interaction takes place (Goffman, 1959)). At other times, he identifies with others seemingly dispassionately. Identification and "recurrent primary identification" (Sandler, 1993) are processes that underlie man's interest in observing or watching those who populate his "real", fantasised, or virtual surroundings (that is, any implementation of social space). When observing a group of individuals, watching a film or a play, or when dreaming or daydreaming, the subject transiently assumes desirable qualities of an object (by unconsciously imitating the object (Sandler, 1993)) and, thereby, comes to experience the security of the object's position within the object's framework of social relatedness. The subject, in his fantasies and dreams, identifies with another person—that is, he projects aspects of his self into a fantasised replica of an internal object—so that he himself can become the object of others' approval and benevolent interest. Objects with whom the subject identifies (by whom the subject sees himself represented), and through whom he establishes fantasised relationships with derivatives of the primary object, are instantiations of the ego ideal.

The ability to identify with (and project aspects of the self into) another object may be relevant to the evolution of more complex forms of goal-directed social behaviour. If efforts to induce external objects to assume roles defined by the subject's internal object relationships are likely to be frustrated (and if, in other words, approval and benevolent interest are unlikely to be obtained from any object present in the here-and-now), then instances of secure relationships between the ego-identified-with-the-object and an object that is a derivative of the primary love object may be recalled in imagery. This may act as a simulation of an outcome of behaviour—a simulated image that incentivises appetitive behaviour. Imaginary recollection of internal objects may in itself have a reassuring or *partially* pleasurable effect (Federn, 1952) (as illustrated by the infant's conjuring up of an image of his mother at times of her absence (Balint, 1952) and, perhaps, by narcissistic ruminations of the schizoid individual (Fairbairn, 1952)), however, by offering the *prospect* of reward in the form of approval or care, imagery of internal objects may produce incentive motivational arousal and direct instrumental efforts to reach a social situation that would be *more secure* and more favourable to the actual receipt of rewarding social contact. Actualisation of the potential of others to supply approval to oneself (based on the recollection and enactment of an internal object relationship) is equivalent to realisation of one's potential to *attract* others'

approval (self-actualisation (Horney, 1950)). One's potential to attract others' approval is defined by one's admirable qualities. This is the origin of narcissistic ego feelings and feelings of self-worth. The self, especially self-esteem, encapsulates the organism's *potential*, at any one time, to derive approval from objects that populate the current "external" social environment. The self or ego may be sustained transiently, and anxiety may be alleviated, by the experience of narcissistically cathected objects (positively inclined "good" objects) in conscious fantasy, however, as Federn (1952) realised, the gratifying or *pleasurable* (rewarding) receipt of interpersonal signals of approval can not be substituted in this way.

The subject can gain *full* gratification of libidinal and narcissistic needs (needs of care giving and care receiving, respectively) in the context of a secure relationship with an object (a derivative of the primary object) (Figure 7-2). Second, the subject can gain *partial* gratification, and relieve his anxiety, by establishing a secure object relationship, that is, by establishing conditions conducive to caring and affectionate interactions and inhibitory to aggressive interactions. Third, the subject can gain partial gratification, and relieve his anxiety, by casting himself (or part of his ego) into a *fantasised* third object that has an ego-sustaining relationship with an object that is a derivative of the primary love object; but, fourth, the subject can also do so by identifying with an *external* third object (involving subtle imitation) and, through it, establishing an ego-sustaining relationship, in the external world, with a derivative of the primary object.[6] The derivative of the primary object with which the subject establishes a link via identification with a third object may be an instance of the superego. The superego is essentially an internalised object with which the subject (or ego) has a relationship (Fairbairn, 1952). Being an abstract object to the self—an object that can be approving or

---

[6] The concept of "ego-identified-with-the-object" has been used to shed light into the dynamics of melancholia and narcissism (Freud, 1917; Ogden, 2002).

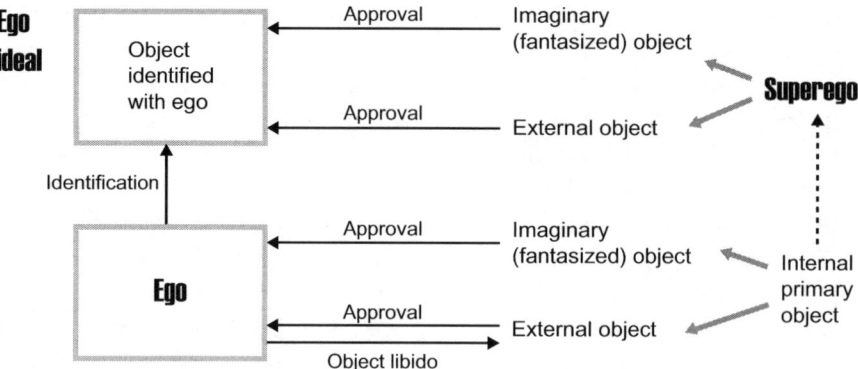

Figure 7-2.    The external object that is an instance of the superego can adopt various abstract forms, such as audiences, legal bodies, or the public at large. It was the receipt, by the primary love object (usually the mother), of attention from a third party (usually the father) in the triangular constellation of the Oedipus complex that precipitated the differentiation of ego into ego ideal.

disapproving towards the self-, the superego can be regarded as a repository of templates of interpersonal experience between the ego-identified-with-the-third-object and the primary object (hence, its origin in the oedipal period). The ego-sustaining relationship, formed in the here-and-now, between an external object with whom the subject is identified and an approving or disapproving derivative of the primary object can be more abstract, in that the derivative of the primary object can take any form of audience or social formation representing the superego. Many social behaviours are designed to enhance one's approvability and attractiveness in the eyes of others, that is, in the eyes of external objects that exert, and encapsulate, the approving and admiring functions of the superego. We, quite naturally, act in ways that ensure that others are positively (acceptingly or appreciatively) inclined towards us; and we may do so by unconsciously identifying (through our actions) with an object who is seen to possess desirable and admirable qualities. The part of the ego that employs behaviours intended to please replicas (incarnations) of internal objects—insofar as they represent aspects of the approving superego (including the subject's Gods)—is the ego ideal. Although the ego ideal is usually considered to be part of the superego, referring especially to its approving and admiring functions (Bergler, 1952), it derived from *identification* of the child with the parents (especially the same-sex parent) during the oedipal period; and it is, later in life, reenacted by the object with which the subject identifies (in a quest to reexperience approval by the opposite-sex parent and its derivatives) (Figure 7-2).

# CHAPTER EIGHT

# Social structure

Culture as it appears as a more or less complete gestalt is more than it is conscious of itself. It has to be deciphered like a neurotic symptom or like a dream. (Schilder, 1951, p. 350)

... a cultural pattern and an economic process, once created, although fundamentally related to the psychology of the participant, follow their own laws. They become in some way part of nature which can be modified by human endeavour but not in the same way as psychological processes. (Schilder, 1951, p. 264)

Aggressive impulses, which are partially inhibited and expressed indirectly in culturally ritualised ways, play a crucial role in how we relate to each other in social groups (Lorenz, 1963). In most cases, aggressive impulses that instinctively compel us to "attack" others in competition for rank and resources are intertwined with other impulses, fear impulses in particular. Thus, in the sociocultural context, ubiquitous aggression assumes a complex spectrum of manifestations that are socially adaptive and culturally conditioned. The effect of intraspecific aggression is to dynamically maintain our social status and position (Lorenz, 1963). Developmentally, competitive aggression that underlies group dynamics is related to the Oedipus complex; and its product, social rank or position, may be related to our ability to monopolise the primary object's (the mother's) attention and devotion in competition with the father. Avoidance and fear impulses that curtail intraspecific aggression exerted in competition for attention or devotion from a replica of the primary object (for instance, the group leader) may thus be related to the potential of others' aggressive retaliation (or retaliation by the group as a whole) to remove us from the abstract primary object on which we depend and, thereby, to reawaken our basic anxiety. By dynamically maintaining our rank or position in social networks, we may control both: (i) access, on an abstract level, to maternal resources that satisfy our needs and (ii) basic anxiety, which expresses itself in feelings of insecurity or inferiority or low self-esteem. Anticipation of aggression by others or the group, as a whole, keeps interpersonal behaviour on a habitual trajectory aimed at appeasement and conformity. It is an awareness of others' aggressive potentials that continually shapes interpersonal behaviour and contributes to a fluctuating sense of self—partly an apprehensive sense of potentially being a target of aggression. The self becomes a vehicle through which we control others' aggressive impulses towards us. Whatever we do or do not do in a social situation, we cannot but actively control self-referential patterns predictive of others' aggressive, but also libidinal, impulses towards us; and it is these self-referential patterns of social information obtained from the environment that constitute our sense of self.

Smith (1813) spoke of our "endeavouring to view [ourselves] with the eyes of other people". In the company of others, an individual is immediately provided with a "mirror" "placed in the countenance and behaviour of those he lives with"—a mirror that always registers "when they disapprove of his sentiments" (Smith, 1813). We observe others, and appraise the social situation of which they form a part, with a variable degree of self-reference. The degree of self-reference varies between the extremes of derealisation (others appearing wooden, life-, and meaningless) and delusions of reference. Participation in ranking order presupposes that we are able to differentiate between individual members of the group and, more specifically, that we are able to recognise each individual's potential for aggression or willingness to submission towards ourselves. Our sense of self may, in part, derive from a sense of the probability, specific to each social situation, of becoming the target of others' aggression, together with a situationally specific awareness of when to inhibit and how to channel our own aggressive impulses. In addition, or alternatively, the sense of self is dynamically assembled from cues relating to the situationally specific likelihood of receiving approval and appreciation from others. The self would be a means for controlling the receipt of others' positive attention and a measure of our positive relatedness to the social environment. Functioning as a protective shield, the self would indirectly represent the degree of protection against hostile impulses emanating from the social environment. Self-esteem may be a measure of both, our

relatedness to the social environment and our protection against conspecific attack, while low self-esteem (and self-consciousness), much like anxiety, would be a measure of our vulnerability to attack.

## 8.1   Cohesion

Eibl-Eibesfeldt (1970) discerned two principle roots of sociability in vertebrates: flight motivation and parental care. First, contact seeking is motivated by anxiety or flight motivation. Insofar as the proximity of conspecifics has been associated, in the course of evolution, with security, conspecifics act as a "goal-in-flight"—a goal that is sought and approached at times of anxiety. Given that this motivational process also underpins the seeking of shelter and the retreat to places of high familiarity and predictability, conspecifics and their congregations can be said to have "home valency" (Eibl-Eibesfeldt, 1970). Second, group cohesion is maintained, in part, by behaviour patterns derived from the realm of parental care interactions. Parental care-giving (cherishing) behaviours and infantile care-soliciting signals, which activate parental care-giving behaviours, unite parents with their offspring and are "excellently suited to reinforcing the bond between adults", too (p. 124). Owing to their aggression-inhibiting effects, care-giving and care-soliciting signals are innately understood as friendly (Eibl-Eibesfeldt, 1970). Appeasement gestures, partly derived from care-soliciting signals, play an equally important role in group cohesion. In humans, smiling plays an important role in overcoming barriers of aversion and "bringing us aggressive creatures closer together" (Hass, 1968, p. 131). By smiling, "we ingratiate ourselves with other people and bind them to us" (p. 131). Civilisation, according to Hass (1968), "can be said to owe its cohesion to a myriad-and-one such smiles" (p. 131).

In our primitive forebears' communities it must have been extremely important to a child to know when it was permissible or inadvisable to approach an adult. The same applied equally to adults encountering strangers. The angry, ill-tempered, sick individual could be dangerous if approached too closely by those who encroached on his private territory. In this context, it was extremely important for man to develop an innate recognition mechanism which would give him suitable warning on sighting such a face. It was just as important for man to develop an appropriate signal for the contrary mood—a sign of approachability. And this, as we have seen, became further strengthened into a means of inhibiting aggression and actively enlisting fellow feeling. (Hass, 1968, pp. 130–131)

### 8.1.1   Gregariousness

In many species of mammals and birds, animals readily approach, join, and follow their conspecifics (Moynihan, 1998). These movements are called friendly, gregarious, affiliative, or "distance-decreasing". Joining and following patterns in gregarious mammals and birds are evolutionary extensions of familial reactions between parents and offspring. In mammals and birds (but not "in the gregarious cephalopods and some fishes"), friendly or gregarious patterns of behaviour are derived from patterns preexisting within the behavioural repertoire of the species—"patterns that were originally evolved to regulate and encourage family (possibly including sexual) relations" (Moynihan, 1998, p. 89). Gregariousness modifies the expression of hostility. Crowding can lead to intensification of intraspecific aggression; it, therefore, requires "hypertrophy" of the controls of aggression (p. 84). Gregarious behaviour patterns not only facilitate the congregation of animals but, owing to their signal function, serve to inhibit aggression of conspecifics. Gregarious patterns of behaviour, "and the derivatives thereof", when performed in potentially hostile situations, "are used for appeasement and soliciting" (p. 100).

Familiarity between individuals (based upon individual recognition) is another mechanism of control that establishes "relatively peaceful social bonds" among members of a group (Moynihan, 1998, p. 85).

> In species with parental care, birds and mammals, all or most of the numerous friendly and gregarious patterns, so often used to control or canalize aggression, seem to be derived from familial reactions. They include joining, following, and helping, at the nest and elsewhere. These patterns can be shown, by extension, to all sorts of potential cooperators, competitors, rivals, opponents. The results include the formation of groups of different sizes ... of different levels of structural complexity ... (Moynihan, 1998, p. 100)

### Cooperation and competition

Gregariousness increases protection from predators (for instance, by making detection of predators easier) and facilitates cooperation between individuals in processes that exploit resources (Moynihan, 1998). Gregariousness is advantageous in species that have no need to set up feeding territories and no difficulty to find nesting sites. Groups or colonies may be established because resources occur in patches. However, access to these resources often has to be regulated within groups or colonies. The exchange of specialised signals, both gregarious and hostile, between individuals organises social groups and, thereby, regulates the utilisation of limited resources. Competition for resources involves the discouragement and aggressive control of competitors. In monkeys (and humans), another method of coordinating social groups can be observed: individuals monitor each other's movements and overt expressions of attention (Moynihan, 1998). Competition for access to resources is regulated "by facilitating, even ensuring, that associates can monitor one another's activities", so that no individual "is likely to get much of a head start in exploiting a resource when and if its companions are watching with interest at the time" (Moynihan, 1998, p. 100).

### 8.1.2    Communal defence

Individualised bonds, including individualised bonds that contribute to group cohesion, serve the purpose of protecting the young, however individual bonds and group cohesion could not have evolved from protection of the young alone (Eibl-Eibesfeldt, 1970). Protection and defence of the young evolved before "true parental care"; in those fishes and reptiles that look after their young, care for the young is limited to the defence against predators. True parental care behaviour also includes feeding and cleaning of the young. Eibl-Eibesfeldt (1970) suggested that the partner bond "has arisen with the evolution of parental care" (p. 123). Group-uniting mechanisms, too, have evolved alongside the development of care for the young. Cohesive defence communities are only formed in species in which animals provide true parental care to their young. Only animals that truly care for their young "have succeeded in forming a bond in spite of the 'aggression barrier'" (Eibl-Eibesfeldt, 1970, p. 124).

> Joint brood defence or group defence is a force for cohesion. Amongst the animals that do not look after their young, such as reptiles or amphibians, we know of no group defence and no fighting partnerships. (p. 123)
>
> Brood care, on the other hand, calls very early on for individual partnerships and individualized cherishing of the young and thereby offers the necessary basis for a differentiated social life. (Eibl-Eibesfeldt, 1970, pp. 123–124)

Via the defence of the young, aggression became a force for group cohesion in species with true parental care. Aggression aimed at protecting the young has to be inhibited within the group. The cry of fear emitted by a young primate is a signal that unconditionally releases innate attack and threatening behaviour in members of a group (Eibl-Eibesfeldt, 1970). When the group's aggressive potential is mobilised, which would have originally been limited to situations representing a threat to the young, aggression has to be inhibited effectively *within* the group. Familiarity between group members, underpinning individualised relationships, is an effective mechanism for inhibiting aggression. Eibl-Eibesfeldt (1970) pointed out that groups are strengthened by fear of a common enemy. This effect is mediated in two ways. On the one hand, fear unites the group by activating flight behaviour towards one another (conspecifics acting as goals-in-flight). On the other hand, it is the release of collective aggression toward a common enemy that unites the group. Scapegoats, towards which members of a group jointly discharge their aggression, serve to increase cohesion of the group (Eibl-Eibesfeldt, 1970).

> As primates living in closed groups we are disposed to close our ranks in danger. Common defence or common aggression establish an exceptionally strong bond. This is true of primitive peoples and there is no question but that we follow the same pattern. Groups are even united by ritualized mock battles (football etc.). (p. 161)
>
> We often defend our ideals with a commitment that is similar to that with which we defend our children and in a certain sense our ideals *are* our spiritual children. (Eibl-Eibesfeldt, 1970, p. 162)

A common threat "welds gregarious creatures into a fighting unit" (the "social defensive reaction"), "a phenomenon exhaustively studies in rhesus monkeys, baboons, and howling monkeys" (Hass, 1968, p. 197). The welding together into a fighting unit is illustrated by the phenomenon of laughter. With regard to its evolutionary origin, laughter is an innate ritualised threat behaviour that has a cohesive effect. It evolved from mobbing behaviour—the rhythmic emission of threat sounds by groups of apes or monkeys (Eibl-Eibesfeldt, 1970).

> The person who is laughed at experiences the laughter as aggressive. But the people laughing together feel themselves to be bound together via this ritualized "mobbing". (Eibl-Eibesfeldt, 1970, p. 162)

### 8.1.3 Libidinal ties

> What appears ... in society in the shape of *Gemeingeist*, *esprit de corps*, "group sprit", etc., does not belie its derivation from what was originally envy. ... Thus social feeling is based upon the reversal of what was first a hostile feeling into a positively-toned tie of the nature of an identification. (Freud, 1921, pp. 87–88)

Intraspecific aggression, in the form of envy, rivalry, or assertiveness, is an essential factor in the process of group formation. Intraspecific aggression is responsible for the dynamic structure of a group or society but does not, in itself, explain social cohesion. The "urge to become a member of a group" has likely been "programmed in the pre-human phylogeny of man" (Lorenz, 1963, p. 256), in part by endowing mammals with a separate affiliative drive or gregarious instinct. Schilder (1951) recognised that "there is a definite purpose which binds the group together" (p. 287). In the setting of group analysis, "the connection between the leader of the group and single members of the group is particularly strong, whereas the bond between the members of the group is otherwise comparatively weak" (p. 287). The analyst, as the leader of the group, "represents father and mother", and so "the importance of family ties" becomes apparent (Schilder, 1951, p. 287). Freud (1921) considered that "a group is clearly held together by a power of some kind: and to what power could this feat be better ascribed than to Eros, who holds together everything in the world" (p. 40). Thus, the binding force in a group, the emotional

tie that holds together members of the group, is an expression of libidinal striving.

Having recognised that "libidinal ties are what characterize a group" (p. 54), Freud (1921) went on to argue that, in love relationships connecting a group, "object choice has regressed to identification" (p. 64); identification being "the earliest and original form of emotional tie" in which the ego "assumes the characteristics of the object" (p. 64). In other words, not libidinal cathexis of the leader (members considering the leader as an external libidinal object), but more primitive "introjective identification" with the leader (identification through introjection of the object) provides the group with a common tie.[1] Through identification with the leader, group members overcome their rivalries and hostile attitudes towards each other (Freud, 1921). In a regressive development, each "member of the group substitutes [the leader] for his superego" (Hartmann, 1964, p. 51), or for a part thereof. In each member of the group, "a splitting of the superego takes place, and as a member of the group the individual accepts moral standards that as a private person he would reject" (p. 51). Regressive tendencies that can be observed in members of a group "intensify the individual's readiness for cooperation" (Hartmann, 1964, p. 54).

### 8.1.4 Flight to safety

> ... panic arises either owing to an increase of the common danger or owing to the disappearance of the emotional ties which hold the group together; and the latter case is analogous to that of neurotic dread. (Freud, 1921, p. 48)
>
> Opposition to the herd is as good as separation from it, and is therefore anxiously avoided. (Freud, 1921, p. 83)

The insecurity or dangerousness of a situation an individual occupies is captured by his anxiety.

---

[1] At the same time, sharing the same "ego ideal", group members identify with each other (Freud, 1921).

In many species, anxiety is innately linked to situations of relative isolation from conspecifics. The presence of the mother or inclusion into a group, flock, herd, or shoal has a calming effect (Eibl-Eibesfeldt, 1970). Anxiety can be measured by an animal's defensive readiness. Animals, including shoaling fish, are much more inclined to take flight when alone. Primate infants take flight from unfamiliar objects when alone but watch them with interest when they are in the presence of their mother (Eibl-Eibesfeldt, 1970). Seeking protection is an old and powerful motive for association with conspecifics. Bond formation motivated by the flight drive "is very old" and derived from the tendency of the child to go to it's mother when in danger (p. 119). A primate infant looks to his mother for protection. He takes flight towards her and clings to her when frightened. Later in life, the animal seeks refuge with a high-ranking member of the group, whereby the highest ranking male is the most common "goal-in-flight" (Eibl-Eibesfeldt, 1970). Thus, the protective function of the mother is transferred onto the group as a whole and particularly its leader.

> The conspecific becomes the "goal-in-flight", its proximity means security. That is why the bond with a member of the group can be cemented by means of a fear motivation. (Eibl-Eibesfeldt, 1970, p. 118)

Eibl-Eibesfeldt (1970) spoke of "appetitive behaviour for security which is activated by flight motivation" (p. 118). In the case of gregarious animals, "the conspecific becomes what the mousehole is to the mouse or the hiding place in the reef is to the coral fish" (p. 118). The conspecific adopts "home valency", inasmuch as this can be said about hiding places (Eibl-Eibesfeldt, 1970). Animals orientate themselves to their surroundings and learn escape routes to a burrow, nest, or other place of safety. When an animal feels insecure, it retraces, guided by familiar landmarks, along a previously learned route to a safe place. Once the animal feels safe again, it can embark on other activities (Eibl-Eibesfeldt, 1970). This may point

to a link between spatial orienting, navigation, map learning, anxiety, and the hippocampus.

By analogy, "social orientation" and a sequence of actions complying with social norms and expectations (active avoidance behaviour) guide us from a situation of social anxiety to a situation of security. Every person has "the need, motivated by fear, to know where one stands" within the social environment (Eibl-Eibesfeldt, 1970, p. 164). Moreover, we have an innate disposition to obedience. A subordinate position in a dominance hierarchy guards against anxiety, and, for this reason, "human beings submit to the cruel ruler and give him their allegiance" (p. 164). When the overriding need is for security, adoption of a subordinate position and acceptance of others' dominance is preferable to a potentially higher but uncertain social position. A subordinate position guards against anxiety because it allows the person occupying this position to reenact a parent-child relationship: "the dominant individual acts in a fatherly manner and the subordinate in a childishly dependent manner" (Eibl-Eibesfeldt, 1970, p. 164).

> Our own desire for order has its roots in flight motivation. Order means orientation in time and space and indeed not only in relation to events outside our species. It also gives us a sense of security if we can tell in advance what other people will do, and if we know what we should do. Even a small child will ask firmly what it should and should not do: in this way it acquires social orientation and with this a sense of security. (Eibl-Eibesfeldt, 1970, p. 164)

### 8.1.5   Intrapsychic defence

Individual mechanisms of defence pool in social processes. Pooled defence systems in organisations develop as a result of interaction between members. Common defence systems, such as the culture or structure of a social organisation, are used by individuals to reinforce their own defences against persecutory anxieties. Jaques (1955) thought that the defence against persecutory anxiety is one of the primary mechanisms that binds people together in an organisation. The cohesion of individuals stems from the pooling, within a social organisation, of their defence mechanisms against their persecutory anxieties (reviewed in De Board, 1978).

## 8.2    Competition and norms

Intraspecific aggression fulfils three functions: the balanced distribution of animals of the same species over the available environment, selection of the strongest in a group by rival fight, and protection of the young (Lorenz, 1963). Mutual repulsion of individuals of the same species prevents overcrowding and exhaustion of nutritional resources and, thus, fulfils an important survival function for the species. While territorial animals use intraspecific aggression to prevent others from exploiting the resources of their territory, gregarious animals—whose survival depends more on membership of a group or herd—may have come to use aggression for the defence of their position in the group—a position which, like a territory, would determine the individual's access to resources for the satisfaction of needs. Ranking order is an important principle of organisation of social life in higher vertebrates (Lorenz, 1963). The "state of tension arising inside the community from the aggression drive and its result, ranking order" bestows on society a "beneficial firmness of structure" (p. 41). Ranking order implies that "every individual in the society knows which one is stronger and which weaker than itself, so that everyone can retreat from the stronger and expect submission from the weaker" (Lorenz, 1963, p. 40). Ranking order limits fighting between members of the society, although it also has the consequence that "there is always particularly high tension between individuals who hold immediately adjoining positions in the ranking order" (Lorenz, 1963, p. 41).

Rado (1956) understood that "competition is adaptive only to the extent to which it *improves cooperation*; ruthless competition tends to destroy the group" (p. 342). Importantly, dominant status in primate societies is not determined by aggressiveness alone (Eibl-Eibesfeldt, 1970). In fact, status will be withheld from a purely aggressive animal. In various species of monkeys, "the ability of a male to make friendships with others is a prerequisite for a high ranking status" (p. 83). It is often the especially friendly male "that knows how to win the sympathies of the others" (p. 83). A positive correlation between aggressiveness and status is, however, seen in monkeys living in "cramped conditions of zoo life" (p. 84). Another factor determining the attainment of status in groups of apes and some monkeys is the individual's age and experience (Eibl-Eibesfeldt, 1970). Ranking order tends to ensure that older, more experienced animals remain in charge of the group and provide the templates for imitative learning by younger, less experienced members of the group. Ranking order, established partly through aggression, thus allows individual experience and learning to play an increasing role in the evolution of higher vertebrates (Lorenz, 1963, p. 42).

### 8.2.1    Disguised aggression

Freud came to recognise the role of aggression as a separate instinct relatively late in his life, having previously adhered to the notion that aggression is not an elementary force but secondary to narcissism (Freud, 1921). Self-assertion, commonly displayed in social situations, is not only a derivative of intraspecific aggression; it also serves to regulate self-esteem and self-love (by increasing the receipt of selfobject experiences). Intraspecific aggression is suppressed in the social context and channelled into socially acceptable outlets (such as self-assertion and strivings for prestige, possessions, and power), thereby facilitating the formation of libidinal ties in groups; but it can readily become undisguised, then reemerging in the form of antipathies, aversions, and intolerance.

> In the undisguised antipathies and aversions which people feel towards strangers with whom they have to do we may recognize the expression of self-love—of

narcissism. This self-love works for the self-assertion of the individual, and behaves as though the occurrence of any divergence from his own particular lines of development involved a criticism of them and a demand for their alteration. We do not know why such sensitiveness should have been directed to just these details of differentiation; but it is unmistakable that in this whole connection men give evidence of a readiness for hatred, an aggressiveness, the source of which is unknown, and to which one is tempted to ascribe an elementary character.

But the whole of this intolerance vanishes, temporarily or permanently, as the result of the formation of a group, and in a group. So long as a group formation persists or so far as it extends, individuals behave as though they were uniform, tolerate other people's peculiarities, put themselves on an equal level with them, and have no feeling of aversion towards them. Such a limitation of narcissism can, according to our theoretical views, only be produced by one factor, a libidinal tie with other people. (Freud, 1921, pp. 55–56)

In *Civilisation and Its Discontents*, Freud (1930) gave credit to the "fundamental hostility of human beings to one another" (p. 49); he appreciated that "the tendency to aggression is an original, autonomous disposition in man" (p. 58) and acknowledged that he could "no longer understand how we could have ignored the ubiquity of non-erotic aggression and destruction and failed to accord it its due place in the interpretation of life" (pp. 56–57).

The reality behind all this, which many would deny, is that human beings are not gentle creatures in need of love, at most able to defend themselves if attacked; on the contrary, they can count a powerful share of aggression among their instinctual endowments. … As a rule, this cruel aggression waits for some provocation or puts itself at the service of a different aim, which could be attained by milder means. If the circumstances favour it, if the psychical counter-forces that would otherwise inhibit it have ceased to operate, it manifests itself spontaneously and reveals man as a savage beast that has no thought of sparing its own kind. (Freud, 1930, p. 48)

Freud (1930) came to the conclusion that "contention and competition" in human activity are "indispensable" to civilisation (p. 49). Nevertheless, he thought that "multitudes of human beings are libidinally bound to one another" and that "man's natural aggressive drive" opposes the "programme of civilisation" (Freud, 1930, p. 58). Lorenz (1963), by contrast, emphasised that culturally ritualised expression of the aggressive instinct plays a central role in cultural evolution. What Freud (1930) did see is that inhibition of the aggressive drive, as called for by the social context, contributes to the formation of the superego (being, in part, a symbolic representation of learned avoidance behaviour and the anticipation of punishment or retaliation from others) and to psychopathology (in that, "any restriction of this outward-directed aggression would be bound to increase the degree of self-destruction" (p. 56)).

### 8.2.2   Fear of aggression

Anxiety, reflecting our existential dependence on others, provides an important motivational impetus to group membership and interpersonal relationships. While companionship and social inclusion keep existential anxieties at bay, we expose ourselves, at the same time, to a situation that breeds intraspecific aggression and related fears. Aggression pervades many aspects of social behaviour in groups and gatherings. Aggressive impulses arise naturally in the social environment with which we engage; we cannot avoid them. Unless we can tolerate the aversiveness, insecurity, and anxiety associated with loneliness, or unless we can withdraw from the world defensively, we have to develop complicated adaptive behaviours aiming at appeasement, submission, and assertion—behaviours that in fluctuating group constellations respond to a multitude of symbolic and paralinguistic cues indicative of others' social ranking and aggressive potential and intentions.

> Dependence is felt to be dangerous because it involves the possibility of privation. ... Our dependence on others is manifestly a condition of our life in all its aspects: self-preservative, sexual or pleasure-seeking. And this means that some degree of sharing, some degree of waiting, of giving up something for others, is necessary in life. But though this brings a gain in collective security, it can mean a loss of individual security as well. So these dependent relationships in themselves tend to rouse resistance and aggressive emotions. (Riviere, 1937, pp. 7–8)

It may be difficult to distinguish between fear of aggression that behaviourally results in conformity, appeasement, and submission, on the one hand, and existential anxiety, or separation anxiety, that manifests in the seeking of others' attention and group membership, on the other. Conformity with the norms of the group may be motivated directly by fear of aggression but also, indirectly, by fears of rejection by, and separation from, the group. Rejection by others may be avoided because it leaves the individual with the prospect of resurging existential anxiety. Although the individual's realisation that non-conformity would invite aggression stabilises the group more proximally, it may be that his or her existential anxiety, that is, the anxiety first experienced by the infant in the mother's absence, is what imbues the *prospect* of rejection from the group, or loss of social status therein, with emotional significance and ensures the individual's membership of the group in the first place.

> Man's need for the society of his fellows is of course no simple manifestation,

and every single element and every mechanism in his psychology will be found to contribute to it; but it is probably true that where this instinct is strongly developed it represents more particularly the need to collect and accumulate a specially large measure of love, support and so security, which will be available as a perpetual reserve to be drawn upon at need. ... Thus by collecting goodness all round them, which they can dip into at any moment, they re-create for themselves (by their unconscious phantasy-attitude) a kind of substitute mother's breast which is always at their disposal and never frustrates or fails them. (Riviere, 1937, p. 24)

### 8.2.3   Conformity

> Our seemingly non-homogenous society with apparently great latitude in behavior consists of a mixture in space of different groups which in themselves are not less homogenous than primitive tribes. (Schilder, 1951, p. 289)

Recognising that "human beings are continually afraid of the hostility of the others", Schilder (1951) thought that "one function of society is to relieve human beings of the fear of mutual hostility and to divert the hostility toward outside groups" (p. 272). In a group or society, aggressive tendencies are diverted not only "toward the outside enemy" but also "toward work and toward nature" (p. 276), especially work concerned with the advancement or protection of one's social position. Schilder (1951) thought that work, "which is aggressive in nature", is also "self-punishment for aggressiveness" (p. 323). By neutralising mutual hostility and putting rivalries "into a definite form which is no longer dangerous", the group or society provides "an opportunity for the expression of human curiosity" (Schilder, 1951, p. 287). Mutual aggression in a group is absorbed, averted, and suppressed in part by members' adherence to "an average rule of conduct"; whereby such conformity guarantees "to all members a reasonable security in getting the essentials of life—food, protection and sex gratification" (p. 288). However, complete conformity is impossible, "and the individual will always fight against conformity created by others" (Schilder, 1951, pp. 289–290).

Maintenance or elevation of one's ranking position within an established group presupposes one's conforming to the group's norms. We are successful in competing with others for access to resources only insofar as we avoid rejection and maintain our position within the group. Conformity with the group's rules and norms is a form of active avoidance behaviour from the perspective of the individual; it is designed to actively inhibit others' potential for aggression. Any temptation we might experience to infringe upon social norms evokes in us an anticipation of aggression by others or the group. We can monitor the extent to which our social actions and attitudes conform to the group's norms and expectations by paying attention to others' attitudes and expressions of disapproval, which function as early warning signs of overt conspecific attack and which are condensed within ourselves into a sense of dissonance or anxiety. The self is partly a manifestation of this process. The price of defying social norms is anxiety, which we have to keep at bay with elaborate defensive systems that may test to the limit our higher cognitive abilities. Any failure to conform to the complexities of social rules and demands would make us vulnerable to attack. Others' aggressive impulses, which are otherwise invested into the maintenance of culture and norms, would thus become disinhibited. Our fear of rejection by the group may explain why we tend to hate in others common behaviours or attitudes that, if expressed by ourselves publically, would make us vulnerable to social rejection and exclusion by the group.

> It is one of the strangest laws of our nature that many things which we are well satisfied with in ourselves disgust us when seen in others. (James, 1890, p. 314)

### 8.2.4 Victimisation of the outsider

Cultural rituals and norms inhibit aggression between members of the group, which is why there remains the potential for aggression stored-up in the group to be released towards the individual who deviates from the group's rituals and norms. Any "deviation from a group's characteristic manners and mannerisms" elicits overt aggression, which "forces all its members into a strictly uniform observance of these norms of social behaviour" (Lorenz, 1963, p. 76). The "nonconformist is discriminated against as an outsider" (Lorenz, 1963); and it is the individual's anticipation of such treatment by the group—his fear of rejection or punishment—that keeps interpersonal behaviour on a habitual trajectory aimed at appeasement. In established groups and societies, we are afraid perhaps not so much of being attacked competitively by other individuals but more so of becoming the target of aggression by the group as a whole.

> The ganging up against an individual diverging from the social norms characteristic of a group, and the group's enthusiastic readiness to defend these social norms and rites, are both good illustrations of the way in which culturally determined conditioned stimulus situations release activities which are fundamentally instinctive. (Lorenz, 1963, p. 251)

When writing his *Group Psychology and the Analysis of the Ego*, Freud was not unaware of the role of aggression in society. He spoke of the "uncanny and coercive characteristics of group formations", the intimidation of the individual by the group, and the fact that, unconsciously, the "leader of the group is still the dreaded primal father" of the primal horde (Freud, 1921, p. 99). Later, Freud (1930) acknowledged that it is "clearly not easy for people to forgo the satisfaction of their tendency to aggression" (p. 50). The aggressive drive seeks an "outlet in the form of hostility to outsiders" (p. 50). He observed that binding "a large number of people together in love" might even require that "others are left out as targets for aggression" (p. 50); aggression against outsiders has the effect of "facilitating solidarity within the community" (Freud, 1930, p. 51). Discussing religious communities, he wrote:

> Therefore a religion, even if it calls itself the religion of love, must be hard and unloving to those who do not belong to it. Fundamentally indeed every religion is in this same way a religion of love for all those whom it embraces; while cruelty and intolerance towards those who do not belong to it are natural to every religion. (Freud, 1921, p. 51)

### 8.2.5  Cultural ritualisation

> These deep strata of the human personality are, in their dynamics, not essentially different form the instincts of animals, but on their basis human culture has erected all the enormous superstructure of social norms and rites whose function is so closely analogous to that of phylogenetic ritualisation. (Lorenz, 1963, p. 240)

Phylogenetically evolved patterns of social behaviour are interrelated with cultural tradition. Culturally evolved social norms, as expressed in customs and taboos, "motivate behaviour in a way comparable to that of autonomous instincts". In their institutionalised form, they function "like a supporting skeleton in human cultures" (Lorenz, 1963, p. 258). Phylogenetically evolved signals and culturally evolved symbols have in common that they "both originate in the emergence of a creature's ability to 'understand' those behaviour patterns which allow it to predict how a fellow creature is going to react" (Lorenz, 1973, p. 214). Patterns of social behaviour developed by phylogenetic or cultural ritualisation serve to curb man's aggressive tendencies. Norms of social behaviour developed by cultural ritualisation started to play an important part in human

society "when invention of tools was beginning to upset the equilibrium of phylogenetically evolved patterns of social behaviour" (p. 249)— the "equilibrium between the ability and the inhibition to kill" (Lorenz, 1963, p. 242). Cultural ritualisation "has converted aggressive tendencies into the form of contest that we call sport" (Lorenz, 1973, p. 221). The fulfilment of a variety of common tasks and the performance of a variety of customs, of which competitive sports is an example, use up aggressive feelings or divert aggression (Eibl-Eibesfeldt, 1970). Aggression "is to a great extent neutralised through rivalry and striving for dominance" (Eibl-Eibesfeldt, 1970, p. 217). Both, phylogenetic and cultural ritualisation, foster group cohesion and the distinction of one group from another, however "the distinctive properties of any group which make it coherent and exclusive are norms of behaviour ritualised in cultural development" (Lorenz, 1963, p. 256). Larger groups and societies owe their cohesion "to symbols which have been evolved as a result of cultural ritualization and are felt by all members of the group to be of value" (Lorenz, 1973, p. 230).

### 8.2.6  Breakdown of traditions

> What we are faced with, to employ the jargon that corresponds to our approaches to man's subjective needs, is the increasing absence of all those saturations of the superego and ego ideal that are realized in all kinds of organic forms in traditional societies, forms that extend from the rituals of everyday intimacy to the periodic festivals in which the community manifests itself. We no longer know them except in their most obviously degraded aspects. (Lacan, 1966, p. 29)

In modern society, personal acquaintance became less important in its function of appeasing aggressive feelings (Eibl-Eibesfeldt, 1970). Man had to learn to live with strangers. Groups have evolved into an anonymous mass society, where it becomes problematic that "we feel a markedly weaker bond between ourselves and unknown fellow men than between ourselves and people we know" (p. 221). As a result, conflicts are more bitter, which is "evident in the struggle for positions of rank" (Eibl-Eibesfeldt, 1970, p. 221). Men, in particular, have to be inconspicuous in order to avoid becoming the target of aggression. While traditionally ordered groups evolved into anonymous societies, the aggression-controlling functions of traditions were undermined politically and philosophically. Eighteenth-century Enlightenment "has resulted generally in critical attitudes towards the old cultural patterns of order" (Eibl-Eibesfeldt, 1970, p. 221).

> Customs are no longer inherited uncritically: we try, rather, to base the conduct of our lives upon reason. This means that our own values are regarded as more relative, while other systems of values are regarded with more openmindedness: there is thus a true process of liberalization. Nevertheless traditions are the basic skeleton of a culture. However they are constituted they underwrite social order and lend conviction and credibility to the leaders of a culture (Eibl-Eibesfeldt, 1970, p. 221)

A more sceptical attitude towards cultural tradition and authorities and, ultimately a break with tradition, causes uncertainty. Anxiety aggravates the struggle for positions of power. Authorities are not recognised; and "people in authority are no longer certain of their role" (Eibl-Eibesfeldt, 1970, p. 222). Since people continue to feel the need for authorities, they seek substitute authorities who are "as far away as possible, or already dead, and can therefore easily be idealized" (p. 222). The growth of ideologies—at a time when traditional value systems are being undermined—is an expression of our tendency to form exclusive groups (closed groups). Eibl-Eibesfeldt (1970) recognised that "in creating an 'enemy schema' and clothing it in an ideology we are following certain thought processes quite involuntarily" (p. 220).

## 8.3  Group therapy

Individuals wish to be *accepted* by members of their group. In therapeutic groups, too, members experience a "fear of being left out or not being accepted" (Parloff, 1968, p. 503). Mutual acceptance increases the self-esteem of members; members feel increasingly secure as a result of others' acceptance. The "collusion of mutual good fellowship and a pressure to accept group norms" may be "antagonistic to analytic psychotherapy" (p. 505). Group therapy "provides more opportunity than individual treatment does for experiencing wholesome, loving feelings, sympathy and positive relatedness", although "patients in groups occasionally treat each other with harshness and cruelty" (Parloff, 1968, p. 504). Members of a therapeutic group are provoked into expressing their agreement or disagreement with the ideas or attitudes of others, whereby "members are particularly sensitive to behavior in others which they tend to reject in themselves" (p. 508). The group's cohesiveness arises due to subtle pressures to conform to the group's standards, norms, and goals. Patients must deal with the opportunity of controlling others and with the possibility of being controlled by others (Parloff, 1968).

Freud (1921) observed that members of a group show heightened suggestibility and readiness for mutual identification, including identification with the leader. The group is bound by libidinal ties that members establish with their leader (Freud, 1921). The therapeutic group setting engenders intense rivalries for the therapist's attention and approval (Parloff, 1968). In the course of all of these interactions, patients reveal their anxieties, sensitivities, resistances, and defences. The therapist helps patients to become aware of their reactions to others (including feelings of sympathy, resentment, and hostility) and of others' reactions to them. Analytic group psychotherapy entails the analysis of observable interpersonal relationships and transactions. Analytic group therapy is more "reality-focused" than *individual* psychoanalytic therapy. The group setting may not be conducive to deep regression and the emergence of unconscious fantasies. The presence of other individuals diminishes the transference that can be established with the therapist. Thus, the level of insight a patient can attain in analytic group therapy is less deep than in individual psychoanalysis. Patients with severe psychoneuroses, who require the establishment of a transference neurosis as part of their treatment, generally do not benefit from analytic group therapy (reviewed in Parloff, 1968).

## 8.3.1   Phases of development

The behaviour of an individual in a group is a function of his or her perception of the social situation, which, in turn, depends on the phase of group development (Agazarian & Peters, 1981). Individuals experience heightened anxiety when they enter a therapy group. In the early phase of group development, when the emphasis is on rules and regulations, group members are driven by the wish for conformity. Members readily engage in "dependence behaviour" (mechanisms of avoidance), becoming compliant followers of the leader's real or imagined wishes. The group's *status quo* offers security to its members; and the leader (the therapist) is seen as a saviour "whose power will protect the group from anything bad happening to them" (Agazarian & Peters, 1981, p. 136). Group members also display "flight behaviours", which "lead to a retreat to some place else in time and space into the past or the future and far away from 'here' and 'now'" (p. 132). Members start to pair in alliances, which "are based partly on the similarities and support that members see in other members" (pp. 133–134). Members are supportive of each other or perceive others as nurturing and protective (Agazarian & Peters, 1981).

In the second phase of group development, members tend to challenge other members of the group. Aggressive behaviour ("aggressive dependence behaviour") "induces the conformity of other members to the leader's imagined or real leadership" (Agazarian & Peters, 1981, p. 135). Members "look to certain members for support and alliance, to others for contention and

disagreement" (p. 135). Competitive subgroups scapegoat each other or a particular member. Then, the emphasis in group dynamics shifts to nonconformity and rebellion ("counterdependence behaviour") against the leader's rules, whereby, again, "the inferred wish of the leader is the reference point around which group process revolves" (p. 135). The "projections on the leader turn 'bad', and the leader is seen either as malevolent" or incompetent (p. 136). The leader becomes an "object of rage". Questions are asked that cannot be answered to the group's satisfaction and that are, in fact, an act of power ("confrontation questions"); what the group wants is not an answer but to control the leader (the therapist). The group consolidates in their power struggle with the leader. Scapegoating "becomes a unifying group force that unites the members against the leader" (p. 136); and, however the group raises the "authority issue" "the effect is to continue to build a strong family feeling among the members" (p. 137). At this point, the "group as a whole provides surrogate ego support for all members", while the leader is left to experience annihilation anxiety, a state of terror (Agazarian & Peters, 1981, p. 138).

Eventually, some compromise is reached with the authority (Agazarian & Peters, 1981). As the group resolves the "authority issue" and continues to develop, new alliances are formed that allow members to receive positive and affirmative feedback. Members strive "to become fused with the group, and to merge their identity into the group identity" (p. 141). This "phase of enchantment" "provides a repetition of early symbiotic gratification" (Agazarian & Peters, 1981, p. 141).

## 8.3.2   Basic assumptions

"Basic assumptions", which are unspoken assumptions that are tacitly accepted by all members of a group, influence and direct the activity of the group (Bion, 1961). Basic assumptions, describing the group's covert culture, demonstrate how principles of early object relations pervade and determine group dynamics. There are three forms of basic assumption groups, only one of which will be evident at any one time. Bion (1961) postulated that we have an innate capacity ("valency") to enter into one or another of the basic assumptions. There is "a force which irresistibly draws group members into participation in any of the basic assumptions once they have been manifested in members of the group"; "the very fact that some members move into a basic assumption attitude might be sufficient to induce other members to follow" (Parloff, 1968, p. 516). The group "stimulates each member to adopt a particular role which corresponds to his own way of defending himself against unconscious fears" (p. 517). For example, one member's striving for dominance is complemented and supported by the submissiveness of the other. Group members are impelled to seek security by submergence in the group, while, at the same time, fearing to sacrifice their independence. Thus, members may experience an anxiety-provoking conflict between participation in a basic assumption and the contradictory wish to maintain their individuality. Groups tend to shift from one basic assumption to another, which may be "due to the fact that the assumptions are unrealistic and cannot be met satisfactorily" (p. 517). Whenever intense anxiety is aroused in the group, this anxiety will force the shift to another basic assumption (Parloff, 1968).

## Dependency

Under the basic assumption of "dependency", the group's purpose is to seeks nurturance and protection from a leader. Members behave as if they are inadequate, immature, and helpless, whereas the leader is endowed with godlike qualities of wisdom, knowledge, and power. Through their behaviour, group members underscore their "desperate need for an omniscient and omnipotent leader" (Parloff, 1968, pp. 514–515); moreover, their behaviour is designed to *induce* the leader to fulfil their dependency needs. "Introjective identification" with the leader is part of the group process. The leader, or perhaps an idea or symbol representing the group,

serves the function of the primary object for each member, becoming the target for libidinal and aggressive impulses, which members generate as they try to keep at bay their primitive anxieties. For the group to function under the unspoken assumption of "dependency", someone has to play the role of a leader in the way that the group desires. When the leader fails to live up to the group's expectations, the group reacts with disappointment, rejection, and hostility towards the leader. The group then instates someone else as their leader or oscillates between believing that the leader is good or bad. Through "projective identification", each member splits off bad parts of his ego and projects them into the leader or part of the group. Being projected into others, bad parts of the self can be persecuted and punished. The realisation that the badness, such as cruelty and greed perceived in others, actually originates in the self can be terrifying, laying bare one's primordial psychotic anxieties (Bion, 1961; reviewed in de Board, 1978).

## Fight or flight

The second of Bion's basic assumptions is called "fight or flight". The group governed by the basic assumption of fight or flight acts as if it has to protect itself, as if it can only engage in attack or flight behaviour. The group is preoccupied with self-preservation and consumed by paranoia. The realisation that the danger that threatens the group may be within and not outside the group is resisted. The group creates its common enemy and "seeks out a leader who can mobilize it for attack or for flight" (Parloff, 1968, p. 515). The leader is entirely a creature of the group, and once the danger is felt to have passed, the leader is ignored (Bion, 1961).

## Pairing

When a group is governed by the third of Bion's basic assumptions, that of "pairing", it behaves as if it has the purpose to produce a new leader and saviour. There is an air of optimism and hopeful anticipation that two people within the group will come together and produce a new omnipotent leader. The group hops for resolution of its fears in the future. The hoped-for leader will inevitably fail to deliver the group from its fears, again bringing about destructiveness and hatred in the group (Bion, 1961).

### 8.3.3    Work groups

Bion (1961) contrasted basic assumption groups, which represent attempts to escape from reality (into group-shared assumptions), with what he called "work groups", that is, groups concerned with reality. Group cultures characterised by "basic assumptions" are alternatives to a culture concerned with "work" (Bion, 1961). "Basic assumptions" are expressions of psychotic anxiety within the group and are defence mechanisms against this anxiety (de Board, 1978). To protect themselves from persecutory (or "psychotic") anxiety, the individual regresses to defence mechanisms characteristic of the paranoid-schizoid position of infantile development. The group, in this process, plays the role of the primary object in the mind of the individual. A group that is guided by basic assumptions stagnates or regresses (akin to the paranoid-schizoid position in infant development), whereas Bion's "work group", which has an overt task to perform, achieves growth and development (akin to the depressive position). In a group that functions as a "work group", members cooperate to achieve a common task (Bion, 1961). A group that operates as a "basic assumption group" does not produce effective output but uses its energy to defend itself against its own internal anxieties. The "basic assumption group" is a closed system, ignoring external reality, whereas the "work group" maintains a balance with the forces acting outside it, thus functioning like a Freudian ego that mediates between instinctive anxiety and external reality (de Board, 1978).

### 8.3.4    T-groups

Laboratory-based "T-groups", based on Lewin's (1947) work, allow participants to learn and appreciate the effects that their behaviour has on others. When a new group commences, the main feeling among members is anxiety and the need to find and retain a role in the group. The questions that arise in each member's mind are: will I dominate others in the group or will I face the group's hostility? Consciously or unconsciously, the question "who dominates whom" is on all members' minds. Most of the behaviour exhibited will be that which has gained approval from authority figures in the past. Subgroups emerge and the trainer is likely to be bullied or ignored as he abstains from giving directions to the group (refusing to adopt a leadership role in accordance with any of the "basic assumptions"). Once the trainer reveals his authority, the group experiences a sense of euphoria. The group now tends to subdivide into those who are overpersonal and feel they must establish and maintain a high degree of intimacy, and those who tend to avoid intimacy. In this phase, fears of rejection prevail, although they gradually diminish as they are tested against reality as the end of the group approaches (reviewed in De Board, 1978).

## 8.4    The myth of free will

The flourishing of capitalist methods of production in the nineteenth century went hand in hand with the progressive destruction of restrictive social conventions and values and a corresponding growth in values of liberalism and human rights. At a time when macroeconomic mechanisms started to fundamentally depend on equal opportunities and consumerism, human beings were increasingly conceived of as responsible for their actions and able to make "informed decisions". Decisions made by consumers and voters had to be seen as quasi-technological acts, similar to those arrived at by machines devoid of irrational instincts. Psychology, being firmly embedded in the political and social culture of society, could not but press ahead on the assumption that humans are guided in their behaviour and decisions by rationality, free will, and an inherent striving for goodness and progress. The whole spectrum of humanities relentlessly developed in a manner that was both necessitated and inspired by technological advances. Already Nietzsche (1886) analysed these cultural processes emerging in nineteenth-century capitalist society. Free will implies moral responsibilities and rights, which are thought to separate us from the rest of the animal kingdom. Free will is cited as evidence for the higher standing attained by human beings in nature. Yet, "freedom of will", as Nietzsche (1886) understood, supposes a *causa sui*—a "pull[ing] oneself up into existence by the hair". The realisation that there is no free will in any of our beliefs, moral decisions, and intellectual pursuits, is resisted, not least because it challenges our socio-political belief system. Lorenz (1963) thought that there are "certain inner obstacles which prevent many people from seeing themselves as part of the universe and recognising that their own behaviour too obeys the laws of nature" (p. xiii). Our reluctance to "recognize the causal determination of all natural phenomena, human behaviour included", "comes from the justifiable wish to possess a free will and to feel that our actions are determined not by fortuitous causes but by higher aims" (p. 215). People are afraid of "causal considerations" lest they could "expose man's free will as an illusion" (Lorenz, 1963, p. 224).

> The best definition of man is that he is the one creature capable of reflection, of seeing himself in the frame of reference of the surrounding universe. Pride is one of the chief obstacles to seeing ourselves as we really are, and self-deceit is the obliging servant of pride. (Lorenz, 1963, p. 286)

Psychology and sociology are complicit in perpetuating a model of the mind that serves technological progress but is conceptually questionable. Insights into the nature of human behaviour gathered by Lorenz, McDougall, Freud, and others have been met with much ignorance, if not hostility, by a world of science that, up until recently, tended to ridicule anybody who ascribed

emotions to animals. The fundamental animal nature of humans was ignored; and metaphors were adopted in psychology that cemented this denial. Cognitivist and information-processing accounts of the mind firmly displaced instinct theory of the mind that was anticipated by Nietzsche in the late nineteenth century and developed from different perspectives in the early twentieth century by McDougall and Freud. Lorenz (1996) tried to return us to a grounding of human psychology in instinctual mechanisms that are common among the animal kingdom, yet, in a climate dominated by liberalism and emphasis on human rights, psychologists and sociologists did not receive this with enthusiasm. Cognitivism became a dogma and monopolised resources in research despite the fact that much of its theorising implicated an inner homunculus (the self as an agent).

### 8.4.1   Enlightenment

In Marxist sociology, the modes and methods of production ("base") are seen as conditioning the social, political, and cultural life-processes of a society (art, law, morality, ethics, mass media, politics)—collectively referred to as "superstructure". The realm of culture and politics serves to reinforce capitalist relations of production, e.g., by producing a certain conformity—of opinion, satisfaction, ambition (reviewed in Abbinnet, 2003). The thriving of capitalist methods of production depended on a progressive destruction of restrictive social conventions and traditions. Notions of individual freedom and self-determination are not absolute but—according to the Marxist dialectic of base and superstructure—flourished insofar as they played a useful role in the advancement of capitalist methods of production. Enlightenment, as part of the superstructure in early capitalism, played an important role in advancing notions of free will in conjunction with values of equality and responsibility.

Kant recognised that, insofar as humans are considered from the standpoint of biology and act in accordance with desires, they are not free.

He saw that the presumed rationality of free will stands opposed to every manifestation of nature in the individual (i.e., the "passions" and "inclinations"). The "empirical" or "phenomenal" self (i.e., the self revealed to us in introspection, which Kant distinguished from the "transcendental" self) is "as completely determined as the movements of matter in the physical world" (reviewed in Joad, 1955, p. 390). However, from a moral point of view, humans have to be seen as being capable of rational self-determination; humans should not simply surrender to the forces of blind necessity. Kant regarded freedom along with mortality and God as improvable but indispensable postulates of ethics. Although there is no way of demonstrating that anything exists outside the world of causally determined phenomena, Kant thought that obligations of morality compel us to think of ourselves as free agents (Passmore, 1957). The possession of a rational will places us under an obligation to control the "inclinations" that bind us to nature and allows us thus to participate in the moral order of society. According to Kant, the bourgeois individual is the embodiment of rational abstinence, which constantly asserts itself against the instinctual life of nature (Passmore, 1957).

James, too, recognised that there is an irreconcilable conflict between the postulate of deterministic natural law, which governs science, and the postulates of free choice and personal responsibility, which govern moral or legal operations. He was unwilling to accept the pessimistic conclusion of determinism that "we are wholly conditioned, not a wiggle of our will happens save as a result of physical laws" (James, cited by Passmore, 1957), a conclusion to which his empirical studies and empirical philosophy inevitably led him. James saw that psychology could not settle this conflict since it involves areas of life outside science. It was James's pragmatic conclusion then that we are *entitled* to believe in free will, like we have a right to believe in God. We are entitled to oppose any suggestion that we are "forced" to act as long as this belief cannot be ruled out as logically impossible (Passmore, 1957,

p. 111). Nietzsche disagreed with Kant's position, insisting that there is "no independent faculty of pure reason, constructing its demonstrations in isolation from the passions" (Passmore, 1957, p. 98). Free will presupposes the existence of an autonomous self but ultimately, no agent can be held responsible for our thoughts, feelings, and actions—a view that was supported by Lorenz (1963).

> In reality, even the fullest rational insight into the consequences of an action and into the logical consistency of its premise would not result in an imperative or in a prohibition, were it not for some emotional, in other words instinctive, source of energy supplying motivation. Like power steering in a modern car, responsible morality derives the energy which it needs to control human behaviour from the same primal powers which it was created to keep in rein. (Lorenz, 1963, p. 239)

### 8.4.2    Modernity

In conjunction with rising ontological insecurity and the loss of authenticity in modern times, notions of free will became the basis for an increase in awareness of personal rights, partly as a compensation for the loss of value orientation. The growing emphasis on personal rights and freedom of choices was accompanied by a decline in emphasis on compliance and responsibility. People have become "reluctant to force their children to conform to external controls and standards, fearing that imposing such authoritarian controls will stifle their creativity and create low self-esteem" (Baumeister, 1997). On a political level, antiauthoritarian, liberalist, and feminist movements, borne out of consciously disavowed persecutory beliefs, had the effect of further undermining traditions and enhancing insecurity. Modern notions of autonomy and self-reliance (according to which the individual as a consumer of technological services acts freely, knowingly, and with full agency) are at odds with the existential reality of being, that is, our existential dependence on stable interpersonal and social arrangements that replicate our dependence on benevolent objects. Even though economic progress has depended on the progressive erosion of limits placed on the exercise of freedom, Griffiths (1982) argued that the inhumanity of capitalist societies results from a "failure to assert certain absolutes and so place proper limits on the use of freedom" (p. 29). Griffiths (1982) thought that religion could still provide the values which are crucial if the market economy is to survive, however "the pursuit of freedom at the personal level [leads] to abandonment of traditional morality based on the concept of right and wrong and good and evil" (pp. 36–37). It now seems that the pursuit of absolute freedom and the destruction of traditional morality have become preconditions for economic existence in the West.

> Ever since the Renaissance, but particularly since the Enlightenment of the Eighteenth century, Western culture has become imbued with a humanistic and libertarian spirit. As a religion humanism affirms some important absolutes. It starts by proclaiming that God is dead or what comes to the same thing, that if he exists he is irrelevant. From this it follows that "man is the measure of all things". Man is free and autonomous. He is independent of all authority except that of his own choosing. He is free to choose anything and everything. In no area of life is choice restricted. Because of this faith in the perfectibility of Man, liberalism fostered a great belief in progress—history was seen as the emancipation of mankind from ignorance, taboos, constraints, crime and war through the process of education and increasing material prosperity. … Alongside the emphasis on knowledge, great faith was also placed in the power of science to discover the laws of the physical universe, society and even human personality itself, so that the world and individuals could be improved

by being controlled. (Griffiths, 1982, pp. 27–28)

## Consumptive self-indulgence

The expansion of notions of instrumental reason and free will played an essential role in the early development of capitalist modes of production, yet the Enlightenment project was seen to be collapsing in late capitalism, with its ideals of freedom and self-determination being lost to the "functional-systemic necessities" of the capital (Adorno & Horkheimer, 1986, reviewed in Abbinnet, 2003). Necessarily, the historical condition, economic role, and metaphysical meaninglessness of these ideals had to become more apparent. What had been an ethic of freedom and self-restraint turned gradually—on economic grounds—into self-indulgence and relativism. Consumptive self-restraint, along with the protestant ethic of saving, became "the enemy rather than ally of the main economic forces" (Baumeister, 1997). In late capitalism, the limiting factor on sales was not manufacturing but consumer demand. Culture, as the counterpart of corporate capitalism, became a matter of technological media reproduction being used effectively for rendering the desires of the masses stable and predictable, thereby completing the integration of the masses into the economy of corporate desire (Adorno, 1991). Marketing techniques aim "to depreciate a man's property as quickly as possible, use every available means to destroy his pleasure in what he has already acquired, and enhance the desirability of what he does not already possess", thereby reducing man "to a permanent condition of wanting more" (Hass, 1968, p. 183).

> Every conceivable form of demand is explored and stimulated, and the products or services suggested by this research are offered for sale. Progress receives a powerful fillip in this way—not in its true guise, however, but in its capacity as a sales product. The result is endless activity and an incessant stimulation of new demand.

Because the individual is constantly offered aids to happiness, he has little time to reflect whether such aids bring him genuine and lasting contentment. Ultimately this trend will create, in biological terms, a spongelike social structure whose components are inextricably entangled, each at one and the same time operating on the others and being influenced by them—a system which feeds upon, erodes, and paralyzes itself, a system in which the individual is just as surely lost as in the Communist one. (Hass, 1968, p. 184)

## Media

According to Baudrillard (1999), agentic categories (will, choice, judgement, transgression) are constantly "recycled" by the media in the production of "simulated" political meaning. Constant solicitations by the media, e.g., to be responsible consumers or informed users of services, have ceased to refer to anything beyond the "simulation" of social relations and have come to recreate the indifference of the masses the media "seek" to overcome (Baudrillard, 1996). The media present themselves as authorising the individual and its rational will, but, under their solicitations, the masses revert to a state of total suspension of will, deliberation, and judgement. The seductiveness of the media lies in the abrogation of individual responsibility, communicating with an unconscious desire to be relieved of choice and be diverted from one's own "objective will" (Baudrillard, 1999).

Baudrillard (1999) argued that the signifying codes of "the social" have become independent of their referents (the essential wants, needs, and responsibilities of human beings). The system of signs (moral, legal, economic, and political norms) does not refer to a reality beyond its autonomous self-generation. "The symbolic" is expanded into an operational version of itself and all that remains is the circulation of different modes of interpretation (Baudrillard, 1999). Any destabilisation in the relationship between the masses, the ideals of deliberative democracy,

and the media responsible for the transmission of these ideals merely provokes further simulation and "hypersimulation" of political relations. Total simulation deters every real process via its operational double, bypassing the vicissitudes of "the real". The masses, according to Baudrillard (1999), retain a certain short-circuiting potential; their inertial conductivity can short-circuit the total simulation of "the real" to produce unforeseen effects of ironic hyperconformity, thus reducing the logic of the system to absurdity.

### 8.4.3   Unintended consequences

Lorenz (1963) recognised a lack of appreciation in modern society that "man's whole system of innate activities and reactions is phylogenetically so constructed … as to need to be complemented by cultural tradition" (p. 256). He warned that the "social organisation of any culture is a complicated system of universal interaction between a great many divergent traditional norms of behaviour"; and the "cutting out of even one single part" may have unpredictable "repercussions … for the functioning of the whole" (pp. 252–253). The "extreme speed of ecological and sociological change wrought by the development of technology causes many customs to become maladaptive within one generation" (p. 255); and "industrialisation that prevails in all sectors of human life produces a distance between the generations which is not compensated for by the greatest familiarity, by the most democratic tolerance and permissiveness of which we are so proud" (Lorenz, 1963, p. 254).

… scientific enlightenment tends to engender doubt in the value of traditional beliefs long before it furnishes the causal insight necessary to decide whether some accepted custom is an obsolete superstition or a still indispensable part of the system of social norms. Again, it is the unripe fruit of the tree of knowledge that proves to be dangerous; indeed I suspect that the whole legend of the tree of knowledge is meant to defend sacred traditions against premature inroads of incomplete ration-alisation. (Lorenz, 1963, p. 255)

Liberalism and other social-utopian ideologies are not based on a biologically and evolutionarily sensible model of human behaviour: they fail to see humans for what they are. Propagation of liberalist political ideals serves the self-esteem of the propagandist, but their literal implementation may destroy social structures serving to balance man's aggressive potential, undermine social cohesion, and, as a result, increase man's self-obsession and vulnerability to mental illness. Our preoccupation with human rights, to the extent of sparing people from responsibilities, and our pursuit of "freedom" of choices and speech, to the extent of relinquishing discipline and curtailment, will unleash destructively the natural, because instinctive, tendencies of intraspecific aggression. Society has evolved on the basis of complex systems of ritualisation of aggression, thus diverting these tendencies to the benefit of the community; but if traditions and customs continue to be undermined, aggression will seek other outlets, and selfishness and greed will prevail in a manner that does not serve the common good. The climate in Western societies is becoming harsher: people are becoming more self-centred, aggressive, and depressed—and this, again, inasmuch as social policies seek to conform to ideologically motivated ideas about what people *should* be like. Collective self-deception about the essential goodness of human nature is related to our belief in the special status of humans above all other creatures. Goodness implies free will, an ability to chose between good and bad, yet the more we cling to such evolutionarily meaning-less concepts out of "pride", the more we are at risk of ignoring the derailment of culturally complex systems that have, throughout cultural evolution, served to restrain and constructively divert instinctive aggression (Lorenz, 1963).

These cautions to not only apply to society as a whole but also to psychiatry, which is torn between catering for the consequences of break-down of social networks and traditions, on the

one hand, and political imperatives for service development informed by ideological misconceptions about the nature of human beings, on the other. Many of the approaches used in psychiatry and psychotherapy, including approaches to service development, implicitly or explicitly centre on notions of free will and free choice, yet, as long as society, at large, and the psychiatric and psychotherapeutic establishment, in particular, remain suspended in collective self-deception about the nature of human behaviour, patients' true needs will remain unmet. Kant postulated "free will" in order to maintain compatibility with the world of morality and social relations as it developed under new economic conditions, but he could not foresee that the adoption of his essentially pragmatic stance would exert such lasting influence on the science of human behaviour and philosophy of the mind. To this day, science of the mind remains under the hegemony of ideology. Models of mental functioning have to pay tribute to a culture of liberalism where personal rights and freedom of choice have acquired the status of absolute truths and values in an otherwise increasingly valueless society. Balancing demands for "political correctness" in behavioural and mental health sciences, psychoanalytic theory and Lorenz's work could help us to reassert the principle of causality against the demands of morality.

### 8.4.4   Moral treatment

The antipsychiatry movement is a good example of how concerns about human rights, based, in part, on misconceived ideas about the mind, were accentuated by the media in order to demonise and destroy institutions, that, on the whole, provided safety and routine for the vulnerable (asylum closure and emphasis on "community psychiatry"); which is not to say that problems did not exist. Thus, paradoxically, while we have created in modern society conditions for the flourishing of neuroses, mental illness, and antisocial behaviour—a development of which already Lorenz spoke—, we were keen, at the same time, to dismantle effective retreats from an increasingly pathogenic cultural environment. Approaches to the care of the mentally ill should be formulated on the basis of an evolutionarily feasible understanding of human behaviour. Such understanding seems less available today than it was in previous times. For example, Tuke (1813), who described "moral treatment", as practiced in the Retreat Hospital in York in the early nineteenth century, argued that, in both mental health and illness, self-restraint (social conduct) is regulated according to the "desire of esteem" and the "principle of fear" and that treatment needs to address these normal human propensities.

> The principle of fear, which is rarely decreased by insanity, is considered as of great importance in the management of the patients. But it is not allowed to be excited, beyond that degree which naturally arises from the necessary regulations of the family. ... There cannot be a doubt that the principle of fear, in the human mind, when moderately and judiciously excited, as it is by the operation of just and equal laws, has a salutatory effect upon society. (Tuke, 1813, pp. 141–142)
>
> ... and though we allowed *fear* a considerable place in the production of that restraint, which the patient generally exerts on his entrance into a new situation; yet the *desire of esteem* is considered at the Retreat, as operating, in general, still more powerfully. This principle in the human mind, which doubtless influences, in a great degree, though often secretly, our general manners; and which operates with peculiar force on our introduction into a new circle of acquaintance, is found to have great influence, even over the conduct of the insane. (Tuke, 1813, p. 157)

Importantly, Tuke (1813, 1815) recognised that we have a natural tendency to reject those who are different and appear vulnerable and that a condescending attitude and other forms of subtle rejection are likely to fuel the vicious cycle of anxiety, maladaptive social behaviours, and social rejection that has seized many patients. Tuke (1813) spoke of ...

> ... the difficulty of entirely subduing the vindictive feelings, which the inconsistent, but often half rational, conduct of the patient, frequently excites in the minds of the inferior attendants. It is therefore an object of the highest importance, to infuse into the minds of these persons, just sentiments, with regard to the poor objects placed under their care; ... and to remind them, that the patient is really under the influence of a disease, which deprives him of responsibility ... But even this view of the subject is not exempt from danger; if the attendant does not sufficiently consider the degree in which the patient may be influenced by moral and rational inducements. ... To consider them at the same time as both brothers, and as mere automata; to applaud all they do right; and pity, without censuring, whatever they do wrong, requires such a habit of philosophical reflection, and Christian charity, as is certainly difficult to attain. (pp. 174–176)
>
> A perpetual desire to lessen personal exertion exists on the part of the servants of these establishments; and those who have not almost lived in an asylum can but faintly conceive the temptation to neglect, oppression and cruelty, which present themselves to those who have the care of insane persons ... The business of the attendant requires him to counteract some of the strongest impulses of our common nature ... I have rarely met an attendant, however humane and well-informed, who did not in greater or lesser degree err in this respect. It is evident that the only security of good conduct on part of the attendants is more frequent inspection. (Tuke, 1815, p. 26)

"Moral treatment" appears to have been successful not simply because of the absence of cruelty, as we may wish to think, but crucially because treatment with kindness, friendship, and occupation had the effect of making the patient feel valued. Mental illness is often a reaction to social rejection and marginalisation, leaving patients chronically frustrated in their natural desires for esteem, affiliation, and interpersonal security and instilling in them excessive fear of aggression from others or increasing their own aggressive tendencies. It is usually those who are ill equipped with regard to social competitiveness or ability to secure permanent relationships who develop manifestations of mental illness in accordance with their specific biological predispositions. "Moral treatment", as described by Tuke, sought to address patients' inability to attain interpersonal security in their conventional social environment by offering, in a protective environment, a balance of enhancing self-esteem and judicious induction of the principle of fear (in form of clear and firm boundaries, which operate through anticipation of punishment rather than punishment itself).

### 8.4.5   Psychiatric service development

Abolition of cruelty, as Samuel Tuke realised, does not mean that kindness becomes the natural attitude by default. Our approach to the mentally ill is not automatically endowed with kindness and genuineness, which is hard to appreciate from a perspective of liberalist notions of human nature and cognitivist models of the mind. There may be several reasons why the importance of genuine appreciation (valuing) of the patient as a paramount treatment principle is neglected in modern psychiatry. First, biological psychiatry and the availability of modern psychopharmacology can lead to the neglect of the impact of societal and interpersonal processes on mental health and illness. Moreover, in psychoeducation, care is taken to emphasise that rejection by the familial or social environment (and, to a lesser extent, early attachment deficits) do not cause mental illness. Second, biological and evidence-based psychiatry tend to reduce mental suffering to an instance of a disease process caused by neurotransmitter

imbalances. The disease model of mental illness artificially contrasts self and mental illness, suggesting that the self can suffer from or be afflicted by something that is external to its nature. Even when they are acknowledged, social stress and psychological conflict are demoted to precipitating or perpetuating factors that interact with pre-existing vulnerability factors ("biopsychosocial models").

> We are commanded to love our neighbour. … One cannot love a conglomeration of "signs and symptoms of schizophrenia". … What the schizophrenic is to us determines very considerably what we are to him, and hence his actions. (Laing, 1960, p. 35)
>
> As long as we are sane and he is insane, it will remain so. But comprehension as an effort to reach and grasp him, while remaining within our own world and judging him by our own categories whereby he inevitably falls short, is not what the schizophrenic either wants or requires. We have to recognize all the time his distinctiveness and differentness, his separateness and loneliness and despair. (Laing, 1960, p. 39)

Third, excessive concern with policies and procedures ("clinical governance" and "integrated care pathways") bears the risk of reducing patients to items in a technological process. In a climate characterised by governmental, societal, and media preoccupation with risk aversion and mistrust of professionals, treatment processes are dictated more by fears of litigation or inquests (institutionalised versions of anxiety) rather than attempts to empathetically understand the patient's suffering. The system of central control and managerially imposed user-centeredness favours a superficial, formalistic, and nongenuine attitude towards the patient. Community psychiatry with its modalities of assertive outreach and home treatment could only have been developed with a degree of ignorance of the true extent to which the "community" is pathogenic.

Few were warning against the process of deinstitutionalisation (which had assumed that institutional care for the mentally ill is inherently abusive and destructive) and, in efforts to keep alive the fantasy of community psychiatry, staff are burning out and large resources are spent. Not only does the history of the Retreat demonstrate that institutional care can be conducted in a manner that prevents abuse, but also that institutional care may be a more humane treatment alternative for many patients who cannot but face ridicule, abuse, and other forms of rejection in a "community" that itself undergoes disintegration. In fact, increasing tendencies of fragmentation, competitiveness, materialism, and moral decay in today's society may render well-run institutions particularly valuable as environments that integrate and consistently value the mentally ill.

## 8.5   Cultural construction of self and identity

> Every old-fashioned farmer knows who he is—and is proud of it! The desperate search for an identity—a subject often discussed in our newspapers and a problem that besets modern youth is a symptom of a hiatus in the continuum of our cultural tradition, and it is extremely difficult to help those who are caught up in this predicament. If a man loses contact with the culture in which he has grown up, and finds no intellectual substitute for it in another culture, he has no chance to identify with anyone or anything: he is a nobody, a nothing, as one can see in the despairing emptiness of so many young people's faces today. A man who has lost his cultural inheritance is indeed disinherited. Small wonder that he frantically takes refuge behind a protective wall of dogged autism and becomes an enemy of society. (Lorenz, 1973, p. 206)

Lorenz (1963) spoke of "the ever-increasing danger of human society's becoming disintegrated by the misfunctioning of social behaviour patterns"—a danger, which he felt demanded insight into the causation of human behaviour, yet his prediction that "in the very near future … people will consider as an obvious and banal truth all that has been said … about instincts in general and intraspecific aggression in particular" (p. 267) has not come true. Freud (1930), in view of man's reluctance to consider the true mechanisms underlying social behaviour, was similarly pessimistic; he refrained form the "enthusiastic prejudice" that the path of civilisation "will necessarily lead us to heights of perfection hitherto undreamt of"; but, considering the direction of our "cultural endeavour", he felt more inclined to conclude that "the whole effort is not worth the trouble and can only result in a state of affairs that the individual is bound to find intolerable" (p. 81).

Questions that need to be asked are: (i) how do humans, and society at large, adjust to, or metabolise, intraspecific aggression in the absence of clear value systems and ranking order that were characteristic of more traditional groups; and (ii) how is existential anxiety, which has become uncontainable as a result of erosion of culturally evolved norms and rituals, negotiated intrapsychically, and how does it dissipate into structures and institutions of society. Understanding the nature and origin of heightened self-awareness or self-concern of the individual in modernity is relevant to these questions; and it would pave the way to a fuller understanding of psychopathology. Mental illness is not an individual phenomenon, not a disease that, in the common sense, afflicts the individual, but, in most cases, essentially an interpersonal phenomenon that cannot be seen in isolation from cultural processes.

### 8.5.1   Erosion of traditions

Technological progress and the resulting economic growth contribute to an erosion of cultural traditions and, hence, increase ontological insecurity. Concepts such as agency, choice, and rationality are not only an illusion, albeit a systemically (economically) necessary one, they, in themselves, contribute to a rise in existential anxiety—a rise that cannot be contained any longer by traditional forms of human relatedness and that, therefore, has to spill over into new social and psychopathological phenomena. Technological progress fosters attitudes of rationality and efficiency, compounding the effects of Enlightenment on how humans view themselves. The problem with technological progress, according to Jacques Ellul, "is not just one of machines but also of technique with its emphasis on rationality and efficiency being applied in every field of human activity" (Griffiths, 1982, p. 24).

> But when technique enters into every area of life, including the human, it ceases to be external to man and becomes his very substance. It is no longer face to face with him but is integrated with him and it progressively absorbs him. (Ellul, 1964)

Mishan (1967) suggested that "it is now reasonable to believe that, despite the abundance of man-made goods produced by continued growth, its net effect on human heath and happiness could be adverse and possible disastrous" (p. 9).[2] The starting point of Mishan's analysis was that "despite periods of sustained economic growth and increasing prosperity all social statistics indicate a growing sense of malaise and unfulfilment" (Griffiths, 1982, p. 18).

> Modern economic growth, and the norms and attitudes it establishes, have produced a highly complex industrial and urban organisation, albeit one that is increasingly vulnerable, largely because the spread of affluence and the sheer rapidity of change, have combined, unavoidably to undermine the complex of institutions and myths that invested all pre-industrial civilisations with stability and cohesion. The existing libertarian order in the West is no longer rooted in a consensus that

drains its inspiration ultimately from a common set of unquestioned beliefs. The legitimacy of all its institutions are perpetually under assault. Social order is visibly disintegrating. (Mishan, 1977, p. 265)

Schumpeter (1942) thought that the self-destruction of capitalism as a system is inherent in its success (reviewed in Griffiths, 1982, p. 22). He predicted that the process of expansion would "destroy the protecting strata—aristocracy, farmers and small business—on which it depended"; and "it would foster a rational spirit and criticism which would turn in on itself and which is highlighted by a class of intellectuals who … have a 'vested interest in social unrest'" (Griffiths, 1982, p. 22). Reviewing Schumpeter, Griffiths wrote:

> The problem with capitalism was not that that it would fail, but that it would continue its remarkable success in raising real output and real consumption per capita, which in turn would have the effects of undermining those very social institutions on which its success depended, and creating a civilisation hostile to its continued existence. (Griffiths, 1982, p. 22)

### 8.5.2   Self as a substitute value base

In adapting to socio-economic forces unfolding in the context of technological advances, Western selfhood underwent major changes (Baumeister, 1997). As social relationships have become temporary and unstable, the need became paramount to have an attractive, likable, and competent self to serve as a tool for gaining access to groups, attracting partners, and retaining relationships. Transience of social relationships, as a pervasive feature of modern Western society, gave rise, according to Baumeister (1997), to the belief that the self is "a hidden entity that exists inside the person" and that is independent from society. Self-esteem, which is a "private measure of one's suitability for interpersonal relationships" and eligibility for inclusion into social groups

[2]As cited by Griffiths (1982, p. 18).

based on one's characteristics, became a modern preoccupation. Social pressure to construct and maintain a highly attractive, competent, and successful self that is worthy of admiration by others is a continuous source of stress; and a crisis may ensue if something happens that casts the self in a less desirable light (Baumeister, 1997). Western society has gradually undermined its value basis in tradition, family and religion; the "important cultural response to the value gap" was "to transform the self into a major value base"—a value base that is inherently fragile (Baumeister, 1997). The self in modernity has come to replace one's sense of relatedness to others, to a stable social order. Self-culture and individualism increase, through further destruction of traditions and norms, the very existential anxiety on which they thrive.

> If individuals are no longer bound by rigidly circumscribed conventions, they are free to maneuver among different patterns of conduct, always intent on choosing the alternative that promises the best return from others and from one's reflected self-esteem. (Danziger, 1997, p. 146)

The loss of traditional social distinctions and the loosening of common social expectations (common standards) has caused increasing uncertainties in self-evaluation, at a time when "the normative pressure on individuals to engage in self-assessment is stronger than ever" (Danziger, 1997). People in modern Western society are constantly vigilant against potential threats to their positive self-image, even if they do not encounter major humiliation or disgrace, so that self-awareness takes on "an aversive aspect" and is often "tinged with worry or stress" (Baumeister, 1997). To deal with these stresses, people engage in self-seeking (with the aim of disentangling trends of self-deception) and self-actualisation (self-realisation through hobbies, work, or other pursuits). Modern society "must motivate people to work by mobilising the self as a relevant, potent value base". Thus, work, as a "vital means

of glorifying and fulfilling the self", can reduce the sense of interpersonal insecurity arising from fragmentation of traditional social networks and loss of traditional value systems (Baumeister, 1997).

> [T]he careerist aims to accumulate a record of promotions, achievements, and honours that will reflect favourably on the self. Hence people work very hard at things they personally may care rather little about in order to gain respect and esteem through their achievements. The value that drives them is the value placed on the self. (Baumeister, 1997)

The self in modern Western culture has become a basis for making moral decisions. The process of choice in modern society has become one "involving looking inside oneself to discover the correct attitude or nature of one's inner self" (Baumeister, 1997). These processes in society fostered by technological progress have heightened the sense of self as vulnerable and fundamentally anxious; and they have helped to enshrine in culture the conviction that the self is a free and responsible agent.

### 8.5.3   Self as a life project

Giddens (1997) argued that "abstract systems" and "expert knowledges", which pervade every aspect of social, economic, and personal life in modernity, have undermined forms of local control and self-determination (local disempowerment). Insofar as "abstract systems" and "expert knowledges" generate uncertainties (low-probability, high-consequence risks), risk assessment has become the dominant mode of subjective experience. Giddens (1997) conceptualised "reflexive self-consciousness" as the counterpart of risk, much as self-esteem may be the counterpart of anxiety (which entails risk assessment behaviour, in general). The growing concern with risk evaluation in modern society goes hand in hand with the loss of sense of social belonging, as recognised by Giddens (1997), however it can be objected that ontological insecurity in modernity may *not* be the product of risks borne out of technological progress but, on the contrary, risk awareness, risk aversion, and "reflexive self-consciousness" are manifestations of ontological insecurity due to the loss of a sense of belonging. Only inasmuch as traditional sources of collective identity (the traditional narrative of collective beings) are being replaced in modernity, does selfhood of the individual emerge as a "reflexive project". Giddens (1997) recognised that the self emerges inasmuch as the individual is freed from the restraints of traditional societies, yet its concern with risk is a manifestation of increasing ontological insecurity and cannot be seen as evidence for its liberation or emancipation. What Giddens described as liberation of social relations from local contexts of interaction (disembedding) can equally be seen as enslavement by existential anxiety, compelling the individual to pay incessant attention to his reflection in an increasingly fluid and uncertain environment.

Giddens (1997) argued that individuals involved in operations of modern society must actively determine their personal goals and commitments. Individual "life politics" (concerned with these determinations) is the project of sustaining "authenticity" in the context of demands imposed by "abstract systems" and "expert knowledges". In one's pursuit of self-realisation, "abstract systems" give rise to fundamental questions about the authenticity of one's life project. Giddens (1997) maintained that "life-political issues supply the central agenda for the return of the institutionally repressed". Not only debates about risk and concerns with life politics, but political and social debates, in general, can be regarded as processes of social redistribution of anxiety, processes that emerge, through self-organisation, from an interplay of individual adaptations to the transience and fragility of relatedness. Modern society has found mechanisms to channel, and effectively neutralise, the rising tide of ontological insecurity in the masses: the media. Baudrillard (1999) illuminated some of the system-theoretical dynamics in this respect. He concluded that

Western experience in late capitalism has become one of weightlessness and lack of reality rather than progress and Enlightenment. There can be no true choices or responsibilities for individuals other than those "recycled" in self-referential, autonomous systems through which existential anxiety dissipates on a societal level. The self has been infinitely extended through the interface of the human and the technological, as Giddens (1997) proposed, but only insofar as we take "reflective self-experience" as a manifestation of increased anxiety driving the proliferation of defences. The self in modernity has not suddenly become an agent. Decisions made by an apparently reasonable agent—one's self—are guided, in fact, by unconscious forces that aim to defend against ontological insecurity and to ameliorate the "aversive aspect" (Baumeister, 1997) of self-awareness.

## 8.6   Summary

What binds the group together is "the connection between the leader of the group and single members of the group", which "is particularly strong, whereas the bond between the members of the group is otherwise comparatively weak"; the leader of the group "represents father and mother" to members of the group (Schilder, 1951). The leader, serving the function of the primary object for each member of the group, is the target for libidinal and aggressive impulses, which members generate as they try to keep at bay their anxieties (Bion, 1961). Group members have a "desperate need for an omniscient and omnipotent leader" who can fulfil their dependency needs (Parloff, 1968). Group membership offers "to all members a reasonable security in getting the essentials of life—food, protection and sex gratification" (Schilder, 1951), replicating some of the functions of the child's relationship with his primary object. A primate infant looks to his mothers for protection; later in life, the animal seeks refuge with a high-ranking member of the group (Eibl-Eibesfeldt, 1970). Flight towards a high-ranking member of the group or the leader replaces the infant's flight towards the mother. Fear unites the group by activating flight behaviour towards one another (conspecifics acting as "goals-in-flight")—behaviour that is a developmental extension of infantile attachment behaviour. Dominance relationships in the group replicate the parent-child relationship, given that "the dominant individual acts in a fatherly manner and the subordinate in a childishly dependent manner" (Eibl-Eibesfeldt, 1970).

We have a need for approval and praise from the "dominant other" or leader of a group, which, in part, motivates our belonging to a group (Arieti, 1973). Similarly to the "idealised parent imago", the leader of a group or the "psychological image" of the organisation to which one belongs can provide self-confirming selfobject experiences. We have a desire to *merge* with an object or organisation that would provide "idealizing selfobject experiences" (Kohut, 1971; Wolf, 1988). Members of a group strive "to become fused with the group, and to merge their identity into the group identity"; their identification with the group is "a repetition of early symbiotic gratification" (Agazarian & Peters, 1981). Early symbiotic gratification is afforded by primary identification with the object. "Introjective identification" (primary identification) with the object is based on empathy and affective attunement with the object. Introjective identification with the leader—a form of intermittent attunement and merger with the leader—is part of what holds the group together. Object choice by members of the group "has regressed to identification", wherein the ego "assumes the characteristics of the object" (Freud, 1921). Introjective identification of members of the group with their leader (identification through introjection of the object) provides the group with a common tie (Bion, 1961; Freud, 1921).

Introjective identification (primary identification) means that self and other are indistinguishable. The distinction between self and other arises as the individual's relationship with the group and its leader becomes looser or more flexible. In cultural history, the self emerges, as the primal group disintegrates, from "something greater". Conversely, enthusiasm for a common cause and participation in "something greater" dissolves one's self (and one's individuality) (Horney, 1937). Surrendering oneself to a common cause, and feeling "at one with a greater whole", overcomes one's sense of isolation and affords protection against anxiety (Horney, 1937). The sense of self—which is what tends to dissolve in a stable and well ordered group—manifests the organism's *striving* for relatedness, it's need for predictable social order ("social orientation"). One's preserved potential to be included in flexible social constellations is experienced as self-esteem and a guard against anxiety. Enthusiasm for a cause may be similar to the experience of elevated self-esteem. This is to say that the feeling of elevated self-esteem may be equivalent to the feeling that arises when one *loses oneself* in something greater, in the group or society one associates with. Thus, anxiety associated with unrelatedness to the social milieu and unpredictability of the social situation can be overcome in one of two ways: by enhancing one's self-esteem through the accretion of symbols of approvability (ensuring the receipt of approval from others) or by dissolving one's self in the group. It appears that anxiety is both the counterpart of self-esteem and a condition for the emergence of the sense of self.

The group setting engenders rivalries for the leader's attention and approval (Parloff, 1968), not unlike the rivalries for the object's attention and approval that occur in the oedipal period or between siblings. Through identification with the leader, group members overcome their rivalries and hostile attitudes towards each other (Freud, 1921). In the oedipal period, similar rivalries are overcome by way of *secondary identification* with the paternal object. In group processes, members may overcome rivalries for the leader's attention by identifying with each other (secondary identification). Secondary identification, in a group context, is one's identification with other members of the group who have a relationship with the leader. Secondary identification in the group process is similar to the child's identification with his father in an unconscious attempt to retain the libidinal relationships with his mother. Competition in the group for access to resources—including resources administered by the group's leader and narcissistic gratifications provided by the leader—is regulated "by facilitating, even ensuring, that associates can monitor one another's activities" (Moynihan, 1998). Member's of the group monitor others' adherence to a common standard, others' attitudes, and others' intentions with regards to access to resources. Such monitoring involves identification (based on empathy) of group members with each other. Secondary identification enables group members to emulate role models who have been successful in attaining the leader's attention and approval (Figure 8-1).

Each member of the group adopts a "common standard" and a common *ideal* in order to harness the leader's approval and be close to the leader's centre of attention. Moreover, diversion from common standards and traditions is responded to aggressively. The group setting relieves members of the group of their fear of mutual hostility (Schilder, 1951), but only insofar as members adhere to an "average rule of conduct". The aggression of group members is absorbed (and suppressed) by their adherence to this "average rule of conduct" (Schilder, 1951), and aggression is released by divergence

from this average rule. Inasmuch as aggression is inhibited from within the group, it is diverted towards outside groups. The release of collective aggression toward a common enemy may be a symptom of cohesion in the group, or it may be a mechanism through which cohesion of the group is maintained (Eibl-Eibesfeldt, 1970; Lorenz, 1963; Schilder, 1951). Thus, intraspecific aggression and the need for approval and attention from the group leader are two mechanisms that enforce common standards and normative behaviour—two mechanisms that, in child development, underpin the formation of the punitive superego and the narcissistically cathected ego ideal. The ego ideal and superego are developmental achievements dependent on the process of secondary identification. The relationship between ego ideal and superego transposes onto another level the developmentally earlier relationship between ego and object—an earlier relationship that was founded on (emerged from) primary identification (introjective identification). The superego can be seen as the internal representation of derivatives of the primary object, including the group leader and earlier teachers, with which the ego, acting as ego ideal, has or has had a relationship (on Lacan's "symbolic" plane). The superego

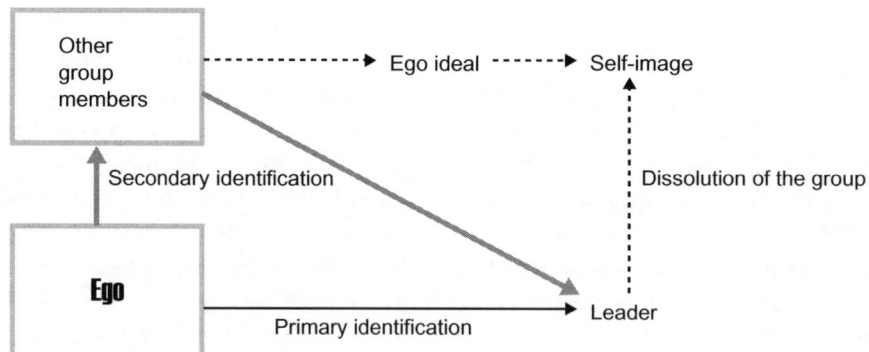

Figure 8-1.   The process of identification is related to, and may have evolved from, functions of imitation and empathy. Primary identification (characterising Lacan's "mirror stage") underpins one's relationship with the leader of a group. Secondary identification, in a group context, is one's identification with other members of the group who have a relationship with the leader (Oedipus complex). Secondary identification contributes to the formation of ego ideal and self-image (the latter being an instantiation of the ego ideal). While primary identification operates in the dyadic context, secondary identification operates when one monitors one's social environment.

is, in part, an internalised abstraction of the leader of the group, and, in the formation of a group, each member of the group *regressively* substitutes the leader for his superego (Hartmann, 1964). In other words, the leader becomes an external replica of the superego, while the group member adopts the role of his own ego ideal. Sharing the same ego ideal, group members can identify with each other (Freud, 1921). These regressive tendencies in members of a group "intensify the individual's readiness for cooperation" (Hartmann, 1964).

Imitation of, and, especially, affective attunement to, a conspecific with whom the subject is directly engaged is involved in the psychodynamic mechanism of primary identification. Subtle imitation of conspecifics with whom the subject is not directly engaged may be related to secondary identification. The ability to imitate conspecifics, to emulate their attitudes towards others, and to ascertain their social intentions plays a role in the acquisition of social knowledge from conspecifics and in the propagation of culture. Secondary identification with conspecifics may have enabled the cultural propagation of complex social attitudes and standards without the need to undergo repeated punishments for deviant attitudes and standards. The superego and ego ideal are formed by many secondary identifications; the superego, it appears, is not simply a representation of accumulated social avoidance learning. The superego would have formed in phylogeny when members of a group started to use secondary identification (over and above avoidance learning) as a means of acquiring standards that avoid exposure to social punishment. Owing to secondary identification, compliance with norms could be acquired not only as a result of exposure to social punishment (avoidance learning) but also through subtle imitation of others' social behaviour—imitations that would be reinforced by rewarding approval and attention from the leader of the group.

With the evolvement of civilisation, closely integrated social groups were gradually replaced by looser social formations. Identification with others in the group was replaced by *identification with an image of the self*, an image formed in a process of recurrent identification with different conspecifics acting as role models in different social situations and at different stages of personality development. The contention is that individuals started to identify with an image of themselves (derived from their ego ideal) when, historically, they were taken out of a context of close and stable groups (hordes). Thus, the self-image, that is, the individual's identification with himself in imagination, derives from the individual's identification with others in the group. The self replaces, and is a substitute for, the individual's close integration into his group. The self became a cultural phenomenon in itself insofar as social networks disintegrated and insofar as, in an increasingly fluid society, individuals had to associate themselves intermittently and more transiently with variable social formations. At the same time, self-esteem, that is, one's experience of security in a social situation, became more elusive, facilitating the repeated simulation in imagination of self-images that act as goals or desired outcomes of social behaviour. Security in a social situation, and, hence, self-esteem, are defined contextually by one's relatedness to others and others' position in the social hierarchy as well as by others' adherence to norms and standards. Other's failure to adhere to norms and standards, or a sudden shift in norms or standards for other reasons, undermines one's relatedness to the group and, hence, one's security and elicits one's offensive aggression, inasmuch as it pierces the boundaries that define one's "territory" in a hierarchical social system. Ones's sense of social position or territory (ascertained through social orientation), one's sense of one's capacity to attract narcissistic supplies (self-esteem), one's anticipatory self-image (indicating a desired social position associated with a desired security of narcissistic supplies) (Horney, 1950; Moore, 1926), and the self as a "reflexive project" (Giddens, 1997) or "value base" (Baumeister, 1997) (a narcissistically cathected object) appear to be reflections of different degrees of ontological insecurity and social unpredictability.

# CHAPTER NINE

# Mental disorder

Shapiro (2000) thought that "it may be possible to understand the varieties of psychopathology, with their enormously diverse symptoms, as variations of the mind's organizing and regulating systems" (p. 6).

> It is well known that in nonpsychotic pathology, at least, the defense organization and the attitudes it involves also have adaptive aspects. The compulsive's productiveness, not infrequently even the hypomanic's productiveness, the hysteric's social appeal, in some circumstances the psychopath's capacity for quick action and, up to a point, the suspicious person's eye for the hidden irregularity all may have adaptive value. These adaptive capacities reflect the essential nature of the defense processes. In other words, the adaptive advantages of defense styles … are capacities intrinsic to those styles, and their adaptive value may well have been important in their development. (Shapiro, 2000, pp. 43–44)

The form of neurotic symptoms and, if we are correct, the form of schizophrenic symptoms as well, require for their understanding a more inclusive picture of dynamics, a picture that recognizes the *forms* of thinking and modes of activity as central to the mind's regulatory system. That regulatory system, the individual character organization, … may indeed be affected by variations of individual biology as well as by personal history, but the existence of a psychological mental apparatus that includes the individual forms of cognition makes the assumption that cognitive deficiencies must have direct biological causes unnecessary. (Shapiro, 2000, p. 135)

Existential anxiety (ontological insecurity), attributable to the developmental persistence of the infant's separation distress, propels us to establish and maintain relationships with others (relationships on the basis of mutual approval or affection), however membership of groups and participation in social gatherings exposes us to the potential of intraspecific aggression. The contention is that the instinctive "ganging up against an individual diverging from the social norms characteristic of a group" (Lorenz, 1963, p. 251) lies at the heart not only of social conformity but also importantly contributes to mental illness in those who are vulnerable. What is most effective in attracting others' aggression is our failure, for one or another reason, to conform to the group's norms and expectations. Our ability to conform may be limited as a result of a disturbed early childhood or due to organic brain impairment. Excessive fear of others' aggression may not only be the result of adverse early-life experiences but also a manifestation of constitutionally heightened sensitivity to aversive stimulation in general. Others' aggression threatens our membership of groups, excludes us from sustaining object relations, and leaves us with uncontained existential anxiety, which mobilises our own aggression and escalates our drive to relate, thereby adding to our vulnerability to become the target of others' aggression. Ultimately, chronically high levels of existential anxiety and fear of aggression channel into one form or another of defensive organisation or mental illness in accordance with individual biological predispositions.

> We all suffer to some extent from the necessity of controlling our natural inclinations by the exercise of moral responsibility. Some of us, lavishly endowed with social inclinations, suffer hardly at all, other less lucky ones need all the strength of their sense of moral responsibility to keep them from getting into trouble with the strict requirements of modern society. According to a useful old psychiatric definition, a psychopath is a man who either suffers himself from the demands of society or else makes society suffer. Thus in one sense we are all psychopaths, for each of us suffers from the necessity of self-imposed control for the good of the community. The above mentioned definition, however, was meant to apply particularly to those people who do not suffer in secret, but overtly break down under the stress imposed upon them,

> becoming either neurotic or delinquent. (Lorenz, 1963, p. 246)

### 9.1   Neuroses

> As we know, it is not in the actual structure of his mind that the normal man differs from the neurotic, but in the quantitative factors at work. (Klein, 1932, p. 201)

Fixation in the paranoid-schizoid infantile developmental position or failure to resolve the depressive infantile developmental position render individuals vulnerable to psychological suffering. Inability to save and repair internal loved objects remains a lifelong problem for those who have not successfully overcome the depressive position (Klein, 1940). Lacking secure internal objects, individuals are engaged in lifelong attempts to overcome anxieties resulting from the loss of the primary object (mother/breast). Lack of close and happy relationships confirms fears of annihilation from inside (and persecution from outside). External reality cannot provide proof for the groundlessness of the individual's insecurities and worries about his internal world. Insecurity and worries constantly incite a need to observe the world of external objects. Defences used to avoid the suffering of the depressive position include an excessive turning to external good objects, which can manifest as neurosis (Klein, 1940). The neurotic person is totally dependent on others for self-evaluation; his self-esteem (pride) rises or falls with the attitudes of others towards him (Horney, 1950, p. 137). Individuals with a neurotic disposition are inclined to make pleasant experiences part of their self; they "introject" parts of the outside world (Ferenczi, 1916). Those with a paranoiac disposition, by contrast, get rid of unpleasant feelings by "projecting" them onto the external world. Paranoiac projection and neurotic introjection are extreme cases of psychical processes that can be demonstrated in every normal human being (Ferenczi, 1916).

Instead of developing a basic confidence in self and others the child developed basic anxiety, which I defined as a feeling of being isolated and helpless toward a world potentially hostile. In order to keep this basic anxiety at a minimum the spontaneous moves toward, against, and away from others became compulsive. (Horney, 1950, p. 366)

Fragility of self-esteem (corresponding to inner insecurity and liability to feel anxious) is the starting point for "the compulsive drive for worldly glory through success, power, and triumph" (Horney, 1950, p. 368). Compensating for an inner insecurity (inferiority), the neurotic person strives for power and superiority (Adler, 1965). In order to satisfy the innate need for affection and admiration (the need for narcissistic supplies), the child "must cultivate within himself" qualities and attitudes "in the service of such a need" (Horney, 1950, p. 367). From the ego ideal (the precipitate of such qualities and attitudes) formed in the oedipal period (as an aspect of the superego), an idealised self can emerge in imagination. The person is "bent on actualizing his idealized self"; and, under "the tyrannical inner system" of dictates (the "shoulds and taboos"), "he tries to mold himself into a godlike being" (Horney, 1950, p. 368). Being driven to actualise his idealised self, the neurotic patient is "liable to expect an unreasonable amount from others"; he is liable to make "claims" on others, to the fulfilment of which he feels entitled (Horney, 1950, p. 370). Idealising his self in imagination, the person is bound to fail in his efforts to actualise his anticipatory self image and, therefore, to hate his actual being (for not being able to "make himself over into something he is not") (p. 374). This is what Horney (1950) thought lies at the heart of neurosis. The more a person idealises himself (and the more he is, thus, "alienated" from his real self), the more he hates and despises himself "for being as he is" (p. 373). The neurotic process "is a process of abandoning the real self for an idealized one; of

trying to actualize this pseudoself instead of our given human potentials; of a destructive warfare between the two selves" (Horney, 1950, p. 376).

Some, instead of accepting the situation as it is, blind themselves to reality and dream that they are what they only wish to be. These are proud and vain pretenders whom the world recognizes as such, but who have no insight into their own disability. Others, unable to accept the situation as it is, unable to compensate by dreams, unable to find an outlet in any other channel, react to an intolerable situation by some one of the many types of mental breakdown. At the root of every mental breakdown—every parataxis, every psychoneurosis, every psychosis—is the conflict over the realization of the self-ideal. (Moore, 1926, p. 175)[1]

### 9.1.1  Reproaches

"Claims" (to be given a higher social position or to have one's needs met by others) are means of actualising the neurotic person's "idealised self" (representing his prospect of future possibilities, of a glorious future); "*claims are his guaranty for future glory*" (Horney, 1950, p. 62). The idealised self encapsulates the neurotic person's "desire to have his many compulsive needs fulfilled by others" (p. 63). The neurotic person, "raising his needs to the dignity of claims" (p. 63), responds with indignation and hostility to a frustration of his "justified" claims. If he feels frustrated by somebody, "that person suddenly becomes untrustworthy, nasty, cruel, contemptible—i.e., this indignation drastically influences our judgement of others" (Horney, 1950, p. 56). The person to whom a "wrong" has been done and who is convinced of his righteousness ponders "the hateful qualities of somebody" and "feels

---

[1]Moore (1926) defined parataxes as abnormal emotional adjustments.

the impulse to get back at others" (p. 57). Thus, frustration can turn via anger into aggression. If the expression of anger is not warranted by the situation or is socially unacceptable, "one will have to exaggerate the wrong done; one will then inadvertently build up a case against the offender that looks logic tight" (p. 56). If anger cannot be expressed, one becomes despondent or plunges "into misery and self-pity" (p. 57), or anger may "appear in psychosomatic symptoms" (p. 56). Then, suffering may become "the medium to express reproaches" (Horney, 1950, p. 57).

### 9.1.2  Social anxiety disorder

Patients with social anxiety disorder ("social neurosis") react to social situations with a high degree of anxiety (Schilder, 1951). The danger which is feared by the patient is indistinct and uncertain. When a patient becomes sure of the hostility of others, or when he blames others, rather than himself, social anxiety disappears and outspoken paranoia emerges. Erythrophobia and stammering are conditions related to (but not identical with) social neurosis (Schilder, 1951). The fear of being seen or observed by others and a resulting paranoid attitude play a greater part in erythrophobia than in social neurosis. In stammering, the patient's counteraggression comes into the foreground; whereby speech "becomes the weapon which the patient would like to use" (p. 90). In social neurosis, symptoms of shaking, sweating, and dryness of mouth as well as the giving way of the voice serve to deny (unconsciously) that aggressive action (including "oral aggression") is intended; instead, "the superiority of the other person is acknowledged" (p. 93). Inhibition of social conduct, a characteristic feature of social anxiety, occurs especially "in the presence of specific persons socially or professionally superior" (Schilder, 1951, p. 77). The patient with social neurosis tends to avoid all situations in which he "has to meet other persons and especially groups" (p. 78), however, even when social contacts are avoided, "the patient is usually surrounded by an imaginary society in

which he lives intensely" (p. 93). The patient may drink alcohol excessively in order to escape his social difficulties (Schilder, 1951).[2]

> It is characteristic that social contacts are all of the same level. Everybody has an importance. He wants everybody's admiration and appreciation. Sensitiveness and irritability may follow, and harmless remarks may provoke the full impression of complete rejection. A reactive hostile reaction follows in some cases, but this is comparatively rare. The symptoms will multiply in proportion to the number of individuals present. Persons who otherwise do not show symptoms of this type when faced by an audience may show symptoms of stage fright in which the speech phenomena and forgetting or inability to think clearly are outstanding. In approaching heterosexual love objects, the symptoms are very often present, especially in cases in which the parent of the same sex was the aggressor. (Schilder, 1951, p. 93)

> In many cases the shyness leads to a more or less complete blocking. The patient may be unable to clearly formulate any thoughts and may remain silent against his will. The patient may also prefer to remain silent instead of saying banal and unimportant things. (Schilder, 1951, p. 77)

#### Pathogenesis

Narcissism (self-love) is of paramount importance in "social neurosis" (social anxiety disorder) (Schilder, 1951). Healthy or pathological self-admiration and self-love are contingent upon "a continuous stream of appreciation coming

---

[2] In Schilder's time, treatment with "benzedrine, which intensifies interhuman relations and gives the feeling of being appreciated and loved, has been successful" (p. 94).

from other human beings" (p. 91). Moreover, "self-appreciation of the individual is dependent upon the appreciation given by early love objects" (p. 94). The child "builds up the consciousness of itself by the love and appreciation it gets from its surroundings" (Schilder, 1951, p. 91). The patient with increased narcissism and heightened demands for appreciation insists "that he should get the same exaggerated admiration from himself and others that he received from his parents" (p. 90). If, due to adverse infantile experiences, "demands for self-appreciation" are heightened, "the amount of appreciation offered in social contacts will become insufficient" (p. 91). Social neurosis first manifests at the time of puberty, "when the individual demands not only social but also sexual recognition and finds that he cannot get them in full measure" (p. 92). As the socially anxious individual "becomes dependent upon the social surroundings which take the place of the parents", his "exaggerated infantile demands concerning recognition in the widest sense are no longer satisfied" (Schilder, 1951, p. 92).

> Self-appreciation can only be sustained when supported by the continuous approval of others. The appreciation of others becomes insufficient in this respect when the individual demands from himself an extraordinarily high degree of self-admiration and self-love. (Schilder, 1951, p. 94)

Patients with social neurosis "have the ideal of having poise and social grace" (Schilder, 1951, p. 93). They have strong wishes for beauty or intelligence and harbour a "fear of an impairment of attractiveness or narcissism of a high degree" (p. 82). Patients are concerned that others might consider them unattractive or intellectually inferior; and their concerns about inferiority are often increased as a result of their inadequacy in social situations. These wishes and fears may act as "safeguards against a too dangerous submission and masochism" (Schilder, 1951, p. 82).

Complete submission is an alternative, albeit for some people dangerous, way of gaining the love of the object (or of its derivatives). Patients with social neurosis are unable to submit to others (in order to not admit, to themselves and others, their inferiority and vulnerability); they also find themselves unable to control or dominate others (fearing others' retaliation). Patients find it difficult to actively solicit appreciation or affection from others. Schilder (1951) noted that the position adopted by these patients in social situations is a passive one. In childhood, they may have been "pushed into a passive position" by their "parents' strictness and aggressiveness" (Schilder, 1951, p. 91).

### 9.1.3  Obsessions and compulsions

Klein (1932) thought that "anxiety belonging to the early danger-situations" is "closely associated with the beginnings of obsessions and obsessional neuroses" (p. 231). Order and cleanliness are reaction formations against an anxiety that originates in the child's earliest danger situations. Obsessive acts serve the purpose of mastering anxiety (p. 231). Anxiety, being allied with uncertainty, "gives rise to an obsessive desire for knowledge", that is, for certainty (p. 231). The individual seeks to overcome doubt and uncertainty, and hence anxiety, "by being overprecise" (p. 231). Anxiety, or rather the uncertainty that is inherent in it, gives rise to "inclinations towards exactness and order and towards the observance of certain rules and rituals" (Klein, 1932, p. 231). The early danger situations, against which order and cleanliness are reaction formations, arise from primitive superego pressures, signifying an uncertain expectation of social punishment. The severe superego which figures in obsessional neurosis "is no other than the unmodified, terrifying super-ego belonging to early stages of the child's development" (Klein, 1932, p. 229). Kernberg (1996) suggested that, in patients with obsessive-compulsive personality disorder, "inordinate aggression has been neutralized by its absorption into a well-integrated, but excessively sadistic superego, leading to the perfectionism, self-doubts, and chronic need to control the environment as well as the self that are characteristic of this personality disorder" (p. 125).

Obsessional ideas and compulsive behaviours in patients with obsessive-compulsive personality disorder are considered to be ego-syntonic. By contrast, in obsessive-compulsive disorder *per se*, compulsions and obsessions are characteristically "egodystonic": they are accompanied by inner resistance reflecting a conflict between drives. Conflict may arise between an urge to escape a hazard and a fear of punishment for doing so. Expectations of punishment, conceptualised as fear of the superego, relate to the patient's preserved insight into the abnormality and social unacceptability of his compulsions and are the source of much of his suffering. Obsessive thoughts about harming or offending others elicit fears of social ostracism, representing an acute conflict between the individual's aggressive impulses and a fear of attracting attack or punishment from others (the latter being an externalised fear of punishment by the superego). The point is that obsessive and compulsive phenomena are not just exaggerated versions of risk avoidance behaviour, but are crucially intertwined with fear of attack from others (for performing these behaviours).[3]

## Sense of precariousness

The obsessional person always watches out for danger. He "has to be ready to avoid any danger from the world outside and to parry, like a fencer in a duel, any possible attack from others"; "the dangers he fears are dangers seen from the perspective of pessimism and distrust; the attacks he fears often have to do with blame and rejection" (Schachtel, 1973, p. 45). The obsessional person is prepared for a battle with the other, whereby his "readiness to fight about logical points and his search for the right rules are intensely emotional" (p. 46). He is preoccupied with fault in others and in himself. He is ready "to detect any fault or mistake in them; but he must be equally or even more on the alert and watchful about himself, about any fault or mistake in himself" (p. 45), presumably because any fault or mistake would make him vulnerable to attack. An alternative explanation is that "he has to be irreproachable, so that he be spared the painful and repressed possibility of feeling unacceptable" (p. 46). Obsessive persons may isolate their sense of precariousness from its source in the interpersonal sphere "and experience it primarily in relation to the world in general, to daily routines, to things, to technicalities of their work, and in such well-known phenomena as excessive preoccupation with orderliness, exactness, and the like" (Schachtel, 1973, p. 45).

> But even where it is consciously related to people, it is often isolated from its real source and experienced mostly with regard to minute questions of etiquette and similar details of behavior, both in the other person and in the self. The real source of the uncertainty, precariousness, and doubt in the obsessive-compulsive's life … is to be found in his pervasive confusion whether the other person and the world in general are friendly or hostile, accepting and approving or rejecting and blaming. This doubt originates usually in relation to a parent whose behavior is such as to make it difficult or impossible for the young child to experience any understandable and reliable pattern of acceptance or rejection, hence interfering with the development of trust and reasonable certainty. And it makes it equally impossible for him to know whether he is good

---

[3]The motivational conflict between drives, ultimately between existential anxiety urging relatedness and the fear of punishment or aggression, would be expected to activate, in patients with obsessive-compulsive disorder, cortical areas critically involved in conflict monitoring, especially the anterior cingulate gyrus, consistent with findings by Fitzgerald et al. (2005).

(lovable) or bad (unlovable). (Schachtel, 1973, pp. 45–46)

## Attentional focus

The obsessive person inhabits "a world pervaded by a sense of uncertain danger and risk" (Schachtel, 1973, p. 45). His concern with remote or minor dangers requires broad attentional scanning with a narrow focus; "his attention searches a relatively wide area with a narrow and intense focus, looking for danger and cautionary cues, for mistakes and the like" (p. 47). Freud noted that it is difficult for the obsessional person to freely associate. Schachtel (1973) contrasted the attentional mode of "broad scanning with a narrow focus", which is characteristically used by the obsessional person, with a mode of "open attention" employed in the service of global perception and global knowing.

> The motive underlying such open attention does not have any particular, partial purpose; it is the wish to relate to the object, to know it as it is, out of interest in the object. There are many different kinds of interest, but the type of interest I am describing here does not want to use the object but to experience it, to know it fully by relating to it. (Schachtel, 1973, p. 48)

One may wonder whether both, anxiously focused monitoring and "open attention", are modes of activity of the default-mode network, or whether anxiously focused monitoring is a derivative of default-mode activity. Default-mode activity enables us to survey the environment prior to engagement with it; it terminates when we identify an object in relation to which we feel compelled to act. At this point, the obsessive person would likely switch his mode of activity from anxiety to compulsive interaction with an object, restoring certainty to the situation in which he finds himself. Obsessive-compulsive behaviours are varieties of appetitive behaviour, whereas defensive behaviours (fight and flight), which are also facilitated in a state of anxiety, are

instinctive. The former type of anxiety-related behaviours may involve an interaction between hippocampus and ventral striatum, whereas the later would be mediated by an interaction between the hippocampus and hypothalamus via the lateral septum (Figure 10-1).

## Displacement

Miller (1948) suggested that compulsions are habits which are motivated by fear or anxiety and reinforced by a reduction in fear or anxiety. Anxiety forms an important context of compulsive actions. Certain cues or objects, when perceived or imagined by patients with obsessive-compulsive disorder, elicit fears of contamination and washing or cleaning rituals. Other cues may elicit fears about natural hazards endangering one's environment or intrusion by others, leading in vulnerable subjects to compulsive checking. Perception of threats and ideas about possible threats may represent displacements, that is, unconscious attempts to convert anxiety into more concrete forms of fear that allow specific responses. The subject's attention to potential threats may be heightened inasmuch as his anxiety cannot be regulated through secure interpersonal relatedness. Compulsive actions, then, may relieve a specific fear, the immediate motivational impetus behind these actions, but would not substantially alter the background of existential anxiety. Specific fears can be abreacted under most circumstances, but existential anxiety often cannot, because secure social relatedness is often beyond reach for the individual. Anxiety may in fact increase in the course of illness due to social debilitation and stigmatisation. Conversely, helping the patient in therapy to develop secure interpersonal relatedness addresses his anxiety and can reduce obsessions and compulsions (Gabbard, 1990).

## Reparative efforts

Compulsive repetition of actions may be due to the fact that the ultimate motivational force is not addressed: existential anxiety. In the infantile depressive position, attempts to repair loved objects that are damaged by ones destructive impulses may be defeated repeatedly (Klein, 1940). The child cannot trust his constructive and reparative efforts and, hence, the need for compulsive repetition of actions arises. If the depressive position has not been worked through successfully, then, upon reactivation of the depressive position later in life, the subject may compulsively repeat his constructive and reparative efforts, manifesting in obsessive-compulsive disorders (Klein, 1940). The development of obsessive and compulsive phenomena to defend against unbearable anxiety represents an alternative scenario to the development of persecutory delusions. Paranoid psychosis can only develop if the superego regresses to the primitive paranoid fears that were once its origin. If the superego is too strong, resisting any such regression, displacement of anxiety into obsessive or phobic fears may be the only alternative.[4]

### 9.1.4   Conversions

Intolerable ideas or impulses and the resulting emotional conflicts (arising, for instance, from a fear of retaliation for uncontrollable urges) can be "converted" into behavioural, functional, or somatic symptoms (Laughlin, 1970). Converting an unbearable idea or impulse into a physical symptom renders the idea or impulse innocuous. Through conversion, conflicts, which would otherwise give rise to anxiety, can be held in abeyance. The unconscious intent of conversion is to defend against anxiety and to preserve repression (Laughlin, 1970). Repression of an inacceptable and consciously intolerable impulse or idea may be threatened by failure, however conversion can maintain the repression by allowing "the return to consciousness of elements of the

conflict … in a converted and disguised form" (p. 51). Conversion symptoms "allow some measure of disguised external expression" and, hence, partial gratification of disowned impulses (p. 31). Consciously disowned impulses and unconscious conflict over them can be transmuted into loss of sensory or motor function. Paralysis of a limb, loss of the ability to speak (aphonia), functional loss of vision, and other neurological symptoms may be intended to express an intolerable impulse in a consciously more tolerable form and "to secure a position of dependency" at the same time (p. 43). With regard to the related somatoform disorders, hostility can be converted into headaches and other somatic symptoms. Emotional pain can be converted into experiences of bodily pain (Laughlin, 1970).

The "primary gain" associated with conversion is the defence against anxiety (and, hence, maintenance of self-esteem) (Laughlin, 1970). There may be a "secondary gain" for the patient in terms of material advantage or fulfilment of dependency needs. Primarily, conversion symptoms allay anxiety (by maintaining repression) and secure some resolution of, or relief from, the pressure of unconscious conflicts. Conversion symptoms express unconscious impulses and resulting conflicts in symbolic form; which is to say that conversion symptoms convey a message (Laughlin, 1970). Elucidation of the unconscious meaning of a conversion symptom in psychotherapy leads to its dissolution. Elucidation of the symptom "results in the surrender of the symptom, as it becomes more patently an inappropriate means of attempted solution" of the unconscious conflict (p. 36). Maintenance of the patient's self-esteem is a necessary prerequisite for the gradual relinquishing of conversion symptoms through therapy (Laughlin, 1970).

### Behavioural conversion

Consciously disowned impulses and the resulting emotional conflicts can be converted into symbolic behaviour. "Behavioural conversion" is the expression of intrapsychic conflict in

---

[4]If the patient is, at the same time, endowed with heightened aggressiveness, a strong superego may render the development of depression or self-destructiveness as the only possible outcome.

the form of "acting out" (neurotic behaviour). "Behavioural conversion" may be motivated by "inner insecurity, and inferiority and by the need for approval and love" (Laughlin, 1970, p. 41). Patients who are thought of as "acting out" "may express significant hostile or loving feelings in some self-concealed and disguised form of outward action" (p. 39). Again, behavioural conversion allows partial gratification of concealed impulses, and partial resolution of emotional conflicts over them, through one's outward behaviour. Through behavioural conversion, concealed impulses (repressed wishes) can be expressed, and conflicts can be resolved, in a consciously more acceptable form (Laughlin, 1970).

### 9.1.5   Secondary gain

Secondary gain, which "consists in getting attention by being sick" (Fenichel, 1946, p. 461), plays an important role in maintaining illness, especially conversion and somatisation disorders. Illness is "frequently perceived as a right to privileges", such as in the form of loss of responsibilities, and it may bestow intrapsychic economic advantages "by provoking pity, attention, love, the granting of narcissistic supplies" (p. 461). Being ill entails a "longing for the time of childhood when one was taken care of" (p. 461), a "regression to childhood times, when one was still protected" (p. 462). What is often reactivated at times of illness is a "need of a sign of parental affection and of assurance against abandonment" (p. 461). The expression of this need through illness "may in turn arouse guilt feelings, creating secondary conflicts and vicious circles" (p. 461). Finally, some secondary gain may derive from "evaluating symptoms as punishment" (Fenichel, 1946, p. 461).

## 9.2   Personality disorders

The love object is instrumental for attainment of a "feeling of safety", that is, an "ideal state of well-being" (Sandler, 1960). When the love object is lost, the "feeling of safety" or "ideal state of well-being" is lost, too. In relationships, partners unconsciously assign roles to each other and induce each other to respond in certain ways (Sandler & Sandler, 1978). These role relationships (involving mutual manipulations) are motivated by a need to restore feelings of well-being and safety and, thus, to avoid *psychic pain*. Interpersonal relationships, and the individual's relationships to social groups and society at large, all of which represent developmental continuations of early object relations, operate according to the same mechanism. If there is a discrepancy between the "ideal state of well-being" and the actual state of well-being, psychic pain (which is related to physical pain and the sense of frustration) ensues. The individual may react in a variety of ways to this pain, e.g., by "acting out" (through the variety of behaviours that feature in personality disorders) or consumption of drugs or alcohol (reviewed in Mendelson, 1982). If these fail to relieve the pain, helplessness, and depression develop. The "feeling of safety", or "ideal state of well-being", is related to self-esteem, the lowering of which is regarded as central to depression. It is the absence of feelings of safety or well-being that produces psychic pain and eventually leads to depression (Mendelson, 1982).

### 9.2.1   Disorders of the self

"Disorders of the self" (narcissistic and borderline personality disorders, in particular) appear to have become more prevalent over recent decades, while presentations with conversion hysteria and obsessive-compulsive rituals have become less frequent (Wolf, 1988). These "changing patterns in psychological symptomatology" may reflect a historical shift in child rearing patterns from excessive repression of sexuality to breakdown of the extended family and changing social expectations towards women, which resulted in relative scarcity of appropriate self-object experiences in early life. In recent times, the tendency has been for children to feel "uncared for and unresponded to", representing a lack of self-sustaining and self-supporting selfobject experiences in early life (Wolf, 1988, p. 25). Individuals with narcissistic personality structure excessively rely on external supplies of love and approval to maintain their precarious self-esteem. The model advanced by Kohut (1971) and Wolf distinguishes between two types of abnormal personality structure characterised by low self-esteem due to lack of selfobject experiences in early life. First, "mirror hungry personalities" are "impelled to display themselves to evoke the attention of others, who through their admiring responses will perhaps counteract the experience of worthlessness" (p. 78). Second, "ideal hungry personalities" try to find "selfobjects to whom they can look up and by whom they can feel accepted" (p. 73). Alternatively, an individual may have "no expectation of any real interest in him from anybody" manifesting as chronic depression (Wolf, 1988, p. 71).

> The intense suffering associated with pathology of the self impellingly motivates toward amelioration by forcing the environment to yield the required comfort-giving experiences. Intensity of need combined with expectation of rebuff causes deep shame. Stridently expressed demands may alternate with total suppression of them. Demands, whether expressed in fantasy or in behavior, whether they are related to grandiosity or to being accepted by idealized figures, are not derived from the normal healthy self-assertive narcissism of childhood, but from the fragments of archaic selfobject needs or from the defences against them. (Wolf, 1988, p. 74)

Traumatic selfobject experiences in early years predispose the individual to use schizoid mechanisms in later life to keep involvement with others shallow, or to use paranoid mechanisms in order to surround himself "with an aura of hostility and suspicion that will keep noxious selfobjects at bay" (p. 68). Finally, the individual's fragile self-esteem may be protected from

further damage "through perverse, delinquent, or addictive behavior" (Wolf, 1988, p. 69). The incidence of violence and impulsive crime increases inasmuch as society lowers its standard for self-control, whereby low self-esteem can be identified as a mediating factor (Baumeister, Smart & Boden, 1996). Low self-esteem is compensated by "some highly favourable view of self" (egotism), which is easily threatened by "external, unfavourable evaluation" (Baumeister, 1997), leading to increased aggressiveness.

### 9.2.2  Narcissistic personality structure

> In certain rare cases one observes that the ego takes itself as object, and behaves as if it were in love with itself. For this reason we have borrowed the name of "narcissism" from the Greek legend. (Freud, 1933, p. 133)

The capacity of the narcissistic individual for love and emotional relations is impaired. He longs for relatedness to an object, but he cannot maintain object relations in reality. He has to employ defences to prevent depression that would otherwise result from an insight into the absence of real object relations. These defences establish and control object relations internally in fantasy. Freud (1917) thought that, in patients with narcissistic personality structure, libido is withdrawn form external objects and directed at internal, "introjected" objects with which the ego "identifies".

The narcissistic ego has to deny its dependence on real objects, depreciate its objects, and exert "tyrannical mastery" over them in all situations. Omnipotence, which, as the central feature of the patient's "manic attitude", relates to the ego's omnipotent denial of its dependence on its objects and to the ego's omnipotent control over its objects, allows the narcissistic person to attain security and defend against depressive anxieties (Riviere, 1936). The narcissistic patient is unconsciously convinced that any lessening of control on his part will bring back to life his depressive anxieties. The narcissistic patient dreads the depressive position in which he gains insight into his lack of real object relations and into his fundamental loneliness. In the depressive position, the internal objects on which he depends are destroyed; his internal objects die and there is no one to love and no one to feed him. The narcissistic patient is always close to being aware that he lacks real object relations and his narcissistic and omnipotent defences are an attempt to avoid the pain and depression that this insight brings (Riviere, 1936).

> For his object-relations are not real people, his object-relations are all within himself; his inner world is all the world to him. Whatever he does for his objects he does for himself as well; if only he could do it! and in mania he thinks he can. So it is the overwhelming importance of the inner world of his emotional relations that makes him in real life so egocentric, asocial, self-seeking—so fantastic! (Riviere, 1936)

## Superego functioning

In the narcissistic personality, "an integrated, but pathological, grandiose self" goes hand in hand with "a lack of integration of the concept of significant others" (Kernberg, 1996, p. 124). Kernberg (1996) argued that "both real and idealized self and object representations" are absorbed "into an unrealistically idealized concept of self, with a parallel impoverishment of idealized superego structures" (p. 124). This is to say that processes of idealisation and identification fail to make sufficient contributions to later stages of superego development. As a consequence of impoverishment of the idealising layer (the second layer) of the superego, persecutory superego precursors (constituting the first layer of the superego) predominate, and these persecutory superego precursors can be "reprojected" "as a protection against excessive, pathological guilt" (Kernberg, 1996, p. 124). If weakening of more integrated superego functions, which

is characteristic of the narcissistic personality, is combined with an increased disposition to aggression, then the patient may present with "malignant narcissism". In the "malignant narcissism syndrome", features of narcissistic personality disorder exist alongside "antisocial behaviour, ego syntonic aggression, and paranoid tendencies" (p. 124). Kernberg (1996) viewed the "malignant narcissism" syndrome as "intermediate between the narcissistic personality disorder and the antisocial personality disorder proper", the latter being characterised by a total absence of superego functioning and "severe underlying paranoid trends" (p. 124).

## Malignant narcissism

In patients with "malignant narcissism", the earliest sadistic superego precursors dominate the process of superego formation. In this case, prohibitions and expectations from parental objects are devalued or transformed into persecutory threats (Kernberg, 1992). Sadistic superego components are idealised and drawn into a pathological grandiose and sadistic self, "which then militates against the internalization of later, more realistic superego components" (p. 82). For these patients, object relations "contain the seeds for an attack by the omnipotent cruel object" (Kernberg, 1992, p. 82)—unless they show total submission. Subsequent identification with the cruel omnipotent object "gives the subject a sense of power, freedom from fear, and the feeling that the only way to relate to others is by gratifying one's aggression" (p. 82). Patients may alternate between submitting masochistically to the cruel tyrant and identifying with him. Patients with antisocial personality disorder, in contrast, do not idealise, and do not identify themselves with, a cruel tyrant. Unlike patients with malignant narcissism, those with antisocial personality disorder proper do not attempt "masochistic submission" to a sadistic authority (Kernberg, 1992).

Patients with malignant narcissism "are totally convinced of the impotence of any good object relation", which are week and unreliable, whereas powerful and cruel (bad) objects are the ones that "are needed to survive" (Kernberg, 1992, p. 82). The pain of having to depend upon powerful sadistic parental objects is expressed as rage. Excessive envy of good objects is a related feature of narcissistic personality structure. Envy of the object, that is, the need to destroy anything good that may come from contact with the object, may be due to "unconscious identification with the originally hated—and needed—object" (p. 25). Patients with "malignant narcissism" resort to self-mutilating behaviour or show suicidal tendencies "when their pathological grandiosity is challenged, resulting in their experiencing a traumatic sense of humiliation or defeat" (Kernberg, 1992, p. 40).

### 9.2.3   Narcissistic resistance in therapy

Riviere (1936) argued that manic and narcissistic resistances in therapy are a defence against a more or less unconscious depressive situation that needs to be uncovered in therapy. The inaccessibility of the narcissistic patient in analysis is an expression of his omnipotent denial of the reality of object relations. The patient consciously or unconsciously refuses to freely associate and maintains a flow of carefully selected and arranged material, which is calculated to deceive the analyst. He accepts no alternative point of view or anything that he has not already said himself, except with lip service. The patient denies the value of everything the analyst says and implicitly claims to supersede the analyst and do the analytic work better himself. He does not develop true positive transference. In contrast to other patients, the narcissistic patient's hostile tendencies do not even amount to a negative transference (Riviere, 1936). The patient manages to control the analyst and the analytic situation in a way that is masked very cleverly and often not apparent to the analyst. Under a mask of feigned compliance, superficial politeness, and intellectual rationalisation, he remains self-satisfied and defiant. Such deceptiveness is characteristic of

the manic defence; it is a cover for the narcissistic patient's attempts at securing exclusive control (Riviere, 1936).

The narcissistic patient is determined to keep the upper hand in the analytic situation and resists any progress in treatment for fear that the analyst will gain power over him. If he were to freely associate, admit to his failings, or develop a positive transference, he would expose himself to the analyst's mercies. The patient cannot endure any praise of progress; and any partial solution or insight produces an exacerbation of symptoms. This is the "negative therapeutic reaction" seen in patients with a narcissistic type of character resistance (Riviere, 1936). These patients do not wish to change or get well, but need to preserve things as they are. They do so because of an inherent assumption that there only can be a change in one direction if their equilibrium is upset, namely for the worse. Patients with narcissistic character resistance are highly sensitive to experiencing anxiety and become easily mortified; their depressive position is stronger insofar as their unconscious reality is more unbearable than in other cases (Riviere, 1936). Analysis is about realising this despair and uncovering the depression underneath their manic defences.

> ... it is the love for his internal objects, which lies behind and produces the unbearable guilt and pain, the need to sacrifice his life for theirs, and so the prospect of death, that makes this resistance so stubborn. And we can counter this resistance only by unearthing this love and the guilt with it. ... So it is the positive transference that we must bring to realisation; and this is what they resist beyond all ... What is underneath is a love (a craving for absolute bliss in complete union with a perfect object for ever and ever), and this love is bound up with an uncontrollable and insupportable fury of disappointment, together with anxiety for other love-relations as well. (Riviere, 1936)

The narcissistic patient has been destructive towards his objects all his life for which he unconsciously fears analysis will bring him punishment (Riviere, 1936).

> All the injuries he ever did them in thought or deed arose from his "selfishness", from being too greedy, and too envious of them, not generous and willing enough to allow them what they had, whether of oral, anal or genital pleasure—from not loving them enough, in fact. (Riviere, 1936)

Although it is the control of his objects that defends against his anxieties (his fears for his own ego), the resulting destructiveness adds, in a vicious circle, to his inability to establish real object relations.

> His egoistic self-seeking attitude corresponds accurately enough to one side of things in his unconscious mind—to the hatred, cruelty and callousness there, and it represents his fears for his own ego if the love for his objects became too strong. We all fear the dependence of love to some extent. (Riviere, 1936)

### 9.2.4 Antisocial personality disorder

Patients with antisocial personality disorder are exploitative and greedy; they tend to appropriate others' ideas or property and show an attitude of entitlement. They have "a remarkable incapacity for empathy with and commitment to others" (Kernberg, 1992, p. 74). These patients are unable to invest emotionally in nonexploitative relationships with others. Patients with antisocial personality disorder experience stimulus hunger, impulsively try to "reduce tension by achieving immediately desired goals" (being unable to "conceive of their life beyond the immediate moment") (p. 75), and fail to learn from adverse experience. Interactional behaviours are typically aggressive. The "basic ego state" of patients with antisocial personality disorder is characterised

by a chronic sense of emptiness and "a diffuse sense of the meaninglessness of life" (Kernberg, 1992, p. 74).

In the nonaggressive ("passive-parasitic") type of antisocial personality disorder, parasitic and exploitative, rather than aggressive, behaviours predominate. Patients with "passive-parasitic antisocial personality disorder" deny the importance of all object relations and regressively idealise "the gratification of receptive-dependent needs—food, objects, money, sex, privileges—and the symbolic power exerted over others by extracting such gratifications from them" (Kernberg, 1992, p. 83). For the patient with passive-parasitic antisocial personality, the meaning of life consists in getting "the needed supplies while ignoring others as persons and protecting oneself from revengeful punishment" (p. 83). Aggression is denied and transformed "into ruthless exploitation" (Kernberg, 1992, p. 83).

Patients with antisocial personality disorder are inordinately envious. They protect themselves from their rageful envy "by aggressive, violent appropriation or passive-parasitic exploitation of others" (Kernberg, 1992, p. 83). Alternatively, patients with antisocial personality disorder defend against envy by devaluing others. Patients with antisocial personality disorder typically meet criteria for narcissistic personality disorder, too. Antisocial personality disorder includes narcissistic features, such as self-centredness, excessive self-reference, "grandiosity and derived characteristics of exhibitionism", an attitude of superiority, and overdependency on admiration (p. 73). Patients with antisocial personality disorder manifest severe superego pathology. Narcissistic personalities, too, show some degree of superego pathology. This is characterised by an "incapacity to experience self-reflective sadness", "a predominance of shame as contrasted to guilt in their intrapsychic regulation of social behavior, and a value system more childlike than adult" (p. 74). Features of more serious superego pathology in antisocial personality disorder include untruthfulness, insincerity, lack of remorse, stealing, swindling, assault, robbery, and other criminal behaviours (Kernberg, 1992).

## Differential diagnosis

Patients with narcissistic personality disorder, especially those with "malignant narcissism", can present with passive and/or aggressive antisocial behaviours, however, unlike patients with antisocial personality disorder proper, narcissistic patients have some capacity for feeling guilt and remorse as well as some capacity for nonexploitative object relations (Kernberg, 1992). While superego functions are largely absent in patients with antisocial personality disorder, early superego formation in those who develop narcissistic personality disorder, especially "malignant narcissism", is faulty, in that it is "dominated by the earliest sadistic superego precursors", which cannot be neutralised by "the subsequently idealized superego precursors" (that is, "the more realistic superego introjects of the oedipal period") (Kernberg, 1992, p. 81). Sometimes, antisocial behaviour occurs in the context of neurotic personality organisation. In these cases, and in neurotic adolescent rebelliousness, antisocial behaviour "derives from an unconscious sense of guilt and a corresponding unconscious search for punishment" (Kernberg, 1992, p. 72). Some neurotic patients may unconsciously expose themselves to the humiliating consequences of being caught and punished for their crimes. Patients with antisocial personality disorder, however, do not experience guilt and do not operate out of an unconscious sense of guilt (Kernberg, 1992).

### 9.2.5 Fixation in the paranoid-schizoid position

Klein (1940, 1952) described how, in the paranoid-schizoid infantile developmental position, the infant's feelings of frustration are split off and projected into the object which is then experienced as "bad" and persecutory. Fixation on the paranoid level of development has the defensive effect of preventing the emergence of depression and guilt, however persecutory fears continue to disturb the ego's ability to establish representations of good objects inside (Klein, 1952; Rosenfeld, 1965). Inability to integrate and repair internally loved objects remains a lifelong problem, so that the ego remains locked in futile attempts to overcome anxieties resulting from the unavailability of his objects (Klein, 1940). Patients who are fixated in the paranoid-schizoid position have not retained a good internal relationship with their primary object. The infant's failure to progress to the depressive position, in which a stable internal object relation is established, may be due, in part, to the unpredictability of the mother's attitudes and responses. Alternatively, the infant may have mistrusted his mother's motives early on, leaving him to search continuously for the "ideal" object and to never be quite satisfied by the object's responses. Inability to create good internal objects and ongoing search for the ideal object cause lasting behaviour problems related to the splitting of objects into ideal and all-bad ones (Main, 1957).

Patients who are fixated in the paranoid-schizoid position deal with frustrations by turning away form their objects "with intense hostility, leaving [them] entirely bad and persecuting and turning to secondary objects as entirely good, or rather idealised", however "the primary persecutory anxiety soon re-asserts itself and even the secondary objects soon turn bad" (Rosenfeld, 1965, p. 204). Good and bad objects are interrelated so that if bad objects are extremely persecutory, good objects—as a "reaction formation"—will become highly idealised (Rosenfeld, 1965, p. 70). In situations when love and hate come nearer together, which is when aggressive impulses are directed at a good object, the patient who is fixated in the paranoid-schizoid position does not experience guilt and depression, which would have led to greater integration of his objects, but experiences confusion between good and bad objects (p. 209). The patient who is fixated in the paranoid-schizoid position will thus be compelled to "act out" excessively (and aggressively) in a desperate attempt to keep good and bad objects, or love and hate, separate (Rosenfeld, 1965, p. 214).

## Splitting amongst staff

Main (1957) eloquently illustrated the interplay of affiliative (libidinal) and aggressive impulses in patients who were fixated in the paranoid-schizoid position. A series of patients referred for intensive inpatient psychotherapy who were felt to have been failed by others in the past became "special" soon after admission. These patients arose in staff unusually strong wishes to help and were felt to warrant a special therapeutic effort. Initially these patients made helpless and child-like appeals to nurses. They were able to evoke feelings of omnipotence in selected nurses who came to feel that they possessed a special quality and had a deeper understanding of the patient. Often, these patients would impart confidential information to her favourite nurse that inhibited her from communicating freely with other members of staff. Other staff were deemed not good enough, and the nurse engaged in a closer than usual relationship with the patient. Thus, favourite nurses made omnipotent attempts to be "ideal", which reflected their patients' need for an ideal object. The patients' behaviour was designed to create an exclusive relationship with somebody who would take responsibility for them and their needs (Main, 1957).

These patients were very sensitive to negative feelings in others. If they detected any ambivalence or reluctance in their object's willingness to provide for their needs, they induced feelings of guilt. Patients managed to imply, by subtle means, that, unless the favourite nurse did well, favour would be withdrawn form her and she would be classed among those who had failed them in the past and proven untrustworthy. By inducing guilt, these patients exerted omnipotent control over their object, which could be seen as a defence against betrayal of primitive love. Once they were in doubt, these patients had to seek "regular reassurance that their object is still alive,

reliable and unexhausted". As a defence against anxiety about the inconstancy of their object and for the purpose of "reassurance against the possibility of retaliation" by their object, the patients demanded from their favourite nurse more and more attention—attention that had to be given with the right attitude, with exclusive devotion to their childlike wishes and needs, and even in anticipation of their wishes without them having to express these (Main, 1957). It was their care by an ambivalent object or an object who misunderstood their needs—in the context of an unsatisfied and unsatisfiable longing for the ideal object— that caused distress in these patients. Patients went on to express their distress through trying to secure their object's exclusive devotion in a more aggressive manner. Patients punished their nurse or doctor by showing increasing aggression or self-destructive behaviour (thereby threatening the very feelings of therapeutic omnipotence they had induced). These aggressive manifestations could be seen as "sophisticated versions of the signals an infant uses to dominate his mother and bring her to help him" (Main, 1957).

Main (1957) suggested that, in the early phases, these patients caused splitting among staff through their primitive appeal for help. Patients were able to pick up on latent staff splits and rivalries, causing staff to compete with each other for the honour of being the patient's favourite and being allowed to care for him or her. Patients, in search for security, amplified rivalries between members of staff that already existed latently within the group. Initially, nurses who were chosen by the patient for a special relationship felt honoured, indeed, and did enjoy giving care to the patient. Those who remained in the out-group were left feeling envious. However, due to these patients' sensitivity to disharmony in those around them, competition among staff increased their insecurity and mistrust. The suspicion of these patients grew that they will remain helpless in the future, leading to increasing demands and induction of guilt in the staff who cared for them. Guilt-driven obedience in the favourite nurse is disturbing to the patient, adding to the vicious circle. Moreover, the nurses dealt with their increasing feelings of guilt by denial and projection, with consequences of more obvious staff splitting and burn-out (Main, 1957).

### 9.2.6   Borderline personality organisation

Individuals with a schizoid tendency have gained the conviction, early in life, that "their mother did not really love them and value them" (Fairbairn, 1952, p. 23). As a child, the schizoid individual would have interpreted the apparent lack of his mother's love in the sense that it was *his hate* that destroyed his mother's affection towards him; he would have gained the conviction that the *destructiveness* of his "incorporative needs" (in the oral phase of development) was responsible for the disappearance of his mother or the destruction of her love and affection for him (Fairbairn, 1952). Importantly, "anxiety attached to this situation persists in the unconscious, ready to be reactivated by any subsequent experience of an analogous kind" (p. 24). The individual's "anxiety over a situation which presented itself as involving a threat to the ego" renders his libidinal attitude "highly self-perseverative and narcissistic" (p. 23). He has learned that "he can only permit himself to love and be loved from afar off" (Fairbairn, 1952, p. 26). A persistent fear of rejection by an unresponsive (retaliating) object—in combination with a longing for a relationship with a caring object (seeking to avoid pain and anxiety)—may be responsible for the compulsion, experienced by the schizoid individual, to keep his external objects at a distance from him; and it may explain the inhibition of efforts to induce, within them, a loving or care-giving attitude.

Having become "subject to a compulsion to hate and be hated", the schizoid individual nevertheless "longs deep down to love and be loved" (Fairbairn, 1952, p. 26). Splitting appears to occur between fantasised (internally experienced) all-good objects and external all-bad objects, which—because of their tendency to reject—are forced to stay away from the self,

that is, from their internally fantasised all-good cousins with which the schizoid individual attempts to maintain a relationship conducive to libidinal interactions. Kernberg (1996) considered schizoid, paranoid, and borderline personality disorders to be instances of "borderline personality organization". Excessive endowment with aggression interferes with the integration of all-good and all-bad internalised object relations and, thus, hinders the establishment of object constancy in early development, preparing the psychostructural ground for emergence of a "borderline personality organization" (Kernberg, 1992). In patients with "borderline personality organization", "primitive defensive operations centering on splitting" predominate, while reality testing is generally preserved (p. 120).[5] Splitting and related defence mechanisms (including projective identification, denial, primitive idealisation, and omnipotence) serve "to maintain separate the idealized and persecutory internalized object relations derived from the early developmental phases" (that is, phases normally preceding the establishment of "object constancy") (p. 118). As a consequence of this separation, interpersonal relationships are impoverished (Kernberg, 1992).

In patients with schizoid personality disorder, the impoverishment of interpersonal relationships is associated with social withdrawal and "a defensive hypertrophy of fantasy life" (Kernberg, 1996, p. 122). Splitting *per se* dominates in patients with borderline and schizoid personality disorders, compared to patients with paranoid personality disorder. In patients with borderline personality disorder proper, the predominance of splitting (and related defence mechanisms) is clinically expressed "in impulsive interactions in

---

[5]By contrast, in patients with "psychotic personality organization" (that is, patients conventionally considered to be suffering from atypical forms of psychosis), reality testing is severely disturbed, in addition to the predominance of splitting and related defence mechanisms that can also be seen in patients with "borderline personality organisation" (Kernberg, 1996).

the interpersonal field" (Kernberg, 1996, p. 122). Patients with paranoid personality disorder show increased aggression (compared with patients with schizoid personality disorder) and a resulting "dominance of projective identification and a defensive self idealisation related to the efforts to control an external world of persecutory figures" (Kernberg, 1996, p. 123).

## 9.2.7  Moral masochism

Patients with "depressive-masochistic personality disorder" or "moral masochism" are exposed to excessive superego pressures (Kernberg, 1992). They are responsible and reliable personalities, but "tend to judge themselves harshly and to set extremely high standards for themselves", failing which they may become depressed. They can "show harshness in their judgement of others, a harshness that may be tinged with justified indignation" (p. 37). Patients with "depressive-masochistic personality disorder" also show an "overdependency on support, love, and acceptance from others"; they often go "far out of their way to obtain sympathy and love" (Kernberg, 1992, p. 37). These patients "show an abnormal vulnerability to being disappointed by others" and have "difficulties in the expression of aggression", although they may resort to "attacks on those they need and feel rejected by, followed by depression and abject, submissive, and/or compliant behavior" (p. 38). They have "a tendency to feel inordinately guilty toward others because of unconscious ambivalence toward loved and needed objects" (Kernberg, 1992, p. 37).

> The sense of being rejected and mistreated in reaction to relatively minor slights may lead these patients to unconscious behaviors geared to making the objects of their love feel guilty. A chain reaction is set up of heightened demandingness, feelings of rejection, and an unconscious tendency to try to make others feel guilty; consequent actual rejection from others may spiral into

severe problems in intimate relations and may also trigger depression connected to loss of love. (Kernberg, 1992, p. 37)

### Self-idealisation and infatuation

Masochistic behaviour patterns help to neurotically maintain self-esteem, that is, they ensure the ego's narcissistic supplies (Kernberg, 1992). Patients with depressive-masochistic personality disorder obtain "narcissistic gratification from the sense of being unjustly treated and thus implicitly morally superior to the object" (p. 48). Self-idealisation in fantasy is a narcissistic consequence of the masochistic personality structure. Self-idealisation of these patients contributes to their masochistic infatuations. The masochistic personality becomes "irresistibly attracted" to an idealised object "who is clearly unable or unwilling to respond to love" (Kernberg, 1992, p. 41). Infatuation with an unavailable object "represents submission to the ego-ideal aspects of the superego that were projected onto the object" (p. 42). Through love for the unavailable object, the masochistic patient gains "a sense of narcissistic gratification and fulfilment" (Kernberg, 1992, p. 42).

Narcissistic and masochistic personality features often coexist. The patient with narcissistic personality disorder, too, pursues an impossible love relationship masochistically ("while all his or her other object relations are narcissistic" (Kernberg, 1992, p. 42)). The narcissistic patient projects his or her "pathological grandiose self" onto the unavailable love object, "with an effort to establish a relationship that unconsciously would confirm the stability of the patient's own grandiosity" (p. 43). Through pathological infatuation, the patient seeks to acquire for him- or herself the idealised object's attributes of physical attractiveness, wealth, prestige, or power (Kernberg, 1992).

### Submission

At the deepest level of masochistic pathology, "early sadistic superego precursors" exert a lasting influence (Kernberg, 1992, p. 50). Patients with *severe* masochistic personality pathology grow up with a sense that any object relationship renders them vulnerable to attack by the object. They learn that total submission to the cruel and powerful object "is the only condition for survival" (p. 49). Submission and suffering become essential conditions for any object relation later in life. This also means that ties to good and weak objects have to be severed. Moreover, unconscious identification with the primitive sadistic object results in a need to destroy all good objects. Identification with the patient's cruel and powerful early object leads to the use of aggression as the only way of relating to others; "love can be expressed only as destruction" (Kernberg, 1992, p. 49).

## 9.3   Affective disorders

Whether aggressive impulses are prevented from external expression by the subject's fears that his attack on the object would lead to its permanent loss (depressive position) or by his fear of punishment emanating from an external authority or his superego, aggressive impulses do arise. Instincts, including intraspecific aggression, have intrinsic spontaneity and need a target or outlet. Similarly to our choice of food, some targets are more suitable than others but if we run out of habitual targets, then less appropriate targets will suffice, unless the inappropriateness of targets is enshrined in cultural prohibitions. The fear that compels us to conformity is the same that inhibits our aggressive impulses towards others. Prevention of overt aggression directed at significant objects or other individuals around us developmentally leads to the adoption by the subject of a great variety of ritualised forms of aggression, which importantly contribute to the cultural fabric of society (Lorenz, 1963).

If aggression is excessive, such as at times of stress, but can still not be expressed directly or overtly, images in our mind may manifest transient abreactions. Aggressive fantasies (which are "unconscious" in that we do not like to admit to them or remember them after their occurrence) are common, however images of others or ourselves that are not utilised as goals for aggressive behaviour do not permit an abreaction of the aggressive drive. If others who are perceived "externally" cannot be used as targets to abreact aggressive impulses, due to a watchful superego, and aggressive impulses are too intense to await delayed and socially appropriate expression, then, sooner or later, images of self-harm and ruminations about self-recrimination have to give way to actual acts of self-harm or other self-destructive behaviour. Self-harming behaviour would occur when transient fantasies of aggression against self-representations in imagery (suicidal ideation) do not provide sufficient relief for accumulating instinctive energy. There will be a point at which aggressive energy is greater than the ultimate inhibition, the inhibition against killing oneself. Suicidal ideation, parasuicidal behaviour and other forms of self-directed aggression are important problems in psychiatry yet cognitive psychology, from which contemporary psychiatry draws its inspirations, fails to elucidate their mechanism.

> Caught in the clash between their own defiant rage (violence from within) and the retaliatory rage of their parents (violence from without), these patients have emerged from childhood with an established pattern of adaptation that forces them unawares to damage themselves in order to avoid the dreaded danger of damaging others. (Rado, 1956, p. 344)

### 9.3.1   Cyclothymia

Every person's mood oscillates between states of elation (hyperthymic states) and states of depression (hypothymic states) (Lorenz, 1973). The pathological exaggeration of this oscillation can be seen in the alternating phases of mania and melancholia in manic-depressive illness (bipolar affective disorder). The normal fluctuation between hyperthymic and hypothymic states is "a biologically necessary process which reflects a search, on the one hand for potential dangers, and on the other for opportunities that we can exploit to our own advantage" (p. 239). Mood fluctuations are often related to the time of day. Low mood in the early hours of the morning is accompanied by unpleasant thoughts, typically preoccupations with regrets or guilt. In this state, the individual is prone to "discover all kinds of dangers" of which he was previously unaware (Lorenz, 1973, p. 239). Passivity at times of depression may serve a purpose that is related to the motionlessness of an animal that is "on the look-out for foes" (p. 240). If a hypothymic state arises after a personal loss, the individual is "acutely alert to the new dangers which are sure to arise from his changed situation" (p. 239). In a hyperthymic state that arises following a personal gain or success, "it is very sensible to look for ways to profit from [the] good fortune" (p. 240). Physical hyperactivity that accompanies a state of elation enables the individual to take advantage of new opportunities. Lorenz (1973) summarised that the reciprocal oscillation between hyperthymic and hypothymic states "fulfils the dual role of guarding against potential dangers and looking for new opportunities to exploit" (p. 240).

### 9.3.2 Mourning

Psychoanalytic theory conceptualises depression as a consequence of the loss of a loved object, however, loss of object is not a necessary condition for depression. We could argue that what is lost in depression, more generally, is a stable supply of selfobject experiences. The sufferer may have become unable to control the stream of selfobject experiences from his social environment, explaining the sufferer's low self-esteem. Depression would be a reaction to incessant disapproval (negative reflection of the self in the eyes of others) or lack of approval. This may, at first, seem inconsistent with Freud's and Klein's model of melancholic depression, yet we need to remind ourselves that the social environment from which selfobject experiences are drawn is developmentally continuous with

the primary object, so that, unconsciously, it is the primary object, indeed, that is lost in depression. According to Klein (1940), when a loved object is lost, the infantile depressive position is reactivated. Not only features of the depressive position, namely feelings of guilt toward one's primary object (parent), but also fears of persecution (fears to be punished by one's parents) come to life again. Objects that would have been established securely in one's infancy turn into persecutors again (Klein, 1940).

> This feeling of being persecuted by bad objects while "pining" for the lost good objects is what constitutes the essence of the depressive position, which is reactivated in melancholic states. (Gabbard, 1990, p. 179)

The mourner has to work through the depressive position again to achieve what he had achieved previously in childhood: integration and repair of the lost object internally (Klein, 1940). Not only the lost love object is repaired internally (reintrojected), so are the mourner's primary objects. The internal world is rebuilt, populated by the good parents and the internal lost object (and, crucially, by one's relationships with them). Trust in external objects is gradually regained. As the connection with the external world is reestablished, the pain of loss is felt again and again; finally, connection with the external world is reestablished without the threat of annihilation of the internal world. As the depressive position is worked through, mourning ends (Klein, 1940).

### 9.3.3 Melancholia

One way to conceptualise depression is to regard it as an extreme form of help-seeking behaviour. Patients prone to depression (or those who have learned in childhood that to be good and accepted is to be weak and helpless) respond to threats or anxiety by placing significant others in a care-taking role. Patients with severe depression who are unable to perform basic tasks of self-maintenance force others to take over basic care-taking functions. Others are "drawn into a relationship in which they are asked to provide things that only a mother could reasonably be asked to provide" (Cashdan, 1988, p. 63). "Projective identification of dependency", which may be reinforced by statements of suicidal intent, is used to reconstitute the early infant-caregiver relationship. On the other hand, depression may arise if projective identifications aiming to induce care-giving behaviour in others and to enhance self-esteem are frustrated (Cashdan, 1988). Depression has defensive and manipulative aspects; it "is a complex way of simultaneously acting angrily, fearfully, self-punitively, even protectively or lovingly" (Schafer, 1976, p. 349). The depressed patient is "protecting loved ones from directly destructive actions" and "attempting in these and other ways to regulate both self-esteem and relationship with others" (p. 350).

> ... in acting depressively one is unconsciously engaged in affirming or enacting the following propositions: I hate those I love (ambivalence); I interact with them lovingly insofar as they support my precarious self-esteem by being loving, admiring, attentive, and steadily available to me (narcissism), and I interact with them hatefully, even to the extent of wishing them dead, insofar as they do not relate to me in the way I desire (ruthless destructiveness); ... I cannot altogether control how they actually behave (hopelessness), ...; I seem to be reproaching only myself when in fact I am simultaneously reproaching these others as well, so that secretly it is my esteem for them as well as self-esteem that is at stake (self-punishment and latent persecution of others); ... (Schafer, 1976, p. 350)

Klein (1940) saw the origins of pathological mourning and manic-depressive states in failure to establish good internal objects in childhood. Individuals who develop depression have never resolved the infantile depressive position. If the infantile depressive position had not been worked through successfully and internal objects were never securely established in early childhood, lost objects cannot be repaired successfully later in life. Those prone to depression remain unconsciously concerned that their greed and destructiveness have destroyed the good objects on whom they depend. As a consequence of that destruction, patients feel persecuted by bad objects (Klein, 1940; Gabbard, 1990). Freud thought that patients who are liable to develop melancholic depression have a severe superego. A severe superego is related to feelings of guilt over having shown aggression toward loved ones (reviewed in Gabbard, 1990). A severe superego represents expectation of severe or frequent punishment by authority figures for aggressive impulses against love objects or objects on whom one depends. Hostility and aggressiveness may be unacceptable and have to be disowned due to unconscious fears of retaliation and rejection or because anger is consciously felt for the lost object. Both, fear of punishment by internalised authority figures and concern about one's destructiveness towards one's good object, would prevent external expression of aggression. Aggressive impulses, which continue to seek expression in situations of frustrated object relationships, would have to be redirected.

## Paranoia versus self-recrimination

One solution would be to project the threat of punishment by the superego onto external persecutors who would then become justifiable targets for aggression. This is in accordance with the continuum that Klein noted between parents, superego, and fantasised persecutors (Laughlin, 1970, p. 177). Guilt feelings have strongly paranoid elements and, if paranoid fears emerging from the superego gain the upper hand, the patient regresses to the paranoid-schizoid level of functioning. In patients who have regressed to the paranoid-schizoid position, external persecutory objects can take on superego func-tion (Rosenfeld, 1965, pp. 70, 206). Another solution—one that is especially relevant to mel-ancholic depression—is to discharge instinc-tive aggression onto the self. According to both Freud and Klein, the internal representation of the self becomes the substitute target if it takes on aspects of the lost object. What is being "introjected" into the ego are aspects of the dis-appointing or unreachable object. "Introjection" provides a "defense against the conscious recog-nition of intolerable hostile aggressive impulses" (Laughlin, 1970, p. 183). Punishment of the intro-jected object manifests as self-recrimination and self-depreciatory attitudes, that is, harshness and criticism directed towards oneself. Punish-ment of the introjected object forms "the essence of the pathogenesis of depression" (Laughlin, 1970, p. 183). Aggression that is redirected inter-nally manifests in self-destructive behaviour. Suicidal ideas and threats not only manifest the redirection of aggression onto the ego but also contain an element of safe externalised dis-posal of aggression. Suicide is often designed to destroy the lives of the survivors; it can be the only satisfactory or tolerable avenue for revenge (Gabbard, 1990).

### 9.3.4   Narcissistic identification with the object

In narcissistic object love, the loved object is not experienced as separate from the ego, so that the pain of loss can be avoided (Ogden, 2002). "Identification" with the object is the first way in which the ego "picks out an object", develop-mentally preceding object cathexis (investment of libidinal energy into a chosen object) (Freud, 1917). In a patient suffering from melancholia, object cathexis is abandoned and love, which as an instinctive drive cannot be given up, takes ref-uge in narcissistic identification with the object, which thus "becomes a substitute for the erotic cathexis" (Freud, 1917). A regression to narcis-sistic identification with the object renders the patient incapable of accepting the irrevocable

loss of the object which would normally occur in the process of mourning (Ogden, 2002).

> Self-reproaches are reproaches against a loved object which have been shifted away from it to the patient's own ego. (Freud, 1917)

While part of the ego regresses to narcissistic identification with the object, another part, the split-off "critical agency", establishes a sadis-tic object tie with the "ego-identified-with-the-object" (Ogden, 2002; based on Freud, 1917). Hate emanating from the "critical agency" or conscience makes the substitute object (identified with the ego) suffer, thereby taking revenge on the original object. Freud (1917) observed that the melancholic patient's indulgence in self-reproach, self-tormenting, and self-denigration, which may culminate in delusional expectation of punish-ment, are not directed, in fact, at the self but at "someone else, someone whom the patient loves or has loved or should love". Outrage directed against the object seeks to detach libido from the object so that the subject can live, while, at the same time, love seeks to maintain the narcissistic object tie (ego-identified-with-the-object) so that the pain of loss can be avoided. Thus, the patient unconsciously loves the same object he hates (ambivalence), a combination that is similarly encountered in sadism and stalking and that is characterised by high durability (Ogden, 2002).

Freud (1917) thought that object choice (choice of love object) in those prone to melancholia is made on a narcissistic basis. Object relation-ships of those predisposed to melancholia are characterised by ambivalence toward the loved object. Riviere (1936) noted that the narcissistic individual is always close to being aware that he lacks real object relations and his narcissistic and omnipotent defences are an attempt to avoid the pain and depression that this insight brings.

Modern psychoanalysis

Spotnitz (1985) thought that not self-directed love but aggression directed against the self is the main problem narcissistic patients have. Redirection of aggressive impulse against the self is defensive in nature, motivated by a fear of destroying or losing the object. Aggressive impulses that are not discharged externally accumulate in the ego where they can have destructive effects, pushing the ego towards depression and even schizophrenia later in life (Spotnitz, 1985). Insofar as depression is a preoedipal disorder where hatred, that is aggression, is turned on the self, patients require a different psychoanalytic approach. "Modern psychoanalysis" aims to resolve the "narcissistic transference" before the focus of analysis can shift to object transference. While in classical analysis, concerned with oedipal patients, the analyst facilitates the development of object transference leading to transference neurosis and allowing its interpretation, the analyst working with preoedipal patients is concerned primarily with creating an atmosphere that allows the patient to externalise his aggressive feelings. While the "classical analyst" uses interpretation to resolve resistances, the "modern analyst" seeks to strengthen the patient's ego defences and resolve his narcissistic transference by methods of collusion, mirroring, and reflection. Resistances need to be mobilised first before they can be analysed and resolved. Not insight or the resolution of resistances are what modern analysis tries to achieve, but the strengthening of the patient's ego through fostering a sense of security, a sense of freedom to say anything without fear of rejection. Spotnitz (1985) suggested that the therapist avoids questions, comments, and observations that relate to the internal sphere of the patient and instead provokes the patient to express aggression externally, that is, against the therapist. Verbal attacks of the patient are to be welcomed as long-awaited external projection of what earlier were poisonous introjections.

### 9.3.5   Self-blaming versus claiming depression

Patients with depression unconsciously experience a sense of failure in relation to one person in their immediate environment, the "dominant

other" (Arieti, 1973). The "dominant other", with whom the patient "is in a relation of dependency", "is symbolic of the mother, as she appeared to the patient in very early childhood" (p. 129). The depressed patient "is always afraid of losing or of having already lost what she needs from this dominant figure: love, affection, praise, admiration, approval, a precious supply of intangible things that only he can give" (p. 129). Arieti (1973) distinguished between "self-blaming depression" and "claiming depression". "Self-blaming depression" is characterised by prominent self-accusations and guilt feelings. In patients prone to this type of depression, "some attitudes of the mother, as she originally appeared in childhood, and later of the dominant other, are internalized" (p. 129).

> The attainment of the parental ideal would ensure parental love, affection, and praise. The depression occurs after the realization by the patient that she has not lived up to what the dominant other expected of her. The patient feels responsible and guilty for not having met these expectations. Inasmuch as some real or assumed aspects of the dominant other are introjected, the patient feels deprived of love, affection, admiration … A profound feeling of guilt confers to the depression the particular self-blaming aspect. (Arieti, 1973, p. 129)

In "claiming depression", all the symptoms seem to signify the patient's need for pity and an expectation and demand on others to relive the patient's suffering. Even the suicidal attempt or prospect is an appeal to others and an attempt to attribute to others a power to prevent the patient's death. The patient prone to "claiming depression" "did not necessarily try to obtain gratification or fulfilment through her own efforts", but obtained gratification and fulfilment "by receiving support, praise, admiration from others, especially from the dominant other" (Arieti, 1973, p. 130). The person prone to "claiming depression" "is not able to transform an important part of the interpersonal into the intrapsychic" (p. 130). Therefore, she "must depend on interpersonal contacts for gratification"; and even if she praises herself, she would do so "only after she has been admired by others" (p. 130). Thus, the patient suffering from "claiming depression" "needs an external agent from whom to extract praise and approval" (Arieti, 1973, p. 130).

> In some cases, there is an apparent variation in the symptomatology, inasmuch as the patient tries desperately to submerge herself into work and activities, hoping that eventually she will find something to do that will make her worthy of recognition from other people. The patient may hate and depreciate herself, but not with a real attitude of self-blame. Her sorrow derives predominantly from the fact that she cannot obtain gratification from others. (Arieti, 1973, p. 130)

### 9.3.6  Mania

Failure, in childhood, to overcome the depressive position can not only lead to depressive disorders and an inability to experience mourning in later life, but may also predispose to paranoia and mania. Any loss of external objects in later life, either as a result of ambivalent attack on the object or actual loss, will reawaken early depressive anxieties of losing the good internal object. Manic defences are a way of defending against depressive feelings of loss and guilt (Klein, 1940; reviewed in Gabbard, 1990). Manic defences avoid unbearable depressive anxieties principally by suppressing any acknowledgement of dependence. If love objects, damaged by one's destructive impulses, cannot be "repaired", the subject may turn away from his internal objects and omnipotently "deny" his dependence on them. Such "denial" is integral to mania and hypomania. Denial of dependency on internal objects is an attempt to offset depression and prevent depressive affect and

grief arising from the loss of an irreplaceable object—a loss that is still unconsciously mourned (Klein, 1940).

Through the use of mechanisms characteristic for the paranoid-schizoid position, the patient keeps at bay feelings of pining and mourning and, instead, experiences feelings of triumph, contempt, and control. Triumph is the denial of concern for the object; contempt arises through devaluation of the object. Control of the object allows the denial of dependence (Segal, 1973). The subject's ability to control his object depends on the persecutory nature of his object. Persecutory fears strengthen paranoid and manic mechanisms of defence. Manic defences entail a need to constantly observe and check on bad objects, so that inner bad and persecutory objects can be manically subordinated. The need for persecution creates a dependence on bad objects (Klein, 1940). Superiority over, and humiliation of, one's objects provides sadistic satisfaction, but the triumph over one's objects delays the working-through of mourning. While the object is treated with contempt, controlled, and triumphed over, reparative activities cannot be carried out. Instead, attacks on the object increase its destruction, "thereby deepening depressive anxieties and making the underlying depressive situation increasingly hopeless and persecutory" (Segal, 1973).

### 9.4  Schizophreniform psychoses

Mature defensive systems against anxiety and guilt are cognitively demanding. Elaborate neurotic defences, maintained in the interest of continued social adaptation, can, at times of heightened stress or anxiety, disintegrate and give way to psychosis. Any decline in cognitive capacity, as it occurs in old age, particularly with the onset of dementia, will undermine mature defensive systems, leaving the individual vulnerable to maladaptive regression to the paranoid-schizoid position. Minimal cognitive dysfunction or nonspecific organic brain alterations in old age are associated with late-onset psychosis (paraphrenia). Individuals who are in the process of developing schizophrenia are often handicapped by minor cognitive dysfunction, too. Under these conditions, defences seeking to metabolise guilt or existential anxiety may regress to primitive levels. Persecutory beliefs and reactive outrage help the individual to reduce existential anxiety at the cost of loss of social adaptation.

Some patients with incipient schizophrenia and those with schizoid personality disorder are paralysed by a motivational conflict between existential anxiety urging human relatedness and an excessive fear of rejection (reflective of a severe superego). Fear of rejection by others and fear of others' aggression may prevent the attainment of security in schizoid and schizophrenic developments (Laing, 1960), whereby avoidance of situations that could expose the individual to others' expressions of hostility increases, in itself, the risk of exposure to ridicule and aggression. The socially excluded individual may develop a compromise solution: interaction with fantasy objects, this being a safer or more successful option than interaction with external objects. Thus, the suffering of social isolation and the craving for interpersonal relatedness and security may find temporary relief in fantasy by conjuring up an image of an attentive and devoted object.

### 9.4.1  Paranoid delusions

Delusions, in general, serve to maintain or recover the psychotic patient's self-esteem. Deluded patients wish to be in the public eye or in the centre of world-wide attention; they wish to be acclaimed for possessing supernatural powers or foreseeing the future (Adler, 1965). Patients with paranoid schizophrenia "attempt to maintain self-esteem by grandiose phantasies", fantasies that not only sustain grandiose delusions but can also contribute to the generation of persecutory delusions. The patient who elaborates delusions of persecution sees himself as "a person of consequence" insofar as he has become "the subject of

widespread attention, even if this be malicious" (Storr, 1968, p. 95).

Excessive guilt is another factor implicated in the mechanism of persecutory delusions. Guilt over aggressive impulses against objects on whom one depends can be avoided if aggressive impulses can be redirected either against the self or at justifiable external targets. Depending on the patient's constitution, intolerable guilt emanating from a severe superego can either be replaced by self-recriminations and suicidal ruminations, characteristic of melancholic depression, or be transformed into persecutory delusions. The feared persecutor can be hated without guilt, so that, through the mechanism of projection, a patient may secure "a substitute and more tolerable target for his resentment, accusations, and recriminations" (Laughlin, 1970, p. 228). Self-recriminations may secondarily give way to delusions of persecution. The patient may project his self-critical feelings and self-condemnation for failed responsibilities onto others (Laughlin, 1970). In any event, excessive guilt channels into a psychopathological constellation that is optimal with regard to an individual's intrapsychic economics.

> Denial and Projection are often the basis of delusional jealousy and belief in persecution. In these psychotic manifestations, it is often a basic sense of guilt which the person is unable to tolerate, and against which he calls into play ego defenses of Denial and Projection. (Laughlin, 1970, p. 69)

To appreciate the evolution of paranoid psychoses, it is important to be reminded that fear of the superego, according to Klein, derive from the fear of retaliation or counterattacks by the "bad breast", a fear that characterises the paranoid-schizoid infantile developmental position. Persecutory fears that are too strong undermine the infant's ability to work through the depressive position and establish good objects inside; the split between the loved and hated objects remains rigid. Failure to work through the depressive position, later forces the ego to regress to the paranoid-schizoid position, which reinforces earlier persecutory fears (Klein, 1952). Regressively, fear of the superego, which manifests as intolerable guilt, can turn into a more tolerable fear of persecution by external agents. Regression of the superego to its more primitive stage linked to the paranoid-schizoid position allows aggressive impulses to be directed at fantasised external persecutors. Thus, internal redirection of aggression attributable to a severe superego can be avoided. It was Freud who thought that, in paranoid disorders, "the evolution of the conscience is reproduced regressively". Persecutory delusions present the superego in a regressive form and reveal its genesis (Freud, 1914). Paranoid indifference, a phenomenon similar to *la belle indifferance* described in patients with conversion disorders, may accompany persecutory delusions (Laughlin, 1970) and attests to the economic benefit the patient derives from his beliefs. Superego fears are essential for normal social functioning, so that the economic advantage of regression to the primitive superego is achieved at the cost of loss of social adaptation.

### 9.4.2 Schizoid personality structure

Personality features that characterise individuals with a schizoid tendency include an overvaluation of thought processes (intellectualisation), preoccupation with inner reality, an attitude of isolation and detachment, the repression of affect, a sense of difference from others, and an attitude of omnipotence or superiority (which can be conscious or unconscious) (Fairbairn, 1952). Schizoid individuals have difficulty in expressing their feelings naturally towards other people, finding it difficult to act "naturally and spontaneously" in their relations with others (p. 20). In embarrassing or paralysing social situations, schizoid individuals experience a transient sense of looking on at themselves. Being seen by others in social situations may "give rise to acute self-consciousness" (p. 17), indicating that "an actual splitting of the ego has occurred" (Fairbairn, 1952,

p. 51). Withdrawal of libido from external objects has the effect of intensifying the splitting process that manifests in "intense self-consciousness and a sense of looking on at oneself" (p. 51). Schizoid individuals try to work out their "emotional problems intellectually in the inner world" (p. 20). Their attempts to circumvent their difficulty over emotional relationships are commonly directed "towards attainment within the intellectual sphere" (Fairbairn, 1952, p. 23). Schizoid persons concentrate "their often considerable libidinal resources on pursuits which minimize human contact (such as interest and work in the area of aesthetics; or the study of abstract, theoretical topics)" (Kohut, 1971, p. 12). Schizoid individuals tend "to look down from their intellectual retreats upon common humanity" (Fairbairn, 1952, p. 21). Schizoid individuals have "a sense of inner superiority", "even when, as is commonly the case, this is largely unconscious" (p. 22).[6] Their attitude of superiority or omnipotence may be "concealed under a superficial attitude of inferiority or humility; and it may be consciously cherished as a precious secret" (p. 7). Similarly, the attitude of isolation and detachment "may be masked by a façade of sociability" (Fairbairn, 1952, p. 7).

Individuals with a schizoid tendency tend to treat objects "as means of satisfying their own requirements rather than as persons possessing inherent value" (Fairbairn, 1952, p. 13). The schizoid individual "takes active measures to drive his libidinal objects away from him" (p. 26). He mobilises hate and directs aggression against his libidinal objects with the aim of inducing "them to hate, instead of loving, him; and he does all this in order to keep his libidinal objects at a distance" (p. 26). Schizoid individuals experience difficulty "over expressing emotion in a social context" (p. 15); in particular, they "experience considerable difficulty over giving in the

---

[6]Fairbairn (1952) pointed out that the schizoid individual's attitude of superiority "is based upon an orientation towards internalized objects", while their attitude in relation to objects in the outer world is one of inferiority (p. 50).

emotional sense" (Fairbairn, 1952, p. 14). They are, however, "able to express quite a lot of feeling and to make what appear to be quite impressive social contacts" by "playing a role or acting an adopted part" (p. 16). Exhibitionism is another defence employed by schizoid individuals, since exhibitionistic activities provide a "means of expression without involving direct social contact" (p. 16). Exhibitionism, which unconsciously motivates artistic and other socially constructive activities, is often related to the tendency of schizoid individuals to adopt or play roles. Fairbairn (1952) saw the origin of schizoid personality problems in the mother's failure "to convince her child by spontaneous and genuine expressions of affection that she herself loves him as a person" (p. 13). This renders it difficult for the child "to sustain an emotional relationship with her on a personal basis" (p. 13); he "keeps his love shut in because he feels that it is too dangerous to release upon his objects" (p. 26). As a consequence, "the child tends to transfer his relationships with his objects to the realm of inner reality"; his "objects tend to belong to the inner rather than to the outer world" (Fairbairn, 1952, p. 18).

The schizoid individual's behaviour may resemble that of "a timid mouse, alternately creeping out of the shelter of his hole to peep at the world of outer objects and then beating a hasty retreat" (Fairbairn, 1952, p. 39). "Giving" in the emotional sense, that is, attempting to establish libidinal contact with an external object, "has the effect of depreciating values, and of lowering self-respect" (p. 18). Individuals with a schizoid tendency build up the libidinal value of their objects in the inner world, and "they tend to identify themselves very strongly with their internal objects" (Fairbairn, 1952, p. 18).[7] Identification with internalised libidinal objects (and a secret sense of possession of internal objects) leads to "a narcissistic inflation of the ego" and, hence,

the individual's secret sense of superiority. Secret possession of internalised objects also causes "the individual to feel that he is 'different' from other people—even if not, as often happens, actually exceptional or unique" (p. 22). The need for secrecy is partly "determined by fear of the loss of internalized objects which appear infinitely precious (even as precious as life itself)" (p. 22). The tendency of schizoid individuals to libidinise their thought processes, and a further tendency "to make libidinal objects of the systems which they have created" (p. 21), are particularly evident in "schizoid infatuations". The libidinisation of thought processes and the substitution of ideas for feelings (intellectualisation) are "carried to extreme lengths" in patients with schizophrenia (Fairbairn, 1952, p. 20).

### 9.4.3   Schizoid beginnings of schizophrenia

> The case histories of many schizophrenics emphasize that the patients had shown some signs of peculiarity from early on in life and were never able to express strong feelings. There had been a tendency to turn away from the outside world at the least provocation. (Rosenfeld, 1965, p. 167)

For Rosenfeld (1965), patients with schizophrenia have a particularly severe superego of a persecutory nature. The clinical picture of schizophrenia "often reflects some of the most brutal morality", attributable to an archaic superego "in which the primal identification (incorporated figure of the mother) holds forth only the promise of condemnation, abandonment and consequent death" (Rosenfeld, 1965 p. 66). Schizophrenic individuals are fundamentally lonely because for them human relatedness is fraud with terror. They cannot overcome their fear and distrust of others because of adverse experiences early in life (Gabbard, 1990). Arieti (1973) suggested that adverse experiences of early childhood (giving rise to the "original" self-image) are repressed but can be reactivated later in life when—as a result of recurring adverse experiences—the patient

---

[7]These are internally fantasised objects (experienced in the inner world), as opposed to unconscious representations of object relations, which Kernberg defined internal objects to be.

comes to feel "that the segment of the world that is important to him finds him unacceptable", and when he realises "that as long as he lives he will be unacceptable to others" (p. 126). As the patient realises that he does not fit and is alone, he experiences a state of panic (Sullivan, 1953); he "now sees himself as totally defeated, without any worth and possibility of redemption" (Arieti, 1973, p. 127). Laing described the motivational conflict of the schizoid individual, a conflict that may eventually carry him into psychosis.

> His longing is for complete union. But of this very longing he is terrified, because it will be the end of his self. (Laing, 1960, p. 97)

Overwhelming anxiety, which, according to Laing (1960), may be elaborated by the schizoid individual as a fear of death or fear of irrevocable loss of self, increases in anticipation of rejection. It causes the individual to avoid relationships or to relate to others in a depersonalised manner, as described by Laing, and to hold on tight to the defences employed against dependence on others.

> In phantasy, the self can be anyone, anywhere, do anything, have everything. It is thus omnipotent and completely free—but only in phantasy. Once commit itself to any real project and it suffers agonies of humiliation—not necessarily for any failure, but simply because it has to subject itself to necessity and contingency. It is omnipotent and free only in phantasy. The more this phantastic omnipotence and freedom are indulged, the more weak, helpless and fettered it becomes in actuality. The illusion of omnipotence and freedom can be sustained only within the magic circle of its own shut-up-ness in phantasy. (Laing 1960, pp. 88–89)

## Self-consciousness and conformity

Participation in life is possible "but only in the face of intense anxiety" (Laing, 1960, p. 95).

The schizoid individual "feels more 'vulnerable', more liable to be exposed by the look of another person" (p. 79) than anyone else. His "heightened sense of being always seen, or at any rate of being always potentially seeable", an exaggeration of normal self-consciousness, assumes a tormenting quality and "compulsive nature" (Laing, 1960, p. 113). For the schizoid person to enter into essential exchange with others means to expose himself to the possibility of attack, insofar as he cannot conform. Our persona is constructed from compliance with others' expectations and designed to keep in check fears of aggression, yet conformity is precisely what is difficult to achieve for various reasons by those who have schizoid tendencies, allowing existential anxieties to come to the surface during their being-with-others and resulting in their "inner" withdrawal to be established ever more firmly. From the "false self" or persona, which is our "identity-for-others", arising "in compliance with [others'] intentions or expectations" (p. 105), schizoid individuals separate a secrete "inner self", which is the self that "is occupied in phantasy" (Laing, 1960).

Indeed, many mechanisms can undermine our ability to conform. Schizophrenia is a neurodevelopmental disorder that apart from mutation loading (Keller & Miller, 2006) is associated with prenatal exposure to viral infections (Brown & Susser, 2002), obstetric complications (Verdoux et al., 1997), and childhood brain disease, manifesting not only in abnormal brain development with morphological and cytoarchitectonic alterations, but also in postural and movement deficits in childhood (Walker, Savoie & Davis, 1994), minor physical abnormalities, cognitive impairment, and developmental delays (Jones, Rodgers, Murray & Marmot, 1994). Although it is often argued that aberrant early development is part of the schizophrenic process, it is clear that if children or adolescents thus affected lack compensatory strengths and alternative sources of support, they may be placed on a trajectory of social rejection, fears of rejection, social maladjustment, and unappeasable existential anxieties that may lead to and, at times of additional social stresses and insecurities, clinically present as schizoid or schizotypal, perhaps paranoid, personality disorder or, indeed, schizophrenia if the individual has a hallucinatory predisposition in addition (Behrendt & Young, 2004).

## Existential anxiety and omnipotent fantasy

The schizoid individual is locked in a futile struggle to overcome his existential anxiety, and it is this anxiety that may eventually carry him into psychosis. In an attempt to preserve the compensatory "inner self" from "destruction from outer sources", the schizoid individual has to eliminate "any direct access from without to this "inner" self" (Laing, 1960, p. 152). Withdrawal into omnipotent fantasy affords some lowering of existential anxieties, however this comes at a price of increasing estrangement from the reality shared with others.

> Hence what was designed in the first instance as a guard or barrier to prevent disruptive impingements on the self, can become the walls of a prison from which the self cannot escape. (Laing, 1960, p. 150)

The schizoid individual, "in order to be safe from the persistent threat and danger from the world, has cut [himself] off from direct relatedness with others" (Laing, 1960, pp. 149–150). His withdrawal into an omnipotent "inner self", manifesting to us as oddity, becomes one of the reasons why he struggles to achieve conformity and hence relatedness. While visibility is avoided for fear of attack, invisibility is dreaded for fear of existential annihilation (separation distress). As Laing noted, the schizoid individual's "fear of being invisible, of disappearing, is closely associated with the fear of his mother disappearing" (p. 125). His "schizoid nature is partly a direct expression of, and occasion for, his ontological insecurity, and partly an attempt to overcome it" (Laing, 1960, p. 115).

The "self-conscious" person is caught in a dilemma. He may *need* to be seen and recognised, in order to maintain his sense of realness and identity. Yet, at the same time, the other represents a threat to his identity and reality. (pp. 121–122)

What he longs for most is the possibility of "a moment of recognition", but whenever this by chance occurs, when he has by accident "given himself away", he is covered in confusion and suffused with panic. (p. 122)

He is constantly drawing attention to himself, and at the same time drawing attention *away* from his self. His behaviour is compulsive. All his thoughts are occupied with being seen. His longing is to be known. But this is also what is most dreaded. (Laing, 1960, pp. 122–123)

## Environmental contributions

Children who later develop schizophrenia are more anxious at school and more likely to play alone (Jones *et al.*, 1994). Poor social adjustment and lack of confidence are common characteristics in children and adolescents who later develop schizophrenia (Jones, Murray & Rodgers, 1995). Vulnerable children are at risk of attracting their peers' aggression quite naturally through their being slow, weak, unattractive, or simply different, and this would be even more so if they were anything but content with the lowest rank in their peer group. Failure by others to conform disinhibits our instinctive aggression, which is why those who are about to develop schizophrenia start to fearfully observe their social environment, especially at times when parents' and society's expectations as to the individual's commitment to conform and fulfil acceptable roles is greatest, that is, in puberty and early adulthood. The association between schizophrenic relapse and exposure to criticism and hostility in the patient's family (Brown, Birley & Wing, 1972) and the association with urban upbringing (Pedersen & Mortensen, 2001), which implies instability of relatedness to the social environment, attest to the importance of intraspecific aggression and the fear thereof in the genesis of schizophrenia—as do hallucinations of other people's voices during psychosis, which are often critical and derogatory in their content (Birchwood, Meaden, Trower, Gilbert & Plaistow, 2000; Linn, 1977), reflecting patients' fears of rejection and marginalisation.

### 9.4.4 Schizophrenic breakdown into psychosis

> Indeed, what is called psychosis is sometimes simply the sudden removal of the veil of the false self, which had been serving to maintain an outer behavioural normality that may, long ago, have failed to be any reflection of the state of affairs in the secret self. (Laing, 1960, p. 106)

The schizoid individual maintains "his outward semblance of normality by progressively more desperate means" until his "defences against the world fail even in their primary functions: to prevent persecutory impingements", so that anxiety "creeps back more intensely than ever" (Laing, 1960, p. 150). Intense anxiety leads to personality disintegration (lifting the veil of the "false self") and frank psychosis with the emergence of an autistic system of defences (Laing, 1960). The patient "partially removes the influence of the conceptual interpersonal world that has afflicted the recent injuries" by adopting new forms of cognition and new intrapsychic mechanisms (Arieti, 1973, p. 127). He "transforms the intrapsychic danger into an external or interpersonal one" (Arieti, 1973, p. 127).

> During the prepsychotic stages, the patient had, so to say, protected the world from blame and had to a large extent considered himself responsible for his defeat. Now he externalizes again this feeling. No longer does he accuse himself. The accusation comes from the external world. The voices accuse him of being a spy, a murderer,

a traitor, a homosexual. These developments are defensive, though they do not seem so. As painful as it is to be accused by others, it is not so unpleasant as to accuse oneself. Moreover, the patient feels falsely accused. Thus, the projected accusation is not injurious to the self-esteem. On the contrary, in comparison with his prepsychotic state, the patient experiences a rise in his self-esteem, often accompanied by a feeling of martyrdom. The really accused person now is not the patient but the persecutor, who is accused of persecuting the patient. (Arieti, 1973, p. 127)

### Expression of hostility

> If the patient contrasts his own inner emptiness, worthlessness, coldness, desolation, dryness, with the abundance, worth, warmth, companionship that he may yet believe to be elsewhere ..., there is evoked a welter of conflicting emotions, from a desperate *longing* and yearning for what others have and he lacks, to frantic *envy* and hatred of all that is theirs and not his, or a desire to destroy all the goodness, freshness, richness in the world. (Laing 1960, p. 96)

Schizoid individuals and those with incipient schizophrenia are not only unable to withstand or avert the numerous implicit threats that are an essential part of the fabric of social exchange (as a result of their excessive sensitivity to threat and failure to conform to social norms), they are also excessively inhibited when it comes to expression of their own aggression, including the expression of their envy (which they may feel particularly acutely). Once psychosis has established itself, the patient's aggressive impulses against those who (overtly or in the patient's mind) frustrate his longing for human relatedness (and for complete union with an ideal object) may still be inhibited by excessive fear of retaliation, but can now find new indirect outlets.

Much of the eccentricity and oddity of schizoid behaviour has this basis. The individual begins by slavish conformity and compliance, and ends through the very medium of this conformity and compliance in expressing his own negative will and hatred. (p. 109)

The false-self system's compliance with the will of others reaches its most extreme form in the automatic obedience, echolalia, and flexibilitas cerea of the catatonic. Here obedience, imitation, copying are carried to such excess that the grotesque parody produced becomes a concealed indictment of the examiner. The hebephrenic frequently employs guying and mimicry of the persons he hates and fears as his preferred and only available means of attacking them. This may be one of the patient's private jokes. (Laing, 1960, p. 109)

# CHAPTER TEN

# Conclusions

Social interaction is based, in part, on reciprocal induction of phylogenetically evolved (and hence instinctive) affective signals expressed through language and gesture (Eibl-Eibesfeldt, 1970; Hass, 1968; Lorenz, 1973; Moynihan, 1998). Approving other individuals and being approved of by others are instinctive libidinal interactions, interactions that take place in a domain that remains unconscious. Insofar as approval is *sought*, we are dealing with appetitive behaviour and its acquisition; and, here, consciousness may be relevant. When *seeking* approval and recognition, we aim to create conditions conducive to libidinal interactions and affective attunement. Instinctive behaviour, that is, behaviour that automatically is induced in us by others or that we automatically induce in others, needs to be distinguished from appetitive behaviour, including behavioural strategies and attitudes that we use in order to induce certain behavioural dispositions and attitudes in others—dispositions and attitudes that are associated with the release, in others, of affectionate and cherishing signals. Instinctive behaviour is not modulated by learning in the way this can be said about appetitive behaviour. Appetitive social behaviour (comprising again linguistic and gestural expressions) is ontogenetically acquired and culturally transmitted. Performance of an instinctive action can be facilitated or suppressed by appreciation of the situational context in which an instinctive action is called for, but the stimulus configuration that incites an instinctive action (the releasing "stimulus situation") does so outside consciousness. Our innate responses to others' innate affective (linguistic and gestural) displays are released in accordance with the situation in which the interaction takes place (social context), but only insofar as releasing stimulus configurations are encountered in that situation (Figure 10-1). Acquired aspects of social behaviour (behaviours of "the more theatrical and contextual kind") are mainly concerned with the creation and maintenance ("definition") of situations (Goffman, 1959) that favour certain types of reciprocally inductive interactions (those derived from libidinal parent-infant interactions) and that disfavour other types of innate affective interactions (involving offensive aggression). Behaviour that creates and maintains these situations does so by responding to complex contextual information; it is appetitive in nature, in that it is designed to attain "releasing stimulus situations" for instinctive communicative patterns (Lorenz, 1935, 1937).

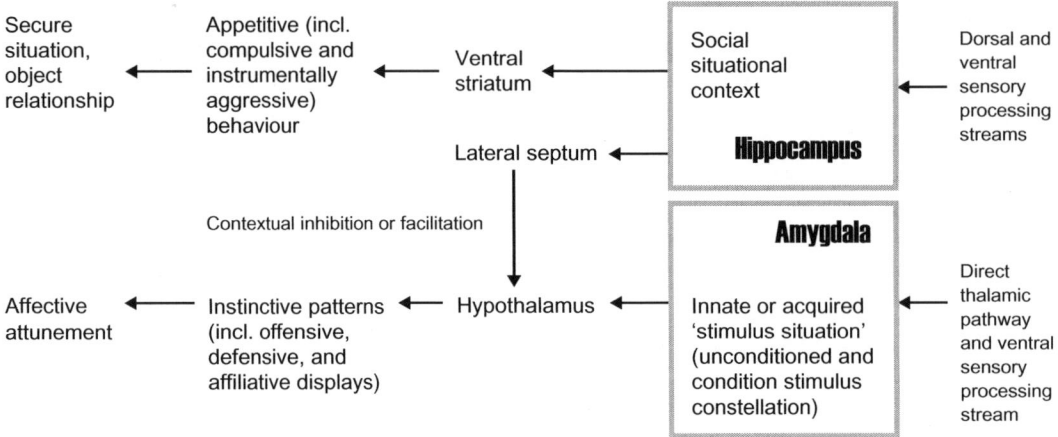

Figure 10-1.    Two dimensions of social behaviour.

Appetitive behaviour advances sequentially by responding to frames of a simulated world—the world that seems to surround us (the consciously experienced allocentric world). Consciousness is uniquely involved in the guidance and acquisition of appetitive (preparatory and goal-directed) behaviours. Appetitive behaviour is composed of (i) orienting reactions that align the organism to releasing stimulus situations and (ii) locomotor activation and navigation to locations in its environment where certain types of releasing stimulus situations are more likely to occur. Appetitive behaviour that moves the organism across time, rather than space, has lost its locomotor component but retained its effort component in the form of assertive and instrumentally aggressive behaviour. One's location in the environment is defined spatially, whereas the social or interpersonal situation that envelops one's instinctive interactions with others is defined temporally and spatially.[1] "Social orientation" to the situation one presently occupies is similar to one's orientation in and to the spatial

environment (Eibl-Eibesfeldt, 1970; Lorenz, 1973). Social orientation may precede, and give guidance to, an epoch of appetitive behaviour (consisting of actions complying with social norms and expectations) that *moves* oneself from an anxiogenic situation to a situation of relative security, much as spatial orientation precedes spatial navigation to a location of a known resource. The former process may depend on neural circuitry and structures (namely the hippocampus) that originally evolved to support the latter process. Social orientation, which is not dissimilar from processes involved in the dynamic formation of one's sense of self in the here-and-now, is accompanied by an *anxiety* concerning one's standing in the present social environment and the social order and rules that apply to oneself (Eibl-Eibesfeldt, 1970). Social navigation not only guides us to a "place" where we feel safe and related again, it also allows us to gain access to resources, that is, access to conditions conducive to libidinal interactions (affective attunement) and other consummatory-type instinctive activities. Role relationships (Sandler, 1976), which one establishes and maintains in "space-time", are situations, persisting for a period of time, within which one is likely to engage another individual in reciprocal care-giving/care-inducing (libidinal) interactions or—depending on formative early life experiences—in reciprocal    dominant/submissive    interactions

---

[1]The close evolutionary relationship between space and time is evident in the process of thought (Lorenz, 1973), which is the process that generates virtual situations—situations that are assessed internally (in imagery) for their potential to provide a suitable framework for libidinal interactions with others. Virtual situations, created by the process of thought, provide a "space" for trial activity (Hartmann, 1964).

(as illustrated by the dynamics of guilt and masochism (Horney, 1937)). There is considerable compulsion involved in the maintenance of situational envelopes learned to be conducive to patterns of dyadic libidinal or dominant/ submissive interactions ("compulsion to repeat" (Freud, 1920)), as illustrated by the various forms of transference and the compulsion, experienced by narcissistic individuals, to tell untruths (Kohut, 1971). These compulsive phenomena are reflective of the appetitive nature of the social behaviour involved (Figure 10-1).

There are two types of self: a self-image based on the ego ideal and a sense of self (self-esteem) derived from others' attitudes towards us. How are these types of self related to each other and how do they interact? In imagery, we picture ourselves in a form that is socially approved and that—if we were to *adopt that form*—would ensure our acceptance and recognition by others. The self of one's imagery is an *object* of others' benevolent attention and approval. In the here-and-now, we employ behaviours and adopt attitudes that are personality characteristics of the imagined self formed by many past identifications (ego ideal). Thus, we can emulate, in the here and now, our own self-image. By emulating our self-image, that is by acting in accordance with our ego ideal, we ensure (or seek to ensure) others' approval and acceptance of ourselves. In this process, we recreate (appetitively) situations in which others' caring capacities can be enlisted and instinctive caring interactions can take place. We may, for instance, set out, in an appetitively driven fashion, to become someone who appears helpless or distressed and who therefore automatically induces caring interventions from others. Progression along a path towards adoption of a helpless or distressed state may be automatically (habitually) induced by the situation in which we find ourselves, or it may be preceded by imagery of a helpless or distressed self receiving attention from others, which actually is an imagery of a helpless or distressed third object (one with whom we identified in the past) receiving care from the mother or a later reincarnation

of the mother (an object that is an external replica of the primary love object).

Self-awareness, the self experienced in the here-and-now, accompanies appetitive behaviour that—when being performed in accordance with social norms and the law—achieves and maintains social relatedness, conditions under which instinctive libidinal interactions can take place. Conscious self-awareness varies between the extremes of anxious self-consciousness, apathy and dissociation, and raised self-esteem, even elation. The acute sense of self-consciousness, associated with anxiety, indicates that our security is low and, here, our appetitive striving for relatedness is most intense. Raised self-esteem, on the other hand, indicates that appetitive striving for relatedness has been successful. The self that senses others' benevolent interest (the self that is infused with esteem) may be similar to a state of pleasure that arises upon consumption of a reward, a state of satisfaction that accompanies reinforcement learning and facilitates further exploratory actions (along the appetitive or "symbolic" dimension of behaviour). Similarly to other states of satisfaction, raised self-esteem (as opposed to a sense of self that is tinged with anxiety) favours exploratory and expansive actions that can lead to the acquisition of new behavioural strategies. Such actions may be seen as arrogant or offensive by others; they may inadvertently challenge the integrity of others' self and the security of their position, inviting them to respond in an offensively aggressive manner. Mania is, of course, a state associated not only with exceedingly high self-esteem—often to the point of pervasive elation—but also with socially expansive and exploitative behaviour (whereas depression is associated with low self-esteem and social withdrawal, and incipient schizophrenia is associated with anxious self-consciousness).

## 10.1  Probability and predictability

The organism's responding to the environmental location or temporal-spatial situation it presently occupies may be evolutionarily related to its responding to discrete external stimuli, which means that principles of stimulus-response relationships and their acquisition may apply to the organisation of behaviour that appears to be responsive and *appropriate to* the environmental context. Research into hippocampal, ventral striatal, and medial prefrontal cortical function provides evidence consistent with a model according to which representations of environmental locations evolved into representations of abstract situations featuring an emotional dimension (i.e., a dimension that relates to the organism's physiological state) (Behrendt, 2011). Spatiotemporal aspects of situations (or locations in the environment), ascertained by the dorsal hippocampus, are suggested to induce or dispose to discriminative appetitive actions, while emotional and nonspatial environmental aspects of the organism's situation, ascertained by the ventral hippocampus, induce or dispose to modes of emotional behaviour that maintain the more or less random generation of exploratory reward-seeking and aversion-escaping behaviours. Emotional behaviour modes involve activation of a general-purpose appetitive drive (incentive state). If transformations of the situational context (with its emotional dimension) into behaviour are initially implemented with a degree of variability, then drive reduction (mediated, for instance, by unexpected reward experience), reinforces the transformation of situations into more specialised emotional behaviour modes or task-orientated action modes (task modes), according to general principles of learning theory (Brown, 1953; Miller, 1948; Miller & Dollard, 1941). Emotional accompaniments of reward-seeking behaviour ensure that learning is specific with regard to the reward sought and obtained. Reinforcement of associations between situational-emotional contexts and emotional or task-oriented behaviour modes underlies the acquisition of instrumental behaviour, which, when henceforth employed in a *situationally appropriate* manner, leads to reward exposure or punishment avoidance with a greater degree of *certainty*. Social situations become meaningful in individual social development in that they acquire the ability to compel us enact

another situation (outcome) in which we are likely to obtain social (libidinal) reward or avoid the exposure to social punishment. Whether the aim of instrumental behaviour is to minimise the probability of punishment or maximise the occurrence of reward, instrumental behaviour, including voluntary social behaviour, is always a repetition of the past, as illustrated by the psychoanalytic concept of transference.

Developing the notion of the dimensionality of social behaviour, direct affective interactions include fearful or submissive responding to social threats (in form of gestural or verbal insults), offensively aggressive responding to insults, and care-inducing and care-giving behaviours (libidinal interactions). It is clear that these responses typically depend on the social context, however they are not primarily responses to contextual information. Appetitive and contextually determined behaviours, unfolding along a separate dimension, include escape from situations in which one likely becomes the target of others' aggression (situations that are associated with anxiety), active avoidance of exposure to offensive aggression (often involving culturally ritualised gestural behaviours), angry responding to intrusions into one's territory (e.g., intrusions that are effected by a challenge to the cultural framework within which one's self is defined), and goal-directed solicitation of others' attentive and caring behaviours (attachment behaviours). Through these behaviours (involving acquired gestural and linguistic expressions), we habitually or exploratively change our situation in such a way that exposure to offensive aggression becomes less likely and exposure to positive social signals that have their ontogenetic and phylogenetic origin in maternal nursing behaviour becomes more likely. We, thus, gravitate towards situations that are familiar and predictable and in which we feel secure, accepted, and socially related.

Defensive attacks against predators involve defensive vocalisations that have a noxious effect on the opponent (Blanchard & Blanchard, 1989). Phylogenetically, offensively aggressive displays, serving an intraspecific communicative function, came to be based, in part, on defensively threatening vocalisations (McDougall, 1924; Moynihan, 1998). While some vocalisations automatically induce withdrawal or submissive behaviours in an opponent, other vocalisations evolved as a means of overcoming separation from the mother or herd. Both, threatening vocalisations and separation cries, must have been drawn into the evolution of appetitive speech behaviour, inasmuch as both control the behaviour of other individuals. More complex speech may have evolved—partly from offensively aggressive displays and partly from infantile separation vocalisations—as a means for soliciting and appetitively *controlling* another's attention and devotion. The purpose of speech is, at least in part, to establish and maintain engagement with another person (originally the mother) and, thereby, increase the probability of rewarding exchange of instinctively affective displays. Thus, speech—as an appetitive, contextually responsive, and culturally transmitted behaviour—enables approach to a situation of relatedness and concurrent withdrawal from a situation of unrelatedness (relative social isolation or exclusion). Not only speech and attention-seeking behaviour but also instrumental (and offensive) aggression are predominantly left-hemisphere-based in humans. Speech and proactive attention-seeking behaviour can be habitual (exploitative) and affectively neutral *or* explorative (random) and affectively charged, being employed in certain and uncertain social situations (giving rise to certain or uncertain expectation of a state of interpersonal relatedness or security), respectively. The right hemisphere may support complementary aspects of appetitive avoidance/withdrawal behaviour; social avoidance or submissive behaviour (behaviour constructed around culturally ritualised forms of innate submissive gestures) is thought to be right-hemisphere based. Explorative (random) avoidance or submissive behaviour in uncertain situations (seeking to reduce the probability of punishment in a more or less random fashion) is accompanied by anxiety. Habitually submissive behaviour inhibits others' aggressive potential in a situationally appropriate manner with a high

degree of certainty (predictability); it is an active avoidance behaviour, and it is not accompanied by anxiety. It can be speculated that, in either hemisphere, modes of explorative behaviour (accompanied by affective arousal) may involve an interaction between hippocampus (especially ventral hippocampus) and the infralimbic region of the medial prefrontal cortex, whereas modes of habitually exploitative behaviour (instrumental task modes) may involve a functional interaction between hippocampus (including the dorsal hippocampus) and the prelimbic region of the medial prefrontal cortex.

## 10.2  Self and defence

Being part of the appetitive system of the regulation of social behaviour, the self captures the current *risk* of becoming a target of others' aggressive displays; it, thus, characterises the social situation one presently occupies. At the same time, the self, particularly self-esteem, represents one's *potential* for attracting signals of approval or submission (Danziger, 1997; Gergen, 1977). The person's self is formed on the basis of reflected appraisals from others (James, 1890; Sullivan, 1953), much as the child "builds up the consciousness of itself by the love and appreciation it gets from its surroundings" (Schilder, 1951). Self-esteem is a marker of relative security in the social or group situation; it is acquired and offensively defended like a territory. Appetitive safety-seeking behaviour, creating a situation in which one can receive signals of approval (self-object experiences, according to Kohut (1971)) and submission, overcomes anxiety (related to infantile fear of strangers) and enhances self-esteem. The essential desirability of being acceptable to others corresponds to the essential undesirability of being anxious (Sullivan, 1953). Appetitive social behaviour, maintaining conditions that suppress others' offensively aggressive tendencies, may also *avoid* anxiety. Loss of self-esteem, which is equivalent to a resurgence of social anxiety, signifies a decrease in social relatedness and an increase in one's vulnerability to being offensively aggressed by others. Pain and anxiety are involved in learning socially adaptive, appetitive behaviour, in that a reduction in pain or anxiety reinforces links between situations and exploratory type social actions immediately preceding a reduction in pain or anxiety. Defence mechanisms, preventing pain and anxiety, and personality styles refer to habitually employed strategies of social behaviour that, in standard situations, more or less successfully solicit approval or interest, on the one hand, and limit the attraction of hostile signals, on the other hand.

We devote energy and behavioural resources (through incentive motivational arousal) to building up and maintaining an image or opinion that we want others to have of ourselves (James, 1890). The aura we create around ourselves, by means of social behaviour, influences others' behaviour towards ourselves, especially their disposition to emit affiliative or aggressive signals. If we lose this aura (and, with it, our sense of relatedness), we enter an evolutionarily dangerous situation (related to a heightened risk of becoming the target of conspecific aggression) and, thus, submerge into anxiety. The aura we create around ourselves—in an effort to influence others' perception of ourselves—can be regarded as a "defensive screen". We deduce this defensive screen from others' attitudes and reactions towards us or, more precisely, from our subjective *perception* of others' attitudes and reactions towards us. Efforts to improve and maintain the image or idea that others form about ourselves lie at the heart of adaptive social behaviour; and the manner in which we direct and prioritise these efforts characterises our personality style and defensive constitution. There are three principle strategies by which we control our reflection in the mirror of the social environment. First, socially normative (including politically correct) behaviours positively influence others' opinion of ourselves (by inhibiting their aggressiveness). Second, exhibitionistic behaviour and the enactment of grandiose fantasies place us into the focus of an admiring audience (Kohut, 1971). Unless exhibitionistic behaviour is adequately tempered by judicious employment of socially

normative behaviour, our self disintegrates and anxiety resurges (Laing, 1960). Third, an objective of social behaviour is to build up and maintain our self (being our reflection in the mirror of the immediate social environment) or defensive screen through the acquisition and display of social attributes (possessions and status signs) (Horney, 1937)—attributes that, by determining the *context* in which we are perceived by others, have an inhibiting effect on the aggressive potentialities in our environment. The defensive aura, actively maintained through (i) socially normative behaviours, (ii) tempered exhibitionistic behaviours, and (iii) the acquisition of socially desirable attributes, forms a secure base (similarly to that provided by the mother) for dyadic exploratory and libidinal engagement with others. The objective of many neurotic behaviours, too, is to improve the image others form of oneself. Neurotic behaviours often fail to achieve this objective, or achieve it less effectively, although self-deception (through repression, denial, and other defence mechanisms) may prevent the neurotic person from gaining insight into his failures. Due to their ineffectiveness, neurotic behaviours are often accompanied by an anxious sense of self-consciousness (Fairbairn, 1952; Kohut, 1971; Laing, 1960; Shapiro, 2000). The greater the anxiety, the greater one's potential exposure to others' hostility (as exemplified by Laing's (1960) dynamic conceptualisation of schizophrenia), and the more effort has be to invested into building a defensive screen—to the point of suffering decompensation and mental illness.

Defence mechanisms and personality types may also describe different ways, acquired in childhood, in which approach-avoidance conflicts (or avoidance-avoidance conflicts) are considered and resolved in social situations. Expression of appetitive social behaviour, in both mental health and illness, tends to be contingent on decision-making processes, weighing conflicting imperatives: the need to be seen and the need not to be seen by conspecifics (Laing, 1960). Trying to solicit positive attention (by emulating the ego ideal) and, at the same time, guard against conspecific attack, we frequently face approach-avoidance conflicts. Approach-avoidance conflicts are associated with "behavioural inhibition", risk assessment, and anxiety; and all of these are facets of hippocampal function (McNaughton, 2006; McNaughton & Corr, 2004; McNaughton & Wickens, 2003). Behavioural inhibition, occurring in intervals of "rest", is a prerequisite for decision-making processes that aim at risk assessment and conflict resolution. The hippocampus is intricately linked with the default-mode network. Speculatively, therefore, anxiety faced in social situations invokes default-mode (resting-state) activity of the brain, which may have evolved to facilitate the competition between alternative interpretations of, and response dispositions to, cues embedded in the environmental situation faced by the organism. Decision making and conflict resolution involve an interaction between hippocampus and prefrontal cortex. The hippocampus may characterise the current situation in contrasting ways and *simulate* possible future situations (outcomes); the medial prefrontal cortex may coordinate behavioural response modes associated with representations of situations ascertained or simulated by the hippocampus. Competition between these response modes (referring to instrumental or emotional behaviour modes) may involve an interaction between the medial prefrontal cortex and ventral striatum—an interaction that is regulated by dopamine (reviewed in Behrendt, 2011).

### 10.3  Object relations

The infant introjects an object (i.e., learns about the object) when the object contains or modifies his distress, that is, when the infant experiences a reduction in his anxiety *vis-à-vis* the object (Bion, 1962). Introjection of an object (or part object) presupposes that an object cathexis (or cathexis of a part object) has taken place. Inner pleasurable states, reflecting the satisfaction of libidinal and other instincts or the dissolution of anxiety, are externalised onto part objects (cathexis), which are then introjected as good internal part objects.

Aggression plays a role in the early formation of part objects. By projecting feelings of frustration onto a part object (cathexis), these feelings can be controlled effectively through aggression directed at the part object. Splitting ensures that, while bad part objects can be totally projected, all-good part objects can be totally introjected (that is, incorporated into the ego) (Kernberg, 1980; Klein, 1940;). Internal bad part objects, which are projected outward at times of distress, are the primitive precursors of the superego. Splitting and part objects are characteristic features of the paranoid-schizoid infantile developmental position. In the subsequent depressive position, good and bad part objects are synthesised into a whole object, which can be reprojected and then reintrojected whenever satisfaction of a libidinal need (implying drive reduction) or anxiety reduction occurs, thereby contributing to the further differentiation of the object world. Reintrojection of good objects also promotes the complementary process of "ego synthesis". From the depressive position on, libidinal aspects of objects are introjected into the ego (thereby maintaining the cohesiveness of the self), while prohibitive and demanding aspects of these objects are introjected into the superego (Kernberg, 1980; Klein, 1940).

"Internal objects" (internal object relations) are unconscious bipolar structures consisting of an object representation, a self-representation, and an affective relationship between them (Kernberg, 1996). When internal objects are projected, and thus experienced either externally (as external objects) or in imagination (as imaginary internal or internalised objects), they establish an affective relationship with the self. The person projects his object representation or self representation (that is, either component of the bipolar structure) onto a significant other person, while enacting the reciprocal self or object representation himself. Importantly, a reactivated affect accompanies the reactivated internal object relation (Kernberg, 1996). "Role relationships" (derivatives of early object relations) develop as a *vehicle* to gratify instinctual needs and wishes (Sandler, 1976), including those to love and be loved. The resurgence of an instinctual wish becomes a wish to impose and experience a particular "role relationship" (Sandler, 1976), illustrating the appetitive-driven nature of behaviours implementing an interpersonal situation in which instinctive motor displays (communicating the giving of affection or the receipt of affection) can be released. An enacted object relationship (or role relationship) can be regarded as the situational context in which selfobject experiences (narcissistic sustenance) are likely to be received and love is likely to be given. An important function of object relationships is to procure narcissistic sustenance. Cathexis of the self with narcissistic libido serves to maintain the cohesiveness of the self (Kohut, 1971), although it could be argued that it is the situation that is conducive to receiving affection or approval that—by dissolving anxiety—enhances self-esteem.

Unavailability or unresponsiveness of one's object causes anger and aggression directed at the object. To make the object compliant with one's wishes, a degree of aggression can be used. The infant learns to exert subtle pressures on the object to force her to adopt a caring attitude towards himself (Cashdan, 1988). Using "projective identification", an individual engages in subtle manipulations to induce those about him to behave in prescribed ways. The object (target of the projection) is induced to engage in an identification with a disowned aspect of the individual doing the projection and, importantly, to behave in ways that enhance the projector's sense of self and reduce his anxiety (Cashdan, 1988). Aggression can be used to control derivatives of the primary object in indirect ways. In patients with histrionic or borderline personality disorder, self-destructive behaviour in association with rage "represents an unconscious effort to reestablish control over the environment by evoking guilt feelings in others" (Kernberg, 1992). Submergence in misery is a related strategy for coercing others to fulfil one's wishes. In masochism, access to narcissistic supplies is gained by denigrating oneself and attracting the object's aggression.

Neurotic persons with a masochistic tendency use suffering and helplessness as a means of "obtaining affection, help, control" (Horney, 1937).[2] Patients with narcissistic personality structure use their objects for the attainment of narcissistic supplies (selfobject experiences) but show few care-giving or affectionate behaviours in return (investing little object libido into their objects) (Kohut, 1971). In order to attain the craved narcissistic sustenance, these patients frequently resort to exhibitionism and grandiosity. In narcissism, there is an "expansion of the ego feeling to cover object representations", resulting in the transformation of object cathexes into secondary narcissistic cathexes (Federn, 1952). Objects are restricted to their functions of providing narcissistic sustenance and protecting the person's self-esteem. The narcissistic person's preoccupation with "inflating his ego" reflects attempts to protect himself against feelings of "insignificance and humiliation" (anxiety), on the one hand, and to repair his "crushed self-esteem", on the other (Horney, 1937).

The child learns to obtain narcissistic supplies (approval and affection)—and to maintain conditions favourable to libidinal instinctive interactions and the satisfaction of physiological needs—by inhibiting the object's potential for disapproval or aggression, specifically by behaving in prescribed ways and showing attitudes that do not elicit the object's hostility.[3] The primary love object (usually the mother) is not only a source of benevolent attention and narcissistic supplies (and can be loved in return)

---

[2] In addition, abandoning the self to "excessive suffering" narcotises the pain of rejection or loss (Horney, 1937).

[3] Aggression, in the form of punishment and firm disapproval, plays an important role in the formation of the superego (and acquisition of social avoidance behaviour). The memory of having been punished for an undesirable attitude or action can be reactivated in form of an external or imaginary bad or prohibiting object, the fear of which then constrains behaviour and shapes further learning. Gradually, curtailment of undesirable behaviour loses its dependence on the experience of prohibiting objects (automatisation) (Rado, 1956). Similarly, the superego comes to sustain self-esteem (narcissistic supplies) independently of selfobjects (Kohut, 1971).

but is also prone to receive benevolent attention and caring signals from a third party (usually the father), as the child comes to realise in the oedipal phase of development. In the classical oedipal constellation, the child learns to preserve its object relation to the opposite-sex parent (providing libidinal and narcissistic gratification) by way of unconscious identification with the same-sex parent (Freud, 1923). Identification with an object means that the individual obtains *this object's* desirable qualities and behavioural templates in order to access *this object's* sources of approval and affection. Subsequent to the oedipal phase, the ego's relationship with its objects is based on an identification of the ego with the "ego ideal" part of the superego (Figure 7-2). The superego is essentially an internalised object—a good object to the ego (Fairbairn, 1952), an object with which *the ego that has adopted the role of ego ideal* has a sustaining relationship. If we assume that the "superego state" is a state of identification with the ego ideal, then it becomes clear why ego and superego (or ego ideal, more precisely) "have an analogous distance from, and potential connection to, the object cathexes" and external reality (Federn, 1952). By adopting socially acceptable (normative) attitudes and emulating the ego ideal, we inhibit the object's, that is, the superego's, potential for offensive aggression; "temporary immobilisation of the Daimonion sector of the superego" is achieved when the ego "allies with the ego ideal" (Bergler, 1952).

In the context of an affect, the subject may experience "an image or representation of the self relating to an image or representation of another person" (prior to imposing an internal object relation on an interaction with an external object) (Kernberg, 1996). Conversations with inner presences may fulfil a function that is related to the anticipation of parental approval or disapproval of actions (outcome simulation). When an action is contemplated by the self, the action (or its outcome) is "subjected to an imaginary audience" (Cashdan, 1988), that is, to a replica or enactment of the superego. The image of the self that receives approval or disapproval in this way may, in fact,

be that part of the ego that is identified with the ego ideal for the purpose of receiving approval from an internally experienced or fantasised replica (derivative) of the superego (Figure 7-2). Some attempts to emulate a third object or the ego ideal do not progress beyond the contemplative stage in which object relations are anticipated (as a form of trial activity for the purpose of decision making). In schizoid developments, the person is compelled to maintain relationships with internalised objects (experienced in fleeting imagery), instead of relationships with external objects, given that, for the schizoid person, relationships with external objects would be "fraught with too much anxiety over separation" (Fairbairn, 1952). Identification with an object for the purpose of securing narcissistic supplies (in the oedipal phase) is continuous with phenomena involving the adoption of a grandiose (but fragile) façade or "persona". In this way, the neurotic person covers up deep feelings of intrinsic weakness and insignificance (low self-esteem) (Horney, 1937).

The ability to observe others in their relationship without hostility, and be benevolent towards them, marks an achievement in ego development (Segal, 1997). Our ability to observe external objects interacting with each other may be related to our ability to identify with an external object in the "here-and-now" (or in a virtual environment, such as a movie or play) or with an imaginary object in thought or daydreaming. We unwittingly adopt the perspective of an individual we observe in a movie or play. When observing others, during wakeful states of rest, the perspective adopted by the self (ego feeling) can be transferred onto an object with whom one identifies. The switching of ego feeling between the self and objects may also occur in dreams. The self-boundary is relaxed in these states (similarly to the phenomenon of recurrent primary identification described by Sandler (1993)). Identification with an object in these states transposes the ego-object polarity onto a new level, whereby the object that is identified with the ego enters into a relationship with a derivative of the primary object. By identifying with (and subtly imitating) an object, we adopt the role of the ego ideal and accesses resources of approving and affectionate signals available to that object and, in an abstract sense, to the ego ideal—resources that are conceptualised as the approving functions of the superego. Both, states of external observation or monitoring and states of daydreaming or thought, are associated with default-mode network activity; and both imply "behavioural inhibition", in that thinking (imaginary trial engagement with an object or an "imaginary audience") is incompatible with "acting out" of destructive impulses (Segal, 1997).

# REFERENCES

Abbinnet, R. (2003). *Culture and Identity: Critical Theories*. London: Sage Publications.

Addis, D. R., Wong, A. T. & Schacter, D. L. (2007). Remembering the past and imagining the future: common and distinct neural substrates during event construction and elaboration. *Neuropsychologia, 45*: 1363–1377.

Adler, A. (1965). *Superiority and Social Interest*. London: Routledge and Kegan Paul.

Adorno, T. W. (1991). *The Culture Industry*. London: Routledge.

Adorno, T. W. & Horkheimer, M. (1986). *Dialectic of Enlightenment* (J. Cumming Trans.). New York: Continuum.

Agazarian, Y. & Peters, R. (1981/2004). *The Visible and Invisible Group*. London: Karnac.

Anderson, M. I. & Jeffery, K. J. (2003). Heterogeneous modulation of place cell firing by changes in context. *The Journal of Neuroscience, 23*: 8827–8835.

Arieti, S. (1970). The structural and psychodynamic role of cognition in the human psyche. In: S. Arieti (Ed.), *The World Biennial of Psychiatry and Psychotherapy, Volume I*. New York: Basic Books.

Arieti, S. (1973). The interpersonal and the intrapsychic in severe psychopathology. In: E. G. Witenberg (Ed.), *Interpersonal Explorations in Psychoanalysis: New Directions in Theory and Practice*. New York: Basic Books.

Balint, M. (1952). *Primary Love and Psycho-Analytic Technique*. London: Hogarth Press.

Baron-Cohen, S., Allen, J. & Gillberg, C. (1992). Can autism be detected at 18 months? The needle, the haystack, and the CHAT. *The British Journal of Psychiatry, 161*: 839–843.

Baron-Cohen, S., Leslie, A. M. & Frith, U. (1985). Does the autistic child have a "theory of mind"? *Cognition, 21*: 37–46.

Baudouin, C. (1922). *Studies in Psychoanalysis*. London: George Allen & Unwin.

Baumeister, R. F. (1997). The self and society: Changes, problems and opportunities. In: R. D. Ashmore & L. Jussim (Eds.), *Self and Identity: Fundamental Issues*. New York: Oxford University Press.

Baumeister, R. F., Smart, L. & Boden, J. M. (1996). Relation of threatened egotism to violence and aggression: The dark side of high self-esteem. *Psychological Review, 103*: 5–33.

Behrendt, R. P. (2007). The subjectivity of the perceived world: Psychopathology and the mind-body problem from a perspective of idealism. In: V. W. Fallio (Ed.), *New Developments in Consciousness Research*. Hauppauge, NY: Nova Science.

Behrendt, R. P. (2010). Contribution of hippocampal region CA3 to consciousness and schizophrenic hallucinations. *Neuroscience and Biobehavioral Reviews, 34*: 1121–1136.

Behrendt, R. P. (2011). *Neuroanatomy of Social Behaviour: An Evolutionary and Psychoanalytic Perspective*. London: Karnac.

Behrendt, R. P. & Young, C. (2004). Hallucinations in schizophrenia, sensory impairment, and brain disease: A unifying model. *Behavioral and Brain Sciences, 27*: 771–787.

Bell, D. (2001). Projective identification. In: C. Bronstein (Ed.), *Kleinian Theory: A Contemporary Perspective*. London: Wiley.

Benjamin, L. S. (1996). An interpersonal theory of personality disorders. In: J. F. Clarkin & M. F. Lenzenweger (Eds.), *Major Theories of Personality Disorder*. New York: The Guilford Press.

Bergler, E. (1952). *The Superego: Unconscious Conscience*. New York: Grune & Stratton.

Berkowitz, L. (1989). Laboratory experiments in the study of aggression. In: J. Archer & K. Browne (Eds.), *Human Aggression: Naturalistic Approaches*. London: Routledge.

Bion, W. R. (1959). Attacks on linking. *International Journal of Psychoanalysis, 40*: 308–315.

Bion, W. R. (1961). *Experiences in Groups*. London: Tavistock Publications.

Bion, W. R. (1962). A theory of thinking. *International Journal of Psychoanalysis, 43*: 306–310.

Birchwood, M., Meaden, A., Trower, P., Gilbert, P. & Plaistow, J. (2000). The power and omnipotence of voices: Subordination and entrapment by voices and significant others. *Psychological Medicine, 30*: 337–344.

Blanchard, D. C. & Blanchard, R. J. (1989). Experimental animal models of aggression: What do they say about human behaviour. In: J. Archer & K. Browne (Eds.), *Human Aggression: Naturalistic Approaches*. London: Routledge.

Bowlby, J. (1973). *Separation: Anxiety and Anger*. New York: Basic Books.

Bowlby, J. (1977). The making and breaking of affectional bonds. *British Journal of Psychiatry, 130*: 201–210.

Bowlby, J. (1988). *A Secure Base: Clinical Applications of Attachment Theory*. London: Routledge.

Breger, L. (1968). Motivation, energy, and cognitive structure in psychoanalytic theory. In: J. Marmor (Ed.), *Modern Psychoanalysis: New Directions and Perspectives*. New York: Basic Books.

Brown, A. S. & Susser, E. S. (2002). In utero infection and adult schizophrenia. *Mental Retardation and Developmental Disabilities Research Reviews, 8*: 51–57.

Brown, G. W., Birley, J. L. & Wing, J. K. (1972). Influence of family life on the course of schizophrenic disorders: a replication. *British Journal of Psychiatry, 121*: 241–258.

Brown, J. S. (1953). Problems presented by the concept of acquired drives. In: *Current Theory and Research in Motivation: A Symposium*. Lincoln: University of Nebraska Press.

Burrow, T. (1949). *The Neurosis of Man*. London: Routledge & Kegan Paul.

Caper, R. (1995). On the difficulty of making a mutative interpretation. *International Journal of Psychoanalysis, 76*: 91–101.

Carpy, D. C. (1989). Tolerating the countertransference: A mutative process. *International Journal of Psychoanalysis, 70*: 285–294.

Cashdan, S. (1988). *Object Relations Therapy: Using the Relationship*. New York: W. W. Norton & Company.

Cassidy, J. W. (1990). Pharmacological treatment of post-traumatic behavioral disorders: Aggression and disorders of mood. In: *Neurobehavioural Sequelae of Traumatic Brain Injury*, ed. R. L. Wood. New York: Taylor & Francis.

Chrzanowski, G. (1973). Implications of interpersonal theory. In: E.G. Witenberg (Ed.), *Interpersonal Explorations in Psychoanalysis: New Directions in Theory and Practice*. New York: Basic Books.

Courchesne, E., Karns, C.M., Davies, H.R., Ziccardi, R., Carper, R.A., Tigue, Z.D., et al. (2001). Unusual brain growth patterns in early life in patients with autistic disorder. *Neurology, 57*: 245–254.

Crick, N. R. & Dodge, K. A. (1996). Social information-processing mechanisms in reactive and proactive aggression. *Child Development, 67*: 993–1002.

Danziger, K. (1997). The historical formation of selves. In: R. D. Ashmore & L. Jussim (Eds.), *Self and Identity: Fundamental Issues*. New York: Oxford University Press.

de Board, R. (1978). *The Psychoanalysis of Organisations*. London: Tavistock Publications.

Dissanayake, C. & Crossley, S. A. (1996). Proximity and sociable behaviours in autism: Evidence for attachment. *Journal of Child Psychology and Psychiatry, 37*: 149–156.

Eames, P. & Wood, R. L. (2003). Episodic disorders of behaviour and affect after acquired brain injury. *Neuropsychological Rehabilitation, 13*: 241–258.

Eibl-Eibesfeldt, I. (1970/1971). *Love and Hate: On the Natural History of Basic Behaviour Patterns.* London: Methuen.

Ellul, J. (1964). *The Technological Society.* New York: Alfred A. Knopf.

Escalona, A., Field, T., Nadel, J. & Lundy, B. (2002). Brief report: Imitation effects on children with autism. *Journal of Autism and Developmental Disorders, 32:* 141–144.

Fairbairn, W. R. D. (1952). *Psychoanalytic Studies of the Personality.* London: Routledge & Kegan Paul.

Federn, P. (1952). *Ego Psychology and the Psychoses.* (Ed. E. Weiss). New York: Basic Books.

Feldman, M. (1997). Projective identification: The analyst's involvement. *International Journal of Psychoanalysis, 78:* 227–241.

Feldman, R., Greenbaum, C. W. & Yirmiya, N. (1999). Mother-infant affect synchrony as an antecedent of the emergence of self-control. *Developmental Psychology, 35:* 223–231.

Fenichel, O. (1946). *The Psychoanalytic Theory of Neurosis.* London: Routledge & Kegan Paul.

Ferenczi, S. (1916). *Contributions to Psychoanalysis.* Boston, MA: Richard Badger.

Ferguson, M. J. & Bargh, J. A. (2004). How social perception can automatically influence behavior. *Trends in Cognitive Sciences, 8:* 33–39.

Ferris, C. F., Meenan, D. M., Axelson, J. F. & Albers, H. E. (1986). A vasopressin antagonist can reverse dominant/subordinate behavior in hamsters. *Physiology & Behavior, 38:* 135–138.

Field, T., Sanders, C. & Nadel, J. (2001). Children with autism display more social behaviors after repeated imitation sessions. *Autism, 5:* 317–323.

Field, T. M., Cohen, D., Garcia, R. & Greenberg, R. (1984). Mother-stranger face discrimination by the newborn. *Infant Behaviour and Development, 7:* 19–25.

Fink, B. (1997). *A Clinical Introduction to Lacanian Psychoanalysis: Theory and Technique.* Cambridge, MA: Harvard University Press.

Fitzgerald, K. D., Welsh, R. C., Gehring, W. J., Abelson, J. L., Himle, J. A., Liberzon, I. & Taylor, S. F. (2005). Error-related hyperactivity of the anterior cingulate cortex in obsessive-compulsive disorder. *Biological Psychiatry, 57:* 287–294.

Floresco, S. B. (2007). Dopaminergic regulation of limbic-striatal interplay. *Journal of Psychiatry & Neuroscience, 32:* 400–411.

Freud, S. (1914/1957). On narcissism: An introduction. In: J. Strachey (Ed.), *The Standard Edition of the Complete Psychological Works of Sigmund Freud, Vol. 14.* London: Hogarth Press.

Freud, S. (1915/1957). Instincts and their vicissitudes. In: J. Strachey (Ed.), *The Standard Edition of the Complete Psychological Works of Sigmund Freud, Vol. 14.* London: Hogarth Press.

Freud, S. (1917/1957). Mourning and melancholia. In: J. Strachey (Ed.), *The Standard Edition of the Complete Psychological Works of Sigmund Freud, Vol. 14.* London: Hogarth Press.

Freud, S. (1920/1955). Beyond the Pleasure Principle. In: J. Strachey (Ed.), *The Standard Edition of the Complete Psychological Works of Sigmund Freud, Vol. 18.* London: Hogarth Press.

Freud, S. (1923/1961). The Ego and the Id. In: J. Strachey (Ed.), *The Standard Edition of the Complete Psychological Works of Sigmund Freud, Vol. 19.* London: Hogarth Press.

Freud, S. (1921/1948). *Group Psychology and the Analysis of the Ego* (J. Strachey Trans.). London: Hogarth Press.

Freud, S. (1930/2002). *Civilisation and Its Discontents.* (D. McLintock Trans.). London: Penguin.

Freud, S. (1933/1967). *New Introductory Lectures on Psycho-Analysis.* (W. J. H. Sprott Trans.). London: Hogarth Press.

Frith, U. & Happe, F. (1994). Autism: Beyond "theory of mind". *Cognition, 50:* 115–132.

Garrod, S. & Pickering, M. J. (2004). Why is conversation so easy? *Trends in Cognitive Sciences, 8:* 8–11.

Gergely, G. (2001). The obscure object of desire: "Nearly, but clearly not, like me": Contingency preference in normal children versus children with autism. *Bulletin of the Menninger Clinic, 65:* 411–426.

Gergen, K. J. (1977). The social construction of self-knowledge. In: T. Mischel (Ed.), *The Self: Psychological and Philosophical Issues.* Oxford, UK: Blackwell.

German, P. W. & Fields, H. L. (2007). Rat nucleus accumbens neurons persistently encode locations associated with morphine reward. *Journal of Neurophysiology, 97:* 2094–2106.

Gerth, H. & Mills, C. W. (1954). *Character and Social Structure: The Psychology of Social Institutions.* London: Routledge & Kegan Paul.

Giddens, A. (1997). *Modernity and Self-Identity: Self and Society in the Late Modern Age*. Cambridge: Polity Press.

Goffman, E. (1959). *The Presentation of Self in Everyday Life*. New York: Anchor Books/ Doubleday.

Gottman, J. M., Jacobson, N. S., Rushe, R. H. & Shortt, J. W. (1995). The relationship between heart rate reactivity, emotionally aggressive behaviour, and general violence in batters. *Journal of Family Psychology, 9*: 227–248.

Griffiths, B. (1982/1989). *Morality and the Market Place*. London: Hodder & Stoughton.

Harris, N.S., Courchesne, E., Townsend, J., Carper, R.A. & Lord, C. (1999). Neuroanatomic contributions to slowed orienting of attention in children with autism. *Brain Research Cognitive Brain Research, 8*: 61–71.

Hartmann, H. (1964). *Essays on Ego Psychology: Selected Problems in Psychoanalytic Theory*. London: The Hogarth Press.

Hartmann, H. & Loewenstein, R. M. (1962). Notes on the superego. *The Psychoanalytical Study of the Child, 17*: 42–81.

Hass, H. (1968/1970). *The Human Animal: The Mystery of Man's Behaviour*. London: Hodder and Stoughton.

Heard, D. H. & Lake, B. (1986). The attachment dynamic in adult life. *British Journal of Psychiatry, 149*: 430–438.

Heidegger, M. (1927/1962). *Being and Time*, tr. J. Macquarrie & E. Robinson. Oxford: Blackewell.

Hobson, P. (1986). The autistic child's appraisal of emotion. *Journal of Child Psychology and Psychiatry, 27*: 321–342.

Hollander, E., Posner, N. & Cherkasky, S. (2002). Neuropsychiatric aspects of aggression and impulse control disorders. In: *The American Psychiatric Publishing Textbook of Neuropsychiatry and Clinical Neurosciences, 4th Edition*, eds. S.C. Yudofsky & R.E. Hales. Washington, DC: American Psychiatric Publishing.

Holmes, J. (2000). Object relations, attachment theory, self-psychology, and interpersonal psychoanalysis. In: M. G. Gelder, J. J. Lopez-Ibor Jr & N. C. Andreasen (Eds.), *New Oxford Textbook of Psychiatry*. Oxford: Oxford University Press.

Horney, K. (1937). *The Neurotic Personality of Our Time*. New York: W. W. Norton & Company.

Horney, K. (1950/1991). *Neurosis and Human Growth: The Struggle Toward Self-Realization*. New York: W. W. Norton & Company.

Hull, C. L. (1943). *Principles of Behavior*. New York: Appleton-Century-Crofts.

Husserl, E. (1928/1973). *Cartesian Meditations*. (Dorion Cairns Trans.). The Hague: Martinus Nijhoff.

Izard, C. (1994). Innate and universal facial expressions: Evidence from developmental and cross-cultural research. *Psychological Bulletin, 115*: 288–299.

James, W. (1890). *The Principles of Psychology*. New York: Holt.

Jaques, E. (1955). Social systems as a defence against persecutory and depressive anxiety. In: M. Klein, P. Heimann & R. Money-Kyrle (Eds.), *New Directions in Psychoanalysis*. London: Tavistock Publications.

Joad, C. E. M. (1955). *Guide to Philosophy*. London: Victor Gollancz.

Johnson, M. H. (2001). Functional brain development in humans. *Nature Reviews Neuroscience, 2*: 475–483.

Johnson, M. H., Dziurawiec, S., Ellis, H. & Morton, J. (1991). Newborn's preferential tracking of face-like stimuli and its subsequent decline. *Cognition, 40*: 1–19.

Jones, P., Murray, R. & Rodgers, B. (1995). Childhood risk factors for adult schizophrenia in a general population birth cohort at age 43 years. In: S. A. Mednick & J. M. Hollister (Eds.), *Neural development and schizophrenia*. New York: Plenum.

Jones, P., Rodgers, B., Murray, R. & Marmot, M. (1994). Child development risk factors for adult schizophrenia in the British 1946 birth cohort. *Lancet, 344*: 1398–1402.

Joseph, B. (1986). Envy in everyday life. *Psychoanalytic Psychotherapy, 2*: 13–22.

Keller, M. C. & Miller, G. (2006). Resolving the paradox of common, harmful, heritable mental disorders: Which evolutionary genetic models work best? *Behavioural and Brain Sciences, 29*: 385–404.

Kemner, C., Verbaten, M.N., Cuperus, J.M., Camfferman, G. & van Engeland, H. (1998). Abnormal saccadic eye movements in autistic children. *Journal of Autism and Developmental Disorders, 28*: 61–67.

Kemper, T.L. & Bauman, M. (1998). Neuropathology of infantile autism. *Journal of Neuropathology and Experimental Neurology, 57*: 645–652.

Kempes, M., Matthys, W., de Vries, H. & van Engeland, H. (2005). Reactive and proactive aggression in children—a review of theory, findings and the relevance for child and adolescent psychiatry. *European Child and Adolescent Psychiatry, 14*: 11–19.

Kernberg, O. F. (1980). Melanie Klein. In: H. I. Kaplan, A. M. Freedman & B. J. Sadock (Eds.), *Comprehensive Textbook of Psychiatry/III*. Baltimore: Williams & Wilkins.

Kernberg, O. F. (1982). Self, ego, affects, and drives. *Journal of the American Psychoanalytic Association, 30*: 893–917.

Kernberg, O. F. (1992). *Aggression in Personality Disorders and Perversions*. New Haven: Yale University Press.

Kernberg, O. F. (1996). A psychoanalytic theory of personality disorders. In: J. F. Clarkin & M. F. Lenzenweger (Eds.), *Major Theories of Personality Disorder*. New York: The Guilford Press.

Klein, M. (1932/1937). *The Psycho-Analysis of Children*. London: Hogarth Press & The Institute of Psycho-Analysis.

Klein, M. (1940/1948). Mourning and its relation to manic depressive states. In: *Contributitons to Psycho-Analysis, 1921–1945* (pp. 311–338). London: Hogarth.

Klein, M. (1952). Notes on some schizoid mechanisms. In: M. Klein, P. Heimann, S. Isaacs & J. Riviere (Eds.), *Developments in Psycho-Analysis*, London: Hogarth Press.

Klin, A. & Volkmar, F. R. (1993). The development of individuals with autism: Implications for the theory of mind hypothesis. In: S. Baron-Cohen, H. Tager-Flusberg & D. J. Cohen (Eds.), *Understanding Other Minds: Perspectives from Autism*. Oxford: Oxford University Press.

Kohut, H. (1971). *The Analysis of the Self: A Systematic Approach to the Psychoanalytic Treatment of Narcissistic Personality Disorders*. New York: International Universities Press.

Krause, R. (1988). Eine Taxonomie der Affekte und ihre Anwendung auf das Verständnis der frühen Stöhrungen. *Psychotherapie und Medizinische Psychologie, 38*: 77–86.

La Barbera, J. D., Izard, C. E., Vietze, P. & Parisi, S. A. (1976). Four- and six-month-old infants' visual responses to joy, anger and neutral expressions. *Child Development, 47*: 535–538.

Lacan, J. (1966/2001). *Écrits: A Selection*. (A. Sheridan, Trans.). London: Routledge.

Laing, R. D. (1960). *The Divided Self*. London: Tavistock.

Lathe, R. (2001). Hormones and the hippocampus. *Journal of Endocrinology, 169*: 205–231.

Laughlin, H. P. (1970). *The Ego and Its Defences*. New York: Appleton-Century-Crofts.

Legerstee, M. & Varghese, J. (2001). The role of maternal affect mirroring on social expectancies in three-month-old infants. *Child Development, 72*: 1301–1313.

Lewin, K. (1947). Frontiers in group dynamics. *Human Relations, 1*: 5–41.

Lier, L. (1988). Mother-infant relationship in the first year of life. *Acta Paediatrica Scandinavica Supplement, 344*: 31–42.

Linn, E. L. (1977). Verbal auditory hallucinations: Mind, self, and society. *Journal of Nervous and Mental Disease, 164*: 8–17.

Lorenz, K. (1935/1957). Companionship in bird life. In: C. H. Schiller (Ed.), *Instinctive Behavior: The Development of a Modern Concept*. New York: International Universities Press.

Lorenz, K. (1937/1957). The nature of instinct. In: C. H. Schiller (Ed.), *Instinctive Behavior: The Development of a Modern Concept*. New York: International Universities Press.

Lorenz, K. (1939/1957). Comparative study of behavior. In: C. H. Schiller (Ed.), *Instinctive Behavior: The Development of a Modern Concept*. New York: International Universities Press.

Lorenz, K. (1952/1957). The past twelve years in the comparative study of behavior. In: C. H. Schiller (Ed.), *Instinctive Behavior: The Development of a Modern Concept*. New York: International Universities Press.

Lorenz, K. (1963/2002). *On Aggression*. London: Routledge.

Lorenz, K. (1973/1977). *Behind the Mirror: A Search for a Natural History of Human Knowledge*. London: Methuen.

Lorenz, K. & Tinbergen, N. (1938/1957). Taxis and instinct. In: C. H. Schiller (Ed.), *Instinctive*

*Behavior: The Development of a Modern Concept.* New York: International Universities Press.

Maestro, S., Muratori, F., Cavallaro, M.C., Peo, F., Stern, D., Golse, B. & Palacio-Espaca, F. (2002). Attentional skills during the first 6 months of age in autism spectrum disorder. *Journal of the American Academy of Child and Adolescent Psychiatry, 41*: 1239–1245.

Machado, C.J. & Bachevalier, J. (2003). Non-human primate models of childhood psychopathology: the promise and the limitations. *Journal of Child Psychology and Psychiatry, 44*: 64–87.

Mahler, M. S. (1968). *On Human Symbiosis and the Vicissitudes of Individuation.* New York: International Universities Press.

Main, T. (1957). The ailment. *British Journal of Medical Psychology, 30*: 129–145.

Masserman, J. H. (1968). The biodynamic roots of psychoanalysis. In: J. Marmor (Ed.), *Modern Psychoanalysis: New Directions and Perspectives.* New York: Basic Books.

McCluskey, U. (2002). The dynamics of attachment and systems-centered group psychotherapy. *Group Dynamics: Theory, Research, and Practice, 6*: 131–142.

McDougall, W. (1924). *An Outline of Psychology, 2nd edition.* London: Methuen.

McEllistrem, J. E. (2004). Affective and predatory violence: A bimodal classification system of human aggression and violence. *Aggression and Violent Behaviour, 10*: 1–30.

McNaughton, N. (2006). The role of the subiculum within the behavioural inhibition system. *Behavioural Brain Research, 174*: 232–250.

McNaughton, N. & Corr, P. J. (2004). A two-dimensional neuropsychology of defense: Fear/anxiety and defensive distance. *Neuroscience and Biobehavioral Reviews, 28*: 285–305.

McNaughton, N. & Wickens, J. (2003). Hebb, pandemonium and catastrophic hypermnesia: The hippocampus as a suppressor of inappropriate associations. *Cortex, 39*: 1139–1163.

Meins, E., Fernyhough, C., Wainwright, R., Das Gupta, M., Fradley, E. & Tuckey, M. (2002). Maternal mind-mindedness and attachment security as predictors of theory of mind understanding. *Child Development, 73*: 1715–1726.

Mendelson, M. (1982). Psychodynamics of depression. In: E. S. Paykel (Ed.), *Handbook of Affective Disorders.* Edinburgh: Churchill Livingstone.

Miller, L. (1994). Traumatic brain injury and aggression. In: M. Hillbrand & L. J. Pallone (Eds.), *The Psychobiology of Aggression: Engines, Measurement, Control.* New York: Howarth Press.

Miller, N. E. (1948). Studies of fear as an acquirable drive: I. Fear as motivation and fear-reduction as reinforcement in the learning of new responses. *Journal of Experimental Psychology, 38*: 89–101.

Miller, N. E. & Dollard, J. (1941). *Social Learning and Imitation.* New Haven: Yale University Press.

Mishan, E. J. (1967). *The Costs of Economic Growth.* London: Penguin.

Mishan, E. J. (1977). *The Economic Growth Debate.* London: George Allen & Unwin.

Moore, T. V. (1926). *Dynamic Psychology: An Introduction to Modern Psychological Theory and Practice.* Philadelphia: Lippincott.

Mowrer, O. H. & Lamoreaux, R. R. (1946). Fear as an intervening variable in avoidance conditioning. *Journal of Comparative Psychology, 29*: 29–50.

Moynihan, M. H. (1998). *The Social Regulation of Competition and Aggression in Animals.* Washington, DC: Smithsonian Institution Press.

Mundy, P., Kasari, C. & Sigman, M. (1992). Nonverbal communication, affective sharing and intersubjectivity. *Infant Behaviour and Development, 15*: 377–381.

Nietzsche, F. (1886/2000). Beyond good and evil. In: W. Kaufmann (Trans. and Ed.), *Basic Writings of Nietzsche.* New York: The Modern Library.

Ogden, T. H. (2002). A new reading of the origins of object-relations theory. *International Journal of Psychoanalysis, 83*: 767–782.

O'Shaughnessy, E. (1964). The absent object. *Journal of Child Psychotherapy, 1*: 34–43.

Panksepp, J. (2003). Feeling the pain of social loss. *Science, 302*: 237–239.

Parloff, M. B. (1968). Analytic group psychotherapy. In: J. Marmor (Ed.), *Modern Psychoanalysis: New Directions and Perspectives.* New York: Basic Books.

Passmore, J. (1957/1968). *A Hundred Years of Philosophy.* Harmondsworth, UK: Penguin.

Pedersen, C. B. & Mortensen, P. B. (2001). Evidence of a dose-response relationship between urbanicity during upbringing and schizophrenia risk. *Archives of General Psychiatry, 58*: 1039–1046.

Pretzer, J. L. & Beck, A. (1996). A cognitive theory of personality disorders. In: J. F. Clarkin & M. F. Lenzenweger (Eds.), *Major Theories of Personality Disorder.* New York: The Guilford Press.

Rado, S. (1956). *Psychoanalysis of Behavior*. New York: Grune & Stratton.

Reddy, V. (2003). On being the object of attention: implications for self-other consciousness. *Trends in Cognitive Sciences, 7*: 397–402.

Riviere, J. (1936). A contribution to the analysis of the negative therapeutic reaction. *International Journal of Psychoanalysis, 17*: 304–320.

Riviere, J. (1937). Hate, greed and aggression. In: M. Klein & J. Riviere (Eds.), *Love, Hate and Reparation*. Psychoanalytic Epitomes No. 2. London: The Hogarth Press.

Rogers, S. J., Ozonoff, S. & Maslin-Cole, C. (1991). A comparative study of attachment behavior in young children with autism or other psychiatric disorder. *Journal of the American Academy of Child and Adolescent Psychiatry, 30*: 483–488.

Rosenfeld, H. A. (1965). *Psychotic States: A Psychoanalytical Approach*. London: Maresfield Reprints.

Sandler, J. (1960). The background of safety. *International Journal of Psycho-Analysis, 41*: 352–356.

Sandler, J. (1976). Countertransference and role-responsiveness. *International Review of Psychoanalysis, 3*: 43–47.

Sandler, J. (1990). On internal object relations. *Journal of the American Psychoanalytic Association, 38*: 859–880.

Sandler, J. (1993). On communication from patient to analyst: Not everything is projective identification. *International Journal of Psychoanalysis, 74*: 1097–1107.

Sander, J. & Sandler, A. M. (1978). On the development of object relations and affects. *International Journal of Psycho-Analysis, 59*: 285–296.

Schachtel, E.G. (1973). On attention, selective inattention, and experience: an inquiry into attention as an attitude. In: E.G. Witenberg (Ed.), *Interpersonal Explorations in Psychoanalysis: New Directions in Theory and Practice*. New York: Basic Books.

Schacter, D. L. & Addis, D. R. (2007). The cognitive neuroscience of constructive memory: remembering the past and imagining the future. *Philosophical Transactions of the Royal Society London—Series B, 362*: 773–786.

Schafer, R. (1976). *A new language for psychoanalysis*. New Haven: Yale University Press.

Schecter, D. E. (1973). On the emergence of human relatedness. In: E. G. Witenberg (Ed.), *Interpersonal Explorations in Psychoanalysis: New Directions in Theory and Practice*. New York: Basic Books.

Schilder, P. (1951). *Psychoanalysis, Man, and Society*. New York: W. W. Norton & Company.

Scholten, M.R., van Honk, J., Aleman, A. & Kahn, R.S. (2006). Behavioral inhibition system (BIS), behavioral activation system (BAS) and schizophrenia: relationship with psychopathology and physiology. *Journal of Psychiatric Research 40*: 638–645.

Schopenhauer, A. (1844/1966). *The World as Will and Representation* (E. F. J. Payne Trans.). New York: Dover.

Schumpeter, J. A. (1942/1976). *Capitalism, Socialism and Democracy*. New York: Harper and Row.

Segal, H. (1973). *Introduction to the Work of Melanie Klein*. London: Hogarth Press.

Segal, H. (1977). Counter-transference. *International Journal of Psychoanalytic Psychotherapy, 6*: 31–37.

Segal, H. (1997). The Oedipus complex today. In: J. Steiner (Ed.), *Psychoanalysis, Literature and War: Papers 1975–1995*. London: Routledge.

Shah, A. & Frith, U. (1983). An islet of ability in autistic children: a research note. *Journal of Child Psychology and Psychiatry, 24*: 613–620.

Shapiro, D. (2000). *Dynamics of Character*. New York: Basic Books.

Sigman, M., Mundy, P., Sherman, T. & Ungerer, J. (1986). Social interactions of autistic, mentally retarded and normal children and their caregivers. *Journal of Child Psychology and Psychiatry, 27*: 647–655.

Skinner, B. F. (1953). *Science and Human Behavior*. New York: Macmillan.

Smith, A. (1813/1759). *The Theory of Moral Sentiments*. Edinburgh: Hay.

Smith, A. D. (2003). *Routledge Philosophy Guidebook to Husserl and the Cartesian Meditations*. London: Routledge.

Smithmyer, C. M., Hubbard, J. A. & Simons, R. F. (2000). Proactive and reactive aggression in delinquent adolescents: relations to aggression outcome expectancies. *Journal of Clinical Child Psychology, 29*: 86–93.

Sokolov, E. N., Nezlina, N. I., Polyanskii, V. B. & Evtikhin, D. V. (2002). The orienting reflex: the "targeting reaction" and "searchlight of attention". *Neuroscience and Behavioral Physiology, 32*: 347–362.

Sparrevohn, R. & Howie, P. (1995). Theory of mind in children with autistic disorder: Evidence of developmental progression and the role of verbal ability. *Journal of Child Psychology and Psychiatry, 36*: 249–263.

Spillius, E. B. (1993). Varieties of envious experience. *International Journal of Psychoanalysis, 74*: 1199–1212.

Spotnitz, H. (1985). *Modern Psychoanalysis of the Schizophrenic Patient: Theory of the Technique* (2nd ed.). New York: Human Sciences Press.

Stern, D. N. (1985). *The Interpersonal World of the Infant: A View from Psychoanalysis and Developmental Psychology*. New York: Basic Books.

Storr, A. (1968). *Human Aggression*. New York: Atheneum.

Sullivan, H. S. (1953). *The Interpersonal Theory of Psychiatry*. New York: W. W. Norton & Company.

Tager-Flusberg, H., Joseph, R. & Folstein, S. (2001). Current directions in research on autism. *Mental Retardation and Developmental Disabilities Research Reviews, 7*: 21–29.

Thorndike, E. L. (1911). *Animal Intelligence*. New York: Macmillan.

Tinbergen, N. (1951). *The Study of Instinct*. Oxford: Oxford University Press.

Toman, W. (1960). *An Introduction to Psychoanalytic Theory of Motivation*. Oxford: Pergamon Press.

Townsend, J., Courchesne, E., Singer-Harris, N., Covington, J., Westerfield, M., Lyden, P., Lowry, T.P. & Press, G.A. (1999). Spatial attention deficits in patients with acquired or developmental cerebellar abnormality. *The Journal of Neuroscience, 19*: 5632–5643.

Tuke, S. (1813/1996). *Description of the Retreat*. London: Process Press.

Tuke, S. (1815). *Practical Hints on the Construction and Economy of Pauper Lunatic Asylums*. York.

Valenza, E., Simion, F., Cassia, V. M. & Umilta, C. (1996). Face preference at birth: Journal of Experimental Psychology. *Human Perception and Performance, 22*: 892–903.

van der Geest, J.N., Kemner, C., Camfferman, G., Verbaten, M.N. & van Engeland, H. (2001). Eye movements, visual attention, and autism: a saccadic reaction time study using the gap and overlap paradigm. *Biological Psychiatry, 50*: 614–619.

Vitaro, F., Gendreau, P. L., Tremblay, R. E. & Oligny, P. (1998). Reactive and proactive aggression differentially predict later conduct problems. *Journal of Child Psychology and Psychiatry, 39*: 377–385.

Walker, E. F., Savoie, T. & Davis, D. (1994). Neuromotor precursors of schizophrenia. *Schizophrenia Bulletin, 20*: 441–451.

Winnicott, D. W. (1971). *Playing and Reality*. London: Routledge.

Wolf, E. (1988). *Treating the Self*. New York: Guilford Press.

Young, P. T. (1959). The role of affective processes in learning and motivation. *Psychological Review, 66*: 104–125.

Yule, W. (2000). Developmental psychology through infancy, childhood, and adolescence. In: M. G. Gelder, J. J. Lopez-Ibor Jr & N. C. Andreasen (Eds.), *New Oxford Textbook of Psychiatry*. Oxford: Oxford University Press.

Zuriff, G. E. (1985). *Behaviourism: A Conceptual Reconstruction*. New York: Columbia University Press.

# INDEX